RES
SHC

SACKING THE FRONTIERS
OF HELL

RESCUE SHOP II

SACKING THE FRONTIERS OF HELL

STEWART & MARIE DINNEN

CHRISTIAN FOCUS

References to dollars are to USA currency

© Stewart and Marie Dinnen
ISBN 1 85792 526 2

Published in 2000
by
Christian Focus Publications,
Geanies House, Fearn, Ross-shire,
IV20 1TW, Great Britain.

Cover design by Owen Daily

Contents

DEDICATION

To RAUL CASTO,
who 'though dead yet speaketh',
and to all those Betelitos*
who are following the example of his life.

Great men are found in unusual places. Myth and history are populated with kings and heroes whose human lineage was humble. Moses, the son of a slave, was drawn out of the river to become a prince and a saviour of Israel. Jesus our Lord, the Son of God and true King of all kings, was born in a manger and raised in a carpenter's home.

Raul Casto, 'Tocho' – the stocky one, the stubborn one, was born in one of Madrid's poorest suburbs. When I first met him he was dirty; his arm was swollen and bandaged to hide the abscesses in the track marks of his veins. But that was in the beginning.

All who later came to know him and observed his life or were touched by his preaching of the gospel knew that they were in the presence of a great man. Raul was the first member of the Betel community. Through the years he grew in grace and stature to become God's champion from San Blas. He left his unique signature in the hearts of that first generation of 'Betelitos'. Shortly before he died he removed his oxygen mask to exhort his wife and the friends who surrounded his bed, 'If we do not surrender, we will conquer.'

This book is dedicated to Raul Casto and to the many other men and women of Betel, all great hearts for God who are laying down their lives, leaving the world behind, and casting off the weight of sin, crime, and drugs. Though many are stricken with AIDS, they are not moved by their own weakness, but rather in their day are fully proclaiming the gospel.

This book is dedicated to them and offered to their posterity in the hope that like men and women will not cease from the earth.

Elliott Tepper
Madrid, January 1999

* See pages 179-180 for definition.

FOREWORD

Where can we find an outstanding model of vigorous kingdom expansion as we move into the 21st century? Look no further than this dynamic and moving little book. Read here of God's transforming power in shattered lives, the dregs of society becoming the cream of the kingdom, and even those at death's door coming into new life. Then, more, see God remould them into co-workers with Him in rescuing others still enslaved.

For Betel staff, hard work, stress, pain, disappointment and heartbreak are the order of the day – but yet there is much fruit. The quality of their efforts and the good success rate of deliverance from drug addiction has drawn admiration from believers, Christian leaders, grateful parents, social workers and many others in public life.

I have watched the amazing growth of Betel in the short space of little over a decade from small beginnings, caring for a few drug addicts, to an impressive church planting movement in a country not known for its welcome to evangelicals and then into a mission outreach to many nations. Betel has become more; it has become a model for many others:

* in methods of ministry to drug addicts,

* in coping with a large number of church members and workers living with HIV and AIDS,

* in a simple faith that God's power can transform lives and release the resources needed for the ministry,

* in effective discipling and training of former addicts to become pastors and missionaries.

I commend this wonderful account to Christians around the world so that by reading, their faith be strengthened, their intercession for this work gained, and their commitment made to the evangelisation of those around the world that are, humanly speaking, too far gone for any expectation of change. This ministry is truly in keeping with WEC's founder, C.T. Studd, whose original words provided the title of this book!

Patrick Johnstone
Author, *Operation World*
International Director for Research,
WEC International,
Bulstrode, Gerrards Cross.
March 1999.

PREFACE

Since *Rescue Shop Within A Yard Of Hell* was written in 1993 Betel has powered ahead both within Spain (where it now has 82 residences) and elsewhere. This second volume details the miraculous developments in Italy, Germany, France, Portugal, Britain, USA and Mexico. These accounts occupy Part II of this book.

But the main feature is, again, the mighty transforming work of the Holy Spirit in the lives of drug addicts, gamblers, alcoholics, prostitutes and criminals, as described in Part I.

The authors, for all their familiarity with the gracious workings of the Lord in many countries, have been constantly staggered by the breakthroughs accomplished in lost lives as a result of God's working through the Betel ministry.

There is a secret to this. There is a pattern. Become a sleuth and see if you can find it! It will bless your heart when you do.

If you fail to discover it then Part III, with its explanation of Betel's principles, will help you further.

Once again we express our heartfelt thanks to Diane Griffiths for computerising our tapes and writings. We thank Elliott for his thoughtful contributions, for his and Mary's gracious hospitality in Madrid, and for lining up many interviews. Thanks also go to Keith Bergmeier, Graham Single and Kent Martin for their helpfulness in translation work and lastly to Dorothy Russell who carefully checked the manuscript.

Stewart and Marie Dinnen
Launceston, Tasmania.
March 1999.

Stewart and Marie Dinnen have fulfilled numerous roles in WEC International, including the leadership of the Missionary Training College in Tasmania, 1960–76, and general leadership of the mission from 1984–87. They continue to have a speaking and writing ministry within WEC and beyond, and are based in Launceston, Tasmania, Australia.

'Some wish to live within the sound
of chapel or church bell.
I want to run a rescue shop
within a yard of hell.'

C.T. STUDD

A Swedish journal, *Svensk Export Strategi,* published
for the benefit of business travellers, ranked nineteen
nations according to seven modern deadly sins –
smoking, drinking, drugs, gambling, lavish eating,
nightlife and prostitution. The clear winner was:
SPAIN

PART I
TRANSFORMATION

1

I FELT AS IF THE ROOF WAS CAVING IN

The story of Reme and Damian

I wanted to die! I could not bear the thought of spending five long years locked away behind bars. I felt so desperate that all I could think of was drugs. I didn't care what drug it was. So long as it made me forget. After all, I had held up that bank only because I was desperate for a fix! And now I was alone.

It was extremely difficult to get drugs inside the prison and my attempts caused me many tears and fights. Friends would send in twenty or thirty amphetamine tablets sewn into clothing when I received my monthly parcel. And I managed to make friends with fellow prisoners who also kept me supplied. But I would often wake up to a new day afraid to get out of bed. I knew it meant coming face to face, yet again, with danger. Doing drugs in jail is playing with death every day!

I managed to keep going like that for eighteen months. My family meanwhile had found a lawyer who was drawing up the necessary documents to take the custody of my young son from me. They, too, had become tired of it all, and were resigned to the fact that I was a daughter without a solution. (How tragic it is that one should be driven to thinking that of one's very own child!)

During this time, Damian, my husband, wrote regularly to me in prison. He repeatedly urged me to reject my present lifestyle and encouraged me to try my hardest to change, assuring me of his love. But the life of a substance abuser really is overwhelming. It produces unreal sensations all day long. Anyway, I had long ago stopped loving Damian and had become involved with another man. I'd even written to him saying that he should forget all about me because I had already chosen my lifestyle, and he formed no part of it.

***

To back-track, half my life has been lived in desperation, knowing neither peace nor love. As a little girl I recall the tense atmosphere at home due to the situation in which my parents co-existed. I remember trying to commit suicide when only eleven years old. I swallowed a huge number of tablets, but failed to achieve my objective. The years passed by and I continued to grow up without the parental love I craved.

I guess that was what made me want to be out with my friends rather than staying at home. By the time I was fifteen my friends and I were spending our weekends at discotheques. I had my own agenda now. My group and I started smoking marijuana daily. It wasn't long before that failed to satisfy us, so we tried amphetamines. Now they really made us feel different. These pills transformed my personality. I felt more attractive, more extrovert, more sociable. I especially liked the way they helped me to forget all my problems.

These sensations satisfied me until I reached adulthood. At eighteen I wanted something more. And I found my answer in heroin. Heroin was a summit experience. But it also held me on the edge of death on more than one occasion due to overdosing. I was admitted and discharged from hospitals at an incredible rate. (Only now I understand just how merciful God was to me through it all.)

At twenty-two a man I had known for years, Damian, and I began a relationship. Together we did the craziest things, deceiving, robbing, and mistreating people. Heroin became an increasingly intimate friend. We were sent to jail several times, but not even this was sufficient to break our 'friendship' with heroin. On the other hand, the relationship that Damian and I had shared became more and more superficial. Our life only consisted of experiencing unreal sensations. We were dominated by a substance that little by little was dragging us down into the mire. We no longer thought of each other. Our only thought was heroin.

Our families were overcome with grief watching our lives disintegrate right before their very eyes. Ironically, Damian and I were oblivious to their pain, hate and love. Nothing in life was important to us any more. All we cared about was getting those daily doses of heroin that our bodies desperately craved.

About a year later I fell pregnant with David, our eldest son. I thought that perhaps this baby might be the incentive we needed to escape from heroin's hold. How mistaken I was! However, with this hope in mind we booked into a Christian rehabilitation centre. I lived with the women, and Damian with the men.

There, I gave birth to my first child. I also had my first encounter with God. Everything was beautiful, and we were very happy at last. We'd been there for nine months and had been given the go-ahead to marry when, one day without premeditation, we spontaneously made the decision to leave the centre and return home to Alicante. We naïvely believed that we were prepared to face life together without help.

So we were married on the crisp spring morning of February 3rd, 1989. It was a wedding with all the trimmings! Family and friends joined in the festivities. After the banquet, we went off to the discotheque with friends to dance the night away. In the euphoria of the evening we celebrated without restraints. Glass after glass of alcohol led to the ultimate trap – a fix. 'Just this once,' we thought! It was our biggest mistake!

Within two months we found ourselves perpetually chasing after that cursed white powder – heroin. For several horrific years we repeatedly and unsuccessfully attempted to break with our addiction. We tried everything. We booked ourselves into rehabilitation centres, we commenced the methadone programme, and we had sessions with psychologists, but all to no avail. Our families did all they could to help us too.

On the 12th August, 1992 I was arrested for armed robbery. It was Damian's birthday. The shock of our separation jolted my husband into booking into the Betel centre, in Madrid, determined that this time he would make it – for the sake of both of us, and our son. Meanwhile, after three months in jail I received my sentence: five years imprisonment! I spent most of it drugged up, constantly getting into fights, and giving the wardens all the trouble I could.

It so happened during this time that Damian had to leave the Madrid centre where he was already a new man. He had been ordered to report to the Alicante prison for a three month sentence because of a previous offence. Ironically the admission cells were situated immediately in front of the women's punishment cells. I happened to be serving two weeks punishment there for pushing a warden. I was busy yelling out to the girl in the next cell as the police brought him in. Damian recognised my voice and shouted, 'Reme, Reme, is that you? It's me, Damian!'

What a shock! But so conditioned was I to my prison lifestyle and friendships that I shouted back. 'Hey, have you got any dope?' And when he once more begged me to leave this way of living, and think of us, I coldly yelled back through the walls that I wished him well, but my decision to go our separate ways was unchanged.

Little did I know how close Damian came to throwing in the towel because of my response. If it hadn't been for some Christian friends from the area, he'd have done so. On return to Madrid, his leader, Juan Carlos, (now the leader in Betel, France) encouraged him to keep going and make the best of his life, even if it meant being without me. His letters to me stopped. When the leadership approached him about forming part of the new pioneer team for Naples, Italy, Damian said yes. He thought that perhaps this was the new beginning God had in mind for him.

In December I received an unexpected letter from Italy. Eight months had gone by. Damian told me of his new venture in a new country. But his message was clear. He told me that for the last time he was writing to ask me to change, because if I didn't, he would, sadly, be forced to make a drastic decision. This was the first time that Damian had spoken of divorce.

My reaction was dramatic. I felt as if the roof was caving in on top of me. I've no idea what took place, but from that moment on, something broke and began to change within me. I actually felt ashamed. Right at that time, my cellmate, Rosa, fell ill. She was in the terminal stages of AIDS. The doctor ordered two weeks of bedrest, and I offered to be her cellmate and helper for that time. I spent those fourteen days weeping. I couldn't explain my tears. All I knew was that I wanted to get out of this mess. Rosa didn't know how to help me. Looking back, I now realise that God's mercy was being poured out on me.

However, simultaneously the Enemy fought to keep me. At times I felt a great desire to leave everything behind and start all over again in my marriage. At other times I wanted to stay as I was. But I didn't budge from the cell and I refused to see anyone. All I could do was cry. It was an inner battle, a spiritual struggle.

One evening after the two weeks were up, I went downstairs to eat in the dining room. We usually stayed on to pass the time playing Bingo or Dominoes. But this night was different. I wanted to go back to my cell. I needed to be alone. I distinctly recall the key turning in the lock. I felt a strong urge inside of me to ask for forgiveness. I fell to my knees and from the very depth of my being asked God's pardon for all that I had done. I didn't know whether He would have mercy on me, yet again, or if He was even listening. I just kept talking to Him, repentant, begging that He give me another opportunity.

As I groaned, a sense of consolation flooded into my being. Never before had I physically felt such a strong, loving, warm embrace as I did that night. I was filled with a burning desire to escape from this hell. I knew that someone loved me. God filled me to overflowing with a new, strong courage to overcome.

I can't explain why, but I began to spend less and less time with my old friends. I left drugs completely and started attending the meetings held by some Christians who visited weekly. In this way, little by little, God began to give me the strength and courage to change. Strangely, from the moment I decided to leave drugs, I felt no desire to return to them. I had thought it would be very difficult, especially as my cellmate was trafficking and using heroin before my very eyes. Many temptations tried to pull me under again but, thanks to the strength that God kept giving me, no temptation succeeded! I am amazed as I think back to this stage in my life. Never would I have dreamed that in spite of being in a prison I could feel so free!

In fact, it was a fantastic time. I had so many opportunities to share about what was happening to me with others. Everyone was so amazed by the change in me. Several times the prison wardens called me to the office and asked me to explain just *what* had happened to me. They had been accustomed to seeing me dragging myself about the yard, drugged up, arguing and picking fights with everyone. They wanted to know what had happened to make me serious, interested in others, and so well behaved!

Their questions filled me with joy because they gave me opportunities to talk about the Lord. Two of my friends in jail also gave their lives to Christ – one of them was Rosa! What a thrill that was! In spite of my lack of freedom, in spirit I was completely free. In fact, the Bible says that 'where sin abounded, grace did much more abound' and it's true, because I've experienced this for myself and now know that *nothing* is impossible for God.

Of the five years I was due to serve, I served only half. God made it possible for me to complete my sentence in Betel, Valencia. My son, David, joined me after several months. I put every effort into making the most of my year with the women there. Then, to my joy, the director in Valencia, Lindsay McKenzie, arranged for us to join Damian in Italy for Christmas, 1995.

My arrival in Naples marked the beginning of a new era – difficult, but special. As a wife, a mother and as a helper to Damian in the ministry, I have been stretched on every level. We shared a flat with another couple for a year and a half. What a lot I learned about sharing and forgiving! I also learned to cook. Each morning I worked with the others, and in the afternoons I cared for David. As a wife I learned about Biblical submission to my husband and to share my thoughts and ideas with him. I had to learn to 'help' Damian. Together we learned to parent our son, on a biblical basis. We had to undo many old habits. The Lord has blessed us with another son whom we have named Samuel, because 'God has heard his servant'.

Damian now gives his side of the story.
In 1965 I was born into a very normal Spanish working-class family and from what I remember of my childhood I did the very normal things that a child does – going to school, playing football and having fun with my friends.

When I was twelve or thirteen years old some friends and I skipped school and began smoking together in a hide-out. It made us feel grown-up. Some time later my friends and I began to visit other suburbs and came to know another circle of friends who began to introduce us to the world of drugs, so we started smoking 'joints'.

Initially it was something new and 'cool'. It seemed like a lot of fun at the time. It was not a daily practice – just now and then – mainly at weekends, but gradually it became a daily habit. Something made me aware that all was not well with this new lifestyle but nothing changed. Later, smoking hashish didn't satisfy me anymore and so I looked for other drugs to fill the void such as amphetamines, speed and cocaine, all this coupled with an ever-increasing alcohol consumption. By this time I was seventeen or eighteen and was completely dependent on these things; they helped me to forget my problems and the heated arguments at home.

I discovered at this time that my father, who was always

lecturing me, was himself an alcoholic. This pushed me further into despair so I resorted to drinking more and taking more drugs in an effort to push all these problems out of my mind.

The 1980s arrived and with them something that would become my constant companion for eleven years – heroin! I had heard about it and had feared it at the same time. But when I finally did try it I realised that this was different; it was special. I liked it so much that I fell in love with it! I began to use heroin almost continually. Whilst I could afford the doses everything was fine but when my wages were used up I began to ask for advances from my employer; finally I resorted to stealing. Problems piled on top of problems as I tried desperately to support my habit. While at first I carefully planned the thefts, before long I didn't care if anybody saw me or caught me in the act.

When I first started on heroin everything seemed fine. I kidded myself that I could leave it whenever I chose to but after a couple of years I knew that I was helplessly addicted to it and that my only escape from it would be my own death. My life continued with each day presenting me with the challenge of discovering new ways of financing my habit. I was arrested by the police on more than fifteen occasions and in ten of those I ended up in prison.

In 1988 Reme became pregnant and so we decided to go to a drug rehabilitation centre. I desperately wanted to leave drugs once and for all, for the sake of the baby. But after the birth of David and ten months in the centre the only thing that changed was our external appearance. Inside we were the same Damian and Reme. Soon after we left that centre we decided to get married. We'd been able to stay off drugs all that time, but after the wedding ceremony when we found ourselves with a lot of cash given to us as wedding gifts, we decided to 'celebrate' by shooting up. Once again we were plunged back into the old addiction cycle but this time it was worse than ever.

Our relationship began to suffer and our marriage fell apart. We each went our own way. David was looked after by Reme's family.

In 1992 I decided to make a last-ditch effort to leave this white powder which had converted me into its slave. I phoned the Madrid Betel centre and asked for help. I had been to Betel in Valencia and before that to Madrid, but this time, I was at the end of myself. I was so bad that I don't recall how I managed the five hour trip from Alicante. Never before had I been so desperate for help as I was that time.

When I reached Madrid they took me in. I remember crying out to God and He answered that sincere cry. I found myself amongst people that were so loving and caring and I found the help that I was searching for. The folk that attended to me had all been where I was. Through them I began to understand that Jesus was the only One who could change my life. These things I had heard before but this time I actually opened my heart to Him and experienced such a peace and forgiveness – something that I had searched for, for so many years.

Now I can say, looking back over six years, that He has restored to me everything that was broken in my life. He has restored my marriage with Reme and brought David back to us. Today we are happily serving God. He has saved us from a certain death and given us a new life. Two years ago Samuel arrived on the scene. We named him Samuel which means 'asked of God' because God has indeed answered our prayer.

Reme concludes, giving an outline of their present situation.
A daughter work in the province of Bari, directly east of Naples, on the Adriatic coast, had been going for two years when the leadership decided that a married couple should go to develop the existing men's house. We were chosen. It was an exciting time, to think we would have a flat to ourselves for the first time, and the challenge of being trusted to care for a group of fifteen men.

It's lonely being so far from the other couples and families at times. And, as in any work, you see men doing well, having commenced a real and vital relationship with the Lord, then without explanation throwing it all overboard and leaving. This saddens us greatly. But the battles and difficulties that sometimes burden us down have also been instrumental in making us go to God to know His consolation, help and direction.

Just recently, during a discouraging time, the Lord lifted my spirit saying, 'Reme, even if only ONE life goes ahead with Me, it's worth it!' He also encourages us daily, reminding us that the work doesn't belong to us anyway. It belongs to God! Together Damian and I, with our sons, continue to serve the Lord here in Italy. We have decided to give our lives to help others, in thanks to Him for all that He has done for us.

2

STABBED THREE TIMES, I ALMOST DIED

THE STORY OF MOHAMMED FROM NORTH AFRICA

In the world of missions, gaining a convert from Islam is a major victory, but to see such a convert discipled and led on to vital Christian living and service is a gigantic triumph.

Reading of Mohammed's troubled Islamic family background and the depth of degradation to which he sank, one can only stand back in wonder, love and praise as the story of how the grace of God reaches this life unfolds.

My parents are from Tetuan, a port city on the northern Moroccan coast midway between Ceuta and Melilla. My father worked in Spain and in 1952 married a Moroccan woman. They then moved to Ceuta during the time of the Spanish colonial rule. She had actually been previously married and brought two daughters with her.

I was the oldest child of that marriage, and three years later my next brother was born, both of us born in Ceuta. After a number of years my mother fled to Morocco taking her two daughters, my brother and me with her. My father was angry; he chased after us and caught us in Morocco. Then there was a big fight. He went to the authorities and they gave the custody of the two sons to him and the daughters to my mother. My parents were divorced and she stayed in Morocco; I went back to Spanish Ceuta with my father.

He went back to Morocco from Ceuta and married another Moroccan woman, bringing her back to Ceuta with him. They had a daughter but later he divorced his wife. Then I discovered that my first two sisters were from an earlier marriage. I had always believed that they were my sisters. In all these problem situations I was present, observing and being part of the rough fights between my parents. It affected me a lot.

As a very young child I was placed in a Koranic school where I sat on the floor with the other students. We had to learn to recite the text of the Koran from memory. We didn't understand what we were memorising but I was conscientious. After seven years I left.

We were very poor. We hardly had anything in the house. My father was a casual labourer, with no rights, or insurance. In those days whenever any employer needed a worker he'd take you on but if he didn't need you, you would be sacked. Dad began to work in the market selling whatever goods he could. When I was nine years of age he took me there with him and taught me how to sell.

After so many divorces and so many fights with women my father decided he would never marry again. When we worked in the markets our life improved because we began to earn money. But even though we had more I felt that I was missing something in life. I would see other people with their families and I felt an emptiness and a longing for affection. I began to seek that by joining gangs and groups of people in the neighbourhood. Dr Dobson says, 'Weak family – strong gang'. I substituted relationships in the street for a mother and family. So I began to drink and get into drugs and misbehave. Along with this longing in my heart for affection there was a growing bitterness and hatred because I felt so left out and wronged.

My father was a very strong Moslem and believed in Allah. He also believed in spiritism, demons, and so on. So from my early years on I accepted my father's Islamic faith. I had a real faith in Islamic supernatural spiritism. I didn't want to do wrong when I was younger because I did fear God and was a good Moslem.

I started off in drugs by smoking hashish, which is easily available in Morocco. I had lots of problems with my Dad about this. He didn't want me to do it. Every time I did it I was condemned by my conscience but bit by bit I ceased to care. Then I began to drink alcohol as well. I read lots of pornography and was obsessed by it and masturbation. I was always an introverted person. I began to build my own little introverted world and live inside it.

I continued working with my father in the market but he was more and more angry with me because I wasn't performing well. I was heading downhill. Pornography really began to destroy my life. I was totally corrupted inside. My mind was totally reprobate. I felt really worthless. I cried a lot and didn't know how to escape from the corruption of my mind. Because of that I didn't care what I did. Nothing mattered – right or wrong.

Then I started to gamble. I put money in slot machines. All the money I earned I put in these machines and for seven years it was hashish, pornography, alcohol and gambling, then heroin.

At nineteen I left home and started sleeping in the streets. One night I was sleeping in an old abandoned car and an older bigger man came by and violated me.

I was in that state for eleven years. My father became old and sickly and eventually died. He left me 3.8 million pesetas, which was a lot of money then. All of a sudden I had lots of friends. Then we all began to buy and sell drugs and I began to shoot up every day.

My father had a big house that he was renting so I assumed the rental contract and lived in it but very soon I had so many problems with the neighbours, they wanted to get rid of me. So I left the house and even with all that money in the bank I lived in the streets. I continued to buy drugs while I had money but it only lasted six months. I just used it all for drugs. I had to start robbing more frequently, had lots of problems with the police, and was in and out of jail. I did have some friends that wanted to take me into their home but I never wanted to live with anybody. I just wanted to be alone. Drugs – jail – solitude. Sickness was a problem too. I began to pick up lots of sicknesses. I was in and out of the hospital – hepatitis, tuberculosis and many other things. Before I had time to get well I'd escape from hospital and get more drugs; so I never quite got over my sicknesses.

After doing a robbery, I would have lots of money on my person. One time some of the street people tried to take it and stabbed me three times in the back. On another occasion they stabbed me in the stomach. Both times I almost died.

When I was feeling so bad I wanted to leave drugs but I didn't know how. I used to follow the dealers to see where they had their stashes, then I'd rob them. I got off heroin and got on to cocaine, but that was worse because it makes you even more anxious and depressed. I really thought I was going to die. An addiction to cocaine, in my opinion, is much worse than an addiction to heroin because you have to rob with more frequency because you're desperate. I was very desperate, robbing more and more. Finally the police caught me and took me to the police station. I was three days there passing through the withdrawal syndrome. I was desperate. Then from the police station they sent me to prison.

After that I was very sick. I was very thin and yellow. Prison was so full that I was put in a little tiny room – not even a regular room. While I was there I found a book called *Light and Guide*. I really had no interest in Christianity. But this book was written in Arabic and it had Arabic decorations and Arabic inscriptions. So I opened it up, I didn't really care what I was reading. As I began to read, all of a sudden I felt myself drawn right into the story, and then I began to weep as I read about the life and death of Jesus. I just wept, and wept. Something entered into me and I began to float. I had a sense of peace. Then I felt as though I was being hugged and I heard a voice saying to me, 'You're going to change, and you're going to be all right.'

I spent thirteen days in the jail and during this time this sense continued. It was like light in the midst of all the darkness. I knew that I wanted to change so I talked to a social worker and said, 'I want to go to a centre.' I left prison, but I didn't go to the centre. I forgot the address and started taking cocaine again. During that week I kept hearing a voice telling me to go to a centre or I'd die. So I went back to the prison to get the address from the social worker. So I entered Betel in Ceuta.

When I got there I said to them, 'Send me far away from here because I've got all kinds of problems with the police and everyone.' But I stayed. The first time they began to sing and worship I began to cry and when they opened the Bible I'd cry. I knew there was something very special in Betel. I knew that I wanted to be like the people there. I sensed God's presence.

Betel opened the Algeciras centre in '93 and I went there with the first group from Ceuta. We rented a big warehouse in the port and built a second hand furniture store there. Some of us lived in this store. About that time, Thomas Spyker, an American missionary, with a group of Mexican missionaries, had a concert in the area and Betel co-operated. I remember being at that concert. There was an altar call and I went forward and publicly gave my life to Christ.

All that happened in Algeciras was just a confirmation of all that had happened before in the jail and in Betel Ceuta. It was almost like a baptism of the Holy Spirit, and a deepening, a public declaration that what had happened was real.

I spent nine months in Algeciras and then was transferred back to the Betel Ceuta. I had so many judgements and sentences against me that I went into jail three times after I was a Christian. The first time was for a month, then I came out; then they put me back in for another month. I said, 'Please put all my sentences together and I'll serve them at once. I want to get them over with.' They sentenced me to two years, ten months and twenty three days in jail.

In view of my good behaviour, after only two months in prison they allowed me to go out on what they call the 'third grade', which means that I had to sleep in the prison but I was free during the day and at weekends to go to Betel. They were astounded at the change in my life. They even gave me a key to my section of the prison. I was almost like a boarder! I simply had to be there at night to check in. I could spend Friday, Saturday and Sunday nights at Betel, and just had to be back at prison Monday night. I really was basically free apart from checking in four nights a week.

I went from being the worst behaved citizen of Ceuta to being an example of a radically changed life. The police said to me, 'We know what you were and now we see how you've really changed.'

Elliott Tepper adds: During this time Mohammed was very hungry for the Word of God. I saw such hunger in him that I went to the Bible Society and I bought him a Study Bible, with notes and cross-references. I came back about three months later and said, 'How are you doing?'

He said, 'I'm having a great time.' I said, 'Have you read the whole Bible?' He said, 'I'm only up to about the middle of Genesis – I follow every one of the references so it takes me a long time!' He had not only read half of Genesis but he probably had a theological education reading every single cross-reference and note diligently. After seventeen months of his sentence they gave him a parole and pardoned him. He's been with us now about six years and during this time he's always been in the leadership team, supervising the new people, and with special ministry to the other Moslems that come in to the programme.

He's a very talented musician. He is one of the most gifted guitarists we have. From the very beginning he has been in the ministry of praise. He's had his personality problems and deep complexes to work through. You have to rebuild the mind of a converted Moslem. They have all kinds of wrong ideas and concepts – about women and society. Even though he was born again and knew God, theologically he had a tremendous intellectual barrier that had to be overcome and we had to explain doctrine after doctrine, point after point, because it was so alien to him. He expressed such a hunger for the Word of God, we transferred him to Madrid for about a year and he did a whole year at our Adullam Bible Institute. After he finished we sent him back down to Ceuta and Algeciras – the two centres work together. He will probably be in the leadership team that develops the Moroccan work.

His health has improved a lot but he still has lots of problems. Strangely enough he doesn't have the AIDS virus; he's cured of his tuberculosis; his hepatitis seems to be dormant. He has problems in his spine and his stomach. His health has improved dramatically but he is still in the process of being physically renewed.

Mohammed concludes:

If I hadn't come to know Christ I would have died. I know God still has a lot to do in me yet and I'm trusting Him to finish His work.

3

COCAINE GAVE ACCELERATION

THE STORY OF CLAUDIO DE ROSA

I am forty-three and I've spent half of my life here in Italy dependent on drugs. From my adolescent days I was a rebel. At thirteen I was expelled from school for playing with knives. Then I did an apprenticeship as a fitter and turner. When I had finished that my brother, who owned a driving school, offered to take me on as an instructor.

My introduction to drugs began with smoking hashish. In spite of that, my one ambition was to make a lot of money and get rich quickly, have a fast, sleek car, and plenty of sex – anything that would give me a thrill. I vainly looked for satisfaction. Life, as far as I was concerned, was only worth living in the 'fast lane'. For this reason my best friend was cocaine. Cocaine gave me the acceleration that I looked for. It enabled me to be the fun-filled, life-of-the-party person that I couldn't be when I was 'normal'. The problem was that the cocaine effect was only very brief, and so in order to continue on a 'high', I had to buy larger quantities. My salary was very limited in comparison with what I needed to keep up the habit. I began asking for advances from my brother, and when that ran out I started borrowing from other family members and friends.

Finally at twenty-six, I lost my employment. I'd pushed my brother too far and after money was missing from the till, he reported me to the police as a thief. When I sought sympathy from my friends, I found that there too the doors were closed. I had abused their friendship just once too often. I was prepared to pay the price of losing their friendship in order to find the satisfaction that I looked for, but instead of satisfaction I was frequently left feeling empty. Something was missing – something vital, but I had no idea what it was, so I kept looking and experimenting.

In 1984 I was put in jail on remand as I was rounded up with a group of pushers in a police raid. I wasn't selling drugs then. I just happened to be buying from one of the pushers when the police arrived. However, soon after that I did indeed begin trafficking in order to sustain my habit. By this stage I had 'graduated' from cocaine to heroin. Heroin enabled me to come down off the cocaine merry-go-round when I couldn't 'come down' by my own means. But soon I was hooked – something I had always sworn would never happen. By this stage I had no friends left. Heroin was my only 'friend'.

One day, in another police raid two years after this, I was rounded up and found to have in my possession fifteen grams of pure heroin and fifteen grams of lactose. The lactose was used to dilute the heroin to make it go further and hence I made more money on each sale. I was later convicted for trafficking and sentenced to five years jail.

Six years prior to this I had formed a *de facto* relationship with a girl. We lived together until I was convicted for trafficking. Just before going to prison she informed me that she was expecting a child. At this moment I couldn't see beyond these five years in prison so I told her not to wait for me, that she needed to begin a new life without me. Nevertheless we wrote to each other for a few months but the letters became less and less frequent until they finally stopped. Later I heard that she had married another fellow. Even though I had told her not to wait for me and to begin a new life, when she did in fact do that I hated her for abandoning me. I desperately wanted to see the daughter that she had given birth to but she refused. That hurt me deeply. Once I did see my daughter very briefly, when she was four years old, but, sadly, I have never been allowed to see her again even though I have tried hard to do so.

I was filled with hate and loneliness. The experience of being in prison usually makes the prisoner more religious and superstitious. He clings to religious symbols like crucifixes, images of the Virgin Mary, etc. One Sunday the prison guard came around as usual wanting to know who would like to attend mass (the chapel was small so only a limited number could attend). That day something inside me made me put my name down. I had not been to mass for years but I felt the need to go and get close to God even if just for a few minutes. At the end of the mass, we all lined up to touch the feet of a marble statue of Jesus. After touching the statue with our hand we were to make the usual sign of the Cross. When it came my turn, suddenly an electric shock went through my hand and arm. It was so strong that I immediately withdrew my hand, as it hurt. I walked away astonished thinking that not even the church accepted me now. That incident, inexplicable as it was, affected me for years afterwards.

My five year sentence was eventually reduced to four because of a new law that had been passed offering a certain amnesty for particular crimes. Mine happened to be one of them. Part of the condition of my release was that I agreed to go to a rehabilitation centre for the year that remained. Soon I found myself in a centre in Foggia on the Adriatic coast. There we could do whatever we liked, as we were given so much freedom: women, drugs, alcohol, tobacco – the works! After two years there I got tired of it and approached my brother who was willing to take me into his house. Whilst there, I asked what happened to my share of our parents' estate. They had both died some years before. I discovered that it had been put in trust for me. When I finally got my hands on it, I blew it all within two months – it all went into my veins. Without a place to live (my brother had since thrown me out of his house when he saw me back on drugs and wasting the inheritance) and with no economic means, I became a beggar living in abandoned buildings, sleeping at night in cardboard boxes. I tried to take my life on a number of occasions by purposely injecting what I thought were fatal doses of heroin, but I always woke again. I felt like a man on death row just waiting for the day when he would finally meet his death.

It was during this time that I was walking in a town called Castel Volturno, near Caserta, when I came across a large circus-size tent with the words 'Christ is the Answer' written in large letters on top. I discovered that it was an itinerant mission that travelled around Italy doing evangelism. During that day, I met many from that tent who invited me to the meeting that evening. But each time I refused. Then an African man, whom I recognised as a fellow vagabond, asked me to go with him, as he didn't want to go alone. So I went just to accompany him.

As I entered the tent, to my amazement, I saw many people praising God together. I had never seen a sight like it before. They were so friendly and genuinely interested in me. Later an invitation was given to go out to the front so they could pray for me. At that moment a female voice from behind me called my name: 'Claudio!' I turned and recognised her as an old friend from years before. She ran over to where I was and hugged me. But at that moment it was more than just a hug from an old friend, somehow I knew that God was embracing me. I was feeling miserable and dejected and that embrace told me that God loved me in spite of all that I was and had done. Part of me wanted to accept Jesus as my Saviour as the folk (including my friend) urged me to do, but my pride welled up inside me and I left the tent to return to my lonely world.

Some months later, I was alone in a ruined house and at the end of my tether. I cried out to God in as loud a voice as I could muster: 'God, I can't stand this loneliness any longer. Please, help me! You who can do anything, make me die, relieve me from this suffering. I can't do any more!' I just sobbed and sobbed. A few days later, on a Sunday morning, I was walking along the street going through horrible withdrawal symptoms, wondering how I was going to make money to buy a 'fix', when I recognised the car of a friend of mine. I waved for him to stop and when he did I asked him if I could accompany him to church. An incredible force took hold of me that morning, because when an addict is going through withdrawal nothing interests him until he has got his 'fix' of heroin. But that day that overwhelming desire made me insist on going with him to church!

The Christians there spoke to me later about a Christian rehabilitation centre called Betel. The next day I went in, although I had decided that the rules were too strict and that I would stay for only a month – just enough time to recuperate physically in order to look for my old girlfriend and my daughter and somehow win them back. I had learnt every trick in the book about stealing and making easy money. I knew that with a bit of help from this centre I could continue on as before, but this time without drugs.

Nevertheless, when I sat and listened during the devotional times, I was astonished at how much they knew about my life. 'I haven't shared those facts with anyone!' I wondered in amazement as they described almost to the last detail what my life was like. The more I stayed and listened, the more I realised that it was God who was speaking to me through His Word. One day I decided that enough was enough. I had to make a clear decision whether to continue on as always or to leave that old life and accept the new life that Jesus was offering me. I chose the second course, and all I can say is that I have had a marvellous experience with my Lord and Saviour, and have found a family, a tremendous peace, joy and above all – hope! That was five years ago!

God has given me so much in these last five years. The verse in the Bible that most describes the change that has occurred in me is when God says to Israel in Ezekiel 11:19, 'I will remove from them their heart of stone and give them a heart of flesh.'

I am currently leading the Betel men's residence in the province of Bari. It is a daughter work from Naples. Each day I see new men arrive at the centre, their lives in ruins, as mine was. As I reflect on how my life was and what it is today, I can say to them, 'You know, there is hope for you too!'

Today God has blessed me with a wife – Isabel, another cured addict sent as a missionary from Spanish Betel. She, like me, has experienced God's 'heart transplant'. God has united us together as husband and wife; He is making two restored hearts into one!

4

DRUGS AND GUNS –
AN EXPLOSIVE MIXTURE

THE STORY OF LOURDES AND EDUARDO ARMESTO

To read the stories of Lourdes and Eduardo is like having a theatre curtain raised on a glorious revelation of the manifold grace of God. Here is a young woman deeply into drugs, playing around with guns which, through an accident, led to her being confined to a wheelchair for the rest of her life.

Here is a young man from a wealthy family fighting everyone in prison and having to be sent to maximum security. Yet both, in desperation over their hellish existence, cry to God – and He hears them and begins a process of transformation. Today they are a team together in Betel, working to help others who need the same release and deliverance that they have found. First we have the story of Lourdes.

I grew up in a divided family where my mother was an alcoholic. I have two brothers but we never lived in the same house. My brothers are older than me and were brought up by my aunts and uncles. I, being the one left at home, suffered from the effects of my mother's alcoholism.

Going back as far as I can remember I always seem to have been alone. My mother was never at home and I never had much of a relationship with her. In one sense you could say my friends and our neighbours were my parents because I was always in their houses and often finished up eating with them and staying the night with them. I felt afraid when mother came home and I didn't want to be where she was. This experience made me feel inferior to other children. I suppose I was looking for affection.

When I was thirteen I became involved in discos, smoking,

and in taking pills and marijuana. When I was sixteen I found out that I was pregnant. At that stage I wasn't sure what to do, whether to have the child or to have an abortion. The father of the child was my boyfriend but we never lived together. Finally I decided to go ahead and have the baby, perhaps for no other reason than just to have someone with me.

After giving birth I began to have problems with depression, and suffered a lot of nervous disorders. Psychiatric treatment didn't help me. A couple of years later, when I was eighteen, I tried heroin for the first time. I didn't really like it but by taking it I could stop taking the other pills and didn't need the psychiatric treatment any more. But of course I became hooked on it. Later I also tried cocaine. This was the drug I enjoyed most. The group of people that I mixed with also trafficked in drugs and played around with firearms.

One day when I was twenty-three I finished up in the hospital because of an accident. I was sitting beside somebody who was playing with one of these guns; it went off accidentally and I was shot. The bullet entered through my left arm, went through one of my lungs, and finished up in my spine. The operation took five hours. It was a success, but the doctors didn't think I would live longer than twenty-four hours.

I remember crying out to God for the first time in my life while in the intensive care ward. Something within me gave me the certainty that I wasn't going to die. After forty-eight hours the doctors saw that I was starting to get better. But I had another problem. They realised that I would never walk again. After five months I was allowed to go home in a wheelchair and I went back to mix with the same group of friends I'd been with before the accident. Once again I was hooked on heroin, and trafficking in drugs as well. But the drugs weren't helping me and I started to feel really bad. I would look at my child – he was six years old at that stage – and I wanted to do something for him, but couldn't. I felt so powerless – I didn't know what to do.

Through one of my neighbours I met an evangelical pastor

who offered to help me and spoke about Betel in Madrid. I was twenty-four years old by then. I was accepted and found myself with a lot of people who had been through problems similar to mine. I was impressed by the number of lives that had been changed and how they were being released from the world of drugs. People in the programme spoke to me about Jesus, telling me He had changed their lives and that He could change my life as well.

Not many days after that I received Christ into my life. When I did this my mind went back to that day in hospital when I cried out to Him and how I had that certainty that I wasn't going to die. I had the confidence that Someone was going to be at my side forever. God has continued to do great things in my life. He is also working in the life of my son. When he was seven he asked Jesus into his life, too!

After some time in the centre God spoke to me and told me I had to share what He had done in my life and to communicate His power and His love to other people. For this reason I decided to stay on in Betel even though I was cured. I became the leader of the girls' house.

After being there a year I met Eduardo. I spent time talking to him as a friend, but I never thought of the possibility of a closer relationship. At that stage I thought God and my son were sufficient for me. But six years later God united us together. We've now been married for a year and a half, and I continue to experience the love of God in my life. I currently work in the Betel office as cashier and secretary.

Now Eduardo tells his amazing story.
I was brought up in a fairly well-off home. We weren't the richest family in Spain but we had all we needed. When I was little I was brought up firstly by my father's parents, my grandfather being a senior army officer. When I was five years old I shifted to the home of my mother's parents. From an early age I was given everything I wanted.

I lived with my grandparents because my parents were going through a process of separation. My father was living his own lifestyle and didn't have much to do with us children. He was a lieutenant colonel in the infantry. My family tried to give me a good education and sent me to the best schools and colleges. But I was expelled from most of those because of my behaviour. There was rebellion in my heart.

We always had the best of holidays at Christmas and Easter. We would go away and stay in the best hotels or go on a pleasant journey somewhere. After being expelled from various places for my behaviour I was sent to boarding school. Deep rebellion began to grow in me; and as a ten year old I wasn't at all interested in studies. During this period I spent some time staying with my mother. She was living with a man whom she later married. He's the man that I suppose I now consider my father.

As I grew I became involved in other forms of delinquency through mixing with the wrong sort of people. When I was thirteen I experimented with drugs and at fourteen my mother told me I could go and find my own way in life. By this time I was hooked on amphetamines and other softer drugs. I mixed with people in a hippie-type world, but it didn't give me satisfaction and I kept looking for something stronger.

I continued for another three years like this until I reached a stage where I thought I was going to die. I was taking so many pills and other drugs that I would go weeks without proper sleep and for long periods without eating. I felt I was losing my mind. The pills weren't very expensive. To obtain them we either robbed pharmacies or stole money from some source or another to buy them. I began to feel delirious and had all sorts of strange sensations. I would see my skin go peculiar and the hairs on my arms would rise up. I had all sorts of strange illusions. When I listened to someone talking it was as if I was far away in a different world. I was very weak physically. I weighed only a little over thirty kilos, and at sixteen years of age I was just like a beanstalk.

I decided to return home and tell them I needed to see a doctor, because I was dying. We went to a psychiatrist the very day I arrived. I was sent to a hospital because my state of health was so grave. They put me under sedation for a week. The only time I was wakened was to eat. I left the hospital having almost doubled the weight I was when I went in, but I wasn't really cured.

After spending some time at home I started taking marijuana and alcohol, and began to experiment with acid drugs. These didn't do anything for me; I didn't like them. Then I went back to amphetamines again. My career as a delinquent continued and I found myself in prison for bigger robberies. Then at eighteen I started to take heroin.

In order to obtain money we broke into shops at night time, and during the day we held up people in the street or shopkeepers. We tackled security companies, travel agencies, and places like that. We began to use knives, pistols and sawn-off shotguns. From these robberies we gained a lot more money; we found it was an exciting life. Meanwhile I was getting more and more hooked on heroin. But finally I was arrested and spent a total of eleven years in prison.

The first stretch was eight and a half years for two hold-ups in which I'd been involved. While I was in jail my heart grew even harder than it was before. Also while I was there I was eaten up with pride and hatred. I continued on with heroin. I was consuming just as much in jail as I was beforehand. I had already done much damage while out of prison but I continued doing damage and hurt while in prison. I didn't care what way or how I did it. I was just determined to get my dose of heroin each day. I didn't have any consideration for anybody else.

In those days it was easy to get heroin in jail. Often the guards themselves would have it available through contacts with the outside world. You had to use some intimidation to get it. At times I even stole it from other prisoners who were weaker than me. There is a 'pecking order' whereby the strong ones live off the weak ones. I made sure I joined the big fish – the ones that were running the place and causing the most trouble.

My behaviour was really bad. I got into many fights and I would stab people; I often had blood on my hands. So I was transferred to a maximum security prison. I was thirty years old when I finally got out of jail. I went back to the same lifestyle I'd been involved in before. But it wasn't the same world any more. Times had changed. There weren't the same people that I'd mixed with before and I was afraid. I didn't have the courage and bravery that I'd had before. I continued taking heroin but my physical state deteriorated so much that I finished up as a vagabond. I didn't care whether I was clean or filthy dirty. I'd sleep in hostels or doss-houses, in the street or in an underground railway station, or under a bridge. All I wanted was to keep on consuming heroin, and carrying out enough robberies so that I could satisfy my craving.

Of course I wasn't happy and at one stage I was sleeping in a warehouse in Madrid. I would go for lunch at a place where they fed down-and-outs like me. It was operated by the Sisters of Calcutta. One day I was talking to someone at the door of the Hostel of St. Isidro. This man spoke to me about a Christian centre. The only problem there was they didn't let you smoke. The other problem was that they talked a lot about God.

At that time I didn't take a lot of notice and I just continued on. But one night in this warehouse I became really desperate. I remembered the words this man said about the centre. I began to talk to my friend about it. He didn't have a drug problem; he drank a bit but not a lot. He said, 'Why don't you go to this centre tomorrow?' So the next day we went to the office of an evangelical church that I knew about in the suburb of Lavapies. I spoke to the pastor and gave him the name of the centre that I'd been told about, but he suggested Betel instead. He rang Betel and we went there that same day.

I entered with a very hardened heart, closed to the things of God; however I saw the love of the people at the centre so I was obedient to those who were over me. But despite my obedience my heart was a long way from God. What had a really big impact on me was their love and devotion, and the way they treated me. I spent a year there and I got to the stage where I had to decide whether I was going to leave or ask God to do a miracle in my life.

One day there was an altar call at the Betel church and I went forward. I started to get closer to God then. But I continued to have doubts, and an inner battle still raged within me. Nevertheless God started to change my heart.

A week later I cried out to Him and actually challenged Him to do a real miracle in this life that had been so messed up.

Well, He is answering my prayer. He is still dealing with my stubborn character – that in itself is a miracle. And He's given me back my family, plus an even bigger family – the fellowship of Betel. Also, He has given me my very own family – with Lourdes. I would never have believed, when I arrived here, that all this was possible.

I'd just like to highlight the fact that God is dealing with my strong nature. Lately He has been challenging me to become more involved in evangelism, and that's my main delight here at Betel at the present time. When I meet with people in the street it's like looking in a mirror – I see what my life was, in other people. The thing that gives me the most joy is the fact that each morning I can give thanks to God for rescuing me from all that.

Elliott adds:
Eduardo is Betel's most active street evangelist. Each month he keeps a log of the people he has picked up and have entered the programme. Most he personally escorts right to our registry office. Hardly a month goes by without him rescuing up to forty addicts.

5

I WAS OLD BEFORE I WAS YOUNG

THE STORY OF PAQUI AND ANGEL

When one realises the depths of degradation to which Paqui and Angel (pronounced Ānhel) had sunk, it is almost impossible to believe that they are now missionaries in Italy. Yet, such is the grace and power of God.

Paqui commences.

I'm from a small city called Badajoz in western Spain, and I'm the second last daughter of eight brothers and sisters. Our parents were poor; my father was a shoemaker and my mum a housemaid. For that reason, four of my older siblings were brought up as wards of the state. Mum and Dad simply couldn't afford to keep them. Another sister lived with an aunt. In fact, only three of us actually lived with our parents. My eldest sister got a job so as to be more independent, while I cared for our little sister. Mum worked all day, and Dad drank too much. When he wasn't drunk he was out with his friends.

Consequently I missed out on family love and discipline; however, I was a very extrovert child. I'd always believed in God and liked going to catechism in the village Catholic church. I found there the love and attention I'd never known at home. Another bonus was that I got to go free on excursions I'd otherwise never have enjoyed!

Dad died in 1974 when I was eleven. His passing opened up the way for me to go and live with an aunt in Barcelona. I saw it as an escape. What I didn't realise was that from that moment on, the devil began to manipulate my life.

47

My aunt's neighbour was a hairdresser, and her husband ran a bar. It was arranged that, in exchange for free board, I would help out in the salon, the bar and in the house. They were rarely at home. I was physically very well developed for an eleven year old girl and the hairdresser's nineteen year old son began fondling me. Finally, the inevitable happened. He found me alone one day and raped me. Overnight I became a frightened, hurt and marked young woman. I felt that what had happened to me was written on my forehead. Over the next two years, however, he repeatedly forced himself on me. I was too afraid to tell his parents. Instead, I began drinking regularly to help me cope. (I'd taken my first sip at eight.) I was only a child who was old before I was young.

At fourteen I decided I'd had enough. A girlfriend and I found work as cleaners in a hotel, receiving lodging as part of our pay. At last we were truly independent. Now we could really enjoy our free time with mutual friends. Smoking pot was part of the scene. One day, when partying in a bar, the police detained me believing that I had escaped from home. They made investigations, but, as nobody claimed me, the head constable suggested that I apply for legal emancipation (release from legal custody of parents). So there I was, free to come and go as I chose at fourteen!

In 1979 I moved to Madrid to stay with my brother-in-law's sister. There I found work in nightclubs. I had become used to living it up on my own, and this was a fast way to make quick cash. I was paid to sit and drink with the men customers. I sure met a lot of men – mostly the wrong sort. I was introduced to strong alcohol and learned to sniff cocaine. Taking drugs just became a normal part of daily living.

A club owner took a fancy to me and forced me to sleep with him one night. Out of fear I submitted to the rape, but after that kept out of his way. When I discovered that I was pregnant, I decided to go home to Badajoz for the baby's birth. Rebeca Vanessa was born four weeks early, but my aunt agreed to have us stay with her. When the baby was six months old, I felt I ought to return to work and with my aunt's consent, left baby Vanessa with her and set off for Madrid, promising to send money and to visit regularly.

I meant well, but my words proved to be empty promises. I was soon trapped in my old lifestyle, becoming emotionally involved with my girlfriend's cousin – a man who trafficked in cocaine. I was soon hooked on the white powder. And once again I ended up pregnant.

A girlfriend was looking for an opportunity to end her affair with a well-known boxer. So we decided to run away together and start again. We packed our scant belongings and set off to find work in the nightclubs of Alicante, enjoying our new-found freedom.

But, unbeknown to us, after several months of detective work, the furious boxer traced us to our flat. We were fast asleep after a night's work when he and his three friends arrived high on cocaine and began beating us up. In his drugged, vindictive rage, he stopped at nothing. I was five months pregnant but this didn't stop him from violently stripping and raping me while the other men looked on. It was the most terrible moment of my life. As I sobbed on the floor he continued to beat both of us until he fell in exhaustion himself. While the four men slept off their doses of cocaine we made our escape – bruised and terrified.

So emotionally traumatised was I that I sat on a friend's bed for a week, unable even to talk. I felt as if I was trapped in a dark hole. Anger and revenge built up inside me, and obsessed with rage, I began searching for someone who would murder the boxer for me. I was even willing to prostitute myself if it meant getting money to pay a hit-man. Mercifully I found no willing person, despite the monetary reward I offered.

Well, I gave birth to my second child – a perfect little son, and decided that this time I would raise him myself although I paid a woman to care for him while I worked. But I hadn't realised that there would be so many bills to pay and finally gave into the temptation to sell my body in order to pay my debts. This was the first time I had willingly sunk to prostitution. I justified my decision, insisting that I was doing it for my son. And so I descended one step further down the ladder to hell.

It was then that I met a man that said he loved me and my boy. We lasted eight years together. We had seen how others had become rich quickly through trafficking heroin, and tried it for ourselves. It really did bring in the money fast. One day, just for fun, we decided to try a snort for ourselves. 'Just once,' we promised. How blind we were to heroin's insidious hold! Once became twice, and twice three times, until we were regularly sniffing. But each time our bodies craved more, which meant we had less to sell. We were forced to begin injecting as, that way, one needs less powder to keep the withdrawal pains at bay – but only for a while. In no time at all we had no powder to sell. We needed every bit we could beg, borrow or steal.

And so, just like all the others we fell totally into heroin's deadly trap. We could think of nothing and nobody else – not even Carlos, my five year old son. I had changed his 'carers' three times by now. They were becoming too emotionally attached to him. And they could see the state I was in. Finally I was reported to the police, and the Family Courts ordered that Carlos be taken away from me. He was eventually adopted into another family. (I live with the longing that one day he will make contact with me. I long to ask for his forgiveness and have our relationship restored.) But right then nothing else mattered: heroin was my master. I was its slave.

After nine long years of heroin addiction someone told me about the Betel centre in the suburb of San Blas, Madrid. Up until then I didn't even know that evangelicals existed! So, with my body, soul and spirit torn in shreds I entered Betel's doors. Betel means 'House of God' and 'Gateway to Heaven'.

At first I thought that everyone was crazy. However, I soon began to feel more relaxed. The leaders actually treated me like a person – something I had forgotten that I was! Betty, a Mexican missionary, spent most of the first weeks with me, constantly talking about Jesus. She gave me my first Bible.

On my twentieth day I set off with some five hundred others for the annual WEC church camp held at the beautiful campsite, 'Peña de Horeb,' near Guadalajara. We all slept in makeshift plastic tents. Tom Spyker, an American missionary to Mexico, was the speaker. He challenged us to try God. I decided that I would put Him to the test for myself. I needed a sign that He really existed after all my hurtful experiences. I simply asked Him to wake me in the night. If He did, then I would follow Him with all my heart. Now, I sleep heavily, but to my surprise, the Lord did wake me. I was so totally awake that I was unable to go back to sleep for the rest of the night! Instead, I was filled with a certainty of His reality and of His presence in my being. There in the tent I knew He was for real. 'Thank You for waking me,' I whispered. 'I promise that I'll serve You from now on.'

You see, I understood in that moment that Jesus was the only One that could save me from certain death. I had known only drug abuse and corruption. I asked myself how it was that I was even still alive! (Today I know why. Jesus had a special plan for my life.) The next morning I began to listen intently to the preaching and entered into the worship with joy, lifting my hands to God in thanks and new liberty.

After I promised to live for Him, God began changing me. It was a tough process, but precious, too. He took away all the hate I held in my heart, all the bitterness and resentment. Even my face began to glow with new life.

After two and a half years at the Madrid centre I was transferred to a daughter work three hours away in Cuenca. It was there that I met Angel. I knew in my heart soon after arrival that he was the man that God had prepared for me. Mind you, it wasn't an easy time, because a year passed by and Angel did not seem to notice me. I kept praying, 'Lord, please put in Angel the same feelings for me as I have for him. But if he is not for me, then take these feelings away from me.'

God finally put those feelings in Angel's heart, and with the blessing of the leadership he asked me to marry him. After six months of engagement we were married in 1993. A friend, Sue Single, lent me her beautiful white bridal gown. I felt clean and pure, forgiven by God for my past. Mum, accompanied by my aunt with my beautiful twelve year old daughter, Vanessa, and two of my sisters, came to the wedding. We didn't have a thing, but God supplied everything! Even our honeymoon was made possible by Christian friends who lent us a lovely little apartment by the beach. This was just the beginning of many other new things God has been doing for us. He continues to work in us both. But He has never thrown any of our past at us. In fact He has made EVERYTHING new.

We had been married for only about eight months when Miguel Jambrina, the leader of the Betel centre in Cuenca, responded to the call to lead the new advance into Italy. He spoke with Angel and me about accompanying him and his wife, Mari Carmen. After praying about it, we replied that we were open to going. Excitedly we applied for our passports. On returning to collect them we were shocked and embarrassed to discover that I was on the police 'wanted list' for two offences – both for trafficking heroin. I was escorted to prison. I would stay there for two and a half years. I panicked.

Angel, too, was frantic with worry. He never stopped praying and doing everything within his power to free me. Miraculously, the judge pardoned me by phone for the first offence on hearing that I was now cured and helping others in rehabilitation work. But the defendant for the other offence refused to budge. Angel made endless trips back and forth to Madrid to talk with the judge and lawyers. Things were not looking good.

In the meantime, the prison director, who knew of Betel, gave Angel special visiting privileges. When it came time for the court case, I told the truth. It could only have been the Lord. I was sentenced to only ten days of imprisonment! The other two years I could complete on a good behaviour bond outside of those four walls. Angel and I fell into each other's arms weak with relief, filled with thanks to God for His unmerited kindness.

After another month in our own small flat we were asked to open a community house for couples. By the time we left, there were four of us sharing the upstairs area of a converted barn. Though not an easy time, it was another important learning experience.

Miguel and his team had been in Naples for a year by the time the Lord freed us to join them. We went in great excitement, but we soon discovered how difficult it was being missionaries in another country. There were so many changes to make, not the least being the language. Being the only woman, and without children and in a men's centre, I had to stay at home for the first year. Angel found it an uphill struggle trying to catch up and feel a part of the original leadership team. We battled often with loneliness, anger and frustration. We couldn't wait to put our feet on Spanish soil a year later when we took our two weeks annual holiday. But to our surprise, we immediately began to feel that we no longer belonged to Spain. Our home was back in Italy! From that moment on we had no doubt that God had truly called us there.

The work has passed through many ups and downs. Miguel became desperately sick with AIDS. He was wasting away in a Naples hospital, hoping to recover and continue the work. We all prayed earnestly for his healing. But finally Lindsay and Tomas had to come over and escort him and his wife and baby son back to Spain for urgent medical attention.

We also saw Damian's marriage restored. When Reme and their son joined him, for financial reasons, we all shared a house. Again we had to learn to share and forgive one another. However, I found that my relationship with the Lord was more intense when we met each day to read the Bible and pray together with them. Besides, after a year of feeling rather useless, I was thrilled when Paco said he was putting us to work. Together Reme and I practised our Italian by offering the Betel calendar to the local businesses. We also helped out in the office answering the phone and typing finances into the computer. Angel and I were sent to Madrid for five weeks to learn about restoring furniture and upholstery.

Now after four years in Italy, we are fulfilled. Although God continues to work in us both, He has never thrown any of our past at us. He encourages us to admit our mistakes, ask forgiveness and move on. My husband organises the work programme for the men and women and sees that the bills are paid. I continue to oversee the upholstery workshop, and together we are learning to care for the new women's work.

Today I have a good relationship with my eighteen year old daughter, Vanessa. We call each other by telephone, and I visit her and my little granddaughter each time we can manage a trip to Spain. We are both longing for the day when Carlos, now sixteen, makes contact with us. Angel and I also have contact with his sixteen year old son, Miguel Angel.

We are open to going anywhere the Lord would want us – especially if it means seeing Italy opened up for Christ. With all our hearts we feel that there is no work more honourable than that of being a servant of Jesus Christ.

I have shared with you many of the unseemly details of my past life but only to give glory to Christ, because, 'where sin abounded, grace did much more abound'.

Now Angel shares his experience.
When I was ten my father died. Losing Dad devastated me so much that I reacted by withdrawing from others; and my personality began to change. At that time I began to smoke and drink alcohol and do all kinds of crazy adolescent things. As I grew into teenage years I left school and began to work as an apprentice electrician. My weekends were filled with discotheques, girls and parties. I felt empty within and tried to fill that inner void with many other things. It wasn't long before smoking 'joints' became a regular part of my leisure time, but

from there it was easy to go the next step to sniffing heroin; then sniffing gave way to 'mainlining'.

This new drug had the potential to destroy my life and everything for which I had worked, up until then – employment, physical health, family, social standing. Eventually heroin took them all! By nature I was a fighter but heroin took all the 'fight' out of me and transformed me into a defeated man. From my viewpoint life made no sense at all. The only thing that I lived for was heroin. I got to a stage where I thought that death would be my only escape from this living hell. Desperately I went to my family and begged them to help me. By then I was living in the street without a roof over my head, without food to eat, and filthy because I didn't wash. My appearance must have been disgusting because people, when they saw me, immediately avoided me. I felt rejected by my family, society, everyone.

One day a neighbour spoke to me about Centro Betel which had an office near where my family lived. When I got there, they told me that it was a Christian rehabilitation centre. This fact didn't impress me as I had attended a school where the teachers were priests and I had received such harsh treatment from these religious men that I vowed never to set foot in a church again. Nevertheless I entered the Betel centre and was immediately astounded to listen to guys like me who had been in the same world of drugs talking about God in such a genuine and personal way that I decided to stay in order to find out what had changed them. Many of them I had known previously on the street.

It was beyond my comprehension, but each day watching and listening to these men gave me an inner strength. I saw something special in them. They loved each other, and new people like me as well, without asking for anything in exchange. By nature I was a very indecisive person but one day I decided that I definitely wanted what they had so I asked Jesus to come into my life and to change me. It wasn't long before I knew that I had been given the opportunity of a life time. That was eight years ago. That day God began such a magnificent work of restructuring in my life – I mean, from the ground up! He is still doing it even today. He has given me so many positive things and I know I haven't deserved any of them.

I never imagined that one day I could be doing what I am doing now, because when my time in the rehabilitation programme was finished I decided to stay on as a staff member and help other men as I had been helped. I am so grateful to God because what He gave to me, and therefore what I am able to give to others, is something that this world can never give – a hope and a future.

Five years ago I married Paqui who came from a similar background. We met at Centro Betel. She is literally a gift from God, not just my wife; she is my companion and friend but even more than that she is a woman who loves God. We are together in this vocation of serving God and serving others. Today we are working with Centro Betel in Naples, Italy, where we feel useful, very satisfied and content as members of a big family in which God has placed us.

I thank God that when every other person and avenue failed, He was there with His hand held out waiting for me.

6

STEALING NEW CARS – PROFITABLE, TILL CAUGHT

THE STORY OF JASON WOOD

I'm from Wigan in Greater Manchester. When I was ten my mother and father were divorced. My father was an electrician and mum was a cleaner. I had a choice of going with either mum or dad. My two brothers went with my father and I stayed with my mother, but she couldn't handle me because I was so wild. As a result I was sent to a children's home in Standish near Wigan. I was there for five years but while there I started to inhale butane gas. It has a hallucinogenic effect; I did it because all the others were into it. That led to glue sniffing.

When I was fifteen I went back to live with my mother in Marsh Green. Then I was into hashish and smoked that for a number of years. At seventeen I started taking amphetamines. After school I went to train to be a builder; this involved working on building sites.

I began to have a relationship with a girl called Joanne, from Liverpool. But I ran into trouble; I was into drink and became aggressive. In court I was given a large fine but failed to pay it – it was a daft thing to do, as I would later discover.

By this time Joanne and I were living together. I was making good money in the building trade, so we were able to have a house. One day just as I was leaving for work there was a knock on the door. Three policemen were standing there and arrested me for failing to pay my fine. In court I was sentenced to twenty eight days in jail. I was taken to Strangeways prison. While I was inside my partner's father came to my house and told her a pack of lies about me. She was four months pregnant but in view of what her father said she decided to have an abortion. While still in jail I had a letter from her telling me about this. I freaked out and because of my behaviour had to serve the full twenty eight days without any remission.

When I came out three of my mates and I went to Liverpool and beat up Joanne's father – he ended up in hospital. I sold our house and used the proceeds for drugs. I don't know what happened to Joanne. From that time I started to take heroin. I was nineteen by then. I went downhill on heroin and crack, using up all the house money and what I had saved for the past two years.

Things went from bad to worse. I began stealing and selling cars in order to have money for drugs. I even stole new cars from dealers' lots and sold them in Manchester.

I used to go to a place called Moss-side to buy heroin. The people there were from Scotland so I made new contacts in Paisley and Glasgow. This led to a job, picking up cars there, and driving them to Manchester. When I was in Glasgow I ran into trouble with the police. I was caught stealing a brand new SAAB and was sentenced to twelve months in jail – Barlinnie, supposed to be the roughest prison in Britain. I lost my remission because of fighting. (I was the only Englishman in a Scottish jail!)

After that I lived in Paisley making a living by delivering drugs. But I had a bad experience there, which I simply can't talk about, and had to leave the area, so I returned to Wigan.

I ended up going back home to see my stepfather and mother, mainly because I had no money. My stepfather was pretty well off so I started stealing from him. (When you are on heroin you have no feelings for others.) My mother had me arrested because I stole and sold all her rings. I was put in a bail-hostel. The doctor put me on methadone, which, I think, is worse than heroin – it makes you feel so desolate. On methadone you can't sleep;

you get more and more depressed, so one morning I just cracked. I cut my wrists. There was blood all over the place. I dropped to my knees and cried: ' There must be more to life than this and if God is there please do something to help me!' Instantly I felt a peace come over me – a sense of relaxation. That's when I knew Jesus was real.

I was sentenced to six months in prison for stealing mum's rings. When I came out, a friend, Andrew Whittle, took me to a church in Wigan – the Christian Community Centre. I went right up to the front as the worship service was starting. I dropped to my knees and cried, 'God, help me!' The pastor, Ray Bellfield, came over to me and prayed for me and I was filled with the Spirit. After that I knew God's hand was upon my life. I made a decision about what things would have to change. Arrangements were made for me to go to a Teen Challenge rehabilitation centre in Scotland but they could not take me immediately.

I met a lady called Pat in the church who was in charge of outreach. She had links with Betel so I called them on the phone. I expected to be told I would have to wait but I was told I could go there that very day!

I decided to wait a couple of days so that I could have one final 'fix'.

I came to Betel and stayed two weeks then left – for three hours! After I came away a cloud of condemnation came over me. I got as far as Birmingham bus station but then decided to phone back and say I was returning.

Since entering Betel I don't even think about heroin. I've no desire for it. I'm free from drugs. Jesus is real! I praise the Lord for what He has done for me. I feel FREE and I've never been happier in all my life.

God has put a vision in my heart to help save young people from the depths that I've been in and I'd like to stay with Betel and work with those who come in.

7

THE WHEELCHAIR FRAUD

THE STORY OF GAETANO CASTELLONE ('NINO')

Born in 1969 into a normal working-class family in Naples, I am one of five brothers. Three of us ended up immersed in the world of drugs. In our inner city suburb, drugs, delinquency and unemployment, sadly, are all a part of life.

From thirteen onwards, I preferred to hang around with friends that were older than me. This gave me a sense of being different, of feeling that I was a cut above others my age. They introduced me to hashish. It made me feel mature and I congratulated myself on having discovered things of which other fellows my age were ignorant. I'd discovered the best that life had to offer and I was still so young! I could hardly wait until the weekends when my friends would take me out and show me the nightlife. I would often not return home until the next day having partied all night. I was 'OK' in their eyes. That was important to me. I thought, as they did, that true freedom manifests itself in rebelling against the social system, the status quo. I honestly believed that real happiness lay in enjoying all the pleasurable experiences that this world had to offer, so I set off to do that at breakneck speed. I was young; I knew I was good-looking, and I had the world at my feet.

When my friends in the neighbourhood 'graduated' from smoking hashish to sniffing heroin, I decided that I wasn't going to be the odd one out! I wanted to prove to them that I was as game and 'mature' as they were. I was amazed at the effects of sniffing heroin. It wasn't like the other drugs. Heroin filled me with a sense of security that I had not known before. Being a shy person by nature, I yearned for this feeling of being sure of myself and being able to confront any problem that came my way. With heroin, I became the person that I always wanted to be. It was great... for a while at least. I was hopelessly unaware of the subtle slavery to which I was submitting myself.

Before long the desire to take heroin so that I would feel secure and 'in control' was replaced with the need to keep sniffing heroin just to do the most basic functions. To get up in the morning, I needed to sniff the stuff. Then in order to be able to go to work, I needed another dose. At lunchtime I needed still another in order to keep going in the afternoon. Then to keep the withdrawal pains at bay in order to sleep, I needed yet another dose. This habit that began as a 'great discovery' now had me in its grip and I had no idea how to escape. Far from being able to confront any problem that came my way, I couldn't even face the new day when the light came into my bedroom. I abhorred the morning because it meant thinking up new ways of finding my next 'fix'.

My so-called friends didn't want anything to do with me; they had their own problems. I felt so alone. Solitude was like a black cloud that followed me everywhere. The lights had gone out in my life – everything just seemed dark and hopeless. I felt reduced to nothing, as if my personality and 'personhood' had been obliterated.

The cost of keeping up the habit made me turn from snorting (sniffing through the nose) to mainlining (injecting directly into the vein). When you mainline you can get by with a lesser quantity. It wasn't now a question of getting 'high' as it had been in the beginning, it was rather a question of just being able to cope with the basics of living. This, of course, had its consequences with my work. I had a good, secure job with the Italian Post Office working at the Central Branch in the heart of Naples. Jobs were hard to come by in our city where the level of unemployment is the highest in Italy. Finally, after many warnings, the Post Office terminated my employment and I was left without any income. I was desperate.

At that time it occurred to me that I could make money begging, and by pretending to be physically handicapped. From somewhere I got hold of a wheelchair in which I sat while a friend pushed me from shop to shop in the main street. Before long, people began to get wise to me so I had to go to other towns and cities. Eventually I made my way around most of the major cities in Italy. My friend and I made a lot of money that way but it all ended up in our veins as we spent it on heroin.

One day in Naples I met up with a friend from the old, drug-experimenting days. I hadn't seen him for years. But I couldn't believe that he was the same person! He was radically changed, very different from the man that I once knew. He told me that he had been in a Christian drug rehabilitation centre called 'Betel', and gave me a tract called 'I am the drug'. It was written as if the drug, heroin, were a person. It was strange, but as I read it, it virtually described in detail my own life. It was uncanny! The tract was a Christian pamphlet printed by Centro Betel. As I read it, something long-extinguished and deep within me came alive as I yearned to change and return to being a real person again. I never once thought that God would have anything to do with giving me a new life, as the tract suggested. Nevertheless, its message touched my heart as nothing ever had before and I went to find this Centro Betel. I immediately asked for admission.

Though I had always believed in God, I had never seen Him as a merciful God and one who deals with each individual on a personal level. What struck me about this Centro Betel was that the leaders, who had all been addicts themselves talked about a *living* Jesus Christ. I had never thought of Christ as a present-day, *living* Person. I was used to seeing Him represented in paintings and statues as crucified on a cross or lying lifeless in Mary's arms – in each case *dead*. But in Betel all they talked about was a living Person who, in spite of all that I had done in the past, put an enormous value on my life, enough to die for me! As I began to comprehend this, for the first time hope began to dawn in my life. I was being offered the chance to recommence my life, taking a new and different direction. But I realised there was a cost – a total commitment to Him and a complete renouncing of my former ways.

Today, three years later, I can say that I am learning what it means to be forgiven and also what it means to serve God. When I think of when I used to go around deceiving people in the wheelchair, and the hundreds of lies that I told every day, and now know that God has forgiven me for each one of those lies (amongst many other things), it just fills me with a tremendous gratitude.

Currently I am a leader in the Betel centre just down the road from where my family lives! My father frequently comes to the church meetings. God has radically changed my life and I am constantly aware of the fact that He demands a radical and unconditional commitment from His followers. He tells us to 'take up our cross' and follow Him. Each day I am conscious of the need of self-discipline in my own life and the responsibility to disciple the lives of those under my care. What a salvation! What a privilege to serve Him!

8

FROM DISC JOCKEY TO DISCIPLE

THE STORY OF PACO GIMENEZ

I am thirty-two now and for the last six years I've been with Betel. My mother died when I was a lad of thirteen, then one year later on the same day in the same month my father died. From that time onward my two older sisters guided me. I was sent to a boarding school for orphans and in the summer my brother would send me to camps. In reality my family relationships were very thin, very scarce.

One older sister was married and I lived with her and her husband in my parents' former house. One night when I was about sixteen I went for a walk. I returned home an hour later than my designated hour and knocked on the door. My brother-in-law answered and asked me why I was so late. 'I told you to come home at 8 o'clock and it's now 9.30 pm!' I went upstairs to my bedroom, took a knife, went down and pointed it at him: and said, 'You're not going to tell me how to run my life.'

Just a few months after that my sister and brother-in-law went to live in Alicante. I was left to live alone. Little by little I established my own pattern of life, doing what I wanted and working at what I wanted. I had some success. I liked working in discotheques. I liked working in radio, and became a disc jockey and a radio announcer. Eventually I was a popular media figure climbing the ladder of success, but actually I started to move towards a precipice. I began to take drugs because of a personal emptiness. After a short period of time all my successes turned to failures and I began to find myself in debt. Creditors were chasing me and people were against me. To escape all this

I went five hundred kilometres away from where I lived – Ciudad Real – to Almería where my second sister was then living.

My sister was aware of my problems. She gave me lodging in her house but after a while she told me to go, because she had her own family to care for. I got a job in a national radio station there and after a few weeks went to live with one of the other employees. It looked as if my problems were now solved: I didn't use drugs, I had a good job, and I lived responsibly. But after three months the temptation to use drugs returned. One day I went to the bar by the beach where I used to buy drugs. In the next six months I used them more than ever and during that time I embezzled 3,000,000 pesetas from the radio station. It got so bad I had to leave the house and live in a hotel. Then I was forced to leave the hotel and went to live in a single room. My world kept getting smaller and smaller, my health started to deteriorate and I felt so trapped that one day I seriously considered suicide.

As people knew me well from the radio, I thought that perhaps my last great stab at fame would be a headline and article to say that I'd committed suicide. I thought of that as my last great success! I was sniffing cocaine which produces a level of anxiety much greater than heroin does. The huge quantities I consumed produced a very high degree of paranoia. I got to such a psychological state of entrapment, that I went to the director of the radio station and confessed that I had been keeping the money from the advertising accounts. I thought that if I confessed but kept working I would have a chance to return the money to him over time. But things went from bad to worse. I felt worse every day and finally I just couldn't stand being where I was, so I went and talked to a social worker in the city and to a lawyer, to see if they could help me. The social worker told me there were centres that could help me. She asked how much I could afford to pay.

Then she asked whether my family could help me. I told her that I had hurt them so much that they wouldn't. As a last resort they gave me the telephone number of Betel (which is free). I decided on Betel in Málaga because that had the best tourist environment with the sea and beach. My idea was just to go there for a few months and have a good time. I thought they would give me pills to cure me then I could go back to selling drugs to recoup the money I had embezzled and lost.

I entered Betel on 18th February, 1993, in bad shape. The only baggage I brought was a little bag of dirty clothes. I just didn't fit in. They would get us up at 7am, and I would ask, 'What are we getting up at 7am for?' But I did have a passion for the songs they were singing. I made my first friend there; his name was Andres. As time went on, I began to have continual tensions with the people; I seemed to live in a different world, and had a way of seeing things that was different to everyone else. So every night I would find my one friend Andres, who was a leader, and would say, 'Why can't we do it this other way? Why can't I talk to the girls? Why do we have to work like this?' He encouraged me. One night I came to him; I was very angry about things that had happened during the day. He said, 'You know what you really need. You need to accept Jesus, as your Saviour and Lord, in your heart and be quiet. Your problems aren't going to disappear. You will see them in a different way.' And that night I accepted the Lord because I didn't have any more defences.

There was no radical change in my life but I noticed that my ego, my person, began to change gradually. I remember one night shortly after that the leader of the house rebuked me in front of all the men. He raised his voice and really had a go at me, but everything he said was true. I remember leaving the meeting, humiliated, and going down to the orange tree; I sat there and cried. There was a war in my heart. I had to decide either to leave or to change. I cried because I wanted to leave. But I knew that this was my last opportunity. I heard the voices of my friends up the hill calling me to go to work but I did not pay any attention. I just kept on crying. I had never cried like that before. By the time I walked up the hill to the houses everyone had left for work except those who were keeping the property. So I went to the responsible person and I said, 'What do you want me to do? I'm willing to do anything.' I believe it was from that day that things changed in my life.

I felt a certain call to serve God. When they asked for volunteers for Italy I raised my hand and said I would go. I was only four or five months old in the Lord, but I continued thinking I had to go. They kept telling me that if I didn't have a call to go I would be a flop. Once a month we would visit the big church which Daniel Del Vecchio ran. He is the grandfather of the rehabilitation movement in Spain.

One particular Sunday I was given permission to go to the evening meeting. Even though I was a very young Christian at that time I said to the Lord, 'If You want me to go to Italy, You'll speak to me and confirm that call.' But in my heart there was a struggle because some were going to the movies to see Tom Cruise in *The Fourth of July*. Would I go to the movies or the tabernacle? I decided to go to the church. It wasn't by chance because Daniel chose to preach on David. He preached about killing giants, and reaching out to others. Sitting in the big tabernacle to the extreme right in the very last row, it was as if everything he preached was for me. Then he made an appeal at the end and said, 'Where are the Davids, to go to the nations?'

I knew God was speaking to me. The start in Italy was delayed because Jambri, the designated leader, was sick. My leader said to me, 'Italy is off now. It's not going to happen, so just forget about it and focus on serving God here.' But I knew that what had happened in the tabernacle wasn't emotion. God had confirmed to me that I would go.

Time passed and eventually a team went to Italy and I went with them. I was the least mature – only seven months old in the Lord.

We began to live in a large old house on the outskirts of Naples. Our team task, at the beginning, was simply to renovate it and make it ready as a centre to receive addicts.

We had a teacher who would come to the house to teach us Italian. We realised the first love we had to have was for our teacher and to communicate with him. The locals used to call me crazy because I would go to work with a dictionary in my hand. That way I learned what a brick was called and what a shovel was called; I began to learn a little more than the other men.

Jambri, the leader, was very much loved by the men. We really appreciated the physical exertion he made to attend all the meetings because he was very sick with AIDS. Even the Italians realised that here was a man who was consumed by a desire to serve God. We saw him as a grandfather even though he was only in his thirties. He had strength to preach for only thirty minutes, but his messages were really powerful and inspiring.

One day when he was preaching he took a tape from Marcos Vidal, a Christian singer, and talked about it, and that had a tremendous impact on us. His sickness was progressive and he had to enter the hospital in Naples which was a very dirty place. Finally Jambri with his wife, Mari-Carmen, had to go to Spain for medical attention because the health care in Naples for AIDS sufferers was bad. As soon as he got a little bit better in Spain, he came right back to Italy. But he didn't last too long and when his health deteriorated further he had to leave.

Elliott continues:
We were left with sixteen single men with no pastor in Italy. We had seven Spanish workers and nine Italians. When Jambri went back we didn't know exactly whom to make leader. It was between another man called Augustine or Paco. Augustine was a little older in the Lord; he'd come from Betel Barcelona and he spoke the best Italian. So he became leader not because he was the best but because he spoke the best Italian at the time. He proved unsuitable so we had to send him back to Spain. This

led to Paco becoming the leader when he was only one year old in the Lord.

His gifting in communications was put to great use by God. He began a promotional campaign by letter and by visits and he really made dozens and dozens of friends for us all over Italy. He really promoted Betel and let the churches know that we weren't coming for money but we were there to serve them and that they could send their drug addicts and their outcast people to us, without any cost to themselves. He was leader for two years and was quite heroic. He was obviously the most gifted person and the best Italian speaker and was the one that had to do it. But the responsibilities were just too weighty and he hadn't had the maturity or the experience of the cross working deeply in his life. The Bible warns us not to promote too quickly. Paco never fell into sin but he was overloaded with responsibilities like pastoring and counselling which he couldn't carry at that time and since he was a gifted person naturally, with very high intelligence, he was able to run the centre in his own natural strength. But a soulish giftedness is not a substitute for a spiritual giftedness. Paco realised that; we realised that; and we agreed that it would be good for him to come back to Madrid to mature, surrounded by other pastors.

Paco lifts the curtain on his inner battles:
I have to admit that those last months in Italy I wasn't being very conscientious. I had reached the place where I was depressed, disillusioned, and I was making errors of judgement. I started to live purely in my own strength. I was at the point of making an appointment with one of the women in the church who was showing some interest in me. While I was dialling her a spirit of heaviness and sadness fell upon me so I hung up and went out and sat on the kerb.

I realised I was going to lose all that I had attained in God up to that point.

Elliott continues:

Paco has come back and he's humbled himself. He's doing more Bible study. He is gaining new skills. He's been very helpful in communications. He has been a big help in programming, in the development of media and church relations, and is designing new literature.

After a year in Madrid Paco has been given responsibility over our Ciudad Real Men's Center and our Betania Conference facilities. God has given him Melanie, a young girl from Naples, Italy, as a wife. They hope to return to Italy one day.

Paco concludes:

One of the reasons why I have stayed here in Madrid is that I don't want to be another failure. I don't want to be a stumbling block to other people. I want to be an example. Every time I go through any doubt or struggle I remember the covenant that God made with Abraham. I want to keep my covenant and be a man of my word.

9

'YOUR CONDITION IS FATAL'

THE STORY OF EDUARDO HERNANDEZ

My parents are Catholics and I had a good Catholic education. My father owned many properties in Seville and we lived off the income derived from them. We had chauffeurs, maids, servants, tutors, but as the costs of our education increased (I had three brothers and four sisters) my father over-extended his business and then it crashed. He had to sell the family home in Seville; my brothers and sisters were separated and my mother went to live in Salamanca with my aunt.

Eventually my father got on his feet again, but I had a lot of rebellion in my heart. I didn't accept authority and just wanted to have a good time.

I was sixteen when I finished high school and it was then that I started to get mixed up with people who were involved in the drug world. I began to smoke marijuana and to take amphetamines. I was very interested in politics and because things like drugs and drinking had been banned in Spain there was a tendency for us young people to take up everything that was prohibited.

I wasn't a communist but I sympathised with them simply because of their rebellion against the government system. I started at the University of Seville but during the first two years I didn't really study at all, I just got involved in drugs. I stole my father's car and wrecked it in an accident. That was the night my parents realised that I had real problems. They offered me the opportunity to leave Seville and go to Salamanca to study. So I went there, lived in my aunt's house and began to study.

But I didn't finish my course. I stole a lot of money from my aunt and then went back to Seville.

I still had one year to finish my degree but I knew that I couldn't complete it because of drugs. I had to do something serious, so I paid to go into a rehabilitation centre.

I was there for twenty eight days but never came free of drugs; I just changed to different ones. I finished up taking morphine and, using that, I managed to finish my degree course at the university. I got some work as a trainee lawyer and that lasted for two years but it was a total disaster because of my drug-taking. I left work and went into a very deep depression. For the next three years I just stayed at home. I hardly went out at all. I closed myself in a bedroom, without any desire to live, just really wanting to die.

I continued taking drugs, mainly pills and morphine. My brother is a doctor so he was able to prescribe these for me. After that a friend of mine came and took me to a psychiatrist. I didn't want to go, but my friend said he'd helped him, so I went. He did some tests and asked me about 500 questions. When I went to get the results he said, 'Your situation is fatal. You've had it.' He said I was so mixed up in my mind he didn't have any solution for me. Then he said, 'Look, I want to be honest with you. I can't help you. I don't want to take your money but if you really want help the only one who is able to help you is Jesus Christ.' He was a Catholic psychiatrist but he'd heard people talking about Christian drug rehabilitation centres. He knew that they were working very well and having a lot of success. He said, 'I don't have a solution for you. The only thing I can give you is pills to make you feel more relaxed. The only one that can change you is God.' He looked for a centre for me and that turned out to be Betel in Málaga.

I entered under compulsion. The friend who had taken me to the psychiatrist and my mother and sister all forced me to go. That was in the middle of 1992. I was so ill when I entered that I didn't realise what was going on around me. I ran off and phoned my mother to come and pick me up, but she said she wouldn't. She said she was sick of me and until I got cured not to bother turning up again.

I either had to live on the street or go back to the centre, so I returned. They put me under discipline for a month. I was unable to sleep for forty days because of my physical condition.

One day I was out working in a house with another fellow, Kiki (Enrike). He was testifying to the lady who owned the house. Kiki said that he was working for love. I hadn't been in the centre very long but something in those words touched me. I believe God touched my heart and tears began to roll down my cheeks. I saw myself as very dirty. I was ashamed. I saw myself as I really was. I had never done anything for the love of anyone. And here was this person saying he was working for love. But nothing really changed.

When I could find an opportunity I would smoke. One of my motives for continuing in Betel in Málaga was that in Seville it is very hot, but in Málaga there are lots of beaches. I thought I could stay here and enjoy going to the beach!

At that stage there weren't many people in the centre and instead of having our own church meetings we went to meetings run by Daniel Del Vecchio who also had a drug centre in Málaga. In one of those meetings they had an altar call and that's when I committed my life to Jesus Christ.

After this happened God broke me. He humbled me. My life changed completely. My first encounter with God really impacted my life. I remember during those early days I spent a lot of time really broken and crying, as God dealt with me.

After being in the centre a year and a half I was given the job of managing our thrift shop. It is a position with a lot of responsibility because I had to control everything – the work, the money, the people coming into the shop and managing the workers as well. The leader, Manuel, put a lot of confidence in me. He has since died. But I realise that during that time there were still things in my life that hadn't been committed to the Lord.

After four years I decided that I was now cured and began to feel a desire for the profession for which I'd studied. I decided to go and work for my brother in his law office. But Manuel died about that time and it wasn't the right time for me to leave. Apart from that there was a secret sin in my life. I felt that the Holy Spirit spoke to me and I realised I had to confess this.

I spoke to Elliott by phone and the elders asked me to go to Madrid because of what I had done. I had to start there as though I was entering for the first time. I came from being the second in charge in Málaga to being like someone who had just come in off the street. I really had to humble myself, but God gave me the strength to continue, and I've experienced that the person who humbles himself God will raise up.

There wasn't any dramatic change in my attitude after this time. It was really something that developed little by little and as time went by I realised that God was shutting doors and that He didn't want me to go back home to Seville for a professional career. He opened doors for me to take on more tasks here in Madrid. I began to develop a burden for the work and God began to give me more responsibility. There's a depth and excitement in this that I love.

Eduardo is now in charge of Betel's legal affairs. He liaises with the local government regarding the registration of the centres; he advises on the constitution; he looks after all the legal aspects of Betel's various ministries.

10

A WEEKLY BANK ROBBERY FINANCED OUR HABITS

THE STORY OF JOSÉ AND TONI

The test of a true transformation is the capacity to re-integrate into normal life. No better example of this can be found than the lives of José and Toni who have been back into city life in Madrid since 1990 and are active members of the Betel church.

Toni shares her testimony first.

My parents worked hard because they wanted to upgrade our house. My two brothers, sister and I really looked after ourselves because they were so busy working. Mum and Dad wanted to give us the best they could but they only thought of that in monetary terms. We were brought up in the Madrid suburb of Vicalvaro. When I was nine we moved to San Blas and at fourteen I left school and started working. I began to drink alcohol and go to discos where I met my husband, José. I started going out with him and when I was seventeen I found I was pregnant. A little while later we were married.

This was the beginning of some of our troubles because we were so young. We hadn't really found out what life was all about. When Oscar was two years old we started going out with our old friends again. We were drinking very heavily and spending whole nights out, leaving Oscar with my mother. That led to us taking soft drugs and then we got on to taking heroin. In the beginning José had work and we were able to buy the drugs we used. At the same time we were able to buy a house in

Mejorada Del Campo. Before that, we were living with my parents but from this time on we were able to live by ourselves. Without parents to influence us our lives became less and less controlled. We just did whatever we wanted.

Even though José was working, we weren't able to pay our debts and we fell behind with our house payments. We moved further and further into the drug world and to injecting heroin. Then I fell pregnant for the second time and our first daughter Ana Belen was born. Even during the pregnancy I was taking heroin. In order to get money for this, we began to hold up and rob people. José was sentenced to jail several times, the last time for nine years, although he served only five. During that time I left the children with my mother so that I could work in San Blas trafficking in drugs in order to support my habit. This was the lowest point in my life because I would do anything to get money.

About this time the Teppers, with Lindsay and Myk began to evangelise in that area.

Myk (later to become Lindsay McKenzie's wife) spoke with me many times in the street and tried to convince me that I should go to a centre, but I kept refusing. I went to a couple of the meetings and I saw what was happening, but my life was such a mess that I didn't believe anything. At the same time Raul Casto was being cured in Lindsay's flat. He also spoke to me in the street, because his life had begun to change. I finally decided to go to a centre in Santander because at that stage Betel didn't have a house for girls in Madrid. The night before I went I injected the biggest quantity of drugs possible and I left myself just enough money to buy the ticket.

I didn't tell anybody in Madrid that I was going to Santander. All I had was the address written on a bit of paper. I found my way to the reception office. They asked who sent me. I said that I'd just come. They didn't want to give me a place in the girls' house there because it was almost full but they rang Lindsay and Myk in Madrid and they recommended that they take me in. The next day when I woke up I wanted to leave. But I know that in some way God took my strength away. I didn't have enough energy to go. The time of passing through 'cold turkey' was difficult for me because my body was in a terrible state. I weighed less than thirty kilos.

During this time I tried to take my own life by cutting the veins in my wrist. They took me to the hospital and the doctors put me on a drip. When I was released the girls asked me if I wanted to give my life to Jesus Christ and I said 'yes' but I wasn't really convinced in my heart. Then one Sunday after the meeting all the girls went to the beach. While I was there I began to feel good; something was happening within me. There was a song that I liked very much – 'Make me into a new vessel.' On the way back I really began to desire that the Lord would make me a new vessel. I began to sing that song with a lot of enthusiasm. I know that that was the day I committed my life to the Lord.

I spent a year there. At that stage my husband was in jail in Vitoria, so I was transferred to another centre there so I could be close to my husband. I spent three years in that location until he was released.

José gives his side of the story now.
We were a big family because my grandparents, parents, brothers and sisters all lived in the one house which had only two bedrooms. There were twelve of us altogether. My parents didn't get on very well so my mother left home and abandoned us. That's the reason my grandparents came to live with us. I was brought up in the Madrid suburb of San Blas. My father was a truck driver and he was seldom at home.

Such was the relationship with my grandmother that I'm used to calling her my mother. With so many people in the house, it was a disaster area. Grandma did her best to educate and bring us up well but there were so many of us it was impossible to keep control. I was only twelve years old when I began working.

I was fourteen when I first met Toni. I hadn't known much happiness in our home so I was very happy with her. I believe that one of the reasons we went back into the world of drugs after we were married is that we were reacting to the previous culture and politics of Spain at that time. After Franco died there was a new age of liberty and everyone wanted to try new things. I had a job but all I thought about was how to enjoy life. I started to deal in drugs as well as my normal work.

Once we started on heroin what we were earning wasn't enough to support us so we had to look for other means. In the beginning I had never robbed anyone but I had friends who were doing it so I began to do it too. We started with shops and restaurants, and then later we went on to banks. I had several periods in jail but each time I came back I got into more trouble than before.

There was a stage in my life where we had to hold up a bank each week otherwise we didn't have enough money. Our lives at this stage were totally uncontrolled. We were injecting cocaine as well as heroin so my mind was absolutely 'blown out'.

I was charged with having robbed twenty-two banks with menaces and finally convicted, but they could only find evidence for me having robbed three banks. I was sentenced to nine years and eight months. Our lives were just a mess. Our relationship began to change when Toni went to Santander and came to the Lord. She spoke to me of what had happened and how God had changed her. When I was released from jail I had everything worked out in my head. Even though she had spoken to me about God I wanted to come to Madrid to look for friends – people who could help me find firearms – and start robbing again.

When I got out of the jail, and reached Santander I thought we would be put in the same house together but it didn't happen like that. She was in one house with the women and they put me in another house thirty-five kilometres away. I really wanted to be with her but we saw each other only at weekends. I began to have feelings for my wife that I'd lost during my time in jail.

I suddenly felt that I didn't want to go back to Madrid; there were a lot of difficulties there. I remember one day we had an evangelistic campaign in the streets in Vitoria. Somebody prayed for me and I felt the presence of God. This was the first time I really felt that God was by my side and I wanted to give my life to Him.

After six months we returned to Madrid with the children. The house that we had before was returned to us! It appears that my in-laws had been paying the bills while we were away hoping that one day we would come back to Madrid. By arrangement with Elliott Tepper I went to work in Betel in one of the boys' houses at Mejorada Del Campo. I worked alongside some of the men like Tito and Raul. I saw something in their lives and I decided that I wanted my life to be like theirs.

While we were in Madrid, working at Betel, God began to reveal Himself and to deal with our lives in a deeper way. I was living and working among people of my own neighbourhood. They were the people with whom I'd been in the world of drugs. They were the people with whom I'd robbed. Now they were off drugs and I was able to see their changed lives.

Toni and I started to build our relationship again. It was not without difficulties, but gradually it got better and better. Rebecca was born in Madrid. Then the people in Betel helped me find work and I had my first job. During this time I've never been without a job and God has always supplied me with what I have needed. We are active in the church and the children are involved in the Sunday School.

Our son Oscar continued attending the church for some time, in fact he went over to Betel in Britain and worked there for a period. Unfortunately he had to come back to do his military service. After that he stopped going to church. We've tried to encourage him to come but at the present time he doesn't want to, so we have to leave him in the hands of God.

Eighteen months ago some of us started to talk about the

possibility of a co-operative. This was a vision that Betel had had for some time, but then we began to discuss it seriously. Setting the co-operative up hasn't been easy but our goal is to provide help for people that come out of Betel and want to work again in normal life, but with the covering of a Christian organisation.

[See the chapter in Part III entitled 'The Biggest Challenge'.]

11

THE ONE-WAY TICKET MISSIONARY
AND THE TROUBLE-SHOOTER

THE STORY OF JUAN CARLOS, ANITA AND 'BETANIA'

*The start of this story is unrelated to Betel but it describes
happenings that led up to Betel's involvement in the end.*

*Juan Carlos and Anita are mature pastoral workers with
Betel in Madrid, but we begin with the testimony of Anita,
daughter of an evangelical pastor who has a huge church in
South Mexico.*

My family lives in the southern part of Mexico. When I gave
my life to the Lord I was ten years old. My father and mother
pastor a big church in Chiapas where they have a building that
holds about ten thousand people. They have one hundred and
seventy branch churches in the state of Chiapas. My culture
was really evangelical and I never learned much about Mexican
culture; all I knew was school, home and church.

I wanted to know about the world outside of Chiapas, so
decided to leave Mexico, learn English, and then experience
other cultures. At seventeen I went to a Bible School in California
which was bi-lingual. After that I went to 'Christ for the Nations',
a college in Dallas, Texas, for which I had a scholarship. That
was when the Lord spoke to me about Spain, in 1981. The course
lasted a year and a half, and as soon as I graduated I flew to
Spain, without returning to Mexico.

I didn't have any supporters; I just had a word from the Lord.
I was sure He was calling me; when I asked Him how I was

going to live, I had an assurance from the Word that if He called me He would sustain me. To this day I don't know how it all happened, but my ticket for Spain came through the mail. I don't know who paid for it. It was a one-way ticket so I came to stay! I told the Lord I would take one step at a time, and I did.

I knew of a missionary couple in Ciudad Real – David and Lyn Myers – so I went to them and offered my services. They were running a radio programme, so I was given the job of secretary – answering mail and sending out New Testaments. There was no church when I arrived but gradually a fellowship developed. We also started women's meetings and I helped the pastor's wife with that. In fact I did any job that needed doing.

Once a lady evangelist came to minister to the church and some people were touched by the Holy Spirit. Nothing like this had happened before; a number were upset and did not understand what was happening. Our numbers dropped from ninety to about a dozen.

We were cast upon the Lord so we started to pray earnestly and asked Him to show us the next step. We felt that God had something different for us, not just a church. As we were walking outside the city we found a property. We thought it looked like a good place for a Christian centre so after a few weeks of praying we went to talk to the owner and asked if it was for sale. At first he said 'no' but after a long time he finally decided to sell it to us. We had a vision for a centre to minister to missionaries, pastors and other Christian workers. Because of the trials we had gone through we felt there was a need for such a place.

After a while some people started to help us and others from overseas gave money to help buy the property which we called 'Betania' (Bethany). God was faithful and we were able to acquire it, and then started to build.

Elliott Tepper explains further.
The original idea was that it should be a retreat centre for missionaries and Christian workers. Others who wanted to

support this venture, particularly from Texas, saw the possibility of it becoming a Bible School. However, in the long run the project was never completed. At a certain point in 1993 the small team felt that they had to discontinue. Considerable finance came from the father of David Myers, namely Wayne Myers, who with his many contacts in the USA and the world, not only raised money but encouraged churches to send teams of workers so that considerable progress was made with the construction.

At the beginning of 1994 David Myers contacted me and raised the idea of Betel taking over the Betania project and turning it into a rehabilitation centre, Bible school or conference centre. We immediately warmed to the idea because it was a wonderful property and his team had done a lot of good work. They had assembled almost all the building materials; they had the roof on and the walls up, and a lot of the main systems were already installed. But it was worth a lot of money and he wanted 45,000,000 pesetas for it (about $350,000). At that point in time Betel had never purchased a property that big. So we said we would consider it. We went to our bank, the Caja de Madrid. They assessed the value at $400,000, (60,000,000 pesetas) which was considerably more than the purchase price. They actually gave us 100% financing and we were able to take over the property. However having the finance is one thing; meeting the monthly payments is another! They were about 700,000 pesetas ($4,500), which was really a lot of money for us to find.

We felt that Betel International could undertake this and we would all support the project. We would set up some stores and businesses in Ciudad Real and what the centre couldn't cover, the rest of the Betel family would provide. Of course we looked for a special person that would be able to pioneer this new work, and we thought of Juan Carlos.

He went there and really raised the centre up from nothing. He started four different stores and at the same time ran a rehabilitation centre while finishing the construction. In fourteen months he had completed the whole thing!

Juan describes the early days.

When I arrived I saw a half finished project that seemed to be part church, part Bible school, and part conference centre. But we realised we were in the purposes of God and that the hand of God was upon us. It was a difficult situation and we had to work closely with the missionary team and the church fellowship.

We interrupt the Betania story to inject a note of romance. Anita tells how she and Juan Carlos met.

Juan came down to Ciudad Real as Betel's representative and we worked together during the takeover.

At a Women's Aglow retreat, a woman felt it on her heart to tell me that 'there was a man coming to my life very shortly.' She gave me a verse: Ecclesiastes 3:11. By now I was thirty-nine years old. Marriage for me was a dream, but it wasn't number one on my prayer list! I was very content with my 'freedom', serving the Lord and surrounded by people that treated me well. A week after the women's retreat Juan Carlos told me he had something important to tell me, and that was when he proposed. What shocked me was that he mentioned the same scripture, Ecclesiastes 3:11. Three months later we were married.

Juan continues.

I had to balance the construction work, the creation and maintenance of the centre, and the producing of income through the Betel businesses, all at the same time. It was very difficult. The only way we could have done it was through the grace of God. I realised that a furniture store rightly organised and run could be a very important economic resource. We began to collect furniture and other used items from people who didn't want them. Then we restored them and sold them.

We opened the first store immediately on our arrival. It very quickly became profitable. We took a second one in the town of Puertollano and it also became very profitable. We started an upholstery shop in downtown Ciudad Real and that functioned very well. Then we set up a fourth one in the town of Manzanares.

Elliott picks up the story.
From those stores we generated very significant income – over $12,000 a month. This more than paid our mortgage and maintained the cost of the community of up to twenty-five young men.

We grew to about thirty people in the centre and in the Betel tradition we maintained good relationships with local churches who began to refer people that had problems to us.

The two buildings slept one hundred and forty people – ninety in the main building and fifty in the second building. There were other facilities – an auditorium for one hundred and twenty people, a dining hall for one hundred and twenty, and lots of individual sleeping areas and small conference rooms. Juan also set up a painting business and a construction business, and had our calendar and poster businesses functioning smoothly.

At that point in time we began to operate as a public conference centre. The WEC missionary team was the first to use it. We had been spending lots of money renting other people's facilities but now we had our own Betel/WEC facilities. Local churches, denominations, and other Christians came to know of us and now use the centre. Almost every month we have groups of up to one hundred and forty people using the facilities. It is becoming almost self-sufficient just through conference work.

It still functions as a rehabilitation place for Betel. Our workers run the conference centre – that's one of our businesses now. We have rented a small house, about a quarter of a mile from the property and so when we have a conference we take all the new people away from the property and put them in that. Then Julio, the leader who is also a professional cook, plus a crew of cooks, cleaners and waiters tend to the people at the conference. When the conference is over they move the people back from the little house. It works very well. We have constructed a large swimming pool and additional toilets and showers for campers. We can now hold our annual 1,300-strong camp meeting there.

Juan Carlos now shares how he came to the Lord.
When I was thirteen I left school and went to work. My first job was as a bus conductor. I began to smoke and drink and by the time I reached sixteen I was smoking hashish, going to parties, staying out at night and taking amphetamines. From there I advanced to cocaine and then to heroin. Then I began to work with my brother in his drug trafficking business. He would bring hashish up from Morocco through Ceuta and we began to earn a lot of money. I went right into the depths of the heroin culture.

At first when I tried to get off heroin I went to the government and tried their methadone programme. Then I got a job with a doctor actually driving an ambulance. But there were times when I would take a sick person to the hospital and then go on to buy some heroin. Even though I was on a methadone programme I was consuming more heroin than ever. I spent about four or five years in this condition.

I lived for six months on the island of Ibiza without consuming heroin, but finally I went back to it and returned to Madrid. I started to live with a prostitute and was with her for two years. She earned a lot of money and we used it for drugs. I was twenty-eight years old then.

I was so sick I dropped down to fifty-eight kilos. (Today I weigh one hundred!) I became incredibly weak. In fact just before entering Betel I visited my parents and did not have enough energy to talk to them.

Someone told me about Betel so I went there and asked to be admitted. I remember that on the fifth day there was a meeting in which an invitation was given to receive Christ. I responded to this and accepted the Lord. Everything changed!

After four or five months they transferred me to Alcalá and I began to assume more and more responsibilities in the house. After eleven months there they made me the house leader at Torres De Alameda. After that, every time they had a problem in a residence they would transfer me and make me the leader of it! I was the Betel trouble-shooter!

Elliott gives this evaluation:
He is a hard worker; he has drive and he's a pusher (in a good sense); he gets businesses running and he inspires people, but more than being just practical he is a real intercessor. Among the pastors in Madrid he more than any takes a personal burden for intercession. He's quick to enter in and he has a sense of the presence of God – a sense of God's working in the heavenlies. That's probably the key to why he has been so successful in the ministry.

Juan Carlos is in his second year back in Madrid now and is supervising approximately one half of the men in the Madrid area – probably over one hundred men; he supervises the six thrift stores in the northern half of Madrid and five of the residential homes. He is one of the three principal Spanish pastors in the large Madrid church.

Juan concludes:
I'm just very grateful for all that God has done in my life – taking me from what I was, saving me, putting me in Betel, giving me my wife and daughter and calling me to the pastorate. I thank Him. He's enlarged my world, allowed me to visit much of Europe, travel to Mexico, California, visit the churches including Anita's father's in Chiapas, and the Amistad churches in Mexico. I'm very grateful for the way God has enlarged my life.

12

BLESSINGS IN BARCELONA:
BEGINNINGS IN BILBAO

THE STORY OF JUAN CARRASCO AND CARMEN

Juan Carrasco and his wife Carmen are one of the ablest couples in Betel. A man of faith, vision, and tenacity, he has seen a great work built up in the Barcelona area. His early testimony appears in Rescue Shop I. He continues his story by describing developments in Barcelona and then the challenge that Elliott put to him about raising up a new work in Bilbao, seven hundred kilometres west on the Atlantic Coast.

We also include two more examples of totally changed lives, reached through the Barcelona work.

Starting a work is slow going for the first few years. After 1992/ 93 – when Rescue Shop was written – the 'boom' began. Then, there were fifteen or seventeen people in Betel Barcelona. We had just obtained a thrift shop with a front section which we used as a church, but hardly anybody from outside attended. Bit by bit some of the families of those who had entered Betel began to attend the meetings. So we started to grow. Then we developed a good relationship with other churches in the area, and they began to see that Betel was more than merely a rehabilitation centre. Numbers rose to the point where we could not fit the people in any more.

After commencing a men's residence we opened up a girls' house in Sabadel not too far from Rubí. We also started another Betel centre an hour and a half to the south in the large city of

Tarragona (200,000 inhabitants). We had a group of visiting Mexicans, and our third leader there, Rafa, fell in love with one of the Mexican girls, Sandra, who was a university graduate in psychology; she returned to Mexico, then came back for their marriage. When it came time for them to be married we couldn't fit the wedding service or celebration in the church so we asked the owner of a large warehouse to lend it to us for the occasion. Out of curiosity we asked the owner how much it would cost to rent this place to use as a church. To pay the contract price and the deposit we would have needed 750,000 pesetas. We were paying only 80,000 for the place we were then using.

At that time we had a girl who had been in an accident. She was referred to us and we picked her up from the hospital. She came on crutches, and we began to take care of her. She was very appreciative. We would take her to the hospital regularly for treatments and check-ups. In court she was awarded 5,000,000 pesetas in damages. The Sunday before this happened I had preached on tithing. The next week I went to the girls' house for a meal. After dinner she said, 'I've got something to give to you.' I thought it was 5,000 pesetas; so I folded it up and said goodbye. When I opened the cheque later and looked at it again I counted the zeros: it was for 500,000 pesetas! We deposited it at the bank immediately. So we had enough money to get the building! The only problem was it was just a warehouse, ugly, unfinished. Then we had all the challenges of the legal work, licences, and building permits. The rules for legalising a church were very rigid because it was to be used as a public auditorium. We had an architect to draw up plans according to required standards, and we had to put in an extra staircase, a second exit, and so on. The final cost was over 2,000,000 pesetas, so now we have a fine church building seating four hundred.

There are now about one hundred and twenty in the three centres that have grown out of the original Barcelona work, plus one hundred and fifty attending church.

The professionalism and the integrity of the programme have been recognised by the Catalonia government, and by the evangelical council of Catalonia. The first congress of an evangelical federation asked Betel to do a presentation on our evangelical rehabilitation centre, so we have very good standing.

* * *

Let me give you just a couple of examples of how God has worked in lives.

Vicente entered Betel in Tarragona. Before coming to us he had been in thirty three other rehabilitation centres but never stayed. He ended up selling everything he had in his house and what he didn't sell, in wrath he threw out the window. His wife and his one child, a son, left him and went to live with her parents. The father of his wife was a member of the federal police. He wanted to give him two bullets in the brain! His wife refused to have anything to do with him. He had lots of legal judgements pending because he had committed many robberies. He received a sentence of over three years in prison but, through an arrangement with the authorities, was able to serve his time with Betel. His wife refused to visit him and refused to let the child visit him. She didn't trust him. Her excuse was that Tarragona was too far away from her home in Barcelona.

So we transferred him to Barcelona. Then we had to work more with her than with him. We brought all the family together for a meal in our own home and invited them to go out with us for walks in the park. We said if she had to miss going to work on Saturday (and thus lose money) we would make it up to her. Little by little she began to attend church. They went out on weekends together either in our home or in the home of another couple in the church. So things began to change.

His parents started to come to our services and relationships between them were restored. The good news of this reached her parents. He finished serving his three and a half years sentence with us so he then thought he would leave Betel and get a job. He was a professional upholsterer and found employment in the company that he had worked for previously, but his boss was dishonest. A creditor of the company would call and the boss would tell Vicente to say that he wasn't there. He could not do it. So he came to me one day and said, 'I really can't continue in this situation.' We had a weekend together to talk it over so I said, 'Well, return to Betel, work with us.' He didn't want any money. He was able to get help from a government programme as a released prisoner. He had a government-subsidised home, and only paid $2 a month (300 pesetas) rent. His wife has a salaried job. Now he just wants to serve God, and so he is a volunteer with us in Betel. Furthermore he has a good relationship with his in-laws.

* * *

Graciela handles accounts in our office. When she was eighteen she was robbing banks. She would pull a ski mask over her head and go in with a knife or a pistol. She would have a man with her, but she'd be the first to go in and put the knife or pistol on someone's throat. When she came to Betel she was like a man. Her face, her expression, and even her clothing, exuded a male appearance. She arrived when she was a little over nineteen. She had lived a life of crime and had a whole string of criminal judgements against her. For one of these the prosecutor asked for seven years in prison but it was reduced to four years and two months. She was able to serve the time at our centre, but after a year and a half the police arrived with another citation and took her to the Barcelona prison for women. She felt deceived; we were upset and felt betrayed. She had been serving God and us for almost two years.

So I went up to Galicia, in the north west of Spain to talk to the judge. Although she was put in prison in Barcelona the crime was committed in Galicia. I was able to talk to the magistrate.

He said, 'I can't re-open the case. What I have to do is give her a pardon.' So he wrote her out a pardon, but said, 'This will take some time to come through.' The prison social worker called us later and asked, 'Will you people give this girl a place in the centre?' We said, 'Of course we will'. I went and talked to the prison authorities and within two months she was out of the prison and back in Betel! We made ourselves responsible for her. She's been with us five years and she does all the cost accounting for Barcelona, Tarragona and other centres.

Elliott continues with a later episode in Juan's testimony.
I was visiting some of our European centres and I had to stop over in the Amsterdam airport for about eight hours. I was trying to read and work on a level up above the crowds of people below, and was thinking about Barcelona. Juan had told me that he felt bored. Here he was – a man with a very successful centre with one hundred and twenty people, a dynamic, pioneer personality, and no more worlds to conquer! I started thinking about what we could give him. Then I thought about Bilbao and the two million people in the Basque country. Bilbao is one of the largest industrial areas in Spain and we had no work there. We had avoided it because there had been other centres in the north and we didn't think they needed us. Then I thought, 'Why don't we start Betel in Bilbao? That would be a challenge for Juan, because it would be very hard, a different language, a different culture, and a very closed society.' So I whipped out my mobile phone on the spot and called him. 'Juan, what do you think about starting Betel in the Basque country? There are millions of people in the area and no Betel. It would be a great challenge for you. Why don't you start it as an outreach from Barcelona?'

Juan continues:
We had been seven or eight years in Barcelona and for the last two God had been saying, 'You've got to move; you've got to do something new.' There was a quickening in my heart when

Elliott called and so the very next day we went to the Basque country, drove round, looked at various towns and left our address with several real estate agents. Actually the day we went was a holiday and everything was closed. So we returned to Barcelona. Then a few days later an agency called us to say that they had a flat for us to rent. So we made the trip. We arrived at the meeting point.

The estate agent said, 'Please forgive me, there's been some mistake, that flat is not available anymore.' I said, 'Wait a second, you can't make a mistake like that. I've travelled seven hundred kilometres for this appointment. It's six in the afternoon, what am I going to do?' He said, 'I don't know what I can do or say. I'm just telling you what my boss told me to say.' So he left and we found ourselves standing in the middle of the street like fools wondering what to do. There were two more hours before everything closed so we got in the car and said, 'Let's see if God has anything for us.' There was one place in Bilbao that we had a lot of interest in because it is a problem area; there's a lot of terrorism there. But it was so wet we could hardly see. We hadn't found anything and at eight o'clock we were just going to give up and go back home. Then we stopped at a stop light, looked to the left and there was a place that said 'Real Estate Agent'. We decided to try one more time. We asked if he had anything to rent and he said, 'Right in this very building we have one'. We asked him how much the rent was and he said, '80,000 pesetas.' 'That's a pretty high price for a little apartment.' He said, 'Let's call the owner.' He called him and then said, 'You can have it for 60,000.' We said, 'Give us the keys.'

Carmen, Juan's wife, describes her turmoil about the idea of moving to Bilbao.

I didn't want to go to Bilbao, I was very happy in Barcelona. We had the church. We had the women's meeting. We had the girls' house. I had a fifteen year old son in school. We had a nice home. Our own families lived here.

For four months Juan travelled to Bilbao every week, leaving on Mondays and coming back on Thursdays. One day after the Monday night leaders' meeting in Barcelona I just gave up and said, 'Well, Juan, if you want to go to Bilbao, it's okay with me, I'll go.' Next day he went specifically to look for a house for us. Two days later he called me and said, 'I have one.'

I started to think about all the nice things we had around us, but God said, 'I'll give you the same or better.' I said, 'Lord, I'll do whatever You want. I'm going to Bilbao.' Then I thought, 'It rains all the time there; there's no sun.' But I am very happy here. There are about fifty in the community already, counting the couples, men and children. Our son is happy. We thought he'd have difficulties but he's settled right in to a good high school and has made friends right away.

Elliott adds:
In less than one year Juan and Carmen and their team from Barcelona and other Betel centres in Spain had established two men's residences, a women's residence, a married couples' hostel, two thrift stores, a carwash, and a large outreach centre in the very centre of the city! During their second year Juan opened a third store and converted an old car agency into Betel's first church in the Basque country.

13

TOWERS OR WELLS?

Chapter one of Rescue Shop I *tells the story of Raul Casto's deliverance from drug addiction, conversion and growth to maturity, as evidenced by his pastoral role at the Betel church in Madrid, with its 500 plus membership.*

But AIDS was taking its toll during the latter years of his ministry. Many said that as his condition deteriorated he had glimpses into eternity that made his ministry uniquely powerful and effective. Here are just a few paragraphs (abridged) from one of his talks at the Betel church.

In Genesis 11, the men of Babel rebelled against God and decided to build a tower. When they came to a place that was flat and easy, where there were fields and water, they said, 'We will build a tower and its highest point will reach heaven. We don't need you, God. We are happy here.'

But the Lord said, 'We will go down and cause confusion.'

I want to say tonight, that if we build a tower in a comfortable place for our own sake, sooner or later confusion will come. 'Why is this happening?' we will say. 'What have I done wrong?' In our Christian lives it is important that we don't stay where the way is flat and without difficulties.

In contrast, Abraham spent his life digging wells. He looked after his people and their livestock, digging wells so that they could have water. And Isaac, his son, also dug wells, working as his father had done. He dug in the valleys and discovered wells of fresh water.

I want to say to you, that if you are in a valley or a desert, or any place where there is no water, where your life seems to be dead, don't try to flee from the situation to construct a tower. Don't look for that small gap to escape through. Stay in the valley and dig a well. The well of Jesus is inside us, deep within, with crystal clear water, with water that quenches thirst. Although we are still in the valley, we can find living water.

Are you building a tower or are you digging a well? It is more comfortable to build a tower, because when you dig a well you are in a confined space. You don't have much room to dig as you go down. It's difficult and it's costly.

Last Saturday, here at the church, there was a funeral – a memorial service for a missionary who had been in Spain for over twenty years. He was in a shop in the middle of Madrid with his wife when he suddenly had a heart attack and died. He left a widow and four children. If you had been in the service without knowing this man, you would have heard what he was like just through the testimonies people gave. Listening to what they said, you could see that this man was a 'well'. In his heart and life he was a well, from which hundreds of Spaniards had the privilege to drink.

What about you? Is your life like this? Are you building a tower or digging a well? By what do you want to be remembered? I decided almost nine years ago that my life was going to be a well, and I want to encourage you to pray that your life will be a well for others too.

At the age of thirty seven Raul passed into the presence of the Lord, leaving his wife Jenny, (née Scantlebury), a missionary from New Zealand, and two daughters, Séfora (5) and Kelly (3). What follows is the poignant story of Jenny's reactions to Raul's death and then the subsequent dealings of the Lord, leading to her re-marriage.

JENNY
Right up to the last moment I believed there would be a miracle of healing even though Raul was on his deathbed, so it was

quite a shock when he died. Towards the end he must have known, because to visitors he would make indications with his hands (he couldn't speak much) that he would be seeing them in heaven.

When he did go there were eight around the bed. I burst into tears and then a peace came over me. I said to everyone, 'I don't understand, but I accept it.' I was quite peaceful. Then for several days I was walking on air, so conscious of the grace of God. It was incredible.

In Spain funerals take place within twenty four hours, so Pastor Luis Pino stepped in and took care of all the details. The State covered the expense of the funeral apart from 50,000 pesetas (about two hundred pounds).

I thought of our girls, particularly Séfora (5) whose relationship with her father had been so close. I had never discussed with her the possibility that her father might die. I went home and told them. They both burst into tears but they accepted it.

I bought a red rose and wrote on a card that Sefi, Kellie and I would see him in heaven. I put it beside his body in the casket. I also bought myself six pink roses, feeling that he would have wanted that for me. I treasured them over the next few days. At the cremation service I felt a sense of exhilaration. I just sang my heart out. I felt Raul's presence so close to me at that time.

When things quietened down after the funeral I told the Lord I would stay where I was for a year. I continued to do the work I had been doing. I visited Elliott to ask what my position would be and he encouraged me to carry on as before. So I continued with pastoral work, hospital visits, Sunday School, organisation of the creche, and began working for one day a week in the reception office.

EDUARDO

I came to Betel seven years ago. I was the first to enter the centre in Ceuta, N. Africa. I came to the Lord there, and after a year I joined the Betel staff and served in various centres – Madrid, Albacete, and Cuenca. Then in 1995 the elders in Madrid felt that I should be part of a team to open up the new work in England under Kent Martin. I had no sense of personal guidance about that but I felt it was right to obey the leaders. Two months after this, and before leaving for England I gave my testimony at the Betel church in Madrid. It was the time of our missionary conference and God spoke to me while I was on the platform and showed me that I would marry Jenny. I felt guilty because Raul had been dead only a few months. I thought, 'Was this just 'the flesh'?'

A month later I came to England, and around Easter Kent told me that Jenny would be visiting Britain! So she and the children came. I hadn't spoken to anyone about my feelings.

JENNY
Each year we tried to get a break around Easter and that year I took the children to England mainly to have a complete change.

EDUARDO
While Jenny and the children were here I spoke a couple of times to her. I asked her if she would like to live in England and she said she would, but she added 'but my place is in Spain.' I found it very hard to open my heart to her and so after a few days she left. My feelings grew stronger and one day when I was talking to Sandra Bautista she asked me if I had anyone in mind. I said, 'Someone like Jenny.'

JENNY
When I returned to Spain I had a strange lack of peace in my heart. I started thinking about returning to New Zealand. A few weeks later, Kent Martin, with Sandra and Victor Bautista (Betel workers in Britain), came to Spain for a conference. During the Friday night service Elliott came up and said to me, 'Jenny, I have a good husband for you. Eduardo in England.' I thought,

'Oh, yes; that's just Elliott'. Afterwards I told Sandra that Elliott had someone for me, but without naming Eduardo. She replied, 'Oh well, I know a good husband for you too.' 'Who's that?' I asked. She replied, 'Eduardo in England. You should pray about that.'

Since Raul's death I had never thought of praying along that line. I continued to have an unrest in my heart so I went to talk to Mary Tepper, Elliott's wife. She encouraged me to think seriously about moving to England. I did this and the Lord confirmed that this was right and that Eduardo was right, too. I was amazed. I told Elliott and he was pleased. He talked to Kent in England and then I had a phone call from Eduardo asking me to marry him. I accepted his proposal over the phone! I just knew it was right. I came over in August and we were married in December.

EDUARDO

When I came to England God took me into a deeper level of fellowship with Himself. Now I was a 'missionary' – away from my own country and out of my 'comfort zone'. I have known dealings from God in these last two years that have been far deeper than the five years with Betel in Spain. It has been God's way of bringing me to maturity.

The culture in England is so different to Spain. I had a lot of fear to begin with. God also spoke to me about my leadership role and showed me that I was producing not fiery 'out-and-out' Christians but 'wishy-washy' ones because I was afraid to offend aspects of their culture.

I remember speaking to Elliott about it during one of his visits. He said, 'Don't confuse culture with Biblical principles. Take a stand on what is right and what is Biblical.'

JENNY

The girls were fearful about going to school in England but they have adjusted beautifully and within four months they were speaking English fluently. They have made friends and they enjoy their school. They miss the Betel church life where they had lots of little friends, but that will develop here too in time. They have taken to Eduardo so well.

14

SEVEN YEARS FOR A HATCHET JOB

THE STORY OF JOHN KAVANAGH

My home was in Dublin, where I was born in 1966. From the age of fourteen I took valium and temazepam tablets. That led on to stealing. Then I started drinking as well as taking pills – the two together were a powerful combination. I became very difficult to live with and eventually left home to get away from my father, who was a foreman builder, because he wanted to discipline me.

I lived rough – sleeping in derelict houses and wherever I could find shelter. Mother would come looking for me at night but I still would not return home. The police got hold of me and took me home one night but I stayed only a week; I needed 'space' and freedom to continue my habits.

At fifteen I started to take heroin and in order to get money for that I started robbing houses and shops. I was only smoking heroin at this stage. On one occasion I was caught and sentenced to twelve months in a detention centre. I was released after nine months and went straight back on to valium, heroin and drink.

I went to rob a house and hit the owner with a hatchet. I was sentenced to seven years for that. When I was released I managed to stay away from drugs for two years. I met a girl and we came over to England but then I started the drug habit again. After my girl friend had a child we moved back to Ireland where I stayed off drugs for a few months but soon went downhill once more.

My girlfriend and I decided to split up. She applied to the

court for custody of the child. I was high on drugs and never contested this.

In 1996 when I assaulted a tourist in Dublin using a syringe I was sentenced to eleven months jail. My mother visited me as she had done when I was serving the previous seven year sentence. She used to talk to me about God. She said I needed to ask God into my life, but I never took any notice of her even though she brought me cassettes and written prayers. I was aggressive to her and to everyone.

I attempted to commit suicide by cutting my throat – I was so sick of life. I even plunged a syringe full of air into myself but it had no effect. I had no hope – I was just drifting. I couldn't hack it, and no one seemed to be able to help me. But I know now that God preserved me.

One day my mother quoted Scripture to me. 'Ask and it will be given you. Seek and you will find. Knock and it shall be opened to you.' This time I listened and called out to Jesus. Two weeks later my mother came to see me and told me about someone who knew about a drug rehabilitation centre in England where I could get help. When I came out of prison this person gave me the address of Teen Challenge. My mother gave me money and so I flew to Liverpool where I was to take the train to Preston, but when I looked for the piece of paper with the address I couldn't find it.

I phoned home and my sister answered. My mother gave me the Preston phone number but when I called, it was the wrong number. I asked at the police station if they knew where it was but they couldn't help me. (There was a mix-up over the name of the place which had been recently changed.)

So I went into a church service and started praying to God. I was so fed up with life. After the service the pastor came up and introduced himself. I told him about my situation. Well, he knew where the centre was and he took me there. But the people at the centre could not accept me because there was a hold-up regarding it being officially registered with the local council. I was desperate. I knew that if I went back to Ireland I would succumb to drugs again.

At that point the pastor said, 'Well, I know of a new place in Birmingham where you could get help.' He phoned Betel and it was arranged that I should go there the next day.

But there was a snag. My girlfriend was now living in Birmingham and I had a restraint order not to go near her. When I explained this to the pastor he said, 'Look, it would be a million-to-one chance that you would cross her path.' I insisted he ring Betel again to explain the situation. They gave me reassurance, so I agreed to go.

I reached Birmingham, was accepted into Betel and started to listen to the teaching, but I couldn't understand it. I still had this vague belief in God but I could not relate to these folk. I started to become aggressive again and badly wanted to leave.

In my desperation I really cried to God. I said to someone, 'If something doesn't happen to me, I'm gone. I'm going back to the old life.' That night God touched me. I seemed to be wrestling with Him and I know He met me and touched me. That was it. I knew it wasn't just my feelings, it was a real experience. Of course, I had my doubts afterwards but I kept praying and looking to Him.

I heard that there was a 'Grapevine' Conference coming up and I wanted to go. At the same time I was listening to tapes. One in particular by Don Franscisco really spoke to my heart; it was on being a disciple. The Lord was dealing with me. I said to Elaine, one of the staff workers, 'Isn't it true that when we are weakest, God is at His strongest?' She said, 'Yes.' So I decided to fast during this conference because I wanted to be totally changed. On the first night I know that God met me, and on the second day a real peace came. God calmed my heart.

When I came here, at first I was full of worries but I have handed them over to God. I don't worry about my child, or my partner, or my family. I want to stay here because I've found peace. I have a vision for being used by God to help others who have had a similar experience.

God has been answering my prayers and I now have access to my daughter, Natasha, who is six years old. My sister has been in touch with me for the first time in eight years and my father is asking questions about what has happened to me.

Kent Martin, leader of Betel in Britain adds:
John's case is a story of genuine change. The social worker in Dublin who has been handling this matter said to me over the phone, 'I want you to know that the complications with this man – relationships with his partner, his crimes, and his drug addiction – constitute the worst case I have ever had to deal with. If you can make an impact on this man you will really have done something very significant.'

So we are thanking the Lord for His wonderful working in John's life and we rejoice in the changes we are seeing in him.

15

'YOU'RE NOT MY SON ANY MORE!'

THE STORY OF ALEXIS PERES

We lived in the Canary Islands, in the main city of Great Canary called Las Palmas. When I'd finished primary school my father, who had been manager of a factory, asked me what I wanted to do. Because I'd never been a good student and was rebellious I decided to get a job. I'd always been interested in mechanics. In fact, when I was a child, I would pull my toys apart and then put them back together again.

I started my apprenticeship when I was fourteen in a mechanic's workshop and was paid the equivalent of about $3 a month. Very soon after that I started to be involved in drugs. Two of the mechanics were smoking something similar to marijuana, so I joined them. I enjoyed it and little by little progressed into taking higher doses and harder drugs. I also played soccer and met people who were into cocaine, so I started to take that as well. I was good at soccer and my father was proud of me. I reached a fairly high level but then I suddenly realised that I'd become hooked on drugs. In fact I had to take them in order to be able to play football.

But I deteriorated so badly that I had to stop playing. My father was so disappointed. From that point he stopped taking any interest in me. Gradually a separation came between us and as a result I became more rebellious than ever. I resented the attitude that he'd shown towards me. It was rebellion, more than anything, that pushed me more into the world of drugs.

I also left my work and gradually became a delinquent. As time went by my father became aware of all this so he took the final step of kicking me out of home. While he was working my mother used to come and look for me; she'd take me home, give me a change of clothes and generally look after me.

For one of the robberies I committed I was taken to the police station. My mother suffers from heart problems so she couldn't stand visiting me. My father did come and said, 'Because of what you have done, you are not my son any more. As far as I'm concerned you have died.' The neighbours had all signed a petition to say that I was selling drugs in the area. I spent seven months in jail. My father never came to visit me and the phrase that haunted me the whole time I was there was what he had said to me earlier. My mother, with the help of a lawyer, arranged for my release after seven months but I went straight back into the world of delinquency. Through everything that happened, hate was really growing in my heart towards my father.

After that I became involved in what is really the mafia in the Canary Islands. They offered me work driving a truck loaded with drugs from one island to another on the inter-island ferry. One day I tried to rob a kilo of heroin from one of the trucks. Because of that one of the mafia tried to kill me, so I had to leave Las Palmas and go to another island. While I was there I worked in the construction industry and managed to free myself of drugs.

I worked there for two years but then I went back to Las Palmas and I soon fell back into the old world. I went to visit my home but the door was firmly closed. My mother looked out the window and was crying as she watched me. She said, 'I can't let you in, you'll have to go away.' It was seeing my mother in that state that gave me the impetus to do something about my life – to look for a place where I could get help.

So I went to a centre in Las Palmas. It was Sunday and there was a meeting in progress; everybody was singing and it all looked a bit strange to me so I lasted only a day and then took off, but my mother persuaded me to go back again. She even gave me money for a fix so I could get filled up before going in.

I agreed but only to get the money. I left after a day.

I knew I needed to do something about my life so I went and spoke to the leader of the centre again. Since it hadn't worked out on two occasions he recommended that I go to Betel in Madrid. I went there in 1990 and at that stage there were fifty people living in the house at Mejorada Del Campo. Because of my experience in mechanics I was put on to repairing vehicles. In the beginning I suffered a lot from the cold, having come from the warm Canary Islands. Madrid was a very cold place. We also felt hungry during those times because one of the few items that we had in abundance was lentils; I got sick of them after a while!

So as you can imagine it wasn't very pleasant – the cold weather, eating lentils, drinking camomile tea and passing through 'cold turkey' at the same time. The planes that land at Madrid fly over the house. As I was passing through cold turkey I would watch them and hope that one would fall out of the sky so that I could rob the gold and stuff that people had, and then just take off.

But as time went by I began to hear the messages about God and I started taking notice. I also liked the attitude of the leaders. They impressed me. But despite this I realised that to follow God wholly you had to renounce the world. I didn't feel I was ready to do that. Running through my mind was the idea of taking off, finding work, finding a girlfriend, getting married and having a family.

I continued there for a year but after that I left. I found a job very easily; I found a girlfriend; I had everything I needed, but I kept thinking about God and about the centre, knowing that God had something special for me. But, sad to say, after nine months all that went out of my mind and I started to take drugs again.

One time during this period I was on a high but suddenly a phrase that Raul had said came to mind: 'God has something special for your life.' The next morning I went to one of the gypsy houses to buy drugs and on the wall someone had painted the words 'God is love'. This really had an impact on me because I had known something of the love of God at Mejorada and I started to think about going back to Betel but I was afraid because I was hooked on cocaine and I knew that cold turkey would be a struggle for me.

Finally I went back and they took me again to the house in Mejorada Del Campo. The total time I'd been out of Betel was a little over nine months. It wasn't easy going back because apart from the fact that I had to go through detoxification again the person who was made responsible for me was the person who had been under me the time before! It was really hard. I had a terrible time going through cold turkey and I asked the leader if I could go to a doctor. He said, 'No, you are only trying to think up a reason to leave.' It was so bad I couldn't eat, I couldn't even drink, and after six days like this God brought Elliott to the house.

He looked at me and I could tell by the expression on his face that he was concerned about my condition. He prayed for me and told the fellows that I was to be taken to the hospital. While there I vomited blood caused by taking cocaine. A kidney had burst and I also had an infection in my throat. I was taken to surgery, where they put a tube down my throat, then poured water down so as to force the blood out. They continued this for about three hours. Later they took me to the infectious diseases ward. I didn't know, but I then found out I had the AIDS virus, so they put me on drips – one with vitamins and one with antibiotics. I had tubes in each arm and tubes up my nose and down my throat; I had bronchitis as well. I could hardly breathe. Lying there in that hopeless state I remembered God. The doctor that did rounds came and said, 'Look, you are not in a very good state.' At that stage I was urinating blood as well. I was taken back to surgery and again they went through the procedure of taking the blood out of my stomach; they also x-rayed my kidney to see what was happening.

That afternoon, back in my bed, I was crying out to God. Then Antonio El Abuelo (which means grandfather) came to visit me. The doctor came in while Antonio was there. She asked him to leave the room. She said my state was very bad and they were going to call my family because it looked as though I was going to die. I was dehydrated, I couldn't take water and my kidneys weren't functioning. I begged the doctor not to ring my mother – I knew I wasn't going to die. She looked at me and almost laughed but at that stage I began to cry. El Abuelo came back into the room and asked me what was wrong. I told him what she had said and he replied, 'Well, the first thing you need is forgiveness from God.' So Antonio prayed beside me and as we were praying I felt something special. I felt as though God had come into the room. I felt forgiven and then I sensed the power of God come into my body.

As the days went by I gradually improved. I was able to eat little by little and able to take fluid. The doctor came in and said she couldn't understand what had happened but I was looking better. I said, 'Well, God has done a miracle in my life.' At that stage I made an agreement with Him that if I got out of the hospital alive I would give my life to Him. That was six years ago.

Now I'm very happy. I love God a lot and my life is committed to Him. After I was released I went back to Betel and since that time I've sought to do what God wants. After ten months I was made the leader at Mejorada Del Campo, then later at Zulema where I have been the leader for a time. I am also responsible for the mechanical workshop there. In the Alcalá area there are four men's houses under a pastor – Javi. When he is not there I'm his deputy. When I left Betel the first time I mentioned that I'd been with a girlfriend for a period of time but as I got back on drugs the relationship didn't work very well and eventually we broke up.

After I'd been at Betel for two years I found I was able to forgive my father. Since then I've visited my family and I'm now able to hug dad. He accepts me, and my relationship with my mother is good.

I'm very grateful for the six years I have been back in Betel and for what God has done in my life. He knows also that I need a companion and He's given me Marisa; she's also in the programme and is a leader in one of the girls' houses. We plan to marry in the near future.

16

AN ALCOHOLIC FOR THIRTY YEARS

THE STORY OF DEREK (DEL) & IRIS WHITMORE

The following story from England is unique because it takes us away from the world of drugs to the chaotic experiences of alcoholism. In this case Betel became not only the channel of deliverance from drink but the means of salvaging a ruined marriage.

The Whitmores are currently helpers at Windmill House and are making a good contribution there, Iris helping with the accounts and Del training ex-drug users to restore and repair furniture.

DEREK:
For the past thirty years I have been a heavy drinker. Drink ruined our marriage and I moved out of our home four and a half years ago to live in the bedroom of a flat.

A friend invited me to Windmill House which was a Christian centre but not a rehabilitation centre. Its ethos did not involve exercising control or authority so I continued drinking and even got into stealing. When this place was handed over to Betel I was faced with a problem. If I stayed I would have to submit to their programme which was strict. I would have to give up my job, give up my car and give up everything in order to be part of the fellowship. My doctor had warned me that if I continued drinking I wouldn't live for long, so it was either imminent death or Betel!

I had tried going to church in 1983 but that didn't change me. I had no relationship with the Lord. So I got no help. I tried

Alcoholics Anonymous, had non-Christian counselling and so on, but to no avail.

Staying with the Betel programme was very difficult for me. There was no freedom. Every time I walked down the road I had to have someone with me. No TV when I wanted it, and no newspapers; I couldn't even answer the phone!

I had had a good job as a car spray-painter. I made good money – there was always plenty of work and though I say it myself, I was good at my work. Of course I made extra on the side by being dishonest – selling paint that wasn't mine and so on. I even stole from my wife's mum and dad. So Betel meant an enormous change in my lifestyle.

I was the first British Betel resident and had problems submitting to Eduardo. These were compounded by his limited English and I felt like leaving. However as time went on I was given more responsibility and was even put in charge of a group. But on one occasion I had a lapse; I went out and drank and so lost my status as a helper.

I attended the Betel meetings and tried to pull myself together. Again I was given responsibility. In one meeting the speaker talked about the influence of our background and I realised that a lot of my problems stemmed from the hatred in my heart toward my father who was an alcoholic and who had treated my mother so badly. The Lord really dealt with me over that, and I think that was the turning point. Since then the Lord has been real to me.

The Lord showed me that I was to stay here and that my wife would rejoin me. She came to visit me but she wasn't happy about me working for Betel and doing nothing for her around the house. Neither of us had a clear understanding at that stage of what living by faith meant.

I'm now in charge of a department, remodelling used furniture and using my spray-painting skills.

IRIS:

Derek and I were married in 1974 and after a couple of years I began to realise he had a drink problem; I had our first child, a girl, and three years later I had a little boy.

I always kept feeling that Derek would get over his problem and change. I thought of leaving him but also realised the children needed a father. So I went on, putting up with his lying, stealing and cheating as well as the drinking. Thankfully he was never violent but the pattern just went on and on.

In 1983 we sent the children to Sunday School and when we went to a Christmas Carol Service Derek put his hand up to receive Christ. I didn't, because I had enough problems – I couldn't face that as well.

Friends gave me books and just gradually I seemed to move into an awareness of salvation. But we continued to have lots of problems and lots of arguments, because he continued to drink. After seventeen years of that I reached the end of my tether. As a Christian I felt, up to that point, that we should stay together, but I could bear it no longer. I told him to go. He persisted in staying around for another three weeks, but I demanded that he leave, so he went.

I was very bitter, very angry. One of the things that upset me most was the fact that he didn't stop drinking. I thought the shock of leaving may have jolted him, but he just went on as before. So we didn't have much contact.

I kept the children and found full-time work. It wasn't easy juggling work and care of the children who were then sixteen and thirteen. We became very close. I remained very bitter – up until the time he joined Betel. I continued to go to church and actually became secretary to the pastor. Later I was made manager of the nursery attached to the church.

I was talking one day to the assistant pastor and after that discussion I had the overwhelming feeling that we would only ever get together again if I joined Betel as well, but in the meantime nothing actually changed.

About eighteen months ago I reached the point where I said, 'God, I know You exist but I have to say I don't really want You. My life is simply working to live and living to work. It's no life at all. I feel like going the way of the world and getting a divorce.' I was like this for a couple of months. Things got darker and darker, until one night in desperation I said, 'All right, Lord, I surrender. I'm Yours. You can do what You want but I don't want this kind of life.'

A little time later I phoned Kent, the director of Betel, pointing out that Derek was doing lots of work there but nothing for us at home. Kent agreed that he should help me by doing jobs around the house. So we started to come closer again. Betel allowed us to have regular times together.

The result of that was a mutual desire to renew our marriage vows, and the decision was made that I would also join Betel and work at the centre. This happened on July 5 this year and it was a great day – a beautiful service and then a banquet. It was lovely.

I have sold the house. I finished work at the church only recently and I started working in the Betel office today. Liza is now twenty one and Lee is eighteen. Liza has left the church and lives on her own. Lee is at a School of Evangelism with Teen Challenge and next year he will work full time with them.

17

PRISON MADE ME REBELLIOUS

THE STORY OF ROSI AND ALBERTO

Alberto and Rosi carry big pastoral responsibilities in the Madrid Betel church. It has been a long hard road for them both, but, again, the grace and grit that God provides have taken them through. Both have been into robbery and both have been sentenced to jail terms. But the radical change that the Gospel produces has turned wasted lives into wonderful workers.

Rosi gives something of her background.
I was thirteen when I left school and since I didn't have work and didn't want to do further study, I was soon involved in the delinquent behaviour of my peers. I started smoking marijuana and sniffing heroin but after a while they didn't do anything for me, so I started to inject heroin. I was sixteen by then.

For the next seven years I was hooked, and took part in many gang robberies so that I could have money for drugs. I tried to give it up at different times but without success. When I was twenty three I was feeling really bad – it was one of the lows in my life. I also discovered that I was pregnant with my first daughter, Karen. Her father is Alberto who is now my husband. At that stage we were not married.

I was living at home and, being pregnant, I wanted to get off drugs. At one stage I was put into hospital where they tried to get me off heroin but they were unsuccessful. For most of the time my mother had to look after Karen. When she was eight months old I decided to do something about it. Some of my friends in the streets had mentioned a centre called 'Betel', but they didn't speak very highly of it. They said it was run by nuns and monks. At this stage I was beaten up in the street by some of my 'friends' so I was in a very bad state. I had to find help somewhere and the thing that really attracted me to Betel was that it was free. My mother really encouraged me to do something about it. Now in order to get into Betel I had to attend some of their meetings first. My mother took me there, so that I could demonstrate that I was interested in being cured. Finally they gave me a place, but I behaved so badly that they showed me the door after a few days, and advised me to go to another group that had a centre in the North, away from Madrid, where all my temptations were.

After a few months the leaders felt I was getting on pretty well but the truth was that I wasn't.

Then I had to go to a delayed court case for holding up a hairdressing salon. I was given a year's jail, but it was arranged that I serve that year with Betel in Madrid where Alberto, my child and my parents lived. But my attitude still wasn't right, I was still rebellious and after five months I left and went back on the street, and back to drugs. I got so desperate that it was then I realised the only hope for my life was God.

I went back for the third time but with true repentance in my heart because I really regretted what I'd done. I realised how much time I'd wasted and I received Christ virtually straight away. After I'd been back in Betel for two years Alberto and I were married and then Karen came back to live with us.

One thing I look back on as being special for me was the help I received from the missionaries that were working with Betel. They were a real example of what it was to live a mature Christian life. They especially helped me to grow in my prayer life.

In 1990 Alberto and I were married, and a year later we had a son, Daniel.

Alberto now tells his story.

My father was a carpenter and I didn't have much interest in studying because I wasn't a very good student. What interested me most was playing soccer and other sports. When I turned fourteen I became involved with young people who were always getting into trouble. I thought I was creating a 'macho' image, but inside I was afraid and didn't like it, but little by little I overcame that fear. I teamed up with another delinquent in the area and did robberies every day. The normal thing was to break into cars and take things out of them. On one occasion we did a hold up with a sawn-off shotgun.

When I was sixteen I was caught robbing a car and was taken to a reformatory in Carabanchel prison; I was there for only two days. I came out and went back to the same thing. I was also taking heroin by then. I had a fight with another young person and I was put in prison again for two and a half months. Prison made me very rebellious. From that time on until the time I entered Betel my life was one of injecting heroin, visiting police stations, being in jails, and being treated in hospitals.

I became separated from my family. My parents didn't want to have me in the home any more. It was during this time that I met Rosi. I heard about Betel because Elliott and others came evangelising in our area. My health deteriorated and at heart I was sick of robbing. I realised I needed help so I went to Betel because of Rosi's connection with it.

I soon realised it was a Christian centre and I felt everything was a bit strange, however I always had a basic belief in God. After about a month a delayed court case came up and I was put in prison again.

[The legal system moves very slowly and so court cases can come up months or even years after a crime. This accounts for the time lag.]

During the few weeks that I'd been in Betel I'd heard the gospel but none of it had really entered my heart. I did take a Bible to

117

prison with me but I hid it. I was in prison for about three weeks and then I went back to the centre. I started then to seek after God. After three months I was back in prison again. This time I put the Bible on top of my table. Some of my friends asked me about it and I openly shared my faith. They would share their problems and I would try to help them. After a month I was back in Betel.

I started to grow in the Lord. I began to realise and feel that Christ was really in my heart.

I had a hard time for a while and it seemed as though the devil was trying to get me out of Betel. But God gave me the victory and I continued to grow. But because of my previous problems with the law I've had to go into prison a total of five or six times while at Betel. Two of these times were four month periods and during one of them our son Daniel was born.

Rosi and I continued to grow in the Lord and were given more responsibility. In 1992 we were sent to Málaga. Betel opened a new centre there so we went to help in that venture. Then in 1994 we were transferred to Albacete where the leader wasn't very well. In fact he died about a month after we arrived so from that time on until recently I was the leader. We have been called back to Madrid to serve in a pastoral capacity, being involved more with the church than with the centres. One of our main responsibilities is caring for the house church groups. We also have a pastoral role in the church. Rosi is involved in the Sunday school and during the week I'm also involved in street evangelism, and in visiting prisons and hospitals.

18

WORN OUT AT TWENTY-FIVE

THE STORY OF PEDRO & ESTRELLA

The testimony of Pedro and Estrella gives an excellent example of how two lives can be straightened out and then become stable and consistent members of society as well as making a vital contribution to local church life.

ESTRELLA

I was brought up in a humble home and I was a hard worker. I had a father who was strict and wanted everything done right. He was a drinker and gambler and I grew up under the pressure of what my father expected of me. I finished up rebelling against him. And so I began to look for things that I thought would make me happy. I mixed with lesbians and that led on to being involved with drugs. I took heroin for three years. It was a hard time – I was involved in a very perverse world, a world of homosexuality and drugs. One night when I believed I would have to become a prostitute, I cried out to God. I realised that there was a God out there. I went to my father and he said he would help me, and that I could return home. He would help me look for a place where I could be cured.

Betel did not have a centre then but my aunt talked to some of the WEC missionaries and they recommended me to a place in Vitoria. But I didn't like it there and left after seven days.

For the next little while I stayed at home. My family wouldn't let me go out of the house. From time to time I went down to the meetings at Betel in San Blas. Once, I used that excuse to go and buy heroin. When I returned Myk asked me why I had injected heroin again. I felt I was a fraud. I was putting on a good front on one hand but in reality I was doing something else. At the same time I was deceiving my family while they were putting a lot of effort into trying to help me. During that time I went to visit another church in the suburb of Coslada. I talked to a missionary there, Ronnie Deelen, and I believe that was when I accepted the Lord into my life.

Eventually I said to Myk, 'I want to go to Santander.' I spent two years in the community there. After that time I came back to Madrid and later became a leader of the new Betel centre for girls.

After seven months in the Betel community I left to marry Pedro.

Pedro shares his early life.
Like my wife, I was brought up in a humble home. I was born in a city called Leon to the north of Madrid. My parents moved to Barcelona and I lived there from when I was two till I was sixteen. I was a difficult child at home, I suffered from a lot of sicknesses of the stomach. I had rickets resulting from inadequate diet. After I started school they discovered I was dyslectic.

When I was sixteen I started to try drugs, and to get money I became involved in prostitution. Of course I did all this without my parents knowing. When I was eighteen I left home and didn't return until I was twenty when I had to do my military service. My parents knew absolutely nothing about where I was during those two years. I had been living as a prostitute and doing anything that was easy for me. The only things that interested me were drugs and living for pleasure.

When I was twenty five my body was tired and worn out. Once I was in a cinema, watching the hero in the picture dying. The film depicted what he was thinking at that moment, 'I haven't had anything in life; no children, I haven't achieved anything.' I saw my life reflected in that film – I had achieved nothing and I was dying. I didn't know God because I didn't believe in Him, but I knew within myself that someone would have to help me. I thought about the possibilities of someone rich falling in love with me and helping me. Of course that would be the easiest thing.

But I decided to go home. My parents received me with open arms but they warned me that this was the last time they were going to help me. We looked for a rehabilitation centre that would be free and we found one in Vitoria. There I met God. One night I cried to Him and asked Him to change my desires. The following day I was another person. I could hardly believe it. I hadn't liked reading the Bible but the day after I changed I liked it, and from that time on I haven't stopped reading it. This was sixteen years ago.

Estrella and I met each other during an evangelistic campaign in Gijon organised by two rehabilitation centres.

It wasn't difficult to leave a homosexual background when I married Estrella because I never really considered myself to be a homosexual. I only used the relationship I had with other men to get money. The day of conversion was a true conversion – a total change. I asked the Lord to come in and change my desires and He has done just that.

Estrella describes her present situation.
For the past nine years I have been participating in the worship team in the church. For about the same time I've also been teaching in the Sunday school. And for the last two years I've been one of the leaders of the Sunday school team. I also lead the worship in the women's meeting and participate in the worship in our weekly home group. I have a normal weekday job too. I work three hours each morning from Monday through Saturday as a cleaner in a bank.

Pedro explains his present role.
I'm a deacon in the church and I help with practical and administrative matters. With my wife I'm involved in leading

the worship in the Sunday School meetings. We work pretty well together. My weekday job is the most demanding part of my life. I work for a company which has a contract to clean banks, including the airport bank. At times during the year we have to start work at 4am and often don't finish until 5pm or 6pm. We have two children, Marta (9) and Samuel (7). They both go to school and are doing very well. They both get good reports. They like going to the church and the Sunday school with us.

I left the community eleven years ago and Estrella finished a year later. Life out of the community hasn't always been easy. For example there was a time when I was out of work for two years. We were just married and didn't receive any help from our parents. Because we had been in the drug world for so long I didn't have any training. Paco Corrales, who was also in Betel, showed me how to do plumbing and how to install central heating. This was a real help because I was able to get some work at that. I use this knowledge in my present job because as well as cleaning we also do maintenance and installation of heating systems.

19

THE CANCER HAS GONE

THE STORY OF MYKA CONTERAS

My name is Myka and I am thirty-eight years old. At an early age I was sent to boarding school, and had little contact with my family during those years. Consequently, when I left at sixteen, I didn't have a very good relationship even with my mother because we had never come to know each other.

I never had any work, and soon finished up in the world of drug-taking. I got mixed up with a gang that robbed pharmacies. I took soft drugs and pills for about a year. On one occasion I was arrested, taken down to the police station and searched, but I didn't have anything with me, so I was released.

Then I started taking hard drugs and learned to inject heroin. I had to rob to get money and lived with a guy who was doing the same. After six years hooked on heroin I had a daughter, but that was by a different man. When she was three years old I went to a drug centre in Alicante, where I stayed for nine months. When I first entered I didn't believe anything, and I thought it was all just put on. I thought the smiles I saw on the people's faces were false. But through their testimony, I realised where they had come from and could see how they had changed. I realised that if God could help them He could help me, and that I needed a personal relationship with Him.

While I was there the State took my child away to care for her, so after leaving, my only desire was to get her back. But I was soon on the streets and hooked on heroin again. After four months I realised I had lost everything. I was sick and knew I needed help, so I went back to Alicante. This time I was determined to look to the Lord and leave the matter of my daughter in His hands, because I realised I wasn't able to do anything about it. After I had been there for three months the authorities began to let my daughter visit me. Then I was transferred to Betel in Madrid, so that I would be closer to my child who was then about four years old.

After I had been in Madrid for nine months I went with a team to open a girls' house in Cuenca. During this time the rest of the team began to trust me and give me more responsibility. I began to help other girls, and gradually realised that God wanted to use me. He had a purpose for my life. After two years I had the total responsibility of the house, and I was the leader for another eighteen months after that. Altogether I have been in Betel for eight and a half years. I have learned to trust in God a lot more, but I still need to enter into a deeper relationship with Him.

Two years ago I had cancer at the base of my spine. My bodily defences, because of AIDS, were very low. The doctors said they couldn't give me much hope of living very long. They had to give me chemotherapy and injections in the bone marrow. At first I felt very disappointed with God. I wondered, 'Why has this happened to me?' But then God spoke to me from Isaiah 40:31, 'Those who hope in the Lord will renew their strength. They will soar on wings like eagles; they will run and not grow weary, they will walk and not be faint.' From this verse He gave me the promise that I was going to come through. At that stage I was going to hospital virtually every day, very fearful, but He kept encouraging me, giving me strength to get up and walk. Today I am completely healed and the doctors don't know how to explain it! I know it's a miracle from God.

20

GAMBLING RUINED MY LIFE

THE STORY OF ANTONIO FERNANDEZ

I'll cover my early life briefly. I suppose I was a fairly good Catholic – largely through my mother's strong influence. I actually took a course on how to share my faith, although I never really knew the Lord, personally.

My father was a bank manager and I had a good education, later joining him at the bank. After marriage and raising three children we moved to Argentina where I took charge of my uncle's business for seventeen years.

When we returned to Spain I began to be involved in gambling, lotteries, bingo, and things like that – activities I'd never participated in before. This brought difficulties into our marriage so I hid what I was doing from my wife. But she realised from our bank accounts that money was disappearing and that I was taking it to gamble. Relationships deteriorated during this time and my children began to reject me. I realised I wasn't being accepted in my own house so I decided to leave.

I had some money with me so I lived in a hostel till it ran out. Things got so bad I didn't have anywhere to stay so I finished up sleeping in underground stations for three or four nights. One morning I came out of the station and looked in the rubbish bin. I noticed a four-page magazine so I began to read it. I saw an advertisement saying that if you had a need or a problem in your life, 'call us'. There was a phone number to ring. I rang and discovered that it was the Salvation Army. The man on the other end of the phone asked me where I was and said he would come and pick me up.

He took me to the church and on the way there he told me that he heard a note of concern in my voice and he was very worried and thought I might do something desperate. He offered me accommodation in the back of the church where they had a little flat with a bedroom and kitchen. He brought me some food and said I could stay there. After a few days he asked me to come with him because he wanted to introduce me to the director of a rehabilitation centre.

I went with him. That was in April 1989. He took me to Betel which at that stage was in Calle Raza. He introduced me to Elliott Tepper, the director, and Elliott said it was up to me whether I would make a decision to stay or not. My first reaction was that if this was a rehabilitation centre for drug addicts what was I doing here? I was not a drug addict! At that time I didn't realise that I really was an addict too; I was enslaved to gambling.

It was some time before I gave my life to the Lord because when they first started speaking to me about Jesus as Saviour I said, 'Yes, I know this. I've known this for ages.' But when they told me that to be saved I had to commit my life to Christ I was offended because I felt I'd already done that. During this time of doubt something happened that really convinced me. It was listening to the testimony of others who had been involved in a level of sin which to my mind was a lot worse than what I'd done. I could see what God had done in their lives. I saw the change; former criminals were now living honest lives and seeking to help others.

This was the thing that most convinced me and led to my true conversion. After that, my wife saw the change in me and the peace that I had. She began to come and visit me at the centre. She saw the joy I now had but when I told her about what had happened she didn't believe me. She said, 'I know that the evangelicals are honourable and sincere people, but I don't believe what you say, because you've lied to me so much lately.' So I asked God to give me the right things to say to my family, and that God would open her heart so that she would understand that what had happened in my life was really of God. She said to me, 'Look, before you were a leader in the Catholic church but you were really leading a double life. So if you've done that you could be doing the same thing now.' She did start coming to the meetings and she was learning something from them, but as she works and is very tired she does not attend regularly.

I will be seventy this year. Certainly I am the oldest 'Betelito'. While my family has seen the change in my life there has not been the complete acceptance and forgiveness I had hoped for. For the last few years I have been living at the centre during the week and going home at weekends. This may seem awkward, but God has had His purpose in it.

I have been able to develop a close relationship with the men and because of my legal and administrative training have served as their advocate in hundreds of court procedures. In the last decade I have developed Betel's office of legal intervention working on behalf of the community members who still have judgements against them. Hundreds have been pardoned or have had their sentences shortened. At this very moment we have almost one hundred serving their sentences in Betel rather than prison because of the ministry the Lord has committed to me.

Although I lost everything because of gambling, and still suffer from a sense of rejection from my family, today Betelitos call me 'Abuelo' (grandfather) and I feel their love and appreciation. I am a friend on a first name basis with many of the principal judges in the Spanish judicial system. I often represent Betel before the public in various capacities. Recently I was ordained as an elder. So while things have not turned out exactly as I had hoped, God has, in His way, recompensed me and said, 'Well done my faithful servant.'

I would like to say something about the death of our youngest son, Felix. While he was doing his military service, he was infected with AIDS through a blood transfusion. The virus developed in his body and he finished up in hospital. My wife, my second daughter and I would take turns to be at his side twenty-four hours a day. While I was visiting I took him a Bible and said, 'Felix, when you feel well enough and have enough strength just read a little bit of the Bible. God will speak to you through it.'

I asked Elliott, all the Betel leaders, and all my friends to pray for my son. So they prayed daily that he would be healed, and more importantly, that he would be saved and come to know the Lord. One day, at midday, when it was my turn to be there Elliott came in to visit. At this stage Felix was very delicate, very weak. Elliott told Felix that he needed to trust in the Lord and explained how he had lost his own son in very difficult circumstances. At this moment Elliott looked at me as if he was asking me if it was okay to continue. Then he looked at Felix and said, 'Felix, would you like to receive Jesus Christ into your life as Lord and Saviour?' My son said, 'Yes', as though he was just waiting for someone to ask him!

Elliott was on one side of the bed, I was on the other and Elliott prayed. Felix repeated the prayer. He said it with such sincerity and I saw a joy in his face immediately after he said it. When my wife arrived the first thing Felix said to her was, 'You know what's happened, Mama? Elliott came in, and I received Jesus Christ in my heart.'

[Felix went to be with the Lord two days later.]

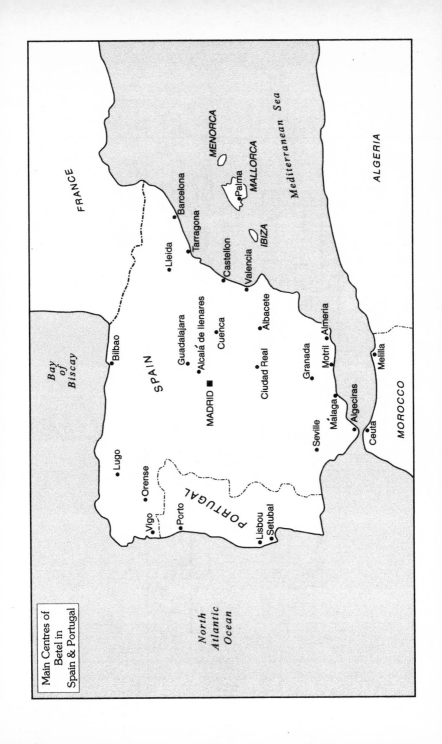

Main Centres of Betel in Spain & Portugal

THE GROWTH OF BETEL

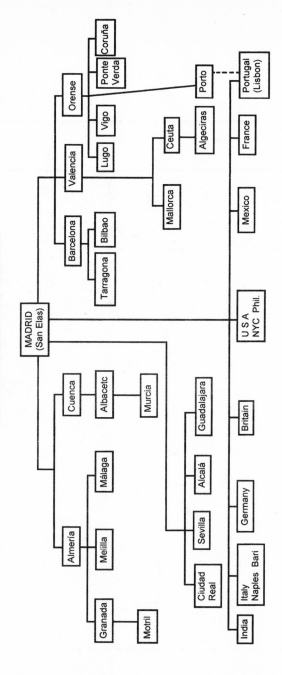

PART II
MULTIPLICATION

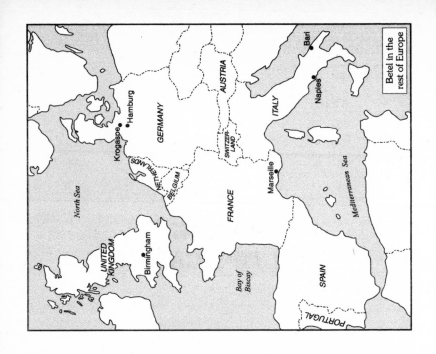

Betel in USA & Mexico

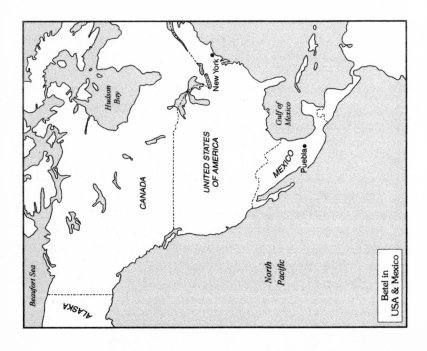

Betel in the rest of Europe

1

A BRITISH CENTRE – READY MADE!

KENT & MARY ALICE MARTIN

Kent Martin is a trained journalist and gifted musician. He and Mary Alice are a great song leading team and made a vital contribution to Betel's worship in Madrid during their first term.

God is constantly looking for faithful couples whom He can stretch by giving them increasing responsibilities, and the Martins were no exception. Faithfully supported and prayed for by their home church in Pennsylvania they relate how God started to prepare them for a big change of ministry.

Kent commences the story.

Roughly three and a half years ago a pastor in USA had a word from the Lord for us and said, 'Kent, you are coming to a sharp turn in the road that you are not expecting.' This was during a short furlough. When we returned to Spain, to our complete surprise the Betel leadership in Madrid asked us if we would consider opening up Betel in England.

We started to weigh this up before the Lord and felt quite positive about this change of direction. I had links with David Partington of Yeldall Manor, a rehabilitation centre in England. He and Terence Rosslyn-Smith set up meetings for me to meet people in Britain. They welcomed us – hesitatingly at first – and then opened the doors wider for us. They arranged for Elliott and me to meet with a wide cross-section of leaders concerned about drug rehabilitation.

So we landed in Britain in May 1995 and came to Birmingham to meet with fifteen church leaders and other concerned people. They asked us, 'What is Betel looking for and how can we help you?'

We had originally thought of opening in Manchester or Liverpool where needs were great, but in this meeting we said we were looking for a property reasonably close to a city where we could establish a centre and have links to the business community. They proposed that we seek a large country property that would meet British regulations. They also recommended that we establish a 'Christian Community' rather than a 'rehabilitation centre'. In other words, have a low profile.

At the meeting we were introduced to Alex Elsaesser, an American missionary, who was in charge of a property leased from the Bournville Village Trust. The group said, 'Alex is going to take you to look at his place while we continue our discussions here.'

While other members of this group were very well dressed, Alex was quite casual and seemed quite detached during the meeting. In fact he had actually spent most of the time reading *Rescue Shop*. We had the impression that we were being politely invited to leave an 'important' meeting to take a tour of an old run down rehabilitation work. But we were very mistaken.

He took us in his van to Windmill House. As we walked through the property we looked at a checklist that we had written up and found that this place fitted the criteria perfectly. We asked how far it was from the centre of town. 'Twenty-five minutes' was the reply, 'and the buildings meet the regulations of the local council.' He showed us through the dormitory rooms, the well-equipped kitchen, the lounge with its adequate seating. Outside was a furniture workshop, and the buildings edged a five acre sports area.

We discovered that he had been running this place as a Christian Community, not a rehabilitation centre – and this, too, fitted our objective. Over a cup of tea Alex opened his heart. He said, 'I invited you here because I would like you to take over this property.' It turned out that he and his large family (a wife and nine children) were hoping to move out to a less stressful type of service. Apparently he had been given authority from the Bournville Trust to transfer the lease to us!

He had been praying and asking the Lord to bring along a reputable group who could take over. When he discovered that we were part of WEC, and after he had read the book, he felt assured that we were the answer. Elliott and I invited him there and then to come to Spain at Betel's expense so that he could see the nature of the work firsthand. Alex finally said, 'When can you come and take over?' We had thought of starting in Britain in eighteen months' time, but he wanted us there much sooner than that, so it was arranged that we come in January 1996 – just six and a half months ahead.

Mary Alice continues.
We were shocked to be asked to go to Britain but God spoke to us separately. I remember I was in Granada for a weekend break with Kent's mother. The Lord wakened me in the middle of the night (amazing – I sleep like a log!) and told me to read Isaiah 62. I came to verse 10: 'Go through, go through the gates, clear the way for the people, build up the highway, remove the stones, lift up a standard over the peoples. Behold the Lord has proclaimed to the ends of the earth, say to the daughters of Zion, Lo your salvation has come; his reward is with him and his recompense before him. And they will call them the holy people, the redeemed of the Lord and you will be called – a city not forsaken.' I felt this was the Lord's encouragement to go forward.

This of course was before Kent visited England and the property was offered. That scripture has been a rock for us. It hasn't been easy pioneering a new work but there has been no escape for us – we know God is in this. He is going to build a work here, so it is not a burden.

Kent explains:

In the Gospels all that Peter needed to move him out of the boat was the Lord's word, 'Come!' The rapid unfolding of God's plan, with the leasing of this property worth millions of pounds, was God's 'come' to us. Once we opened we were in business almost immediately. Within one weekend we had our first man, and within a couple of weeks we had seven.

Unlike what happened in Spain, these men contacted us. This came about through the few contacts we had made and through the Betel literature that we had distributed to churches and groups. It was a good confirmation that there was a need here.

Mary Alice describes how work became available.

Regarding finance, we began to put out flyers indicating we were open for lesser skilled work such as gardening and painting. The jobs came immediately. Initially we had a gift to support us from Madrid Betel but since then we have been financially independent. Lots of work opened up for us. Fortunately we had some men who could do gardening and painting! Then we started a charity or 'opportunity' shop, selling used furniture, clothing and bric-a-brac. It is in a large supermarket-type building that we obtained for a very low rent because we fixed it up ourselves. It has two floors, totalling 7,000 square feet.

Kent describes the march of events.

David Partington and Terence Rosslyn-Smith have both been very helpful in getting us established and giving us a wide variety of contacts. I was introduced to David by an ex-heroin addict. We've been working with these men to develop co-operatives or employee-owned businesses where men can integrate back into society once again.

The most noteworthy aspect of all this is the speed and extent of developments in the two and a half years we have been here. Another major factor has been WEC's reputation in Britain; this has made the fledgling unknown branch incredibly acceptable in churches and fellowships. We've watched faces change when they realise we are part of WEC's thrust.

One hundred and forty WEC prayer groups now have had our printed testimony and we have been invited to speak at WEC gatherings as far north as Edinburgh. The Evangelical Alliance accepted us quickly without requiring the prescribed two year probationary period.

Another group that has given good support is the 'Ground Level' churches – an association of about eighty fellowships largely between the Humber and the Wash in eastern England. They, under Pastor Stuart Bell's leadership, supported us in Spain long before we came to UK. We have been invited for many years to their annual festival where about 5,000 people attend. We have given workshops and presentations there and these have spread the word about Betel.

A number of teams have come from churches in Pennsylvania and Virginia and have done building and maintenance work. They have built us a small house, put in showers, and so on. They pay their own expenses, including food costs, and help finance the projects in which they have been engaged.

Mary Alice describes the family situation.
The children went right into the local school. For Ian, who was ten when we arrived, it was a hard adjustment. We had spent almost five years in Spain and because he spoke Spanish fluently the other children did not realise that he was not a 'foreigner' so he had more 'ribbing' than in Spain. Patricia was six and just starting school when she came so she picked up the Birmingham accent very rapidly. They have both settled well now. Ian recently won the gold medal for the high jump in the local school boy's competition.

In the early years Kent and I had to work very hard for long hours, so we know the tension between the demands of work and family. We have made adjustments in that area for the children's sakes.

Kent discusses the fruit of their labours.

We have started to see some fruit develop. God has told me to take my eyes off 'fruits' and to concentrate on 'roots'. The life-giving organism is what matters. Fruit is the long term result in a healthy tree. During the first two years we had our numbers go up and down rarely passing twenty men in the program – with much turnover and little maturity. But this last year the roots of the tree have found firm rich soil. Today we have about thirty-five men steadily with us, and all our leaders are now British, the last single Spanish monitor having returned toSpain. We have more men now than we have ever had, and a number of these are acting very responsibly. Most of them are now born again. They are eager; they are praying and seeking the Lord – it is such a switch from the early days. We're looking for another place in Birmingham where we can help families and do some church planting. In the last few months we have started a church here in Windmill House. Outsiders are starting to come in and we usually have around fifty at services. There is a sense of bonding and a desire for outreach.

One afternoon at our charity shop in Yardley Wood a gentleman entered and asked what we did. Our men started to talk to him about Betel and the nature of our work. It turned out that he was a director of the Aston Re-investment Trust which is also partially funded by Cadburys. They lend money to charities and new businesses that can't get conventional financing because they don't have a high credit rating.

We told him we needed a truck to move furniture to our warehouse. 'I think we could help with that,' this gentleman said. Within a few weeks we had a loan that enabled us to purchase a suitable seven and a half ton vehicle. It turned out that he was a member of the Charities Aid Foundation which gives or lends up to half a billion pounds a year to deserving charities around the world.

Through him I was introduced to the chairman of this Foundation in London to whom I was able to explain Betel's function; later Elliott Tepper was able to meet him and discuss other ways in which the Foundation could help, namely by brokering a $4,000,000 loan to purchase a building for use as an international headquarters and church, in Madrid.

* * *

We are tremendously grateful to Alex and Irene Elsaesser. They have been so generous not only in handing over the property but also in handing over a lucrative franchise owned by Service Master. This is an American business based in Chicago that franchises the rights and technology to repair and restore quality furniture. One of our men, Derek Whitmore, now handles this department. The name has been changed to 'Furniture Medic' and we now have the franchise for the Birmingham/Coventry area. We would like to see this develop in Spain also.

The Bournville Trust rents this property to us at the princely sum of £33 per month. This lease extends to 2001 with the option of renewing until 2005. The property is worth between one and two million pounds.

We thank God for the contribution of Victor and Sandra Bautista. Victor (from USA) is in charge of the mechanics and Sandra (from New Zealand) has set up the office accounting system. Also for Chris Garrett, a British engineer who gave us two years, working on the sewage system, the well, the computer, and buildings. God has certainly blessed us since coming to Britain!

In July 1999 Kent, Elliott and Mary were invited to Ireland by Bill and Helen Lacy to explore the possibility of opening Betel in Dublin. Betel of Ireland is now in the process of being incorporated as a charity and a search for the right installations is under way. Betel of Britain will sponsor the new community.

2

'I'VE GOT JUST THE PLACE FOR YOU'

BETEL IN ITALY

Elliott Tepper

In 1993 God moved in our hearts and we had a sense that He wanted us to go beyond Spain to other nations. After the start in USA I felt that Italy ought to be one of our next steps; I had a tremendous burden on my heart for that country but I didn't know how to begin. We didn't have any contacts; I knew WEC was there but I didn't know any of the team personally.

One day I was sitting in my office in the Madrid centre. It is on a mezzanine floor that overlooks the main auditorium below. I was praying, 'Lord, how can we find a way into Italy? Whom do we know there that can help us?' Suddenly I remembered that about two years before, Manuel Fernandez, the director of SEFOVAN (which is an evangelical Bible School in Madrid where one of our WEC missionaries, Uwe Hutter, lectures) had been to Italy and had made contact with a church there. In fact it was one of the largest in the country with about one thousand members. Michelle Romeo is the pastor – a former milkman whom God has taken up and used to start a number of churches. Manuel had remarked about the dynamic of this church, and how spiritually-minded the people were. This pastor was seeking more theological understanding for his people and had asked Manuel over to give help and advice. That was two years ago and I hadn't seen him since then.

So I thought, 'That's the man I need to talk to.' Just as I said that I looked out of my open office door, and who was standing in the middle of our sanctuary but Manuel! I shouted, 'What are you doing here?' he shouted back, 'I've just brought a young man in to go on your programme.'

'Manuel, you were in my mind a moment ago. We want to start up in Italy and you are the only person I know who has contacts there! Can you help us?' He said, 'Sure, I have just returned from Italy this week. I'll send a fax off right away and get you an invitation.'

Within a day we had an official invitation from the largest church in Italy to go over, spend a week with the church and investigate possibilities. And that's how we were directed – I believe supernaturally – to Michelle Romeo.

Lindsay McKenzie, a group of Betel leaders and I set off in a van for Italy. We drove along the coast from Barcelona, through France into Italy and down to Naples, stopping for two nights en route.

South Italy is so different from France or Switzerland, or even northern Italy. Everything is neat and tidy as far as Rome but from there on things are different, especially in the greater Naples metropolitan area. Public works show signs of neglect; buildings are in disrepair (because the mafia and often public servants have to be paid before any work can be done). In Naples there is crime and corruption and piles of garbage on the streets. The traffic, confusion and noise are unique in the western world. There is, of course, another Naples. Inside their homes there is beauty, even elegance. The people are very warm and there is a cosmopolitan air to the city. It is hard not to fall in love with Naples despite its 'warts'.

We were well received by the church. They put us up in dormitories in the basement of their building; they gave us access to their kitchen; prepared many of our meals and treated us like family.

The pastor warmed to us and flung his whole weight behind our efforts. He introduced us to Guy Sottile who is an Italian married to an American. He is the director of the principal interdenominational Evangelistic Association in Italy. He is the equivalent of a young Billy Graham to the Italian churches and is one of only a few that can bridge the differences between denominations.

The very week we were there he was in the process of planning a big national conference and had pastors assembled from all over the country. We were invited to give a presentation to them – a unique and strategic opportunity. During the same week Guy was also in the process of organising a city-wide campaign in Naples itself, so we had a further opportunity to speak to all the Neopolitan pastors. Needless to say, we had a tremendous introduction to Italy, and Betel's association with Guy Sottile was not lost on the Italian pastors.

Pastor Romeo introduced us to a lawyer who was a member of his congregation and he immediately started the legal process of obtaining government recognition for Betel.

Of course, we needed a property. The church people showed us a few places but none of them were suitable. I said to the young man from the church who was showing us around, 'Let's follow the ring-road round the city and we'll pray as we go.' At one point I felt urged to say, 'Let's turn off here.' We pulled up at a bar to ask if there was a real estate agent nearby. Someone said, 'There's one right across the street.'

When we explained to the agent what we wanted, she said, 'I've got just the place for you.' We had a look at it and it was quite suitable. The agent said she would arrange for us to meet the owner. The next day we met at the agent's office. But when the owner realised we wanted the property for a rehabilitation centre she was immediately put off and refused to consider a deal. I said, 'Please, we're here from Spain staying in Pastor Romeo's church and...' She broke in: 'Pastor Romeo? Why he's one of my best friends! If you are a friend of his then I'm prepared to rent the property to you.' Out of a population of two million people the Lord led us to a woman who was a friend of Michelle Romeo!

Then when it came to drawing up a contract I suggested we meet at five pm with the lawyer who was handling the Betel registration. When she heard who it was she exclaimed, 'Why, that's my lawyer too! And I have an appointment to see him at four!'

Again we sensed the hand of the Lord in all this. We had brought enough money for the contract (the deposit and first month's rent), but had nothing left to purchase fittings or furniture – and we were leaving the next day.

But here is how God worked. During the week we had paid a courtesy visit to a WEC missionary working in the Naples area. He was a Swiss called Daniel Bachman and had been involved in church planting for many years. On that last day Daniel called on us just as we were loading the van to return to Spain. He said, 'This is a gift from our church to help Betel get started in Italy.' He handed us a large envelope full of money, three million lira ($2,500) to be exact, which was enough to cover the cost not only of fitting out the villa but the charges involved in signing the contract!

One more miracle was the granting of fiscal cards. You can't open a bank account without one, but you can't get this card if you are not a permanent resident.

We went to the taxation office and were referred from one department to another all the way up to the eighth floor. Finally we met a supervisor who simply asked us to fill out a form and issued them on the spot! We then promptly opened a bank account before we left for Spain.

The Lord had worked in every aspect of this new beginning in Italy.

3

IN MAFIA COUNTRY

LINDSAY & MYK McKENZIE

While the previous chapter covers the good things about Betel's entry into Italy, it has to be admitted that there were many problems in the early development of the work. This was to a large extent due to the poor health of the pioneer leader, Jambri, who eventually died of AIDS.

As time went on it became apparent that strong mature leadership was needed and gradually, through having to visit Naples from time to time, the burden came on Lindsay and Myk McKenzie and Armando and Emma Garcia.

Leaving Spain was to be a huge wrench for both families, but, obedient to the leading of the Lord and with the blessing of the Betel leadership in Madrid, they moved to Italy in August 1998.

Space prohibits a detailed examination of the local situation which they faced but the contrasts they encountered in dealing with Italian drug addicts make fascinating reading.

One of the big differences that we noticed between Italy and Spain was the influence of the family. It is a big factor in the life of the Italian people. It is often the controlling factor. In Spain individuals can make personal decisions, but in Italy a decision is conditional on what the family thinks. So when it comes to a basic issue like conversion a person is often hindered by how he thinks the family will react. Also, the families often are more loyal to sons or daughters than to us who are trying to extricate them from the bondage of drug-taking.

Another factor is that the Spanish character is much more

'gungho' – willing to go out and conquer without worrying about details. On the other hand, the Italian wants to know all the details before launching out. That works for good and bad. For instance, in Spain we have terrible trouble maintaining our vehicles. The Spanish driver starts the engine and thinks, 'Let's go; we'll look at the oil later', whereas the Italian mentality is more concerned with details and the aesthetic side of things. 'Let's check the oil, and make sure the tyres are good.' But we may not get off when planned, because there are so many details to be addressed.

Italy is wealthier than Spain and people can afford to cover up their son's drug addiction longer. Some Spanish families will pay for drugs for their sons rather than disclosing their shame to others. Covering up is even more prevalent in Italy where image – what you project yourself to be – is a lot more important. It's very hard to recognise drug addicts in Italy because they will have had the latest haircut, and they will wear designer clothes. In Spain their teeth are falling out, they are unshaven, dirty, unkempt, and are wearing ragged clothes. In Italy their parents will make sure they look good in spite of their drug addiction. The young people play on that too. 'I'll go to a centre if you buy me the latest Nike shoes.' The parents of one lad (a plumber) bought him a three piece suit for our end-of-year celebration. He looked stunning. This is just normal for south Italy.

In the beginning, we received a lot of men through church contacts. They would often come in with a Bible under their arm, spouting verses, and praying, right from the first day. They had been baptised; but they were hooked! Even though going through cold turkey, they wanted to be made leaders! They couldn't be taught anything. More recently we've returned to the old method of going out into the streets, to the plazas, and the stations and bringing them in from there. We would rather have people with no church background because they are far more responsive.

One of the things we had to undo with church contacts was their praying in the meetings. They pray in such a 'religious' way. I have had to say, 'If anyone wants to pray it will be one sentence, about something specific, and in your own words.' We've seen an improvement, but there's still a way to go. I think this is a reflection on the culture more than the churches. Religion is part of the life-style. There is a God-consciousness at every level, even though their practical living doesn't reflect it.

Another feature in Italy is the difference between the northern and southern cultures. The one thing that is apparent in the southern culture is generosity. Initially there is suspicion; you walk into a shop, and you don't get a smile; it's almost a scowl, until they get to know you and the opposite occurs. They are very generous and hospitable.

One thing that most shopkeepers have to contend with is the payment of the local mafia 'tax'. In Naples they are involved in every level of society from politics right down to the man that stands on a street corner selling contraband tobacco. They are the scourge of the local shopkeepers. In the week after we opened our first second-hand shop Miguel Jambrina had a visit from the local mafia (complete with pistols in their back pockets). They made noises about payments that had to be made to them every month. Miguel played ignorant and said that he knew nothing about what they were talking about. Having a heavy accent probably reinforced that; he said he would have to talk to the owner of the premises that they were renting. He gave his name and at that point the two mafiosi looked surprised and said, 'No problem, that's okay.' They never came back! We found out later that the owner of the building was higher up the ladder than they were, so the Lord protected us there.

The other second-hand shop was opened in August, 1997 and began to make a profit from the first day. Elia, one of the Italian leaders, was put in charge. He had spent one and a half years with us in Madrid. Incidentally he was spectacularly delivered from demon control as well as drug addiction, whilst there.

One Monday morning in the beginning of December, a lady from next door came in to the shop and angrily accused the boys of having burgled her apartment during the weekend. (Gold and jewels were stolen apparently). Of course the boys denied such an unfair accusation and finally the lady, unconvinced, left.

Three hours later five thugs stormed into the shop and without warning began to beat the men who were there, throwing them to the ground, kicking and punching them. The customers that happened to be in the shop all fled at the sight. The thugs yelled out, 'Where are the jewels that you stole?' 'Don't resist or we'll shoot!' yelled one, who immediately reached inside his suit coat for a pistol. Elia managed to say amidst the chaos, 'We've come to bless this suburb not steal from it. Even though you are beating us up, we love you and mean you no harm.' Finally the five thugs left threatening, 'If the goods don't turn up we're coming back to give you more!' The four boys were badly bruised and one was treated in hospital for a sprained wrist. Another had only just come out of hospital days before after having been in a diabetic coma.

The rest of the neighbourhood was soon buzzing with comments and opinions. Apparently the man who had organised and participated in the beatings was the lady's live-in companion who was also a member of the local 'camorra', the name of the Neapolitan mafia. He was hooked on cocaine and was consuming ever-increasing amounts. He needed money for his habit so he stole the jewels from his girlfriend but blamed the robbery on the 'addicts' next door! Dealing and trafficking in drugs is OK in the mafia code of ethics, but taking drugs is not, so any mafioso found hooked is immediately kicked out.

Soon neighbourhood support built up for our Betel boys (such was the good testimony that the fellows had created in just four months) and finally the woman came down and apologised to our men. Elia replied, 'We hold no grudge against your friends!' The lady couldn't understand their attitude and asked, astonished, why they didn't hate her and her boyfriend for what they had done. Elia then shared his testimony with her. She began to cry and confessed that some years before she used to attend an evangelical church. Seeing how our fellows had behaved she blurted out, 'But I am going to start attending that church again because I have seen genuine Christianity right here.'

Two days later the boyfriend came by and sheepishly made peace. He stopped short of apologising but that was probably the best that he could manage. He has been back on numerous occasions since then to buy second-hand furniture. A few weeks later the man that had threatened us with his pistol also turned up and (in his own way) showed remorse. He too has bought furniture. What the devil had planned, God has turned to our advantage.

* * *

At a family level there are lots of pressures. We were able to put the girls into a small school so that they could have more individual attention, but we discovered that they were not allowed to go out and play at breaks or lunchtime because of fear that something will happen to them. School authorities don't want to be sued for any mishaps. There's a general fear of kidnapping. We don't allow them to play alone.

Another thing that we are up against continually is ever increasing government regulation. In Spain it took twelve years for local authorities to come upon us with rules governing drug rehabilitation. But in Italy it has come a lot quicker. Fortunately we have had these four years to become established, but now they are making noises about closing us down if we don't have everything in order. They see us as a 'clinic' which we are not. In fact what we do challenges most definitions of drug rehabilitation, because (a) the work is done by the ex-addicts themselves; (b) we take them out into society and (c) we see social insertion as an integral part of the rehabilitation process. So after a fifteen day drying-out period our people are back into the world, always accompanied by somebody. We are facing having to abide by government regulations and either changing our modus operandi or being closed down. We need the Lord's wisdom on how far we go, and at the same time guarding a very precious part of what we do. So far the police and authorities have a positive attitude towards us and are giving us a lot more time than we would normally be given because we have gained a good reputation.

Betel is now part of the principal secular organisation which represents many drug rehabilitation programmes in Europe as well as in Canada and the States. It is based in Europe and acts as a pressure group with governments. We were able to go and speak to members of the European parliament in Brussels in June, 1998. This is part of our duty to be 'salt of the earth'.

The World Council of Therapeutic Communities, based in New York, has also recognised us as authorised counsellors.

* * *

To conclude this account of developments in Italy we now share the recent testimony of Armando and Emma Garcia, a Mexican couple who were members of the initial team that went from Spain to Italy. Armando writes:

Our call to Italy came after nine marvellous years with Betel in Spain. During that time I had the privilege of living in the first residence near Madrid and serving as a missionary through all these years of amazing growth, from the first few men in Mejorada to the establishment of almost one hundred residences around the world.

In the midst of all this, God began to stir my heart deeply for

149

the nation of Italy. One day, as I was seeking confirmation from the Lord, almost as a whim I said to him: 'Show me a reference to Italy in my Bible reading today.' (It had never been my custom to seek guidance in this way.) So I opened the Scriptures and my eyes fell on Acts 27:1. It said, 'And when it was determined that we should sail to Italy....'

The issue was settled for me but I waited for the Lord to speak to my wife also, so that she would be in full agreement with my vision. I knew that that would not be easy. When we had made an earlier exploratory trip she had exclaimed, on seeing the traffic in Naples, 'I could never live in a place like this!' But Emma heard the call from God, too, and it was precisely in Naples that God commenced our training in this culture. We spent two years learning the language. It was a great day when I preached my first sermon in Italian and someone said 'Amen!'. At last I knew I was communicating effectively.

With a vision and burden to advance the Kingdom, God spoke to me through Psalm 72:16: 'There shall be an abundance of corn in the earth upon the top of the mountains; the fruit shall shake like Lebanon; and they of the city shall flourish like grass of the earth.' We visited difference parts of Italy looking for a place to start a new centre, and we felt the promise of that verse lay in the North. Finally we focused very specifically on the city of Genoa and the mountains surrounding it. We knew that it had only six hundred evangelicals in a population of one million. We sensed that that was the land that would 'flourish like grass of the earth', but we never imagined how hard it would be, how violent the spiritual warfare against the forces of the enemy, or how jealous the devil was to preserve his domain.

In April 1999, Emma, Francisco Elia and I made some trips there to explore the region and find a house. There were few houses in the country available for rent and those that were had an exorbitant price tag. The city is located on a very narrow strip of land between the sea and foothills of the Alps and housing is at a premium. Finally, after much searching two possibilities arose, but we discovered that the first house had been destroyed by bombing in World War II and the second – a five storey building with eighteen rooms – had been burned down, so we went to the Lord again in prayer. We just knew he had a house set aside for us and that it was only a matter of time before we would find it.

Sergio, a member of a church in the historic centre of Genoa, told me about a house in the mountains near Torriglia which, in his time, had been used as a Christian conference centre, but had been unoccupied for eighteen years. We went to see it and found that although not bombed or burned, it was not far removed from such a condition. Next to it lived an old man named Gioseppe who for the previous thirty years had been the caretaker. When he found out our intentions he vehemently opposed us and presented us with a long list of impossibilities. But once he came to know us better his attitude changed and he became a good friend and, indeed, a collaborator. In fact he set us on the trail of the owner whom we were eventually able to locate in New York. We reached an agreement to occupy the house and so made a start.

A team of eight with Francisco Elia as leader arrived on June 20th. During the first days the church of the Reconciliation gave the team hospitality and helped us tremendously in restoring the property. Another Christian group called 'Veri Amici' led by Daniel Bachman, a WEC missionary, gave us lots of help also. It was a great adventure fixing up this house, with its leaky roof, broken pipes, fallen walls and so on, and doing it all in the presence of 'girls' – little squirrel-like animals that kept jumping over everything.

We discovered that the water supply did not come from the city or a well, but from a natural fountain in the mountain. It was a marvel of the Lord for us to see it leaping out as if some invisible hand was squeezing crystal clear water out of the rock just for our benefit. It was a constant reminder of Christ our Rock and our Fountain of Living Water.

If we had not had this wonderful base, it would have been impossible to carry on in the face of all the trials and difficulties that we encountered in the next few months. Hell seemed to oppose our advance in every way. The spiritual warfare was intense. My family was attacked. Our goods were attacked. On the first day we went to look for a separate place for my family, my car would not start – the motor had seized up. We had to have it taken to a mechanic who took two weeks to fix it. During that time I borrowed another car from Daniel. It had always gone well but I had driven it only a few kilometres when the motor began to throw out water and smoke. The floor of the car resembled a swimming pool and the engine went on fire. Later, after my car had been fixed I had a phone call from our men to say that their van was stuck in the middle of a highway, and the motor had broke in two. Yes, they had checked the oil and water, but for no apparent reason the engine block had simply broken up, so now we had men living up the mountain with no transportation. I had to give them my car so that the centre could function.

These extra expenses were unexpected and enormous. I remember one night I sat down on the sofa in the home where we were being given hospitality. Without turning on the light I explained the situation to my wife. She tried to encourage me and then said, 'A letter has come for you. Would you like to see it?' I asked her to open it. She said, 'It doesn't seem like a letter; it's a bunch of banknotes.' I said, 'How many? How many zeroes?' She counted, 'One-two-three-four.' I turned on the light and looked carefully at the money. 'This is exactly the price of a new motor for the car.' A Christian, the same morning that the van had broken down, had felt led to donate this amount to Betel!

The story doesn't finish there. The same day on which we picked up the van with its new engine some of our men went to work in my car and on the way the whole transmission broke down – another expensive job.

The material losses were costly but they were nothing to what was to follow – a tragedy in the spiritual realm, and our worst experience. While I was still coming to terms with the transmission failure in my car Francisco Elia called me on the telephone (at that moment I was then in England at the Betel leaders' conference) to tell me that the second leader of the house had taken the van with six others, and had tried to persuade them to 'shoot up' with him. It was so unexpected, unthinkable – diabolical. At the last minute three of them got out of the van and would not participate. Only the newest and weakest stayed with him. They first got drunk and then shot up with heroin. The shock was devastating. We had been like a family. Two of the men who did not take part were so sickened that they left the community, totally discouraged. In the end only two of the original team remained.

From these ashes God has raised up another group. What pleases me most is the fighting spirit and the willingness to co-operate that now exist in the team. There are still battles, but I remember one of the last words of Raul Casto, the first Betelito, shortly before he died: 'If we do not surrender, we will conquer.' The Lord has spoken to us much about 'walking in the light'. When we do that we have real fellowship with one another and give no place to the works of darkness.

Some of the new arrivals have gone through tremendous withdrawal symptoms, with vomiting and convulsions – things that we have not seen for a long time in the older larger centres where our spiritual covering has longer been in place. But all of this has focused our minds on why we are here. We do not want to lose sight of the love of Jesus and his great compassion for the lost. Genoa still has a great place in the plan of God for the blessing of Italy and the world.

4

BETEL'S BATTLES IN THE BIG APPLE

ELLIOTT TEPPER

While we experienced great growth in the eighties in Spain, the burden for the nations was upon our hearts – we worked diligently where we were, but we had a missionary vision as we developed in the Spanish provinces.

It was in our nature to be thinking beyond Spain. The logical step would have been to France, Portugal or Italy – particularly the last two because of the similarities of language. But Portugal was poor (then) and I wasn't sure it could sustain our type of ministry (although I was eventually proved wrong).

In early 1992 we became aware of the great need in the inner cities of America. The media was full of terrible stories. The USA was experiencing the effects of the Savings and Loan debacle, and of recession, rising unemployment, crime, and drug addiction. It appeared that American cities were almost more needy that those in Europe.

Also there was no self-supporting, peer-driven rehabilitation programme in America. Such centres that existed were largely supported by churches and denominations or they were private, expensive and merely psychologically focused. We had a close link with Paul Johannson of the New York School of Urban Ministries (NYSUM); he is also the president of Elim Bible Institute in Lima, New York. Paul had a great burden for the inner cities and through him we were made more deeply aware of the need. We also knew that the USA was home to about thirty million Spanish-speaking people and that the drug problem was greatest among Afro-Americans and Latin Americans. The more we talked about it, the more we investigated the American scene, the more we prayed – the greater the burden grew. Finally the Betel leaders felt that a work among the Spanish-speaking drug addicts in the inner cities of USA was of God. We were sure that the success we had experienced in Spain could be repeated there.

We arrived in early 1993 and stayed with Paul Johannson at NYSUM; we shared our vision with him and he was excited about it. He had visited Spain and knew that our programme was distinct from others in America and that we had something to offer in New York City. Paul took us around; we looked at David Wilkerson's Times Square Church, Teen Challenge (on Clinton Ave., Brooklyn), and other ministries to the marginalised. New York City was full of them, but we felt that Betel had something special to offer.

We found an old curtain factory in Hart Street; a rough area in Brooklyn. We talked to the owner. He still had a factory running on the ground floor but the second floor was empty. It probably had 10,000 square feet or more, so we signed a contract to rent it.

Then we went to visit my home church in Wilmington, North Carolina – Myrtle Grove Presbyterian church – and Robert Warwick who is one of the senior elders and a senior partner in a large accounting firm, offered to help with the legal work needed to register Betel. William Hill, a prominent lawyer, also helped in drawing up a constitution for Betel America.

Within a few months I returned with a team from Spain. It consisted of Tito and Isabel, Ivan and Encarne, Victor and Sandra Bautista, Manuel, Noel, Antonio and some other young people. 'Tito' (Lorenzo Herrera) was one of our first five pastors. He had founded the Almería work and the Málaga work. He was a pioneer type with lots of personal dynamism. He had been a gang leader who lived by his cunning in San Blas – a real 'tough guy'. He had French and we thought he could quickly learn English.

Having rented the Hart Street property we began to remodel it. In the early stages the team stayed in the basement of NYSUM, in the Astoria district of Queens, thanks to the generosity of Paul and his staff. We raised up dividing walls, constructed dorms, a kitchen, dining room, office, toilets, meeting room, etc.

During our first visit Tito, Paul and I had located a three storey building in 79th Street, East Elmhurst, on sale for $169,000. At that time interest rates were low, it was a buyer's market, and so, for 10% down we were able to purchase a home with three apartments. This became the residence for the pastor and his wife, and the other two couples. Then we found a place suitable for a second-hand furniture warehouse on Roosevelt Ave. This we rented for $5,000 a month. It was a busy commercial street underneath an elevated train line. The neighbourhood was almost entirely Latin, though our landlord was Indian. It looked, sounded, and smelled just like Latin America. Our next door neighbour ran a grocery store that specialised in Mexican foods. The owners were from Puebla, Mexico!

In the beginning, progress was slow. Not too many were interested in our programme. We hadn't taken into account the American welfare system or realised how much help was available for the poor. These people would carry a set of cards that told them where free meals, accommodation and clothes were available on each day of the week!

Between the government and the churches, drug addicts didn't have much motivation to be cured. But people started to come in – Puerto Ricans, Mexicans, South Americans and a few African Americans. Many were illegal immigrants with no papers. At its height the community grew to forty or fifty (staff included).

Suddenly city officials started to inspect us – fire department people, housing, gas and water inspectors, etc. (New York City rivals any of the old marxist or socialist states for government regulations, bureaucracy, nomenclature – and tax burden.)

Then the fire department and zoning authorities issued injunctions against us because we had established a residential complex in an industrial area. We tried to get the zoning changed. In court we explained we were taking drug addicts off the street, but they closed us down. We simply could not meet their demanding requirements. Without a doubt we had the neatest, cleanest building in the area; on our street there were stores that sold drugs, and an illegal nightclub/casino, but they ignored them and closed us down.

I remember one memorable day just before we closed, asking the Lord, 'Why New York?' There were so many difficulties. The Lord directed me to Jonah where I read, 'Get thee to that great city.' How could we give up? We knew we were doing what God wanted. But life was hazardous. The team felt, and I agreed, that maybe a better neighbourhood would help. After all, life on Hart Street was like an action movie.

Two policemen were shot in the doorway of our building. A neighbour across the street committed suicide by throwing himself out of the window with an electrical cable wound round his neck. Almost every week someone was shot or killed near us. The walls were covered in graffiti; many buildings were burned out. A high percentage of the people were on welfare.

Once, the police parked in front of our building while they examined a stolen car that had been abandoned nearby. They called for a tow truck to remove it. It was expected in about fifteen minutes, so they drove off but in that short time twenty or so people descended on it and removed everything – windshield, windows, doors, bumpers, even the motor. Only the frame was left standing by the time the tow truck arrived. And they did it all without vehicle tools, because if someone is found with a tool in possession he is immediately arrested. The man who took the engine did it with a piece of pipe.

Yet on every corner there were Latin American missions. There was lots of religion but the salt of the gospel did not seem to be changing things. Of course one wonders how much worse the inner city would have been without these store-front light houses.

We found another house opposite the 79th Street property which Tito's family and the men moved into, Tito in the flat and the men in the back. We turned Tito's old home into a girls' residence, with Marie José and two Mexican missionaries, Josefina and Elba in charge. (Elba had been one of our dentists in Madrid.)

We started another furniture store on Steinway Avenue in Astoria and another men's home in another part of Brooklyn. So it seemed that we were beginning to take off.

But for one reason or another we started to lose workers. Noel felt the Lord's leading to join NYSUM. He was a university graduate and an engineer whom we had sent for Bible training to the WEC Missionary Training College in Holland. Today he is serving Habitat for Humanity. Then a number of single Spanish men left us, some with good reasons, but others just lost heart. We began to realise that New York City was a battlefield.

When Betel of Britain opened it seemed right for Sandra and Victor Bautista, who were English speaking, to go there, so we found ourselves understaffed. After two or three years we had only a few Americans who had gone through the whole programme. They were good fellows; we loved them and I think they loved us but they just did not have that spiritual 'steel' that we were accustomed to seeing in Spain. Perhaps they gave the best they could, given the spiritual climate of New York City. But the fact remained – workers left and indigenous workers were not formed.

Our costs were high – the highest of all Betel centres, yet our housing was in some ways sub-standard. New Yorkers were generally less generous than other cultures. Often we were given junk. The City even charged us $100 for every visit to the dump. It was a struggle. Tito and Isabel and the few remaining

Spaniards were working hard, even sacrificing their own family and personal times to try to make things work. I know that often Tito used his own money to pay Betel's bills. Betel International sent money to our USA work more than to any other outreach. Mary and I tried to help them financially but it seemed at times more like a black hole in space, absorbing energy rather than giving radiance to the dark night of New York City.

About this time a group in Philadelphia was put in touch with us through our WEC headquarters there. It was the Kensington Street mission, and they were interested in us taking over their work. We wondered if this was God's answer because we were realising that New York was not the best place for a drug centre. We should perhaps have gone to a smaller, friendlier, lower cost city first.

We visited this work. There was a large theatre that had been turned into a rescue mission. They had a large dining area and some offices, a small two-bedroomed house plus a small piece of property in the Pocono mountains. So we accepted their offer less the Pocono gift. It had a tax lien on it. The plan was to place Tito and Isabel in one city and Ivan and Encarne in another. We had dreams of sending addicts and resources from one city to the other. We thought that with a little faith and creativity New York and its new frontier in Philadelphia would generate new synergistic energy.

But once again we experienced a set back. Because of moral failure one worker had to return to Spain for discipline and restoration. Praise God he is now fully restored and serving God faithfully in another centre.

So by now we had five properties in New York, two in the Philadelphia area, and inadequate leadership to carry the work. Although we had been up to forty or fifty in New York, including staff, now we were only twenty five between there and Philadelphia.

Another negative factor was that our Spanish workers never really got on top of the English language. We could communicate with the Latin Americans but we cut ourselves off from English speakers. We made no impression in English speaking churches which might have supported us. We took a short cut that turned out to be a long way round. We should have developed church relationships from the very beginning. We were too cocky. We had come out of the boom years in Spain self-sufficient and we discovered later that we needed to relate to the churches – as we have done in Britain and Italy.

Then we proliferated into too many properties too quickly, and we weren't prepared for losses of workers. So we were caught with a number of contractual agreements that we could not comfortably sustain. We did meet and fulfil every obligation – with the help of Betel's international fund.

Finally in the summer of 1998 Mary and I made a trip to New York to talk with Tito and Isabel. We went with the backing of Betel's International Council of Elders. Essentially we told the team that drastic changes would have to be made to save the work and that if in the next year Betel of America was not self-supporting and fruitful, we would have to consider closing it. We were not condemning them. In fact, we felt that Tito would be better used by God in Spain, Portugal or Italy. Of course, Tito and Isabel at first were very reluctant to quit, but came to appreciate the seriousness of the situation.

I told them that we would do everything possible to help them. First, we closed down one house in Philadelphia. Then we closed the men's house and the thrift store in Brooklyn. We also closed the little church in Ozone Park. We moved Tito's family out of the front half of the Queen's men's residence and created one large consolidated men's programme on all three floors of the property. Tito moved across the street into our former girls' residence. There was sacrifice on all levels – and savings. Then God intervened and granted us three new permanent visas for Spaniards. In six months the community was viable and economically sound. They have hope for the future.

Numbers in Philadelphia have been strengthened and some helpers have come from Faith Training Centre in South Carolina. Also in Philadelphia another group sold us a large three-storey house in a better area on very favourable terms, so we have moved the men there, but still retain the Kensington Street property for a furniture warehouse, large thrift store, office, meeting place and welfare centre.

We must thank Glenn Kling and the Baptist church in Wilmington, North Carolina. He and his church have greatly helped us with donations and with work teams that remodelled the theatre.

What have we learned from all of this? Grace – all is grace. When God blesses and enables, that is because He has been at work, not us. When we seem to fail, despite our efforts, then we must count on God's grace again. This time to endure and not faint.

It is very easy to project successful methods from one cultural context and spiritual theatre to another. It is quite different to discover the actual lie of the spiritual terrain and move with God accordingly. It has taken us a couple of years to make adjustments, but we are still there, still on our feet. Tito and his team may not have conquered New York City and Philadelphia but hundreds of lives have been touched for God. They have two living rehabilitation communities and a small Latin church in six years of work. We'll let God decide if it has been worth the battles.

5

HARD LESSONS IN MEXICO

ELLIOTT TEPPER

Around 1994 we began to have an interest in Mexico. We had never considered it as a goal, principally because it was experiencing revival. The church was doubling in size every five or so years. The national church was dynamic and there were thousands of missionaries in the country. All sorts of para-church groups were springing up so I did not feel we had a place there. Neither did I think our kind of activities like selling used furniture, painting, and light construction would fit in a poor economy with very low wages and high unemployment.

Then we received a missionary from the Amistad Cristiana ('Christian Friendship') Church in Jalapa – Dr Carlos Rodriguez, a dentist in his late thirties. He came to set up our first permanent dental clinic in Madrid and quickly became a 'Betelito' at heart. He lived on the farm with the men and he really loved Betel. He kept pushing the idea of opening up in Mexico. One day he came to me and said that there was a family in Jalapa that would lend us a property to get a rehabilitation centre started.

I made a visit but found that the property was tucked away in the mountains. We had thought that there were facilities but the offer was only of undeveloped land, which meant we would have to build buildings and construct a road. We therefore declined.

The Amistad church in Jalapa is pastored by Ricardo Marcello, an American missionary, and a graduate of Faith Training Centre. We visited his church and through him we discovered that there was a large house in the town for sale. We were able to purchase this on very favourable terms. It was a beautiful well-appointed place. So that's where we started. We had chosen Fulgencio Suarez, who was the director in Galicia, to be the leader, and assembled a team around him.

The centre prospered and soon we had twenty people resident. We decided to extend to Vera Cruz, one hour down the mountain on the coast. Things seemed to be going well. Then we commenced in Puebla, an industrial city, five hours away where there was another Amistad church with 5,000 members.

But then we ran into trouble, or rather, a brick wall. We had made the mistake of calling all our young workers 'missionaries'. This gave them a kind of status that went to their heads. After all, even WEC workers with Bible school training and candidate course behind them are still only called 'probationers' or 'new workers' for their first two years! It wasn't all their fault. Out of the goodness of their hearts the church members received them warmly and treated them well. In fact, too much attention was showered upon them by the families and particularly by the young girls.

One of our men who was a plumber fell in love with a Mexican lady who was a doctor, so he left the team and married her. Several others started to have friendships and also left Betel. Remember, some of these were young men just recently delivered from drugs! The two with girlfriends repented and returned so we accepted them back again.

However, in the midst of a calendar-selling campaign they suddenly left again, taking the money and the van with them – $2,000 in cash and our best vehicle! Our testimony in Pueblo was ruined.

We finally located the van. It was in a police compound but they would not release it till we paid certain fees which amounted to the total value of the van! While it was in the compound it was totally stripped. So after paying the equivalent of the price of the van to get it back into our possession we had to pay that much again to refit it. Even the calendars which these men stole were sold on the streets and the money kept for themselves. They lived for a few months as imposters – Betel's ambassadors of 'bad' will.

Finally when they had spent all the money on drugs one decided to return to us. Fulgencio felt it right to receive him but because of what he had done we decided that he should be returned to Spain. He went to one of our centres, is restored and is making good. The other is still begging on the streets of Puebla in Betel's name.

All this brought our work in Puebla to a temporary halt. In addition we came to realise that the centre in Jalapa was too far from sources of hard drug addiction and not the ideal starting point. What we should have done was go to the USA border where there is much drug addiction, high crime, heavy industry, and denser population.

So again through over-extension, economic pressure and the failure of workers we have learned some hard lessons. We have closed Vera Cruz and Jalapa (though we still own the Jalapa house) and have concentrated our efforts in Puebla where we still have friends in Amistad. We rented a farm in Chautzingo, about thirty miles from Puebla, where we have a really successful men's centre with about twenty men. We also have a pastoral residence, an office and a furniture store in the centre of Puebla. So after much struggle we are becoming established.

We are running a small farm in Chautzingo where we have chickens, rabbits and sheep. A government grant is helping us with that and also with a furniture making project. We have even started a small church at the farm for the village people. In this part of Mexico alcoholism is rife, and is relatively a greater problem than hard drugs. In fact, most of the addicts who come to us are on soft drugs like marijuana, hashish, cocaine and glue. Those who sniff glue have usually suffered some degree of brain damage.

We've also started meetings in the centre of Puebla for unchurched people and the parents of the addicts. We certainly could never have started Betel in Mexico without the help of our Amistad friends.

The pastors of the Puebla church have been so co-operative and supportive, even helping us to gain legal recognition. They have generously lent us the help of their accountant and other administrators in the setting up of our office. One of their pastors, Sergio Trevino, is the president of Betel of Mexico and our legal representative before the government. Fulgencio is particularly grateful and appreciative of Amistad's contribution. He has married Cristina, a member of the Jalapa Amistad congregation.

6

HORROR IN HAMBURG

ELLIOTT TEPPER

The story of Betel's beginning in Germany starts with Lutz Damerow – a young man who came to spend a summer with us. He was referred to us by people on the Spanish Decision magazine staff. He wanted to familiarise himself with Spanish language and culture. He was a Lutheran but I'm not quite sure where he really stood then, spiritually. Staying within the Betel community at Mejorada he came into a very vital relationship with Jesus and his life was revolutionised.

He returned to Germany to study at university and prepare for ministry in the Lutheran church. However, he found very few keen evangelicals in the liberal spiritual environment of the university and only a few in the School of Theology. Nevertheless he was hungry for God and sought out and found lively spiritual fellowship in different local churches. He had a real burden to see Betel started in Germany and would talk freely about the value of our work.

He informed us that there was a family near Krogaspé, halfway between Keele and Hamburg, who owned several farm properties. On one of these, which was very rundown, lived a woman who was an unsatisfactory tenant because she had failed to pay any rent for ten years and had not taken care of the place.

Lutz invited us to his church in the nearby town of Nieuminster. Raul Rayes, who had developed a close friendship with Lutz during their time together at the Mejorada farm, came with me. We visited this two-storeyed farmhouse, with some acres of land. It was eminently suited for our purposes although

166

only two rooms were immediately useable. We entered into negotiations with this family and eventually in 1995 sent a team of six with Raul Rayes as leader.

The owners of the farm, Reimer and Helma, did not only allow us to use the property rent free, but, when we started to renovate, supplied us with almost all the materials. They helped us to put in a new septic system, a new boiler, new insulation, and so on. Of course we bought a lot of items too, but they were so generous.

Another German who became a great help was Meyke Pingel. Earlier, her desire to learn Spanish led her to Madrid where she worked as a short-term worker with Betel. She came to know our Mexican Amistad missionaries and when they heard of her desire for Bible training, encouraged her to go to Amistad's Bible College in Puebla. Once in Mexico she met up with Raul Rayes who later came to Betel Madrid as an Amistad missionary. After graduating, Meyke returned to Germany and when Betel began there, was a very active volunteer in the new centre in Krogaspé. The friendship with Raul blossomed and they were eventually married, which was a good thing as it gave Betel natural 'roots' in Germany!

Lutz became the president of the Betel board. When he graduated from the Lutheran seminary he was able to arrange for a year of his probationary period to be spent working with Betel. His wife, Tina – for he was now married – had banking experience, so she took over the books and set us up with a suitable German financial system.

Concerning fruit in the work we had major difficulties. The government's social system provided so much that drug addicts had very little incentive to come to us, and when they did, they expected the moon! They would arrive with their tape decks and videos asking where their private room was! Our system of rising at 7am, devotionals, work without pay, no smoking, etc., meant that very few stayed. We also knew we were not getting the real down-and-out addicts because Krogaspé was an hour from the larger centres of population like Hamburg. Raul and the team made regular trips there. I accompanied them when I would visit Germany and have never seen so many addicts concentrated in one place as at the Hamburg train station. It was common to see upwards to a thousand addicts openly buying, selling, and using hard drugs under the station roof, the police and citizens walking around them as if nothing unusual was taking place.

We made contact with the Salvation Army and another evangelical group that visited this area and they started referring people to us. But we realised that while the Krogaspé farm was a lovely place to live we were in the wrong place, in terms of making contact with addicts. We needed to be in or near Hamburg.

In 1998 Raul found a place suitable for a thrift store and office in one of the main streets. The rent was reasonable so we took it (although it was high compared to Spanish costs). We now have about twenty men. Four of them have been with us over a year and have matured into leaders. Increasingly we are getting men from East Germany and Berlin, and also from the poorer parts of Eastern Europe.

7

GRACIAS, AMISTAD!

ELLIOTT TEPPER

The Amistad connection is primarily the result of the fact that Mary and I were part of the early formation of the Amistad (friendship) church in Mexico. We went there at the invitation of Jack Knowles who was a fellow student with us at Faith Training Centre in South Carolina. Our first book describes how we went to Mexico and worked there for four years. We were involved in a number of projects and developments in the city of Cholula, and during the last year and a half we were involved in raising up a work amongst the university students in the University of Americas where I was teaching economics. God worked graciously and there was a small movement among the university students and some of the faculty and staff, so that we were able to leave a group of about twenty students and other contacts linked to Jack Knowles. He began making weekly trips up from Oaxaca to attend the group. It prospered more and more and Jack had other contacts in Puebla especially through the family of Ernesto Alonzo. Jack, Ernesto and the students from the home group formed the beginning of Amistad Cristiana in Puebla which was related to Amistad Cristiana, a fellowship of churches with similar backgrounds. There are different Amistads now all over Mexico. They do meet and have conferences together but they are all independent. The work didn't just prosper – it exploded, is growing by leaps and bounds, doubling almost every year.

Today, in 1998, the principal Amistad fellowship has 5,000 members in Puebla. Ernesto Alonso was formerly an architect specialising in building auditoriums and large public buildings. He built this incredible centre. Dozens of other daughter groups have grown out of it. Originally it was rooted in the upper/middle class, although now with this mass movement it consists more and more of working class, city people.

I have visited Mexico almost every year, and different members of Amistad have come and visited us here in Spain. The first missionary to join us was Armando Garcia. He arrived when we were just moving into the first house at Mejorada Del Campo, the one that we 'camped' in – with hardly any roof, no lights, no water. He and Raul and other men were camped out under the trees while we built the house bit by bit. Armando has a long history with us.

He was principally involved in developing the worship ministry in Betel. He is a university graduate in science and engineering. He was a Christ for the Nations Bible school student – very well prepared – so he, along with Paul Anderson, built our Bible institute. Paul was the director, Armando was his helper. Armando was naturally drawn to using Amistad's sophisticated and well-developed Bible study materials, so he took these and other Latin American studies, edited them, and produced our first teaching manuals for the Adullam Bible Institute and for our home groups.

Paul Johannson, the president of Elim, also president of NYSUM (New York School of Urban Missions), visited us and recommended that we develop some standardised materials because we were a diverse, widely-spread group with lots of young leaders who didn't have a very strong Biblical base. They needed some materials in their hands. So Armando developed at least half a dozen manuals for this purpose.

Amistad, unlike many indigenous churches, seemed to catch very early the foreign missions vision. They sent missionaries to other places, not exclusively to Betel, but we took the lion's share because of our relationship with them, and also because it was more economically feasible to send a missionary to us than to send them to other parts of Europe where it would have cost two or three times the middle class Mexican salary to support them. But if they came to Betel, and if they were single missionaries and lived in our homes and residences, they could survive very economically. They gave us a lot of assistance in the early formative years and were very helpful. We'd had lots of Americans, British and Australian volunteers and so on and even Mexicans from other churches (non-Amistad). But I have to say Amistad produces the best missionaries. They come with a better attitude; they're servants. They come with a real vision for the nations. They are prepared and educated. Their Bible school gives new workers a good Bible base and a good missionary preparation, like a WEC Missionary Training College. They arrive with anthropological understanding of what it means to be a missionary. They have had good practical experience because they've been taken out to the mountains and to the streets of Mexico's teeming cities to work among the poor people.

Of course, since they speak Spanish they don't have years of language learning like the Americans and British. They are able to move right in. Also we have to recognise that they have a great worship style. Men like Rodolfo Garza, Ernesto Alonzo and Roberto Torres made important contributions to worship. Armando, because he was on the original worship team, brought their worship, and brought their materials, so he designed our first worship manual which, I think, is superior to any other available in Spanish today.

Amistad people have been very wise as regards religious 'labels'. They didn't say they were Baptists or Brethren or Church of Christ. They said they were just Christians. So a lot of Catholic charismatics would come to the early meetings for fellowship because they didn't feel rejected, and they purposely adopted a programme in which they tried to dispense with the religious jargon of Christianity and talk with reality. They never called each other 'brother' or 'sister'; they would use the word 'congregation' rather than 'church'. They would just try to avoid all the catch words that have become clichés. They wouldn't get up and rant and rave against the Catholic church. They would never speak out against Mary as sadly many Protestants do. But on the other hand they were totally reformed in doctrine, evangelical, and eschatologically right. They were just wise, circumspect – all things to all men. In fact sometimes people would ask, 'What kind of Christians are you?' They didn't have people shouting 'hallelujah' all the time. They didn't raise their voices and scream and shout, and there wasn't a lot of emotionalism. It was really what you would call the third wave – freedom in the Spirit, all the gifts affirmed, but no one gift a hobby horse.

So Betel has adopted the Amistad attitude. We have been able to relate to the Catholics and not drive Catholic parents away. We've never in the history of Betel spoken against the Catholic church from the pulpit but rather affirmed what was good. Amistad has made a great contribution to Betel.

8

STRATEGY FOR NORTH AFRICA

ELLIOTT TEPPER

*Rescue Shop I tells how a centre was established in Ceuta, a
Spanish enclave on the north coast of Morocco, and a 'toehold'
gained in Melilla, another enclave four hundred kilometres to
the east.*

Elliott explains:
We have already told how we were able to rent a suitable but
very rundown property in Ceuta. We had strong faith that the
Lord would have us buy it because it was such a strategic centre
for developments in the Maghreb.

Then, in 1993, two groups from my home church – Myrtle
Grove Presbyterian Church, Wilmington, North Carolina – paid
a visit and caught the vision of what Ceuta represented for the
gospel in North Africa – a door to the Moslem world, a launching
pad for ministries in the surrounding area, and a place of rest
for missionaries in the Moslem world. They saw Ceuta as a bi-
lingual, bi-cultural, bi-religious centre. So they went back to
our home church and challenged the mission board to take up
the matter. With great faith and great sacrifice, they elected to
give us the first fruits of their own building project, and
designated $90,000 for Betel's use.

It's the largest gift we have ever received and it makes me
proud to be a member of Myrtle Grove Presbyterian.
Consequently God has blessed them as a congregation with a
real missionary vision and as they have been generous so God
has been generous to them. We paid off the building in three

$30,000 payments. Myrtle Grove gave us $30,000 for three years. During this time we fully restored the big house and now we have new bathrooms downstairs, women's facilities on the second floor, proper windows installed, good plumbing and electricity. Then we restored an out-building and made a hundred-seat dining hall. We raised a metre-high wall round a large sunken area, put windows around the top edge, skylighting in the roof and a big bay window on the fourth wall overlooking the straits of Gibraltar. Now we have a hundred-seat auditorium for conferences. The facility has three buildings, a residence that will hold about forty or fifty people, a dining hall and an auditorium. It's become a very profitable centre both spiritually and economically, with the vision to serve the Maghreb.

We began to collaborate with the Bible Society and the two American missionaries that were resident in the city. We came up with the idea of sponsoring the first Hispanic conference for the Moslem world. There are many English, German, Dutch and French conferences with this goal but no Hispanic. The motive was to create a conference that would minister to and promote the work of missionaries in the Maghreb. They periodically need some refreshing because they are usually isolated, living separate from each other, working undercover using tent-making ministries. There are hardly any churches. If they do have a 'church' it is usually a handful of people in a housegroup. So the goal was, firstly, a ministry to the missionaries, secondly, to inspire the Spanish speaking church in Spain, Latin America, and in the USA to take up the vision of the Moslem world, to call for missionaries to the Moslem world, and to challenge the church to support all this by prayer and giving. We decided to call this effort the Ramon Lull conference. (He lived in the twelfth century, and was the first missionary to have a burden for the Moslem world. I believe he was martyred in North Africa.)

In the first year we had about sixty people. It was a great success. We had Spaniards, Mexicans, Europeans, Americans, and national church representatives. In the second year we had ninety delegates, with Dr. Ehab El Kharratt of Cairo, Egypt, as speaker. He is a member of the largest evangelical church there. He is the director of the Presbyterian Rehab Centre outside Cairo, in the desert. There was great enthusiasm. We had representatives this time from Mexico, Brazil, Chile, Spain, Europe and America. The third year we had more than one hundred delegates with Paul Johannson, the President of Elim Bible Institute, as speaker.

We discovered that Ceuta was not viable economically because it was poorer than the rest of Spain. There was a large Moslem population that worked for very little and our kind of jobs didn't produce the same kind of money as in Madrid. Our store could sell any second hand furniture that we had but we couldn't get it. And we couldn't ship it from Spain because that was too expensive.

About this time, Tom Spyker, an American missionary, had rented a large warehouse in Algeciras but was not finding a use for it. He asked if we could take it off his hands, so we thought we could put a store, an office and a residence right there in the port.

We assumed his contract and began to build a typical Betel office, store and residence complex facing the port where all the Moslems coming from France, Belgium and Holland pass through every season. More than two million take the ferry to Morocco from Algeciras each year. We appointed Juan Capilla as the director of the joint Algeciras/Ceuta work which we treated as one single centre. He commutes back and forth across the straits at least once a week. He supervises both centres, generates funds in Algeciras and transfers the money to Ceuta. He contacts drug addicts in Algeciras and sends them over to Ceuta on the ferry.

As we began to develop the work we realised it was a much more important strategic point than we had thought. Algeciras is the jump-off point for the Moslem world and it is a key location for all the work in the southern part of Spain. As the work grew, there were some pastors in the southern part that began to realise that Betel wasn't just some tiny para-church organisation but was fully involved in the work of church planting and evangelism. We also saw Algeciras was the key for ministry in Gibraltar.

From there we established a house a few miles north of Gibraltar, then we established another store in La Linea – the last Spanish town before you enter Gibraltar. Then we bought a four-storey building in Algeciras that now houses our church, a major antique store, a married couples' hostel and a men's house. We have about fifty people there.

The Gibraltar government social services department sends English speaking Gibraltans to Betel in Birmingham because it knows us. We've had quite a number at Birmingham and because of that I've written a letter to the Governor General asking if he will allow us to open a Betel branch there.

PART III
EXPLANATION

1

THE BETEL ETHOS

ELLIOTT TEPPER

It is *life* not *theology* that begets life – the reality of Christ in you, the reality of the Holy Spirit's presence. That doesn't mean that we don't need theology or the Word or that we don't need to study – we do need a systematic approach to the Christian life – but it is *life* that begets life.

In Betel we can certainly codify our methods in social or scientific terms but that is not what makes Betel work. Unless you have the heart of the matter there can be no success. The fundamental issue is being Christ-centred and having Christ-centred relationships which produce *koinonia* and allow us to enjoy the communion of the Holy Spirit in our communities.

Betel is a church – it is a part of the mystical universal body of Christ. When people come to us we open our hearts to them; we let them live with us, come under our covering and dwell with us. There is no pressure for them to be converted or accept our doctrine, but they need to be part of the fellowship and accept the minimal rules that are in place. We want them to become part of the community and to imbibe our ethos, which is nothing less than Christ living His life through us. 'Ethos' can be defined as a way of life exhibiting a set of values which reveal the love or character that makes a person or a group what it is.

A 'Betelito' is someone who has chosen, for a season, to be part of our community, has been born again, and, we hope, is willing to submit to its authority, take part in the work, contribute to the common good, embrace a spirit of sacrifice, surrender some freedom of individual movement and even be willing to work without remuneration so that the needs of others may be supplied. Of course it must be realised that half the people in Betel do not work in income-generating activities. Part of the community at any one time has just not fully entered in. They are either going through detoxification or are sick and too weak to participate in communal businesses. They stay back in the residences and serve in household duties like cleaning and preparation of food. There are also many young mothers with small children or couples with older children in which the mother's time is at least partly taken up with their care.

From the very first day members encounter in a very personal and practical way the Betel ethos: others serve them unselfishly. The natural response is for them to serve others when they are able. This is not the ethos of the world. When new members savour it they quickly realise that the heart of Betel is not of this world.

One big difference between a Betel community and the usual 'methadone'-based programme or even a psychologically-based counselling community, is that Betel does not provide extensive counselling. We have a minimal number of professionally-qualified people. We do have access to social workers and psychologists whom we can use in extreme cases. We do have doctors and nurses who watch the health of the community. We don't have 'encounter groups' or extensive counselling sessions; what we have, simply, is *Christian community* which means church activities, devotional sessions, regular meetings on Wednesdays, Fridays and Sundays, and Bible school for those who have been in the fellowship for a year or year and a half.

What happens, then, to the individual who joins us? What kind of programme do we have to offer him? I can remember the complaint of an addict who had just entered our farm in Germany. He came up to me and said, 'I thought I was going to a rehabilitation centre, but there is no programme here! All they do is live together, study the Bible, sing and work. Where are the counsellors and the psychologists?' Betel does have a 'programme'. He just could not recognise it.

We have what is called a peer-driven programme. It's a programme that is motivated from below rather than from the top down. When you come in someone who is a bit more advanced helps you. Once you have grown and shown stability in your life, you are allocated to help a new arrival. Everyone who comes has a 'shadow'. There is a dormitory leader, then a house leader, then regional supervisor, and finally a pastor. And the pastor is almost always a cured addict who has been in the fellowship for five, seven or ten years. Every responsible person is someone who has been through the system. Daily encounters with authority are at a 'grass roots' level rather than with professionals or pastors. Of course when there are problems we do step in with a word of pastoral wisdom, even professional counsel as needed.

What we have is a tried and proven structure that puts example and peer pressure before counselling. It has proven to be much more effective and efficient than the mere words of some stranger who comes from a totally alien world (as an addict perceives it). We also make sure that there is plenty of liberty for people to seek God personally and respond to what is being shared by life, example and teaching. The Betel ethos is a spirit that encourages people to believe that there is a way out, that they can change, and *that God* can take a beggar off a dunghill and turn him into a prince. They know that their leaders were once where they are. They have a living hope and example of a peer-leader right before their eyes.

If they look at me – well, I'm from a different planet. I'm American, I come from a different culture and class, but when they look at Luis Pino or Juan or Javi – people they have known on the streets – they realise that they can change too. The peer system works. One of the beauties of it is that there is upward mobility for all. Certainly one of the prime motivating factors is the esteem the recovering addicts seek and receive as they become role models to others.

If the Great Commission didn't exist we would have invented it to give scope through the challenge of new frontiers, and places for pioneers. People need to grow. They need to be offered the chance to scale greater heights and move on spiritually. We've never had a split. Why? Because whenever we find someone who is anxious to develop, restless with strong ambitions, we find something bigger and challenging for him to do.

In the ethos of Betel there is a certain optimism and a certain confidence in the power of God's Spirit. We have no riches but we have faith to believe that God will work for us and through us. Yes, there are charismatic aspects in Betel's worship and practice. Yes, we are Baptistic in practice. Yes, we are Presbyterian in our government. We embrace the whole spectrum of the evangelical church. We are not Roman Catholic in doctrine but we are in sympathy, and willing to co-operate, with Catholic Christians or with anyone in the body of Christ, even those who are far from the reformed position that we take.

This may sound overly broad, but bigness of heart is no threat to true orthodoxy and sound faith. Our roots are in Christ and WEC; we flow in the deep mainstream of evangelical life.

I want to comment on one last attribute in the Betel ethos; that is courage in suffering. We have had so many people suffering physically, mainly from AIDS. I think of Raul Casto and Jambri, of Trini, of Manuel, and many others who kept on ministering even though they were so very weak.

One instance of this that comes immediately to mind involves Manuel El Vasco ('Manuel the Basque'). He was the oldest pastor and was well into his forties when he died. He was the first pastor to manifest full-blown AIDS yet he kept on for four or five years. He served as pastor in Cuenca, then we transferred him to Málaga where he was instrumental in developing the work.

A few months before he died he and I were at the auto-shop where we wash cars and do oil changes. At only half of what his body weight should be he lifted up a five-gallon drum of oil and carried it across the street. I thought, 'How can he do that?' I picked up another full drum and I had a hard time carrying it yet I am a trained wrestler! I said, 'Manuel, I do admire you for your courage and long-suffering.' He smiled and looked at me with his one good eye and replied, 'I don't have any alternative, other than giving in and dying.'

On another trip – just a week before he died – we stayed, at his wife's request, in his home. I got up early to wait on the Lord. I usually have a cup of tea so I went into the kitchen to find the teapot. I found it on top of the fridge. In the early morning light I took it down, put some water in and put it on the stove.

Their little daughter walked into the kitchen. She looked at me and then at the stove and said, 'That's not a teapot, that's a decoration.' Then she ran out shouting, 'Mama, Mama, Brother Elliott is boiling daddy's medicine!' Manuel came in, dressed in a bathrobe and sure enough his medicine was in the teapot. He said, 'Elliott, let me make you breakfast.' Think of it. Here is a man, so weak and at death's door, but he wants to serve me by making me breakfast! He decided to put the coffee pot on instead of tea. After a few minutes there was an awful smell and smoke – the plastic handles on the pot started to melt and then fell off.

Manuel's wife came running out of the bedroom, 'What are you two doing?' There's no water in the pot! You're both like Laurel and Hardy trying to help each other.' (In Spain they are called El Flaco and El Gordo – the thin one and the fat one. I think she was referring to me as the fat one. He certainly wasn't.)

Manuel had a marvellous servant spirit right to the end. He died just a few days later.

BETEL'S LEADERSHIP CONCEPT

ELLIOTT TEPPER

Betel is a complex organisation with complex structures – spiritual, social, charitable and legal. In the nine countries where we operate we have to assume the form that gives the best credibility to the authorities. In Spain, Betel is a charitable organisation; it is also organised as a church, and we have begun an economic co-operative called Cadmiel. As we investigated the possibility of entering Asia we realised that we needed a limited trading company for visas and for the export-import of Asian furniture as an economic support for our community and a new source of supply of furniture for our many thrift stores around the world. That led to the incorporation of a limited company, our trading area. Each of these are separate legal entities. In Britain we are a charitable trust and a trading company. In Germany we are organised as a sportsclub! In France we are a charity. In Italy we are a para-church organisation. In Portugal we are a beneficiary association. In Mexico we are a civil association. In America we are a church. But Betel in its essence, in spite of all the different structures, is an expression of the mystic body of Christ.

All these entities are really governed by the same people, that is, our presbytery or council of elders. We have chosen a presbyterian form of government which is leadership by a group of elders capable of mature decision making. Once you are an elder/pastor you are one for life, if you continue to meet Pauline standards of eldership. (We have had to remove some from this role.) Of course there are elected officials to carry specific responsibilities, and there is a periodic general assembly, but it is really the group of twenty-six national Betel pastors, seven missionary pastors (five from WEC and two from Amistad, of Mexico) and two directors of Kadmiel that govern Betel International. When we talk of a national pastor or missionary leader we consider the couple as a leadership unit. The wives are pastors too. Mary and the other wives participate and make important contributions on all the highest councils.

The guiding principle is found in Proverbs 11:14, 'In the multitude of counsellors there is safety.' We listen to one another, we submit to one another and we take counsel from one another. We may argue; we may debate, but we seek the mind of God together. This is the WEC pattern as established by Norman Grubb and exemplified in the two schools where I trained – at Faith Training Centre with A.S. Worley and at Elim Bible Institute. It is great and wonderful when everyone comes to see the same thing and we have spiritual unanimity and consensus.

I can say that in our thirteen year history only on one or two occasions – and only at the very beginning (when our people were immature) – did I ever go against the counsel of the young Betel eldership. I wanted to start a Bible School and they thought it was not a good idea, but we went ahead and eventually they agreed it was right.

I *do* give direction and I *do* receive the same kind of criticism that Norman Grubb experienced. 'Too strong', 'too dictatorial', 'too directive' are terms used about me. I *do* have strong opinions and I *do* have powers of persuasion, but we really do seek the mind of God as a body. I am not ashamed to provide leadership as God enables. There must be leadership even in a presbytery. Consequently, because of that tension between collectively listening to God, and, at times, to leaders, we do know where we are going. Some of us hear the 'Thus saith the Lord' more quickly than others; some of us are able to articulate it, move people's hearts and persuade others, but that is all part of the presbytery function. Domineering individuals don't get away with anything! Spaniards didn't conquer half the world for nothing! They are not easily led.

Very often when we come together we have no idea about where we are going to go or what decision we'll make until we wait in the presence of God together. Then when we abide in God it is easy to take a decision together and it is very hard to argue when everyone is in the Spirit. It is when we are in the flesh and when there is more heat than light, when there is a conflict of personalities, that we can't make good decisions.

We really do get down before God and humble ourselves before each other. I can think of many instances when God has broken strong individuals and outspoken opinions so that His mind has come through in the end. The presbytery principle really does work if there is a dwelling place for the Third Person of the Trinity in the hearts of those He has called into leadership.

Sometimes I or others feel we do get a word from the Lord and when we share it with the council, others express their views. Many times there is the recognition that it is a word from the Lord so we say, 'Let's do it!' Sometimes we are not sure, so we wait.

People often ask, 'What will happen to Betel when Elliott and Mary Tepper go?' Recently when seeking a large bank loan the very first question asked by the banking official was, 'What will happen to Betel after you go?' The truth is, it will go on because it is not dependent on one man. It does not have a 'corporate' pyramidal shape; it has a mystic presbyterian structure which allows us to rest in a fellowship of love – that multitude of counsellors where safety dwells. The mind of Christ abides in us collectively. Paul said, not 'you', 'but "we" have the mind of Christ'.

I personally seek the advice of the other pastors, firstly because I need it and secondly I want confirmation from them, to make certain that we are doing the right thing. Also it's great to be able to share the blame if things go wrong! Believe it or not, collective error and shared wrong decisions strengthen unity, if they are made in good faith by all together.

We are a faith people and we do take tremendous risks. We've done ridiculous things. Our projects sometimes scare others out of their wits. We take very big leaps of faith where the '0's' in our figures are not just two or three, but often up to six!

Recently we had been negotiating to buy a large international headquarters facility to house our church and all our many departments here in Madrid. We needed millions of dollars for this. Some thought we were crazy but every single Spanish pastor and almost every missionary immediately caught the vision and embraced it. All of the senior pastors came to me individually and said, 'We are with you even if this fails.' Over the eighteen-month period of negotiations and being turned down by a number of banks, and then to have the building stolen from us by speculators at the last moment, all the stops and starts and frustrated hopes certainly contained all the ingredients of a colossal failure and error in judgment. As a testimony to the strength and mutual bond of fellowship that holds the Betel presbytery together, even in the darkest hour when the property was bought out from under us, there was no fracture in our abiding together in Christ – no recriminations, only expressions of consolation and solidarity. At one point, I think Mary and I were actually standing alone and even the most hardy of the Betel pastors had begun to doubt. And yet even then we all stood together.

The details of God's deliverance will have to wait another book. But in short, we bought our new headquarters and entered it on July 18, 1999 – thanks to the heroic efforts of Malcolm Hayday and the CAF (Charities AID Foundation) of Great Britain which provided the guarantees. The Triodos Social Bank of Holland, through the mediation of Esteban Barosso of Proyecto Trust of Spain, granted us a $4,300,000 loan.

To give you a sense of the unity that exists in our hearts, we have never had a division in our midst. Churches split, denominations split, yet we have stuck together.

In our last day of some special meetings at our Betania Conference Centre recently, Juan Carrasco of Bilbao – one of our senior pastors – came to me and said, 'Elliott, I haven't been able to sleep all night. God has asked me to do something I don't want to do, but I'm going to do it.' I asked, 'What is it He's asked you to do?' 'God has told me to support you and to symbolise it before everybody by lying down on the floor lifting my arm and taking your hand. And I really don't want to do it.'

I said, 'Well, if God has told you this, you will have to do it.'

Then after the worship time in the first meeting he stood up and told everyone what God had asked him to do. So he lay down and stretched out his arm. I decided to lie down as well alongside him and we joined hands. After thirty seconds another senior pastor, Luis Pino, came over, lay down and took my other hand. After that every pastor (and most of their wives) did the same. We covered the floor and lay there, not saying a word, in the presence of God for half an hour.

A marvellous sense of spiritual alignment filled our hearts. There was a shifting in the heavenlies that brought us to a higher and deeper place of unity as a fellowship, as a presbytery.

I cannot pretend that that same unity exists at all levels of Betel's government. There are about 1,200 living in our communities. Under the covering of Betel's ruling council we have city, regional and zone leaders. Under each one of these we have a number of house leaders and in each house there are monitors – the 'responsables' or responsible ones. Then there are the shadows, the 'sombras' who are appointed companions who stick with the new entrants. They may have been in the centre only for a few months but even they can take on some measure of responsibility within the Betel family. And then of course there are also the churches with their own local deacons, committees and so on.

One reason it works is because we have a 'peer-driven' programme that fosters respect for servant leaders on all levels of the chain of command. Even our most senior pastors are only ten years old in the Lord. Our pastors have a fresh memory of what it was like when they occupied humble stations.

We require all our leaders from senior monitor upward to have some Bible training. Our 'Adullam' school is only two afternoons, six classes a week, for one year. The studies are not particularly academic. This may seem strange but it is not so by Latin American and African standards. The second and third world church is not particularly well educated. The church in these countries has made major advances with little theological training. The churches in North America and Europe are obsessed with professional training but the growth rate doesn't compare with Latin America or Africa. So obviously while Bible training is very important, under certain circumstances God manages to do quite well with little of it.

In the first few centuries of the church the growth was through inspired Spirit-directed leadership which for the most part was not highly trained academically. It wasn't till the third and fourth centuries that we had highly developed academic structures preparing the ministry. If I were free to choose, I would choose the early church rather than the sophisticated imperial church. Betel is not a true image of the early church, but we would like to be.

BETEL THROUGH OTHER EYES

Graham and Sue Single from Australia and New Zealand and Jim and Sue Regan from Britain are two missionary couples now serving with Betel. Both have had periods of 'straight' missionary work with WEC in Spain.

The authors sat down with them in Madrid and plied them with questions about life in Betel and their evaluation of the Betel ministry generally.

We begin with the Singles.

Graham and Sue, you worked with Betel in Valencia for some years and then you worked with WEC in Madrid. These are two very different ministries. How do you compare the two in terms of job satisfaction, fulfilment, challenge?

GRAHAM: With Betel in Valencia the job satisfaction was high. We were always on the go, there were always plenty of things to do. You are never bored working with Betel! In Madrid, with WEC we served as business agents for the whole missionary team, so we had less contact with the Spanish people. I think our return to Betel has to do with the fulfilment of working directly with people who need us and want our help.

SUE: In the Betel work it was very much building relationships and investing time and energy in people, although of course that was not without its frustrations!

I suppose there is an element of success but also a pretty large element of disappointment dealing with drug addicts.

GRAHAM: Yes. Having spent nine years in Spain we have seen some people who have been in the centres five and six years yet suddenly they go back to the streets; that's most disheartening. But you can see, looking back, that they haven't really given their whole life over to the Lord. One man had been in the centre for seven years and badly wanted a wife. He married a girl that had not been in the centre very long, and then a few weeks later they both went back on drugs. So it is frustrating. But then we look on the positive side, and see the ones that are growing and maturing, so we have to weigh up both sides.

SUE: I remember in Valencia, one of the girls had a very soft heart towards God; one could see God working in her life. She was given certain areas of responsibility and seemed to be faithful in those and then one day she just left. It was quite a shock to everybody and within a short period of time we heard that she had overdosed and died. That's absolutely heartbreaking. Others do go on, become stronger and stronger, and are still serving the Lord today.

As visitors we have been amazed – staggered – at the growth of Betel, both in terms of numerical growth – and spiritual growth – the maturity of the leaders, and so on. How do you feel about this? Has it grown too fast? Are there dangers in the speed with which things have developed?

GRAHAM: I think you can always say there are dangers and I think the leadership knows that too. I think Elliott tries to keep it from growing too fast. God is blessing the work. You have to take risks. You can't just sit back. Having been out of the work for a while and coming back into it, we see the growth of the work and the leaders moving on to maturity. It's thrilling.

SUE: I think a lot of what we call 'risks' are actually steps of faith. It's moving with a God-given vision. The key is to step out at the right time and with the right people. So I see it more as venturing in faith. A few years ago, while we were working with WEC we attended the Betel church in Madrid and Elliott talked a lot about consolidating the work. I think that's where Graham and I felt we could come in and help.

GRAHAM: If these risks weren't taken Betel wouldn't be what it is today. I don't think God would have blessed us otherwise. We've stepped out in faith and sometimes we've failed, but we learn from that and keep on going ahead.

Depending on their progress the men and women are given certain amounts of responsibility. They are not just thrown in at the deep end, they are always with someone else who has been there a bit longer; as they mature they are given more responsibility, and are expected to teach others what they are learning. So it's a learning/teaching situation all the time.

To western Christian standards the leadership training programme seems fairly minimal. What do you feel about this?

GRAHAM: These men and women have come from the street. Their education and understanding are minimal. They are working full time and they have only about six hours of training a week; it's just touching those areas that are needed at that point in time. It's a needs-based thing. It's not an extensive or an exhaustive training. But it's giving them something to use while they are working and learning.

SUE: As Jesus taught His disciples, they used what they had and then they came back for more. That's what I see happening in Betel. They learn something from the Word or from the preaching or teaching, and apply it as they have opportunity. There is accountability, discipline, encouragement and continual training.

Having been in Betel services on a Sunday as visitors we have seen the differences between that and what we are used to in an average church service in Britain, USA or Australia. Would you like to compare the two? What are the dominant features in a Betel service?

GRAHAM: I think it's possibly a simpler service in some ways. There is order and it's usually very similar most weeks, but I think there's a difference in that we are always having people give testimonies of what God is doing in their lives – not just the ex-drug addicts but also those who are part of the church. That encourages people to see that God is working and answering prayer. We might have five or six hundred people in the service and probably only one to two thirds are people from the centre. So a third don't know anything about God, or they haven't committed their lives to the Lord. Then we have addicts' parents and families that come in and they see what God is doing in lives.

Then worship is a strong element and lasts thirty to forty five minutes – just being in His presence and opening our hearts to Him in singing and prayer. This prepares us for hearing the Word.

SUE: I think the fact that at least a third of the people are unbelievers means that there's constantly a focus on salvation and what being a Christian really is. That often comes out in the preaching and testimonies, but not every message is evangelistic.

GRAHAM: In mainline conservative churches at home an altar call isn't the done thing; here we've seen that this helps.

What happens when people respond to an altar call? Are they prayed for? Are they counselled?

GRAHAM: It really depends on why they have come forward. But usually they are prayed for. The pastors and elders of the church come forward and they pray for the various ones, mostly individually. It gives us a chance to sort people out.

As Betel churches are developed, Spanish leadership and Spanish pastors are appointed. You are missionaries within the same group. How does it feel to be there but not carry full responsibility? Can you accept it? Or is it frustrating?

GRAHAM: In some ways it's hard for us, but on the other hand I was sitting in the pastors' planning meeting the other day and listening to their conversation. I thought, 'I'm glad I don't have to do that. I'm glad that I'm not involved in some of these areas.' They have so much insight. Having the pastors take more responsibility is really the aim of a missionary. In a sense we are only gap-fillers.

SUE: We don't feel threatened by the national pastors. We just respect them and thank God for what He is doing in them and through them.

GRAHAM: Some of those gaps pertain more to the church side of things, like following up people that have left, sorting out relationship problems, and visiting people. The national pastors are really managers, running the centres, the men's houses, the women's houses, the marrieds' houses, and the work programme, so they are on the go, supervising and organising.

* * *

Now we quiz the Reagans.

Jim and Sue, for many years you were in a WEC church-planting ministry; now you are working in Betel. How have you handled this change?

JIM: I went through a period of grieving, which I found hard to handle, because we had been church-planting for eight years. But coming into Betel meant working with people who were eager to hear what you had to say about the gospel and interested in having their lives changed. In our other situation it was more a question of trying to stimulate people's interest. So that was a big change.

SUE: It was hard to transfer from a tiny little group to a big city church with loads of people, but we got used to that. It was nice to be appreciated!

What are you doing now?

JIM: My job is the administration of Betel at the Madrid level, at the national Spanish level, and at the international level. We handle all the legal, financial and administrative matters. My job consists of leading a team of about eleven people, mainly ex-addicts who are learning to take responsibility in this area.

So are you at a desk most of the day?

JIM: Yes and no. I tend to move round the office a bit. I have to go out to visit other offices, to banks, to see law firms. Another part of the job is to give pastoral care to the people in the office.

SUE: On the pastoral side, we have team members round regularly for lunch just to see how they are doing, to encourage them, and to pray for them.

I lead a ladies' intercessory group on a Thursday morning. There are so many things going on – people are ill, people in prison, financial pressure, kids' troubles at school; we take all these things to the Lord. But my main ministry is the children's work.

Every job has its pluses and minuses. Could you describe some of the good things?

JIM: We are dealing with lots of Spaniards who are open to the Lord. Another plus is, although we are not really involved in direct evangelism much, we are part of a mechanism that is reaching Spaniards. The plusses for me are that I am in a job that I like. It obviously has its frustrations but I feel as though I am accomplishing something – putting some system into Betel – I suppose it is because I was an engineer at one time.

SUE: It's great to watch little ones whose mothers have just been admitted into the community. The children come with lots of problems, lots of hang-ups and we pray and try to deal with them. Then we see them change over the months and become stable and receptive to the gospel.

JIM: All jobs have their problems! Working with people who are not professional office workers can be a hassle. But then I'm not a professional office worker either! One of the disappointments is when people you get to know leave the centre without coming through to the Lord. You have a relationship with them, then they go. That happens quite often. It's intrinsic to the ministry.

We have difficulties on the admin side, but in one way they are good because they have to do with growth. Betel, in the last four or five years, has doubled in terms of residences in Spain and in financial flow. Trying to put a system in place is like open heart surgery on a man while he is running a four minute mile!

I suppose it's difficult because every centre is having an income from various activities, and at the same time there is expense involved in maintaining the centres, the vehicles, food and so on.

JIM: Yes. The problems come mainly on the accounting side. To help us become, and stay, legal we have to have proper accounting methods. We are dealing with twenty different provinces. Betel is a unity in Spain so we have to bring it all together. There are times when there's not enough money and you have to trust! That's a pressure, but obviously I don't bear that one alone.

Jim, overall is it worthwhile? Is there the lasting fruit that justifies the effort?

JIM: Yes. An example – Tomas, who is now the pastor in Valencia, leads the church and centre there, and also helps to oversee the centre in Majorca. He came to us about ten years ago as a drug addict and we see him functioning now as the father of a family, a responsible pastor involved with other pastors in Valencia, and a leader of the centre and of that area. There is genuine lasting fruit, so it is worthwhile.

SUE: To see families come together again when husband and wife have been apart is so encouraging.

Jim and Sue returned to Britain in June 1999 where they have located in the Midlands. Jim continues as a financial counselor for Betel of Britain and Sue is developing, along with the Selwoods, a Betel sponsored drug prevention program for British schools.

4

BETEL IS GROWING UP

ELLIOTT TEPPER

Betel developed out of a WEC church-planting concept. As the pioneer work in San Blas grew, we realised that we needed to be organised as a social work in its own right, leading to the planting of churches which became part of the AEMC (the WEC-related association of churches).

Over a period of time Betel has gained recognition in the Evangelical Church of Spain and in International Confederations. First we were received into the FEREDE, the Protestant national confederation, which represents all evangelicals before the government. Then we became charter members of the newly formed CEM, the Provincial association of the Comunidad de Madrid, and, over the years, with each provincial evangelical grouping where Betel functions.

Just this year the evangelicals and protestants of Spain have formed 'DIAKONIA' – a national association of evangelical social groups. It would be the equivalent of the Catholic CARITAS – the largest social agency outside of the government in most Catholic countries. We are one of the principal members and organisers of DIAKONIA.

I have been invited to sit on the board of directors – a position that allows us to represent the evangelical community before the government in relation to social issues, and even to help formulate petitions to the government for funding. Our first national conference on social work has just been held in Madrid where I was invited to speak at one of the plenary sessions. The government provided their Pavilion of Congresses as the venue and also underwrote the cost of the event.

Beyond Spain we have been drawn into two organisations. The first is called ISAAC – the International Substance Abuse and Addiction Coalition – started by David Partington of UK. Lindsay McKenzie and I were invited to be foundation directors. Its goal is to form a worldwide coalition of Christian rehabilitation centres. Lindsay made the first trip to Cairo to meet some of the world leaders, then I followed with a trip to a conference in Florida, then another in Cairo. We will be holding the first world conference of Christian Rehabilitation Centres in August, 1999 at the University of Kent. We hope to attract hundreds of representatives. Recently I have been elected president of ISAAC. This is a great honour for Betel and an affirmation of our humble peer-driven model of rehabilitation. Most of the International Substance Abuse and Addiction Coalition organisations are highly professional with doctors, psychologists and trained counsellors as leaders. For ISAAC to choose a 'Betelito' rather than a rehabilitation professional is extraordinary!

We are also part of a secular organisation which is principally made up of European rehabilitation centres. Lindsay has been more involved in that because the push came from the largest rehabilitation centre in Italy. We are on its board of directors.

In June 1998 there was a world conference at the UN of world leaders involved in the war against drugs. The Presidents of USA and Spain were present with departmental heads from many countries. Betel was invited and I attended. So Betel's place and role in the whole area of rehabilitation is being recognised worldwide.

But from the beginning, Betel has always been more than a rehabilitation centre. We are orientated to the goal of church-planting, and we have always kept before us our responsibility to fulfil the Great Commission.

Every three or four years the Spanish evangelical church has held some kind of a national missionary conference, but there has never been an annual conference with this theme.

Because of our world vision and WEC's worldwide involvement we felt we should organise an annual missions conference. Can you imagine it? Here we are – a group of churches made up of cured addicts, ex-prostitutes, former robbers, yet we assumed the mantle of leadership and have had acceptance by the body of Christ in organising the main national missions conference in the country!

We contacted Patrick Johnstone in WEC's International office. His book, *Operation World*, is in Spanish and used by the churches here. He gave us permission to use the Operation World logo and he agreed to initiate the first conference by being our principal speaker. This was held in 1994 and over seven hundred people attended. Thirty different mission organisations were present; we had fifteen workshops organised by YWAM, Open Doors, Pocket Testament League, Wycliffe, Decision magazine, Christian Literature Crusade, Bible Society, and so on.

For the second conference in 1995 we had Rev. A.S. Worley of Faith Training Centre (a missionary statesman in his own right) and Wayne Myers, the grandfather of modern missions in Mexico, and for decades one of 'Christ for the Nations' roving ambassadors.

In 1996 we had Ralph Mahoney of the World Missionary Assistance Plan which produces the Acts magazine that goes to 130,000 pastors, ministers and missionaries, and is published in eighteen languages. Just recently, eight hundred attended, and heard Brother Andrew of Open Doors.

We have had the support and praise of the whole church. Gabino Fernandez Campos – the leading Protestant historian in Spain – has said that Betel is one of the principal agencies for missionary activity in the Spanish church. People tell us that the impact of these conferences has been profound. They certainly have had a great influence on Betel!

Before the first conference in 1994 the only 'foreign mission' point we were maintaining was in New York City, but after that we opened Betel of Italy, Mexico and Germany in 1995 and then Betel Portugal, UK and France in 1996. So it has stirred our own missionary vision. Recently, Betel of India was formally legalised as a charitable trust. In October, 1999 Keith Berghmeier (WEC Australia) and Lauro and Rosane Castelli (WEC Brazil) will begin our first residential programme in Asia.

For these conferences we bring in our own overseas leaders and let them share what God has done, so it has proven to be a forum for us, too. From the onset we felt we wanted to make these conferences as broad based as possible so we invited all the mainline Protestant denominations. That has been significant because that kind of unity and co-operation is not easy to obtain in Spain – or indeed, in any nation.

There has been a notable upsurge of interest in missions by the evangelical church here, and in a small measure Spain has become a sender of missionaries, not just a receiver.

Operation World conferences have also had a significant role to play in stimulating interest in the Maghreb in the North West corner of the African continent. Out of that has come our second effort in promoting world missions in the Hispanic church – the annual 'Raymond Lull Conference' in Ceuta, with its emphasis on the needs of the Moslem world.

5

WHY COMMUNITY?

ELLIOTT TEPPER

We are often asked, 'Why community?' I have given much thought to the question because it is a good one that demands an honest and thorough answer. The question, or better said, the challenge, to community, is usually made because of a misunderstanding of what our community is and does: and of what role community may play in the building up of Christ's kingdom.

The critic almost always assumes that there is a sectish agenda in our community living which robs the individual of his rights and freedoms and imposes unfair or outdated religious restraints upon his or her life. Often there is the insinuation that Betel has a design of entrapping vast numbers of weak and helpless people in its communal web. If that were so, our trap is like a sieve. Of the 33,000 individuals who have passed through Betel's residences over the last years, only 1,200 live with us today, the rest leaving to return to their families or the street. Some choose to live drug-free and some choose to return to drugs. (Our cure rate has ranged between 10% and 15% over the years.) All are free to select the church of their choice or a purely non-religious lifestyle. Of the 1,200 Betel residents only about one hundred and twenty would be permanent or semi-permanent members who exercise some kind of full-time ministry either in the pastorate, as staff, or as monitors in our residences and shops. These are hardly the kind of statistics one would expect from a sect. In reality Betel is really more of a temporary rest stop where weary, broken people can piece back together their shattered lives before continuing on their journey.

Would-be community members usually address the question of 'why' before they take their first step to join Betel and then ask it again and again along the way. When the pressures of their personal journey of faith increase, they naturally ask, 'Is community worth all the trouble and sacrifice? Is it still for me?' I always remind them that Betel has always embraced the refrain, 'Easy entrance, easy exit.' Men and women are free to respond to the hospitality and love we are willing to show them in any way they please.

Being a religious community is not always easy. In general, today, religious communities are looked down upon by the world and by the church at large. Why? There are some good reasons. There have been abuses in the past: extreme monasticism, closed convents, and the deadly religiosity that was at times institutionalised during the Middle Ages. Present day abuses: fanaticism, and sects like those of Jim Jones and Dr. Moon have also coloured popular opinion. The modern mind-set with its obsession for individualism, freedom, and 'rights', with its tendency towards rebellion and the rejection of all authority views a religious community as an affront to human dignity.

The question is: does community deserve this kind of shunning? The answer is yes and no. Each Christian community must be judged by its own fruits and by what it really is and does.

When I challenge Betelitos to consider whether community is for them, I first tell them why I think that the right kind of community experience might suit them. I point out that millions of men, women and children have voluntarily chosen to live in Christian communities throughout the centuries. Some have chosen because of direct revelation, others because of necessity. Why? Perhaps for no other reason than that for them as individuals community was the will of God for their lives for a season. This is not to say that their choice was higher or better, but simply a choice God permitted them to make.

The Bible is full of community. The very first large community was Noah's ark, a veritable floating married couples' hostel, only with a few more pets. To be precise four families lived under one roof and formed one congregation that had everything in common. The world was corrupt, perverse, and destined for judgement. Yet, out of that world one man found grace in the sight of God – Noah. One privileged man and his family were chosen out of all the race to be set apart. He was chosen for the specific purpose of forming that redemptive community which would preserve the human seed from the coming judgement of God.

Most addicts who come to Betel come reluctantly. We are usually the last remedy chosen. Compared to other programmes, both private and governmental, a Christian residential rehabilitation community appears, at least at first sight, to be overly restrictive. When sharing with the new members I emphasise not their 'perceived' plight, but their privilege in being allowed by God to live in Betel's family. Only a fraction of hard addicts seriously seek help and only a fraction of that fraction are willing to live in a residential community long enough to be really changed. We let them know that they are privileged even more than the average Christian who is a member of a normal non-residential congregation. God's purposes and preparation for their lives can be worked out quickly in the intense twenty-four-hours-a-day, seven-days-a-week discipleship programme they have voluntarily and temporarily joined. And, if their attitude is right, and if they are truly seeking God, they may find community to be a kind of spiritual paradise. The mature faith and prayers of the older members of the community, the disciplined study of the Word, and the rich atmosphere of worship create a favourable environment for their growth in grace. While they are privileged guests for a season beneath Betel's spiritual covering, a covering that they themselves would be incapable of finding or building on their own, and if God is gracious, they may from time to time encounter a foretaste of heaven.

At one of our camp meetings our second son Jonathan got up to testify before more than a thousand Betelitos. He said, 'I thank God that I grew up in the Betel Community – a "Chaval" from San Blas. Who would have ever thought that a Rhodes Scholar would come out of Betel?' (Jonathan grew up as one of the community and went on to win a Rhodes Scholarship to Oxford where he is completing his doctorate in history at Christ Church College.

Unlike a possessive sect, if we find a personality that is not happy in Betel and cannot find rest, we make a way for them to leave gracefully. Once we see that their lives are flowing at cross purposes to those of the community, rather than try to persuade them to stay, we try and direct them to some other place better to their liking. Fellowship and calling cannot be forced. It is best that they leave in peace, loved and loving, than that in overstaying they are provoked to criticism and the sowing of the tares of division. As Abraham said to Lot, 'Let there be no strife, I pray thee, between me and thee, and between my herdsmen and thy herdsmen, for we be brethren. Is not the whole land before thee?' (Gen. 13:8, 9).

Sometimes I feel moved by the Spirit of God to strongly encourage some individuals to tough it out and continue in Betel. Certainly the majority of those who leave before they finish the programme leave before God has finished doing in their life what He would like to do. Most addicts have compulsive, obsessive and impatient personalities. The easiest thing to do when things get rough is to quit and run to some other supposedly easier, more sympathetic place. When personalities rub against each other in the community, when the demands and rules of the community start to cut against the grain of a rebellious will, that is when individuals decide that Betel is not the 'will of God for their lives'. If we think that God really has something better for that person, we open the door wide and help them leave. But if they are leaving to escape the dealings of the cross in their lives or if they are leaving for lower reasons, that is, they want to go back on the street, I will do my best in the free market place of ideas and argument to convince them to stay. I like to point out that although Betel's community may appear to be 'hard', they may find, like Jacob, that 'Laban's community' is harder than their father's house. Changing places has never been a successful way of evading the dealings of God. The Lord will manoeuvre His children into the circumstances that will lead them to brokenness and that final stroke of grace that changes a Jacob to an Israel.

Betel's community is certainly not the only place God deals with men's lives, nor is it the definitive place even for committed Betelitos. The world and the Kingdom of God are both much bigger than Betel. Nevertheless, we have tried to do our best to make it a loving and challenging Christian community for the nurture of God's family and the raising up of an army for His glory.

6

THE ULTIMATE CHALLENGE

PETER STEPHENSON & ELLIOTT TEPPER

Elliott explains the crying need for an effective mechanism which will help ex-drug addicts re-enter society.

Right from the beginning of Betel we have known that the people in our programme, the vast majority, have to leave and return to normal life. Only a very small percentage is called to stay in the community as pastors or staff or monitors.

Peter Stephenson from England arrived at Betel as a new WEC missionary. He is a very thoughtful, creative person and became deeply concerned about this problem. It was then that we began to think very seriously about creating a workers' co-operative.

We received valuable help and advice through a visit of Terence Rosslyn-Smith, a specialist in this area with wide experience in Britain.

Peter continues:
What really excited us about the co-operative concept was the idea of the owners being the workers. There's a high incentive for work, for keeping things on the straight and narrow, and for running things legally. There is high motivation for mutual supervision because if your work colleague starts to take drugs and his work performance goes down that starts to affect your end-of-year bonus. Spanish law allows a very strong disciplinary framework for co-operatives because the owners are also the workers, so they don't need protection from the 'owners'. Thus

we were able to put into our statutes that the use of drugs at any time could be a sackable offence, whereas in normal Spanish law an ordinary employee cannot be sacked for drug taking until it seriously affects his work. We used the name 'Cadmiel' which comes from a character mentioned in the book of Ezra who helped in the rebuilding of the temple in the 6th century BC; the name Cadmiel means 'God at the forefront'.

Elliott adds:
Peter did the hard work of drawing up the statutes, of learning the co-operative law, of creating an entity that we could legalise, and of really inspiring the first five founding members to take a step of faith and start a totally legal business. As Peter pointed out, most of the unemployed in Spain usually look for work that's not official, so as to avoid paying taxes and social security. Our method meant that they would have to pay taxes and keep records for the government.

We wanted to keep the membership to people that had the Betel ethos, the Betel experience, because there is a heart loyalty there. So we were taking a risk. On one hand when people graduate from Betel with no chance of work and you create work for them, you are helping the family, and you are also helping the church because it encourages them to form a family, and stay part of the fellowship. But on the other hand there is a certain selfish motive on our part to keep faithful workers and monitors in Betel as long as possible. We can't keep them forever. So we make a doorway out after eighteen months; we make a leak in the system; we are 'bleeding' ourselves in a positive sense to bless families.

One of the chief reasons for creating our own co-operative is a statistic that was passed on to me from Terence Rosslyn-Smith. He noted that in Britain people with a history of drug addiction, criminal background, or AIDS, have only a fifteen percent chance of ever finding permanent work once they leave a rehabilitation programme. A second statistic came to my attention through the *Economist*; it was from an American study in the American Department of Labour. They noted that the lack of skills or lack of professional training was rarely the important factor in unemployment, that most of the people were unemployed because they lacked the social skills and the character necessary to be faithful in whatever job they took. Their problem is lack of character, lack of self discipline, lack of honesty, lack of integrity, lack of punctuality, laziness. We feel that the Betel community puts those qualities into folk.

Peter gives this account of the beginnings.
In June 1997, Cadmiel was legally formed and in September it began trading. It was a very rough ride to begin with. We had a lot of additional costs, families to support and feed, rents on their homes to pay. Betel tried to cushion the blow as much as possible and offered to pay social security for the first year for the five founder members, and we also lent them about seventy square metres of space to set up an upholstery workshop. Its main line of business was in building services, renovating flats and warehouses, bricklaying, plumbing, and heating. The first six months were very much touch-and-go as to whether it would succeed.

There were other sources of external funding that helped. We had a £3,000 grant from the Besom Foundation, which is a Christian charity based in London which provides seed capital for new initiatives. Betel also gave them a permanent loan of a vehicle to help with moving materials and workers.

At the end of the first year there were sixteen owner members; all but two of those being former addicts who have come through the Betel programme. Salaries are still artificially low and they have decided to keep them low to try and guarantee as much as possible the long term stability of Cadmiel. By the end of our second year we should have twenty four members. We already have a waiting list of Betelitos who want to join.

Although we are not out of the woods yet, things are

beginning to look a lot more positive and clients are recognising the work they are doing. They are beginning to get a reputation. They are getting second and third jobs from the same clients and are beginning to have major establishments like the social services and the army as customers. This will increase as they continue to produce good quality work; the future looks bright.

We are very aware that there is always a danger that the whole thing could go horribly wrong and that the original ethos could disappear and turn into pure selfishness and desire for individual financial gain. So we just have to trust the Lord; we have to trust the people concerned, to pray for them and do all we can to influence them correctly.

Elliott mentions a further danger.

One of the dangers is that of losing the ethos and losing the Christian spirit of holiness that is in Betel. We are wrestling with the question of whether the people should be required to go to church, or be strongly encouraged to go to church, or if they choose not to participate in a Christian church should they be on the governing council? All these things we are working through right now because we don't just want to create a mere business organisation.

Peter explains further:

We are anxious that people do not leave the centre until they genuinely are ready. So nobody can even consider joining Cadmiel until they have been in Betel for at least eighteen months without any major hiccups. During these eighteen months they have to have shown a sense of responsibility, a sense of Christian discipleship. Then, even after they join Cadmiel they are on a six month trial period, in which the company can cut the contract whenever it likes if the person fails to perform well morally or spiritually or in the work environment.

We really are right at the front end of thinking in the whole area of rehabilitation, without even realising it. I was recently

210

at a conference on social re-insertion run by one of our brother organisations. The conclusion reached was that unless we have re-integration into the workplace at the front of our minds right from the first moment, then we are really wasting our time. It doesn't matter what you do, in terms of rehabilitation; at the end of the day, if they are incapable of holding down a job, you are failing. So it's ironic that after twelve or fifteen years of being criticised for placing work so central in our Betel programme, everyone is now saying unless work is integral, you are wasting your time!

BETEL INTERNATIONAL

INTERNATIONAL HEADQUARTERS
C/Antonia Rodriguez Sancristan, 8, Madrid
Tel: (34-91) 525 2222   Fax: (34-91) 525 8907

LOCATION	ADDRESS	TELEPHONE/FAX
NEW YORK, USA N.Y. 11372	78-05 Roosevelt Ave., Jackson Heights,	(1-718) 533 9861 T & F
KROGASPE, Germany	Hof Rabenhorst, 24644 Krogaspe	T (49-4321) 53692 F (49-4321) 962780
HAMBURG, Germany	Hamburger Str. 180, 22083 Hamburg	(49-40) 209723385
NAPLES, Italy	Via Roma, 509, 80017 Melito	T (39-081)711 5215 F (39-081) 711 5409
BARI, Italy	Via Flemin, 31 e 33, 70031 Andria	(39-0883) 54 4815 T & F
GENOA Italy	Viale Bernabó Brea No 47 Int.23 16131 Genova	(39-010) 944252
LISBON, Portugal	Rua Do Cruzeiro, Lote 121, Almada, Charneca Da Caparica 2825	(35-11) 225 7691 T & F
OPORTO,	Rua Antero De Quental, 370, 4050 Porto	(35-12) 550 2832
SETUBAL, Portugal	Rua Clube Recreativo de Palhava, 60	(35-065) 573 819

BIRMINGHAM, UK	Windmill House Weatheroak Hill, Alvechurch, Birmingham, B48 7EA	T (44-1564)822 356 F (44-1564) 824929
MARSEILLE, France	198 – Rue De Lyon 13015 Marseille	T (33-4) 9158 7182 F (33-4) 9102 5415
PUEBLA, Mexico	Prolongación Reforma n° 6908, Col. La Libertad, Pue. C.P. 72130	(52-22) 486140

BETEL SPAIN

MADRID	C/Antonia Rodriguez Sancristan, 8, Madrid 28044	T 91 525 2222 F 91 5258907
ALBACETE	C/ Capitán Cortes, 57 – C.P. 02004	T 967 501419 F 967 510410
ALGECIRAS	Avda. Virgen del Carmen, 53 - C.P. 11202	956 587008 T & F
ALMERIA	C/ Doctor Carracido, 19-21 - C.P. 04005	T 950 234127 F 950 276362
BARCELONA	Ctra. Molins de Rey a Sabadell, Km. 13 – nave 91 (Rubi)	T 93 5886324 F 93 6973205
BILBAO	Ctra. De Bilbao a Galdacano, 1 – C.P. 48004	94 4128223 T & F
CASTELLON	C/ Navarra, 119 - C.P. 12002	T 964 203122
CEUTA	C/ Canalejas, 23 bajo – C.P. 51001	T 956 517529 F 956 510744

CIUDAD REAL	C/ Caballeros, 14 - C.P. 13002	T 926 212226 F 9262 15581
CORONA	INÉS de Castro No 9	T 981 247525
CUENCA	Ctra. Alcazar Km. 1,7 – C.P. 16001	T 969 233754 F 969 233371
GRANADA	Avda. de América, 53 B. Elzaidin – C.P. 18008	958 131410 T & F
GUADALAJARA	C/ Wencelao Argumosa, 13 – C.P. 19003	T 949 229769
MALAGA	Avda. de Barcelona, 16 local 1 – C.P. 29009	T 95 2334926 F 95 2355509
MAJORCA	C/ Francisco Friol y Juan, 7 – C.P. 07010	971 753882 T & F
MELILLA	C/ Jacinto Ruiz Mendoza, 13 bajo 129 – C.P. 29805	95 2673614 T & F
MURCIA	C/Ecuador No 37 Archena, Murcia	T 968 608 846946
ORENSE	C/ Marcelo Macias, 48 bajo – C.P. 32002	T 988 253751 F 988 254304
SEVILLA	C/ Asensio y Toledo, 6 – C.P. 41014	T 95 4680845 F 95 4689059
TARRAGONA	C/ Riera de Miró, 27 y 29 – C.P. 43204 (Reus)	977 756618 T & F
VALENCIA	C/ San Vicente Martir, 432- C.P. 46017	T 96 3410433 F 96 3809223
VIGO	C/ Balaidos, 13 bajo - C.P. 36210	986 244541 T & F

WEC INTERNATIONAL

Betel is a transnational department of WEC International, an interdenominational agency with 1,000 members committed to evangelism and church-planting in over fifty countries around the world.

INTERNATIONAL OFFICE

Bulstrode, Oxford Rd., Gerrards   Tel: 1753 880350
         Cross, Bucks SL9 9SZ,   Fax:1753 890830
         England

NATIONAL HEADQUARTERS (English-speaking)
Australia: 48 Woodside Ave.,   Tel: 029 7475577
          Strathfield, NSW.   Fax: 029 7476820

Britain: Bulstrode, Oxford Rd.,   Tel: 01753 884631
          Gerrards Cross, Bucks,   Fax: 01753 882470
          SL9 8SZ

Canada: 37 Aberdeen Ave.,   Tel: 905 529 0166
          Hamilton, ON L8P 2N6   Fax: 905 529 0630

Hong Kong: PO Box 73261, Kowloon   Tel: 02388 2842
          Central PO, Kowloon   Fax: 02388 6941

*New Zealand:*PO Box 27254, Mt. Ruskill, Tel: 09 6302150
          Auckland 1030.   Fax: 09 6386291

Singapore: PO Box 185, Raffles City.   Tel: 250 6455
                                       Fax: 250 1355

South Africa: PO Box 47777, Greyville, Tel: 031 3032533
          4023   Fax: 031 230839

USA: PO Box 1707, Fort   Tel: 215 6462322
          Washington, PA 19034   Fax: 215 6466202

DIRECTORY

BETEL SPAIN
C/Antonia Rodriguez Sancristan, 8   Tel: (34-91) 525 2222
Madrid 28044   Fax: (34-91) 525 8907

INTERNATIONAL

USA
78-05 Roosevelt Ave., Jackson Heights,   Tel: (1-718) 533 9861
New York 11372

GERMANY
Wasbeker Weg, Krogaspe, 24644   Tel: (49-4321) 53692

MEXICO   Tel: (52-22) 486 140
Prolongación Reforma
No 6908, Col. La Libertad
Puebla, C.P. 72130

ITALY
Via Roma 509, (Melito) Napoli   Tel: (39-81) 7115215

PORTUGAL
Rua do Cruzeiro   Tel: (35-11) 297 6109
Lote 121, Almada,
Charneca da Caparica 2825

BRITAIN
Windmill House, Weatheroak Hill,
Alverchurch, Birmingham B48 7EA   Tel: (44-1564) 822356

Rescue Shop Within a Yard of Hell

Stewart and Marie Dinnen

This book takes us to the streets of Madrid – amongst drug users, pushers and prostitutes – where God transformed lives made hopeless by sin. 'Living on the edge of eternity' is a reality in Betel as they take the gospel to those who otherwise would have no hope.

Stewart and Marie Dinnen, with the help of Elliot and Mary Tepper, Lyndsay and Myk Mackenzie, and Kent Martin, describe the origins and activities of Betel. Several, who found Christ through Betel, tell their own stories.

Norman Grubb writes in the foreword: 'I am delighted that Stewart Dinnen...has put together the stirring testimonies which comprise this totally surprising development in our Spanish work. Faith always means shocks, because it causes something to happen – a release of God's power – not as a result of human reasoning but as a manifestation of his purposes for the world....It is just like the Lord to take on what appears to be impossible and turn it into one of the most dramatic responses to the saving truth of Jesus in Europe today.'

First published in 1996, the book has been reprinted several times.

272 pages   ISBN 1 85792 122 4   pocket paperback

Christian Focus Publications publishes biblically-accurate books for adults and children. The books in the adult range are published in three imprints.

Christian Heritage contains classic writings from the past.

Christian Focus contains popular works including biographies, commentaries, doctrine, and Christian living.

Mentor focuses on books written at a level suitable for Bible College and seminary students, pastors, and others; the imprint includes commentaries, doctrinal studies, examination of current issues, and church history.

For a free catalogue of all our titles, please write to
Christian Focus Publications,
Geanies House, Fearn,
Ross-shire, IV20 1TW, Great Britain

For details of our titles visit us on our web site
http://www.christianfocus.com

Explanatory notes

The translation used is the New International Version. Normally, italics are used for the verse under discussion. The reference to the verse being discussed is normally in bold type.

Abbreviations
Bible Translations.

AV	Authorized Version
RV	Revised Version
NKJV	New King James Version
RSV	Revised Standard Version
AMP	Amplified Version
NEB	New English Bible
GNB	Good News Bible

MT means Masoretic Text, the Hebrew text most commonly in use.
LXX (70) is the Septuagint, the Greek version of the Old Testament.

Other abbreviations

f./ff.	following verse/verses
cf.	compare
mg.	marginal reading

Books alluded to.
David Atkinson: *The Message of Proverbs*
Charles Bridges: *Exposition of Proverbs*
Franz Delitzsch: *Biblical Commentary on the Proverbs of Solomon*
Matthew Henry: *Exposition of the Old & New Testaments*
Derek Kidner: *Proverbs (Tyndale Series) Wisdom to live by*
David Thomas: *Commentary on Proverbs*
R.N. Whybray: *Proverbs* (New Century Bible)

© Eric Lane
ISBN 1 85792 451 7

Published in 2000
by Christian Focus Publications
Geanies House, Fearn, Ross-shire, IV20 1TW, Great Britain
Cover design Owen Daily

Poe: Pelted, Pounded, Pummeled and Pulverized

Poe: Pelted, Pounded, Pummeled and Pulverized

By
Jay Dubya

Published by
Bookstand Publishing
Morgan Hill, CA 95037
3079_2H

ISBN 978-1-58909-686-8

Printed in the United States of America

Other Books by Jay Dubya
Adult Fiction

Young Adult Fantasy Novels

Contents

Description

Poe: Pelted, Pounded, Pummeled and Pulverized is a unique collection of eighteen classic Edgar Allan Poe short stories that have been creatively rewritten and satirized into adult parody form featuring adult content and language. When author Jay Dubya was a New Jersey public school English teacher, he often enjoyed teaching and reading E.A. Poe's "influential literature" to his sometimes-enlightened middle and high school students.

Even though Poe (1809-1849) had died at a very young age, he still managed to remarkably write over nine hundred pages of imaginative short stories and poems.

In addition to being a superb writer, Poe was also an excellent editor and literary critic and is widely regarded as one of the most important authors in American literature. The now-esteemed writer is often referred to as "the father of the American short story" and as "the inventor of the detective story."

Edgar Allan Poe was born the son of traveling professional actors and was orphaned at age three to the wealthy Allan family of Richmond, Virginia, and that is how Edgar acquired his middle name. Mr. Allan never adopted Edgar because he disapproved of Poe's literary ambitions, the two often quarreling about authors seldom being able to make a decent and respectable living.

Poe was expelled from the University of Virginia on suspicion of gambling and other misdemeanor behavior. He enrolled as a cadet at West Point but was dismissed from that military academy as a result of poor grades. Realizing that reconciliation with Mr. Allan was impossible as long as he wished to become an author, Poe became disenchanted and depressed and intentionally dropped out of the prestigious school on the Hudson. But today there is a commemorative statue at the academy dedicated to Poe claiming that the famous writer had once attended college there.

Edgar married his thirteen-year-old cousin Virginia Clemm and made a very modest living as a writer and as a newspaper journalist. Poe had a nasty temper, took drugs as painkillers and because of his volatile disposition, couldn't keep a job for any length of time. In 1847 Virginia died of tuberculosis and Poe, underfed, pale and gaunt-looking, passed away two years later.

Poe's detective stories "The Murders in the Rue Morgue" and "The Purloined Letter" made him famous in addition to his classic horror tales "The Pit and the Pendulum" and the genius' eerie epic "The Tell Tale Heart."

"The Assignation"

Ah yes, the seldom used English nomenclature "Assignation," a secret meeting or appointment; a stealthy rendezvous of lovers responding to the accuracy of Cupid's darts. Sounds rather innocuous and idealistic, doesn't it? Perhaps also a tad trite, but if the clandestine meeting is both illicit' and immoral, then *those* elements of ascending suspense greatly add to the maddening intrigue. Allow me to provide some significant background to this story in order to establish character, setting and plot.

Oh yes, Venice, Italy, the city of art, culture, splendid architecture, sophistication, innovation, great canals and the inimitable St. Mark's Square. Many spellbound scholars have described Venice as a duplication of the mythological paradise Elysium, a final destination where the contented souls of the "good among the deceased" are rewarded by eternally and peacefully resting within the splendor of colorful daffodil fields. But the city's landmark canals, those majestic and beautiful watery thoroughfares' that have been privy to myriad secrets of passionate love, the angst of bitter hatred and of the depravity of reprehensible murder and of sudden death, all esoteric subjects belonging first to the young romantics and secondly to the impractical university academics.

Yes, my story of woe begins in Venice near the covered archway over that often traversed branch of the Grand Canal, the classic bridge bearing the appropriate appellation *Ponti di Sospiri*, or translated into standard' English vernacular, "the Bridge of Sighs." It was at that famous place where I unexpectedly and incidentally encountered my remote acquaintance precisely at dusk in late December just at the rise of the full moon, yes, that's precisely when the very odd event occurred. You might say that a full moon begets and engenders lunacy? That crazy people become even crazier under its influence? Well now, perhaps you are entirely correct in subjectively deriving your incisive assessment.

As I presently recollect, it was a pathetically dark night of unusual gloom. The great clock in the Piazza had just struck five and the Square of the Campanile was both silent and deserted. The lights from the Ducal Palace were dimly shining and I recall that I was returning via rented gondola from eating pizza in the Piazza, being awkwardly transported by a drunken opera singing' gondolier weaving his small vessel in a zig-zagging manner on the Grand Canal.

1

But as my leased gondola approached the mouth of the San Marco Canal, a loud hysterical female voice promptly got my attention, the screams originating from the *Ponti di Sospiri*. I anxiously sprang to my feet so that my eyes and ears could better perceive the source of the lady's distress when instantaneously my quick abrupt standing had inadvertently knocked the oar from the inebriated gondolier's hands right into the deep murky stagnant trash-strewn water below. My unintentional action was not immediately appreciated. Indeed, the hiccupping boat pilot was pretty damned incensed at his loss.

"Just look what the hell you've done!" the livid gondolier balked. "I was just about to sing 'Row, Row, Row Your Boat' when you had the audacity to smack my oar from my hands. That'll cost you many gold coins to replace, that's for damned sure! You'll do restitution before I'll ever do destitution!"

"Whatever floats your boat Asshole!" I neurotically yelled at the jerk-off as I then violently tossed the startled oar-less rower overboard. "Now you can get into the swim of things, you pathetic lush! Find your fuckin' oar underwater and you could clumsily paddle your farting ass to the next boarding steps' launch. And of yeah. Keep steering your gondola like *that* and I guarantee that you'll fuckin' wind-up on skid *row*!" I screamed down as the idiot frantically splashed and thrashed his arms about in the filthy canal.

Again my attention was directed towards the 'Damsel in distress.' Luckily the current was guiding the gondola in the direction of the *Ponti di Sospiri*, the aforementioned bridge being where my curiosity needed to learn more about the plight and circumstance of the beleaguered female. A second form was now stationed on the bridge, a fat baldheaded man clad in ostentatious flowing garments who was physically struggling with the woman, a maudlin mother endeavoring to keep her infant separated from the assailant's greedy grasp. Fifteen seconds later the baby plummeted and then plopped into the canal and its tiny body wrapped in a blue blanket quickly submerged beneath the water's surface. I was totally exasperated from what my keen vision had just witnessed. At that insular moment I felt justified in getting involved in the argument.

'Holy shit!' I reckoned. 'That infant no sooner comes out of a birth canal and now winds-up in the goddamned Grand Canal! I've often heard of throwing the baby out with the bathwater,' I hypothesized, 'but where the hell's the damned bathwater in this instance? Not that I believe in third party interference,' I

2

rationalized, 'but I feel compelled to assist in attempting to rescue that child as fast as I possibly can.'

Several appalled eyewitnesses jumped into the deep channel and futilely explored with their hands to locate the drowning infant. Lacking an oar, I maneuvered my own hands, paddling in the water in an alternating manner to guide my gondola closer to the scene of confusion and of potential tragedy.

Upon navigating closer to the historic bridge, I soon recognized that the delirious and inconsolable female was none other than the beautiful Marchesa, or "Marchesa Aphrodite" as she is known in various sophisticated quarters around the city. 'She's the mother of that innocent child/victim and that old fat fuck is the reigning Prince, who's reputed to be a gay faggot that absolutely hates women, especially his vivacious wife,' I logically surmised. 'I'll wager that the rich arrogant asshole has discovered that the Marchesa had had illicit sex with some anonymous lover, had conceived the child out of wedlock and then had secretly given birth without the fat bastard Prince's consent or knowledge. It's too bad I'm not a fuckin' writer or else I could effectively use this dramatic bullshit as the plot basis for a novel! And I'm willing to bet my future that the mongrel kid flung into the canal would grow up to be a lot fuckin' smarter than that renowned corpulent retarded cretin, the dirtball Prince of Venice.'

But from my boat's position on the canal, the weeping Marchesa looked stunningly beautiful despite her excessive grieving and sorrow. Her long black tresses were blowing in the cold early winter wind and her large lustrous brown eyes were gazing down into the water's depth. The Marchesa stood motionless like a statue of Venus, a very emotionally injured and disconsolate Venus at that.

Many stone steps above the Marchesa's position (and well within the arch of the water gate) a Satyr-like figure stood studying the horrendous development play-out below. The onlooker had been more than a mere minstrel strumming his' guitar as he' witnessed the tragic event of the child's demise unfolding. I now reckon that I probably exuded a similar spectral appearance (to him) standing and rocking in my gondola, just as the higher elevation (standing erect) man must have perceived me, or at least *that* was my peculiar impression at that particular moment. 'This might be the child's funeral gondola,' I remember thinking inside my narrow boat. 'Is there no justice in this wicked pathetic world?'

Several more stouthearted men leaped into the dark canal but their valiant efforts at salvaging the child were fruitless. But from that

3

lofty niche that formed a section of the Old Republican Prison the heroic determined figure stepped out of the shadows and then deftly dived into the canal. Amazingly, thirty seconds later the humanitarian savior surfaced, gasping for air with the child being clutched in his arms.

And then a half a minute later the infant began crying and screaming and wriggling about in its saturated light blue blanket. The "messiah" next nonchalantly ascended the stone steps leading-up from the water' gate to the Marchesa's balcony and the dark robed gentleman (resembling the gruesome River Styx ferryman Charon) reverently handed the child to the grateful lady, who immediately brought the infant to her bosom and then gently caressed it.

Only in Venice could such tragedy have an almost comedic ending. The infant boy had been saved and the mother's heart was joyful while her disgruntled husband slammed the palace door in genuine frustration. I heard the then-thrilled Marchesa lowly utter to her benevolent lover, "Thou hast triumphed! Thou hast conquered the evil spirit that rules the Palace! Tomorrow morning, one hour after sunrise we shall have *our* final assignation!" At that moment of temporary exultation, those twenty-five haunting words both puzzled and perplexed me.

* * * * * * * * * * * *

After the canal tumult along with the local gossip about the Ducal Palace incident subsided, I yelled up to my sinister acquaintance that my gondola was available for transportation to his secret secluded apartment if he so chose to accompany me. Seeing that I was deficient my oar, the dark-robed hero promptly pilfered one from an unsuspecting gondolier who was preoccupied discharging and assisting an exiting passenger, and soon the incomparable Mentoni joined me inside my boat.

"Let's get the fuck out of here before I'm assassinated prior to ever having my upcoming assignation with a beautiful lady," my heavily cloaked wet passenger mysteriously commanded. "Row quickly in the direction of the Rialto!"

My Grim Reaper attired rider was tall in stature, muscular in build, keen in intellect and quite frankly, his overall presentation made me a bit envious and also had me wishing that I was a gay bird looking for a suitable canary mate. To me the foreboding rider was a mixture of Hercules and Adonis, or more specifically, of strength and handsomeness. This man was a champion of truth, the

4

Marchesa's paramour who had certainly stimulated the wrath and had aroused the jealousy of the faggot Venetian Prince.

Upon dropping off the drenched rescuer at his newly learned residence, Mentoni requested that I should visit him at sunrise the next morning to engage in what he labeled "some celebratory wine drinking." I said "Goodnight" and then rowed my rented gondola back towards the Piazza where I could again swallow-down some more delicious pizza.

I knew my acquaintance to be wealthy but as to the exact extent of his affluence I had little knowledge. After knocking three raps upon his imported mahogany door the following morning at sunrise, I had the audacity to ask where he had obtained his fortune.

"Are you a merchant having many ships bartering goods all over the world?" I had the courage to ask. "Or are you a slick businessman owning pizzerias all over Italy and Sicily serving both the thin round and the thick rectangular varieties of tomato and cheese pies? Tell me Mentoni, I just have to know this irrelevant bullshit!"

"Well, for your privileged information I've gotten wealthy by aggressively marketing and selling a new invention called Venetian blinds, and I've negotiated distributorships all throughout Europe from London to Berlin and from Stockholm to Vienna. My easy-to-use Venetian blinds' are so utilitarian and they represent a monumental improvement over simple curtains and drapes, you know! The entire enterprise has evolved into a wonderfully lucrative business as you can plainly determine!"

Although the sun was beginning to rise on the eastern horizon, I astutely noticed that Mentoni's living room was bright and well illuminated by an abundance of table and floor oil lamps along with a plethora of candles flickering inside very attractive metal wall sconces. Then my enigmatic acquaintance initiated an odd nebulous-type conversation that tended to bewilder me.

"I was an insomniac last night and didn't sleep a blessed wink," Mentoni divulged, almost guiltily. "But me being a goddamned insomniac is much better than me being a whining hypocritical hypochondriac always complaining about suffering from non-existent maladies. Here my Friend, have some vintage merlot produced from my vineyard outside Verona. We shall drink until the sun has fully risen."

As my chilled lips sipped the delicious wine from my' silver goblet, my eyes surveyed the luxurious apartment and my mind marveled at the expensive Greek canvas paintings and white marble statues, at the alabaster figurines in his specially crafted china cabinet, at the rich tapestries hanging on the walls, at the splendid draperies suspended above the windows and at the exquisite sculptures that were reminiscent of the bygone classical art era of Michelangelo and Leonardo da Vinci.

The distinctive overhead teakwood beams and the glorious and elaborate ceiling cornices were of an attractive and imposing design. A roaring fire blazed upon the stone hearth, effectively neutralizing the winter morning that was persistently attempting to invade Mentoni's most excellent residence from outside.

"Ha, ha, ha!" laughed the superb apartment's exclusive proprietor. "Have a seat upon the ottoman, not the asshole Arab from Turkey statue to your right but instead, I'm referring to the leather footrest situated on the floor to your left," my host giddily laughed before gulping down another mouthful of merlot. "All of my furniture has been recently reupholstered and I assiduously perform that redundant process every single month because I get bored with the everyday appearance of my aristocratic living environment. Here Friend, have another refill of wine. I know you possess the wherewithal to devour it. My vintage merlot is indeed a proven aphrodisiac that affords the drinker an erection a cup-full, at least my homegrown variety accomplishes *that* end!" the suddenly convivial Mentoni cordially explained. "Of course, the said drinker must be a post-pubescent healthy male in order to be capable of developing and sustaining an erection, unless a given woman wine drinker has an exceptionally large clitoris to begin with, ha, ha, ha!"

"What has you in such a jolly mood?" I courteously asked. "Normally you're sullen and pensive. Do you plan on seeing how much alcohol you can consume? Are you going to challenge me to a pissing contest into the gusting wind? If I piss into the back of your head, you'd certainly be wet behind the ears!"

"Ha, ha, ha," my acquaintance boomed in great amusement. "Have you ever heard of the fucked-up Englishman Sir Thomas More, whose followers were often called morons?" Mentoni crazily uttered and then cynically laughed, thereafter pausing to imbibe more red wine. "Well Friend, contrary to popular belief, that ignominious mendacious prick Sir Thomas More was far from being a goddamned saint as the fucked-up British mentality maintains. But the stubborn asshole cleric came to a glorious death. Did you know that *that* dumb-fuck son-of-a-bitch laughed his bloody ass off while he was being executed? Yes, the fucked-up jerk-off charlatan actually died laughing, ha, ha, ha! If there's any fuckin' way to die, yes my Friend, it is to fuckin' die laughing!"

"That's some heavy bullshit you're laying on my all-too-vulnerable thought processes," I nervously answered as I thought about the prospect of becoming a practicing bisexual should Mentoni start becoming amorously affectionate with me. "I must say that your residence affords you much more than a Spartan existence," I nervously uttered.

"Ah yes Sparta, the avowed enemy of Athens during the legendary Peloponnesian War," my partially ripped erudite companion responded. "Those fucked-up militant Spartans had a thousand temples and shrines all over their city-state, each structure dedicated to a different god or goddess. You had Zeus and the Olympians of course, and then there were dumb-shit woodland gods, forest gods, meadow gods, fountain gods, lake gods, river gods, mountain gods, blades-of-grass gods, sea gods and even goddamned god gods, ha ha, ha!" Mentoni squealed and guffawed like an asylum patient during a full moon on a cloudless night. "But those fucked-up asshole Spartans screwed their women like Trojans, yes they did, ha, ha, ha! And they were just like that British fuck-head Sir Thomas More in one major respect: the Spartan mother-fuckers always died laughing. Just think about their fucked-up king Leonidas and the Three Hundred brave warriors sacrificing their lives for historical glory at Thermopylae. Those three hundred mentally deranged cock-suckers all died laughing and relished every shit-eating second of it, just to have the honor of being carried back to Sparta on their shiny bronze shields! Now if *that* type of commitment isn't incredible bullshit, then my Friend, I can't imagine what the fuck is!"

"What are you saying?" I neurotically asked. "Do you intend for me to join you in dying while we both are uncontrollably laughing to death? I don't think so!"

"Not exactly," my extraordinary friend chuckled and snickered before chugging down his expensive merlot and then filling up his goblet again. "You have the honor Sir to be the only stranger ever allowed to inspect my living quarters. That's how much admiration I have for you!" Mentoni sincerely complimented me. "Aren't you fuckin' flattered to be my selection for an intimate companion to trust? Tell me, what the hell do you think of the famous Madonna della Pieta portrait? Give me your honest evaluation."

"It's definitely Guido's own, but as you're well aware Mentoni, there're goddamned Guidos all over Italy and Sicily. Thousands of fucked-up Guidos live in Tuscany alone. I mean," I exaggerated and

7

slurred, "there could be duplicates and counterfeits of that great work of art all over the fuckin' country from Venice all the way down to the ghettos of Naples and Sorrento, not discounting the repulsive antiquated slums of Salerno of course! And if I may add to my loquacious monologue, the entire Amalfi Coast is probably deluged with replicas of the goddamned Madonna della Pieta!" I bellowed, subconsciously mimicking my mentor. "The whole country's teeming with the artificial mother-fuckers!" I accentuated.

"Surely my salubrious Friend who is totally devoid of fine silk haberdashery and obviously deficient in sartorial splendor," Mentoni weirdly addressed and belittled me in a boisterous and demeaning tone of voice, "the Madonna della Pieta is to canvas painting what Venus and Aphrodite are to sculpted marble. Wouldn't you agree with my discreet observation?"

"Well then Mentoni," I bravely answered before sipping some more of the tasty merlot, "what is your candid opinion about the voluptuous and well-endowed Marchesa? Isn't that knockout vixen analogous to being the Venus of the Medici?"

"There is nothing vulgar about the Marchesa except me," Mentoni very strangely answered. "It was the inimitable sage Socrates who had said that the sculptor found *his* statuary image hiding within the marble. So too it is with the Marchesa. I love her dearly but her form and image belong to that homosexual faggot obese baldheaded Prince who thinks that his tiny dick is an asshole stuffer instead of a puny pussy plunger! That insidious snake is a most dangerous viper, at fuckin' worst he's a swamp adder and at fuckin' best he's a potential King Cobra! Here Friend, indulge in some more wine! Partake!" my garrulous inebriated host offered.

My senses then detected a certain palpable *extreme unction* (or discernible paranoia) evident in Mentoni's speech and in his animation, gesticulating with the Sign of the Cross as if he were somehow administering the last rites' sacrament to himself without the benefit or the privilege of a qualified priest.

Once Mentoni's latest oddball reverie had been assimilated into words and orally stated, I wondered about my sorrowed friend's motivation, his hidden motive, his purpose and his objective in warmly inviting me to his residence a mere hour before his scheduled assignation with the Marchesa.

And while Mentoni turned his back to pour himself another goblet of merlot, I glanced down beside the black leather ottoman and noticed a sheet of writing paper containing the flowery words to a love poem, the words written in English, which naturally and

8

automatically led me to believe that Britain was my host's native country in that Mentoni knew so damned many minute details about Sir Thomas More's life and death.

"Well, I see you've uncovered my secret identity," Mentoni noticed and remarked as I examined the romantic poem's verses. "Yes, at one time the Lady Marchesa had lived in London and I had had an exciting romantic interlude with her three years before *our* most recent affair occurred here in Venice," my host sadly lamented. "And contrary to the faggot Prince's awareness," my mercurial host bitterly indicated, "his unfaithful wife is not Venetian but instead she is of British ancestry by birth."

* * * * * * * * * * * * *

"Look my Friend," Mentoni summoned my attention. "There is one rapturous painting that your eyes have not yet viewed." My host yanked open a set of purple drapes and behind them was revealed the full-length portrait of the 'Marchesa Aphrodite' possessing an ethereal short smile that would make da Vinci's Mona Lisa pale in comparison. A set of angelic wings fluttered above the woman's shoulders. And then the emotionally unstable Mentoni carried a silver tray over to me with two full goblets of merlot upon it.

"Come and join me in a toast," the cavalier fellow suggested. "Let us drink to my rare antique Etruscan vases, to my unique Oriental rugs, to my porcelain statuettes from India and to the pulchritude of the one and only Marchesa Aphrodite. And finally, let us drink hardy to the rising sun, whose energy is the source of all life on this fucked-up mundane planet."

"What are you really thinking of?" I interrogated. "What is truly in your heart? And I have but one request. Please don't be too vague or evasive in your answer."

"I am an idealistic dreamer by nature and a pragmatic businessman by occupation," Mentoni haughtily replied. "Around you' is a medley of material embellishments, several perhaps even dating back to Noah's antediluvian era. Each work is an individual pursuit of magnificence, a quest for immortality. At first I was an interior decorator of mansions, and after acquiring substantial wealth, I then became a collector of art and culture. Like *those* arabesque censers over yonder there', my soul has been besieged by a mystery not uncommon to Arabia and its phenomenal tales of magic and wonder. My vulnerable spirit is now entering and writhing in Lucifer's flames. Dear Friend, I'm slowly departing from your

9

midst. I'm journeying towards the designated assignation with the Marchesa Aphrodite to which you alone have been privy."

Before I could utter a sentence of exclamation, Mentoni hurled himself upon the black leather ottoman and soon was dead as a doorknocker. Not fully recovering from my traumatic shock, I quickly responded to a rap upon the door and then was face to face with Mentoni's one and only page.

"Sir," the lad almost incoherently choked out. "Mistress Marchesa is dead! Poisoned by a silver goblet of contaminated merlot!"

I swiftly stepped over to where Mentoni was, his body still lying upon the black leather ottoman. I felt his pulse. I listened for a heartbeat. I checked his lack of respiration.

"Your Master is also dead!" I informed the astonished youth. "It appears that the valiant Mentoni and the beautiful Marchesa Aphrodite have simultaneously departed this world to secretly rendezvous for their final assignation!"

"The Premature Burial"

Both the idealist and the romanticist eschew a certain topic in so-called "legitimate literature," and that seldom-explored taboo subject is the *individual's* death by premature burial. Avid book readers thrill when they vicariously are converted into passive spectators to mass human genocide or even centuries-later are made remote witnesses to the mass destruction of a city like Pompeii in 79 A.D., and many revel in their minuscule minds an author's re-creation of the horrifying Black Plague of London or the stifling of a hundred and twenty-three prisoners in the Black Hole of Calcutta, but to suffer through comprehending the premature death of an *individual* by virtue of a terrifying premature burial, well then, *that* type of reading misadventure is the ultimate in disgust as far as the average American novel reader is concerned.

One can easily tolerate reading about a massive massacre or visualizing thousands of innocent folks dying as a result of a destructive volcano or perhaps perishing by means of a violent earthquake, but for an *individual* to die by being buried alive is indeed evaluated as being grossly repugnant because the horror reminds a person of his or her own mortality and of his own or her own vulnerable demise.

The arcane boundaries that divide Life and Death are thin, shadowy and often quite vague. Where the hell does one condition actually end and the other aspect actually begin? Is this earthly existence of a single mortal soul a goddamned endless cycle governed by reincarnation or, as the sagacious Hindus believe, is it exclusively controlled by karma and/or Nirvana?

But let me now relate out of personal experience that a certain rare disease does exist that makes a victim's vital signs virtually disappear whereby the subject appears to be not breathing while exhibiting a cessation of the pulse and where the *individual's* skin turns gruesomely and morbidly pallid and disgustingly lifeless in character. Yes, all of this graphic description is quite true, and wretched as it may seem, throughout ancient and modern history people, excuse me, *individuals,* have unintentionally been buried alive and have suffered traumatic horror when not being able to successfully escape his or her dreadful entombment.

Indeed, some unfortunate *individuals* have endured a certain temporary cessation of body functions that had been interpreted by their friends and relatives (mourning the *individual's* death) to think

11

and believe that the victim had been in a permanent and unalterable dead condition. But many premature interments have been documented and in this investigative exposition, I will identify and describe some of the more widely chronicled depictions that have been detailed in medical journals and reviewed in various morticians' reports. One recent incident of premature burial had occurred just last year in the neighboring city of Baltimore.

The wife of one of the metropolis's most revered citizens, a prominent lawyer, was stricken with a strange and seldom studied illness and was officially pronounced dead by her attending physician. Why her fucked-up parasitic husband, the eminent politician/defense attorney, wasn't called to the afterlife by Gabriel's horn before his beautiful spouse had been summoned remains both a mystery and a secret that only the Good Lord and His Death-Angel Messenger currently know!

The afflicted wife presented all of the ordinary outward indications of being stone cold dead. Her facial complexion was pinched and chalky and it featured a morose-looking sunken outline, her lips were of a horrid marble pallor, the warmth of her body had completely vanished, her breathing was undetectable and the woman's entire form had assumed a stone-like rigidity. It was determined and decided that burial should commence immediately before decomposition of tissue was to progress.

The dearly departed lady's remains were lovingly deposited inside her family's cemetery vault and the mausoleum was not disturbed for three subsequent years when finally a sarcophagus was to be inserted inside by the rich politician/attorney bastard, who had in the interim married a promiscuous streetwalker from Dundalk, Maryland.

Can you imagine the utter shock of the hired masons and of the remarried shyster husband when the stone structure in the cemetery was again opened and an appalling white skeletal object rattled out into the stunned philanderer's arms, her white bones still covered by her partially decomposed burial shroud.

A death commission investigation was soon conducted and it was determined by the authorities that the wife had revived from her strange rare malady inside the mausoleum several days after her entombment and that her struggle inside her coffin had caused it to slide and then flip off of its ledge. A large fragment of the wooden casket had been broken-off in its impact with the flagstone floor and next the already damaged coffin had been further abused by the frantic burial victim, who apparently, frightened in the extreme dark, then repeatedly smashed the improvised wooden club against the granite tomb's metal portals.

But no one ever heard the horrified woman's desperate banging and her futile cries, the crypt being situated in such a remote area of the expansive burial grounds. The frenzied woman had repeatedly screamed her lungs out in absolute sheer terror while incessantly pounding the rusty iron doors (in total blackness) with her makeshift wooden club and with her bruised fists. In her valiant panic the wife's arms had become entangled in some iron work that projected out from the stone building's interior wall and ultimately, her dead limp body eventually rotted away and detached from her anatomy while her skeleton frame still remained standing erect in an upright position. And the shocked former husband did not even use a skeleton key to open the doors to the mausoleum.

Another distressing and depressing incident involving premature burial occurred in 1810 in France, proving once and for all that truth could often be even more fucked-up than fiction. The story's brave heroine (who incidentally was not on heroin) was Mademoiselle Victorine LaFont, a young attractive lady heiress of a wealthy Parisian family. Julien Bosseut, a poor heart-broken literature student and struggling newspaper journalist dearly loved the Mademoiselle but felt that his lowly birthright could never lure her away from high society to marry for affection instead of for mammon. And besides, Victorine's ruthless family would have Julien Bosseut assassinated before the romantic could ever screw or propose to his love.

Victorine LaFont (whose family had made a killing in the printing business but were never arrested for it) eventually married Monsieur Claude Renelle, a wealthy aristocratic banker and internationally known diplomat having a big ass and a tiny dick. Much to Victorine's emotional despair, the beautiful girl was deliberately neglected and ignored, and possibly even abused by the egocentric sadist Claude Renelle, often forcing his young wife to masturbate herself for his viewing pleasure each and every night he was home in his mansion, which was about once a month.

Having been heinously mistreated and exploited for several years, and after being rejected admission into a Catholic convent for nuns because she was no longer a bona fide virgin, the masochistic girl suddenly swooned in her bed one evening and upon being discovered by a maid several days later, Victorine was pronounced dead by a medic neighbor and by a homosexual veterinarian companion of the evil and sinister Claude Renelle.

Under Claude Renelle's specific directions, Victorine was not buried in her family's elaborate mausoleum in Paris but instead was interred in an ordinary grave near Lyons. Hearing of his love's unfortunate demise, the destitute-but-passionate pauper/journalist Julien Bosseut journeyed from Paris to Lyons and dug up the corpse from its shallow grave, caressing the young woman's tresses and crying incessantly like a colic-suffering baby.

Julien's relentless caresses aroused Victorine from her uncanny slumber and the pair passionately made love in the darkness of a new moon right in the center of the Lyons cemetery. But being totally exhausted from her near-death two-day burial ordeal, Victorine permanently ceased breathing after experiencing a tremendous orgasm that the villainous Claude Renelle could never have rendered. And being a naïve stupid idealistic impractical university-educated asshole, Julien Bosseut all-too-honestly reported the bizarre incident to the local police, who immediately arrested the imbecilic foolish fuck for committing "lady-slaughter."

A relevant hair-raising article was published last month in a Bremen, Germany medical journal describing how an artillery officer of noble birth and outstanding good health had been thrown from an ill-tempered horse and then had fallen on his head, thus sustaining a huge contusion along with a split cranium and an accompanying splitting headache. After falling into a very deep stupor where his vital signs were no longer evident, the officer, Captain Wilhelm Stern, was pronounced dead and he' was scheduled to be buried in a military cemetery plot the following morning.

Two days after the military burial "in full honors," the soldiers' graveyard was swarming with visitors because of an important Armistice Day commemoration. As attendees honoring the anniversary were reverently placing floral wreaths on the graves of recently interred army heroes, a distinct commotion beneath the recently deceased officer's burial site was noticed and soon spades and shovels were quickly inserted into the ground with four men digging feverishly, not knowing exactly what phenomenon to expect as a result of their excavations.

In several minutes the wooden box's squeaky lid had been lifted open and much to the horror and terror of everyone there, the dirty face and grimy head of Captain Wilhelm Stern suddenly appeared. When the resurrected officer mechanically sat up, much to the alarm of already shrieking women and hysterical children, the delirious eyewitnesses to the extremely ghastly event fled in all possible directions away from the frightful debacle.

14

Wilhelm Stern was immediately rushed to a nearby hospital facility. Astounded physicians and coroners on duty extensively examined his body and evaluated his previous head injuries. Even Wilhelm's penis responded to stimuli and stood at erection when a galvanic battery was attached to his reproductive organ and then activated. Two attending nurses skillfully performed a collaborative decent blowjob on his sexual apparatus and the officer's face instantly sported a broad smile of satisfaction. And after volcanically squirting his rejuvenated sperm juices all over the emergency ward's ceiling, Captain Wilhelm Stern sighed and grinned, exposing his pearly white teeth, and then before any pertinent conversation could ensue, the relaxed pervert drifted off in ecstasy into what constituted a very deep (almost unconscious) slumber.

Upon awakening from his lengthy snoring episode twenty-four hours later, Wilhelm revealed to the still-spellbound doctors and coroners that while lying in the grave (which had been filled with porous soil) he had heard the sounds of human conversation and human activity happening above and outside his creepy and gloomy morbid dark environment. 'That's when I finally realized that I had been fuckin' buried alive by you dumb-ass cock-sucking assholes!" Wilhelm yelled at his doctors, coroners and nurses. "How the hell would you jerk-offs and dick-lickers feel if you were buried alive and didn't even fuckin' know about it? I fuckin' hope that all of your hemorrhoids, testicles and tits explode right the fuck off your goddamned bodies!"

Still another significant incident involving the use of a galvanic battery occurred in 1831 at a reputable hospital in Richmond, Virginia, and the sensational saga has stirred much warranted excitement among the general public ever since it had been first reported in several East Coast newspapers. The patient, a young and vibrant prosecuting attorney named Mr. Steven Stapleton was under medical observation for chronic alternating burping and farting spells but then the ambitious barrister suddenly and shockingly expired in his hospital bed. However, the lawyer's scandal-fearful family forbade doctors from performing any standard autopsy to determine the exact cause of death.

Ignoring the family's firm insistence, several audacious doctors at the Richmond hospital took it upon themselves to experiment on their own by attaching the aforementioned galvanic electrode pods to Stapleton's penis and to the inside of his now non-farting rectum, but nothing consequential happened except a delayed reactionary five-minute passing of intestinal gas. Soon after the stench-causing

15

scientific demonstration, the deceased, at the family's convenience, was buried in a nearby Virginia cemetery.

One of the mentally disheveled doctors had remembered that he had left an electrode inserted up Mr. Stapleton's rectum so the idiotic physician traveled with a horse-drawn wagon at midnight to the burial grounds and stealthily dug-up the corpse and then secretly brought the already tampered-with cadaver back to the Richmond hospital laboratory.

After removing the electrode pod from Mr. Stapleton's asshole, the crazed experimenter made a long wide incision inside the body's lower stomach, which a University of Virginia medical journal later aptly described as "an abominable abdominal shank cut." Before proceeding with additional dissecting, the maverick doctor elected to attach one galvanic electrode to Stapleton's shriveled-up testicle sac and the second pod to the corpse's limp penis. The generated volts' current instantaneously made the cadaver open its eyes and upon Stapleton achieving a sizeable erection and subsequently expelling a jet of semen into the delighted physician's face, the recovered patient smiled and then snoozed off into subconscious wonderland as if nothing extraordinary had ever transpired.

The next morning Mr. Steven Stapleton awoke, stretched his arms over his head and boisterously screamed, "I'm alive! I'm fuckin' alive! I've escaped the ravages of voracious underground worms and hungry insects consuming my decaying flesh! It's a good thing I'm a licensed lawyer because now I plan to sue the assholes off of my fucked-up family members for irresponsibly burying me alive and also I'll take litigious action against the fucked-up perverted doctors and coroners who had sexually abused me while I was under the jerk-offs' trusted fucked-up care!"

But now, enough of me' remotely analyzing what unmitigated horrors that have happened to other *individuals*. In the interest of brevity, I myself have throughout my adult life demonstrated overt symptoms of the death condition labeled by medical authorities as "catalepsy," a severe decline in lethargy that virtually duplicates and mimics the onslaught on Death.

* * * * * * * * * * * *

Knowing that catalepsy might make an undesired incursion into my life, I entered into a series of elaborate precautions should I happen to die in a foreign place and the asshole officials in charge should delay in shipping my body back to Baltimore where I would

16

be inadvertently buried alive by some local assholes that don't know their dicks from their scrotums.

First of all, at a considerable expense, I had the family vault remodeled so that my coffin enclosure could be readily opened from within. A handle to my left that extended far into the tomb would cause the iron portals to pry open and a second lever to my right would turn the latches that sealed my casket shut.

Secondly, I also made allowances for the free admission of air into my confined box with a shaft (similar to a small smokestack) penetrating through the coffin's lid allowing some sunlight to also filter down to my horizontal body's eyes. A small receptacle to hold some food was also scrupulously installed in case I required nutrition to eventually have the necessary strength to be able to readjust the two opposite release handles.

And finally, as an intelligently added measure, a large bell attached to a pull-rope had been ingeniously designed and fashioned that would be cemented and mounted on top of the mausoleum to alert any passerby of my agonizing dilemma should all of the preceding (already described) mechanisms or methodologies fail. Suffice it to say, I was prepared to enact any and all possible contingencies.

* * * * * * * * * * * *

A month later I had a unique opportunity to travel with several friends on an adventurous gunning expedition along the eastern banks of the James River. But soon night quickly descended and all was dark save for the shining of a lustrous full harvest moon. A storm was approaching from the south so the three of us sought shelter inside an old abandoned sloop that had been anchored and docked near the riverbank.

We drew straws to determine our sleeping arrangements and the bunk I had been assigned to occupy was only eighteen inches wide, and now as I reflect back on the situation, in retrospect, I believe that it was the severity of the thunder and lightning along with the similarity of my newly deployed confined area of rest to the area inside a standard-sized coffin that caused my spirit and mind to promptly enter into a panic-attack. My two jovial companions were bunking in the other crew quarters located twenty foot down the boat's narrow passageway.

Gradually I became cognizant of a low ringing in my ears as I remained lying horizontal upon the thin mattress. And you think that *you* know what horror is? The persistent irritating noise was soon joined by a prickly tingly sensation very evident throughout my extremities. As I began quivering intensely, I knew quite well that I was entering (or should I say *descending*) into an advanced state of catalepsy, a deleterious disease far worse than (and much more reprehensible than) any overpowering epilepsy.

'Oh my God!' I remember thinking before my mind began to cease functioning. 'I haven't yet told my two friends of my family's modified vault and of my special coffin configurations. If I'm dying, then let me die!' I prayed to Heaven. 'But if I'm having a catalepsy seizure, then please make it an abbreviated one so that I may survive and not be subjected to a horrifying premature burial,' I fearfully wished and prayed.

I recall trying to shriek but my tongue was parched and it was basically immobile inside my mouth. My lungs craved their next breath as I gasped one final time. I knew that my hands and my legs were incapable of movement. Then my eyelids slowly became unbearably heavy and I soon lost all of my sensibilities. Quiet nothingness had stealthily enveloped my being.

The next thing I knew, I had a distinct awareness of my brain's mental awakening. I writhed about for a few seconds and then threw my hands up into the air, my knuckles making contact with hard wood six inches above my face and then hitting firm wood to my right hand side. Immediately I hypothesized that I had been laid to rest in eternal peace inside a solid wooden coffin.

But then I considered that my custom-made "box" would have been insulated (as my will and personal instructions had indicated) with padding as specifically stipulated in my will and *that* rather encouraging optimistic thought afforded me the mental luxury of flirting with Hope. 'I'm not in any damned burial vault or coffin!' I ecstatically evaluated. 'But the smell of fresh earth makes me wonder right here and now in this dark empty stillness whether or not I'm permanently reposing underground in some obscure cemetery plot!'

"Help! Help!" I managed to hysterically scream. "Someone please hear me! My body's paralyzed and I can't move or rise! I'll die from delirium if no one helps me!"

"Hello, hello there!" came a familiar gruff voice. "Don't get your goddamned bowels twisted!"

"What's the matter Edgar?" my second friend's voice demanded as he lit a candle and partially illuminated my environment. "What the fuck's wrong with you Poe? Is this some sort of neurotic phobia

18

originating from your early childhood? I always thought Edgar that you were a rational man and not afraid of thunder, lightning and the dark in any way, shape or form."

My heart, mind and soul were all-together relieved to learn that I had been experiencing a traumatic nightmare in the sloop's bunk-bed with my brain finally registering (after again becoming synchronized with reality) that the overhead wooden-framed bunk was a mere six-inches beyond my nose and that the sturdy wall was a meager six inches from my right hand's grasp.

"The storm has subsided Edgar," my first friend consoled. "Buck up man! There's nothing left that should cause you to have a nightmare. The worst is over!"

"That's right," my second companion confirmed. "You frightened the shit out of me Edgar! You were fuckin' acting like you had been scared to death!"

"Let's get back to civilization as soon as possible," I urgently suggested. "I know a terrific whorehouse in the center of Richmond where some versatile horny kinky bitches can make the three of us be glad that we're still fuckin' alive and wanting to screw every female in sight on this evil and insidious Earth!"

"Metzengerstein"

Several hundred years ago in the primitive interior of what is now geographically Hungary there were many expansive territories that ruthless reigning dukes governed. Still other smaller "estates" were owned and managed by less barbaric noblemen such as barons and counts. But a popular superstition of that backward mountainous land was the strange belief among the uneducated peasants in Metempsychosis, or the silly notion of the transmigration of souls, not only moving from human to human but also possibly from human to animal or from beast to human. So much for advanced academic inquiry among such a totally fucked-up population of morons and ninnies.

Two proud families with century-old traditions were still feuding (ever since feudalism) with each other, namely the Metzengersteins and the Berlifitzings. The two opposing houses' always tried outdoing one other in pageantry, in wealth and in various horsemanship competitions, that is, when their members weren't actively killing each other.

But an old senile fucked-up poverty-stricken prophet once idiotically proclaimed during medieval times, "A lofty name shall have a terrific fall as the rider over his horse, the *mortality* of Metzengerstein shall triumph over the *immortality* of Berlifitzing," whatever the hell *that* gibberish-type embellished phraseology meant. And in terms of simplicity and practicality, whatever the frig' ever happened to common one-syllable last names like Smith and Jones? Among the medieval wealthy landowners in Hungary, four syllable names were the norm and not the exception.

The estates of the two rival families paralleled each other along a narrow heavily forested border that was not graphically demarcated by any particular river, creek, lake or mountain range. And the buttresses, ramparts and turrets of the Metzengerstein castle had been constructed on a high ridge and the resplendent edifice was the equal to the buttresses, ramparts and turrets of the Berlifitzing castle situated on an equally high ridge approximately a mile west.

But over the centuries the fiercely combative Metzengersteins' became much more affluent and prosperous and certainly more politically influential than the declining Berlifitzings, but still the warring clans bickered, argued and quarreled at every available opportunity. And the evolution of the intense antagonistic relationship between the two hostile families seemed to verify the

21

oddball prediction of the daft old-aged prognosticator, who incidentally had died choking on a rotten artichoke.

Elderly Count Wilhelm Von Berlifitzing was an infirmed and doting asshole who' still possessed great antipathy for his principal adversary, the young and handsome power-hungry Hungarian, Baron Frederick Metzengerstein. The mentally feeble Wilhelm had retained a great passion for horses and for hunting and the inane insane old fart especially loved the thrill of the fox chase, mostly because the thrill of chasing foxy harlots and foxy whores no longer could activate any semblance of an erection in the geezer's tight silk pants. Hence, hunting and chasing foxes became more romantic to decrepit Wilhelm than hunting and chasing foxy women.

Baron Frederick Metzengerstein was in his eighteenth year of life and his pampering mother had for a decade considered the audacious brat, who never learned how to read or write, to be very precocious and sophisticated for his age. The adolescent's father had died when Frederick was sixteen, the old man becoming the victim of a horse injury sustained during an atrocious fall from the saddle. And the fortunate only son had not only inherited fantastic wealth but also the ornate "Palace Metzengerstein," plus Frederick gained possession of a regal estate that extended for fifty miles north to south and twenty-three miles east to west.

Despite his great wealth, the manner-less Frederick possessed a nasty temper and he often flogged, intimidated and whipped any vassal under his reign that demonstrated any semblance of independent behavior or exhibited any sign of insubordination. Such "rebellion" on the part of underlings often brought out the tyrannical aspect of Baron Frederick's volatile and cruel disposition. The young ruthless dictator was basically "out-of-control," completely lacking the "cultured discipline" that ordinarily was characteristic of a true gallant nobleman.

One hot summer evening the stables of the Castle Berlifitzings had caught on fire and the macho village people and the country peasants and serfs all attributed the origin of the conflagration to the diabolical Baron Frederick Metzengerstein. While the roaring blaze was in progress and raging on his neighbor's property, the vernal/callow/shallow despot was in a trance-like meditation sitting inside an upper apartment of his magnificent castle.

The strong breeze from an open window made an old tapestry flap against the room's solid stone' wall. The concentration of the egotistical young Baron was suddenly broken as his gaze moved around the room and then briefly studied colorful portraits of rich-ermine-clad priests, pontifical dignitaries and royal European relatives. And to the mentally ill Baron's right were paintings of his glorious fighting ancestors, the muscular mustached Metzengersteins of yesteryear, all impressive-looking cavaliers dressed in knight battle armor with their helmet visors raised to expose their triumphant-looking faces.

But as the commotion and tumult from the blazing stable fire was reaching a culmination, suddenly Baron Frederick glanced up at the familiar ancient faded tapestry still flapping against the stone' wall. The jet-black stallion that, according to local legend, had been ridden by a Saracen ancestor of the Baron's beleaguered neighbor, Count Wilhelm Berlifitzing, old fart extraordinaire, dominated the tapestry's forefront. The awesome-looking horse was represented in the image's bright foreground but in the shadowy background, the steed's discomfited Saracen rider was depicted being mortally wounded and slowly perishing from injuries inflicted by a lethal Metzengerstein dagger.

Viewing that notorious death of a fearsome Berlifitzing, Frederick's countenance immediately expressed a fiendish smirk, but upon refocusing his attention on the ominous tapestry, the black horse seemed to have changed the position of its head from initially being crestfallen and obedient to now being perpendicularly strong and arrogant. The change in the beast's position and the alteration in demeanor momentarily stunned the too-big-for-his-britches teenage son-of-a-bitch.

And then another alteration in the black horse depicted in the faded wall tapestry soon captured the young Baron's attention. The animal was no longer peering compassionately at its dying owner but now it was staring and glaring with exposed clenched teeth directly at the alarmed young Baron.

Feeling terrorized and distraught, the haughty nobleman tottered out of the upstairs' apartment and awkwardly staggered down the long drafty corridor, the flames from the opposing estate's inferno being visible from three separate windows and its intense glare lighting up the entire western night sky. But then Baron Frederick gathered his confidence and exited the Palace Metzengerstein when he heard screaming and chaos emanating from his own courtyard.

Three of the Baron's equerries were attempting to restrain the convulsive plunges and kicks of a huge jet-black stallion, a real-life three-dimensional facsimile to the incredible horse portrayed in the upstairs' apartment's faded wall tapestry.

23

"Whose horse is that?" the Baron yelled to his chief stable vassal with an element of trepidation evident in his tone of voice. "Answer me or else your ass will be thrashed! Answer me disrespectfully and you'll have no fuckin' ass at all!"

"We caught this diabolical beast fleeing the great blaze over at the Berlifitzing barns," the mentally unstable stable vassal answered. "We led the creature back to the old Count's outbuildings but the grooms over there' claim that the black brute doesn't belong to anyone at that estate. How do you explain all of this Master?"

"Who the fuck do I look like, some shit-head Biblical prophet!" Frederick nastily chastised his underling. "Ask me an intelligent question if you value your gonads!"

"The letters W.V.B. have been branded on this stallion's forehead," the second stable vassal testified. "Those three letters could only mean the accursed name of Wilhelm Von Berlifitzing, but all of *our* counterparts over at the burning stables deny any affiliation with or ownership of this formidable black steed."

"He is a remarkable horse with the studding capacity of an Italian stallion, ha, ha, ha!" the egotistical high-and-mighty asshole yelled and laughed. "Yes indeed, the animal is a marvelous hybrid, a very prodigious marvelous hybrid! And his rowdy character is analogous to mine, wouldn't you three penniless jerk-offs agree? Ha, ha, ha! And let it be known to you ignorant dick-lickers that only the incomparable Frederick of Metzengerstein is qualified and capable of taming and riding this feisty hellion! Ha, ha, ha! Some day I'm going to rule all of Hungary with an iron fist, ha, ha, ha!"

And at that precise moment an excited servant dashed down the castle steps and sprinted over to Frederick and anxiously whispered some paranoia into his ear. "Sire, the fierce black horse is missing altogether from the upstairs' apartment's faded tapestry! It's vanished! Completely disappeared!"

"Who gives a shit?" Frederick hollered as he viciously slapped the loyal valet across the face. "Be gone from my midst before I have you executed, yes hung in my courtyard for all to see. Better yet," the maniacal Baron continued his harangue, "I'll send my ferocious hounds after your ass in what I'll call the first human fox hunt! Ha, ha, ha! Isn't that a gas!" the obnoxious Baron yelled to the three dumbfounded stable boys as he loudly farted, blowing a hole in the back of his pants the size of a pregnant grapefruit.

And then the psychopath again addressed his totally humiliated palace servant. "I command you under penalty of death that you immediately lock-up the upstairs' apartment!" Frederick exclaimed

24

to the castle servant. "Do it right away if you value your testicles still being attached to your abdomen. You' craven asshole, you won't be the first Castrati choirboy that I've created with one swift swipe of my sword! Ha, ha, ha! I have to fart again! Get wind of what I'm saying! Ha, ha, ha!"

After the terrified valet hurried back into the castle to fulfill his demented superior's imperative edict, Frederick again turned his attention to his trio of intimidated stable vassals. "Now you three worthless shit-heads," the Baron of Metzengerstein addressed his almost petrified and paralyzed chattels, "get this jet-black stallion into my stables immediately. I wish to begin my taming of this undisciplined creature tomorrow morning!"

* * * * * * * * * * * *

The great fire at the Berlifitzing stables had finally been extinguished the following morning and then a full month passed by, yet the obdurate Baron Frederick Metzengerstein never returned the wondrous black steed to his hated rival, but instead spent his entire energy taming and riding the jet-black horse. No one on the estate dared ask or challenge the nobleman about his clandestine enterprise, pretending that the young jerk's self-imposed isolation was a welcomed novelty.

But as months passed, the black horse became Frederick's most cherished companion and the royal asshole soon decided to loathe and reject his own fellow humans in deference to emotionally bonding with his treasured new friend. Numerous invitations would attempt coaxing Frederick to co-mingle with other aristocrats (other than the detested Berlifitzings) throughout that remote sector of Hungary but on every occasion Metzengerstein refused to interact, preferring the company of his adopted black steed.

One fine day an emissary from the king showed-up at the resplendent castle', formally confronted Frederick while the nutcase was grooming the fearsome black horse and then requested, "Will the Baron have the pleasure of showing-up at His Majesty's annual carnival festival?"

"Get the fuck out of here before I cut your nuts off and you can tell your goddamned fuck-head king to shove his goddamned annual carnival festival up his fuckin' ass and if any goddamned room is left, the lousy bastard could fuckin' shove his cock-sucking queen up there where the sun doesn't shine too!"

On another occasion an emissary from another baron arrived at the castle with the intent of inviting Frederick to a boar hunt and accidentally accosted the royal asshole walking *his* new four-legged friend across the cobblestone courtyard. The all-too-courteous visitor jokingly requested, "Will you Baron Frederick honor us with your presence at my master's upcoming boar hunt? After it is over you and he can drink some fine ale and pig-out!"

"Go home and pork your goddamned old lady and your goddamned mother and your goddamned sister too!" the lunatic Baron insultingly yelled back. "In fact Jerk-off, I'd respect you more if you grew tusks and snorted out of your asshole, you shit-eating swine you, you disgusting old fart hog!"

Subsequent invitations became less cordial, and later on, few and far in between. A full year had now elapsed and Frederick became completely incommunicado in regard to any of his royal peers, for the now laconic Metzengerstein totally distained and shunned the company of his underlings, of his equals and of his superiors alike. 'I prefer the society of my stellar horse and that's the fuckin' long and the fuckin' short of it. I wish I owned a goddamned belligerent donkey so that everybody in Hungary from the king on down could kiss my hairy ass and then have their teeth kicked out!'

Some of the more charitable area gossipers attributed the Baron's recalcitrance to the untimely loss of his parents, thus politely overlooking Frederick's reckless and callous deportment. Even the usually intoxicated family physician, who' valued his head and also his testicles, diplomatically described the Baron's condition as "morbid melancholy" while privately thinking, 'This' stupid young scumbag punk is entirely fucked-up.'

A year to the day after the destructive Berlifitzing stables' conflagration, Metzengerstein awoke from a tempestuous nightmare and speedily descended from his bedchamber like a devil-possessed (and evil-obsessed) maniac. The arrogant impetuous jerk-off swiftly exited the castle, hurried to the stables, saddled and mounted his' unnamed black steed and soon the pair bounded away into the dark forest mazes.

* * * * * * * * * * * *

At noon the following day the dependent peasants living in and around Metzengerstein Castle were shocked to see the palace in a massive blaze with flames jutting out of the structure's windows and dense smoke billowing out from all its doors. Pandemonium reigned supreme as the frantic vassals neurotically scurried about looking for their friends and wondering where their deplored Master was and how he would react to the colossal destruction and personal loss.

All efforts to salvage any portion of the castle proved futile. The entire neighborhood population stood silently and watched in pathetic awe as the magnitude of the calamity progressed and grew. But soon a terrible-looking distraction diverted and riveted the attention of all eyewitnesses, the multitude being privy to the most appalling spectacle that their eyes ever perceived.

A steed bearing an un-bonneted rider leaped and then frantically galloped up the long wide avenue, flanked on either side by stately aged oaks. Soon the equestrian and his black animal arrived at the crumbling structure's main doors. The surreal-looking rider and steed next fiercely maneuvered around in circles, repeatedly revolving in repetitious orbits around the courtyard. The redundant clattering of hoofs was quite disconcerting to the ears and minds of the flabbergasted spectators.

But unexpected to all curious souls in attendance, a mystifying event then occurred. The horrifying black horse and its equally horrifying rider suddenly bounded up the castle's steps and sped directly through the open metal portals, mysteriously disappearing into the rampaging flames. Amazingly, the fury of the blaze soon diminished thereafter, and within several minutes the flames completely died away. Calm and tranquility had finally been re-established.

But still, after the dark smoke cleared away, a strange white illumination enveloped the remains of the Palace Metzengerstein as if the aura was a sacred shroud, giving the astounded onlookers the impression of a glare of preternatural light.

Overwhelmed by the whole incredible ordeal, the very tall chief stable vassal leaned over and said to the often-humiliated palace valet, "The old fart prophet was right when he predicted that the immortal Berlifitzings would ultimately triumph over the mortal Metzengersteins. This fucked-up place really freaks me out and gives me the fuckin' creeps. Sir, now that we're unemployed total paupers, let's go apply for jobs over at the more placid Berlifitzing castle."

"Hop-Frog"

Once upon a time in a fucked-up foreign land lived a very corpulent king who was extremely bored with the monotonous affairs of state and as a diversion from the redundant recurrent matters concerning politics, education and economics, the royal ruler (like his peers in other lands where imperial tyrants and benign emperors reigned) was enamored with the telling and sharing of jokes and also with their attendant jokesters. In fact it was widely rumored throughout the dysfunctional land that the regal nutcase lived exclusively for amusement, recreation, perverted sex, perverted sex orgies, fun and last but not least, games.

And everyone inside the palace, fearing for their mortal lives, imitated this obese overbearing king not only in their appearance, but also in their demeanor, in their behavior and in their interests. And the royal monarch's closest admirers and staunchest supporters were his short fat ministers and his elite corps of jesters, midgets, dwarfs, harlequins and troubadours.

"Fat people are always more jovial than the rest!" the fucked-up senile king was often quoted as saying. "If a particular subject of mine happens to be slender or thin, then that lower-classed dumb shit doesn't have even a *fat chance* of ever achieving modest success in anything, ha, ha, ha!" And predictably, all of the insane king's seven dumb-ass ministers enthusiastically mimicked his obnoxious laugh every time the fucked-up monarch told *that* same stupid joke, which was usually a dozen times each day before noon.

"Who needs to be an intellectual studying astronomy and chemistry and astrology and alchemy like those studious eggheads over in the royal university library when we all could act like ridiculous clowns and preposterous fools just like the legendary jokesters of *jester*year, ha, ha, ha," the fat jolly king yelled and roared, and naturally all of his seven dimwitted key advisors and counselors obediently imitated his facetious deportment out of fear of being either decapitated or brutally compressed into a midget or a dwarf inside the palace's very spacious and seldom used dungeon.

And besides the seven deranged ministers, the king owned a large contingent of motley fools that wore traditional jesters' garb consisting of distorted-in-appearance red and green awkward-looking caps with jingling bells, exaggerated-in-size curled-up shoes and each miniature clown possessed a sharp wit to constantly entertain the fickle-minded monarch and also had plenty of patience to tolerate his incessant ridiculing of them and their colleagues.

However, the zany emperor had one special "fool" that he valued more than any other because wonderful Hop-Frog was a dynamic triple-talented throne room pleaser who was indeed a midget-sized dwarf, a loveable cripple with a lame leg and he had a warm and compassionate heart. In addition, the short stocky fat fellow was a witty conversationalist and skilled juggler as well.

Hop-Frog had never been baptized or confirmed by the royal bishop so his unique name was not given to him at birth by loving parents. The versatile-but-lame dwarf received his I.D. because he was born during a leap year in another kingdom, was kidnapped by one of the fat king's martinet military generals while completing a particular invasion campaign and then thereafter given as a gift to the corpulent fucked-up monarch, who never desired to govern a kingdom in the first place but instead always wished to be a stand-up slapstick vaudeville stage comedian at the Palace.

But Hop-Frog possessed some rather amazing attributes to compensate for his shortness-in-stature and his very evident lameness. The highly motivated dwarf could easily climb any rope, tree, turret or wall because his arms, shoulders and wrists were extremely powerful, and many astounded witnesses believed his grasp to be as strong as those appendages belonging to formidable chimpanzees and gorillas. Consequently, the diminutive-but-dexterous Hop-Frog was actually much stronger than any other human residing in or around the king's extensive domain.

And Hop-Frog had a very cute girlfriend dwarf named Trippetta, who had been captured in an adjacent kingdom's main seaport by one of the fat king's admirals and then transported to the corpulent one's autocratic realm. But unlike her rascally impish boyfriend, Trippetta possessed exquisite charm and grace and always dressed rather elegantly, often better than the all-too-jealous queen herself. And the beautiful lady dwarf was often petted by the pretentious king, and thus subsequently by his mimicking counselors and as a result Trippetta always suffered excruciating headaches caused by large fat hands and fingers constantly massaging her sensitive scalp. But on the plus side of the diminutive girl's ledger, Trippetta's often-abused head was always dandruff-free.

Hop-Frog's greatest strength was organizing beauty contests, parade extravaganzas, castle spire and rampart climbing pageants, inventing novel costumes for court attendees to dress as fabled mythological monsters and finally, arranging masked balls where all that the little-dicked ministers had covered were their tiny testicles.

But now the strong-willed bossy jocular king was planning a spectacular feast and had invited royalty from near and afar to attend the gala festivities. Having confidence in his celebrated lame dwarf, the haughty king put Hop-Frog in charge of coordinating the festive evening's entertainment.

Many of the invitees planning on attending had spent several months selecting just what sort of costume he or she should wear to the highly anticipated masquerade. That is, everyone felt obligated to prepare for the major event except the oversized rotund lazy king, and so the emperor's seven oversized rotund lazy advisors also neglected to get their acts together for the occasion, their diffidence being done out of sheer impersonation of their air-headed leader.

Time flew by on the kingdom's annual calendar and the seven procrastinating wise men finally realized that they should consult the services of the inimitable Hop-Frog to help them navigate through their separate and immediate wardrobe crises.

When Hop-Frog entered the gaudy throne room, he found the derelict king emotionally depressed and in a miserable mood, and the arrogant and omnipotent ruler, knowing full-well that the lame dwarf was not fond of delicious wine because alcohol had an adverse affect on *his* behavior, the insensitive monarch insisted that the dwarf indulge and become equally intoxicated as himself. And so not desiring to insult or disobey his intolerable emperor, the loyal dwarf indulgently drank to the capricious commands and arbitrary imperatives of his fucked-up crowned superior.

"Be merry Hop-Frog, yes, be merrier than Christmas Day," the imbecile king chortled and then imbibed another mouthful of merlot. "And whatever you do, don't sulk or I'll command you to stop your goddamned *whining*, ha, ha, ha!" the vaudeville wannabe' shouted, clapping his hands and spilling his wine all over his majestic throne and imperial clothes. "I relish all jokes and fuckin' hot dogs too, ha, ha, ha! And if it's not a practical joke, I'll fuckin' settle for an impractical one, ha, ha, ha!" the idiot king ranted and raved. "This red wine will no doubt make *you* more creative and novel. Sameness absolutely bores the Hell and the Purgatory out of me. Be dynamic and inventive you ugly deformed dwarf! Come and drink some more so that your senses are dulled and conversely, your fabulous wit becomes even more accentuated, ha, ha, ha!"

It was poor Hop-Frog's birthday and he resented the stern edict for him to provide drunken levity for the amusement of a chubby royal asshole on command. And since the dwarf was alone and not in the company of his absent dwarf friends and his adorable love-mate Trippetta, Hop-Frog was so disconsolate and so dejected that huge tears rolled down his cheeks and then fell directly into the chagrined king's drinking goblet. The seven numbskull ministers in attendance instantly ceased their' excessive laughing and all gasped in unison, not knowing what to expect next.

"Drink your lousy tears mingled with my delicious wine out of the same auspicious cup!" the king ordered the sorrowed lame entertainer.

The humiliated dwarf's eyes quickly scanned the throne room and Hop-Frog immediately perceived the king and his seven mindless ministers boisterously laughing at and ridiculing him. "Yes Hop-Frog, show us your very reputable and famed imagination! Drink some more and give us some intriguing characters to ponder and oh yes, please perform some terrific pantomimes. Come, come, have you' nothing of value to suggest or discuss?" the fat king questioned. "How about a toilet paper float for the royal parade having all fifty women on board rapidly wiping their hairy assholes for all my by-standing subjects and predicates to see and applaud, ha, ha, ha! Say, what the heck's the matter with you Hop-Frog? Did you fall off your water lily in the royal pond?"

"I'm really and truly *endeavoring* to think of something novel, even though I've never before written a lengthy fictional story," Hop-Frog pathetically stated, much to the fat petulant king's annoyance. "I'm presently having serious difficulty thinking abstractly because of the effect of the potent wine on my cerebral activity. Truthfully Your Majesty," the dwarf stated, "I'm quite bewildered at this very moment and at this particular instance I don't know my ass from your grotesque-looking tiny dick!"

"Endeavoring!" belched and bellowed the intoxicated king. "You have the audacity to challenge my authority by uttering the dumb fuck word *endeavoring*? And you brazenly refer to my dick as being grotesque and tiny! I see Hop-Frog. Now I fully understand. You're acting peevishly because your creative appetite desires more wine. Here, drink the remaining liquid in my goblet before I again piss in it, ha, ha, ha!" the insane royal shit bellowed. "Don't just gaze at the metal mother-fucker that's in your warped hands! Indulge and become inebriated so that my illustrious counselors can enjoy themselves by imitating *our* stellar example. Come Hop-Frog, I insist. Partake of some more merlot!"

Hearing that her boyfriend was in jeopardy because of an evolving conflict with the nonsensical tyrannical fat king, Trippetta rushed unannounced into the throne room and her audacity immediately alarmed the seven inane insane ministers. The lewd ludicrous monarch was equally stunned by the beautiful short plump female's abrupt entrance. Then the elegantly dressed girl dropped to her knees and begged the monarch to forgive her beau.

"Get up you ungrateful miniature whore!" the drunken fat emperor raged. "Tell me Snow White, which of the seven dwarfs are you sleeping with tonight besides your little Dopey here? Ha, ha, ha!" And naturally all seven ministers laughed in concert, mimicking their boss. "Get up or else I'll have your cunt shaven and your tits punctured in front of my entire court! Rise I say!"

Trippetta slowly rose to her feet and throughout the throne room one could hear a pin, a leaf or a feather drop. King Guttola then slapped the girl in the face and tossed his goblet full of merlot onto her head and dress. The silence resulting from the monarch's violent chastisement was audibly interrupted by a low-grating protracted sound that seemed to originate from all four corners of the immense chamber. The seven reticent ministers were indeed confounded while pissing and shitting their silk pants.

"Hop-Frog, why the fuck are you making that peculiar gnawing sound? It fuckin' hurts my ears and gives me the goddamned creeps!" the livid king rankled. And his' criticisms were naturally echoed with the parroting incantations of the seven absurd fearful counselors. All the while Trippetta stood in horror, worrying about her beloved boyfriend's life and death situation.

"I couldn't have made those queer noises," the partially drunk Hop-Frog maintained and insisted. "Perhaps the noise had been produced by the royal canary fluttering its yellow wings by the throne room window."

"True, true if one prefers listening to bullshit," the ruler insulted and scolded. Being temporarily pacified, the king gulped down the remaining wine in his goblet. Then he smiled, his grin revealing a set of large repulsive-looking widely separated teeth.

Hop-Frog, somewhat recovering from his and Trippetta's severe admonishments, then felt compelled to make an appropriate announcement. "Your Magnificent Majesty, if it pleases the court, I've just remembered a certain wonderful entertainment that requires the presence of eight stouthearted participants. I ask your esteemed indulgence and permission to enact the fantastic charade."

"Well, you presumptuous microscopic Asshole, there's me and my seven ministers right here! We're perfectly capable of assisting you in your staged *endeavor*," the king observed and then guffawed. "What the fuck are you' waiting for? Come now you little pecker-head, show us your marvelous diversion, you very annoying dumb fuck!" And naturally all seven cowardly ministers (with an abundance of piss and shit in their pants) voluntarily imitated the king's drunken stupidity, just to cover and protect their own asses.

"My talented company of highly skilled performers call our rather exotic enactment the 'Eight Orangutans Going Ape'," Hop-Frog persuasively explained, gaining mock applause from the sarcastic king and his seven amused inebriated ministers. "The beauty of the game, or should I say *comedy* about to be performed is that the melodrama produces fright in the hearts of women, and in fact it generates terror in the hearts of all spectators. I wouldn't be surprised if many of your invited guests crap their pants and dresses."

"Capital idea! Capital idea happening right here in the country's capital! Ha, ha, ha!" bellowed the dizzy fucked-up king. "On with the goddamned show Hop-Frog. Come on now Fool, get your ass in gear! Ha, ha, ha!" And the seven subordinate ministers all concurred in harmonious unison, "Get your ass in gear! Get your ass in gear! Ha, ha, ha!"

"You eight wonderful participants shall all be equipped to look like orangutans and your persona will be to terrorize and astonish the masqueraders in your company by effectively utilizing your authentic-looking monkeyshine suits and your improvised gorilla behavior," Hop-Frog instructed the fucked-up king and his equally fucked-up advisors. "Your' incredible antics and gyrations will certainly scare the crap out of all your guests, especially the constipated women!"

"Oh, this is fantastically exquisite! How novel and how positively original!" the fat king marveled and emoted. "I get to act beastly, I get to act beastly! Ha, ha, ha!" he chortled to the absolute delight of his groggy court, who naturally repeated, chanted and reveled in shouting-out their zany monarch's fucked-up mantra.

"Chains will be implemented in the performance to increase the anxiety level of your royal audience," Hop-Frog informed his eight captivated and enchanted listeners. "The dramatic confusion will be so marvelous and so grand that your attendees will not know whether what they're witnessing is real, surreal or fake. It'll be the greatest event ever to take place in this kingdom's history."

34

"Oh this is stellar, oh this fabulous idea of yours is so absolutely phenomenal!" conceded and congratulated the drunken fat king. "I've always wanted to monkey around scaring the shit out of everyone whose path I crossed. Get me my costume immediately!" And naturally, the seven weak-minded ministers (with piss and shit in their silk pants) all declared and repeated the same shallow verbalizations. And next, amazingly without being prompted or suggested by their king, all seven moronic ministers began chanting all together, "Monkey see, monkey do! Monkey see, monkey do! I want to go ape! I want to go ape! Ha, ha, ha!"

Now orangutans were not-too-common in that remote sector of the known world so the already manufactured red furry costumes were guaranteed to both intrigue and startle the king's invited masquerade audience. And the eight furry costumes were so realistic in appearance that anyone wearing one would automatically instill fear and awe into any earnest eyewitness royally honored to view the astonishing spectacle.

The ornate arena in which the great masquerade was to take place was a circular indoor stadium illuminated by a massive overhead chandelier and further brightened by mammoth-sized mirrors strategically located in the ceiling and also above the circular interior wall. A thick sturdy chain suspended the opulent-looking main chandelier from a huge cupola that had been intricately constructed inside the arena's roof, and the magnificent crystal object could be raised or lowered to accommodate optimal viewing and to achieve a splendid lighting effect during any given entertainment performance. The enormous expense budget that had been required in building the arena had nearly bankrupted the unproductive nation's economy, which incidentally had been mired in a deep recession.

At the stroke of midnight, when the theater was filled to capacity with costumed revelers, the eight clumsy orangutans, all chained together, humorously rolled into the indoor auditorium to the prodigious applause of the somewhat startled audience. Many of the less sophisticated women swooned and fainted while others gently and discreetly masturbated their clit' buttons beneath their expensive jeweled gowns and satin dresses.

A general panic soon ensued with people scampering to the theater's massive doors, but the gates were locked, and assigned armed guards sent the stampeding fleers scurrying back to their seats by menacingly wielding and waving their swords, bows and arrows, limp dicks and spears.

The mentally challenged king and his seven crazy impersonators got all tangled up in their chains and soon the eight buffoons received a well-deserved standing ovation from the assembled crowd of invitees. But at the culmination of the clamorous clapping, Hop-Frog's revenge for the king's punishment of the lovely Trippetta was not to be denied.

The creative dwarf noticed that the eight fools had eventually awkwardly tumbled and rolled to the arena's center. Using his exceptionally strong arms and hands, Hop-Frog swiftly clamped several of the iron chains' links to the already lowered chandelier's extended prongs and then promptly dashed to the control mechanism that would soon hoist the mass of furry orangutans up towards the opened overhead cupola that had been artistically designed to be hollow in its center. Mass hysteria and delirium reigned supreme throughout the entire stadium as the incomparable dwarf's complex imaginative scheme continued to materialize.

All the while the king and his eight imitators regarded the activity as a well-designed farce that was bringing tremendous pleasantry and laughter to the appreciative attendees below. The predicament of the affected elevated apes (literally in suspended animation) again generated an abundance of hilarity. All in attendance (including the eight fraudulent elevated orangutans) were now holding their fat stomachs and laughing incessantly while inadvertently rearranging their duodenums along with their' small and large intestines.

Being the brilliant mastermind of the sensational spectacle, Hop-Frog, brandishing a lit torch, dashed to the partially raised chandelier, deftly clambered up the sturdy hoisting chain and then stared down at the eight furry imbeciles wrapped up below in a massive irregular-shaped ball.

"I shall soon find out exactly who these devilish imbeciles are!" the dwarf screamed to the thorough amusement of his enthralled audience. But then the ingenious instigator blew a shrill whistle, signaling to his chief assistant that the chandelier with its eight furry passengers should be quickly raised to a height of thirty feet above the arena's floor.

The enraged dwarf was soon wildly thrusting his flaming torch in and out of the entangled furry mass, pretending to be attempting to determine the true identities of the eight very encumbered orangutans. But the danger of the stunt seemed so real and so imminent that its spectacular presentation was soon recognized as being intensely frightening. In moments gasps of horror followed by a very palpable silence existed throughout the regal arena, a popular venue that ordinarily presented reputable comedy that was often disguised as fantasy tragedy.

The lengthy hush was broken by the same low grating noise that had infuriated the king in the throne room after he had reprimanded Trippetta by unjustly striking her cheek and then tossing wine onto her face and dress. But this time the source of the unnerving noise distraction was very obvious. Hop-Frog's teeth were grinding together out of anger and vengeance and his mouth was foaming like that of a rabid dog as he gnashed his jaws harder to express his maniacal rage at Trippetta's callous persecutors.

"Ah ha, now I begin to see who these impostor jesters clad in ape attire really are!" the formerly powerless Hop-Frog triumphantly yelled to the stunned spectators.

Pretending to be again inspecting and examining his captured apes, the incensed dwarf repeatedly thrust his flambeau into the incarcerated mass suspended below him, and to the horror of all witnesses, the reddish hairy costumes of the king and his seven incompetent chained ministers caught on fire and began burning fiercely in what constituted a small inferno. The blaze was soon raging intensely and the seated multitude of horror-stricken aristocratic gazers was completely powerless in either rendering assistance or in initiating a rescue.

The excessive heat from the roaring flames caused Hop-Frog to climb higher up the suspended chandelier chain to avoid suffering first-degree burns to his own ass and skin. After ascending to a safer height, the incomparable on-a-mission dwarf again addressed the exasperated masqueraders who were now standing in front of their seats. Meanwhile at *that* phase of the awesome debacle, eight corpses hung in a hideous and indistinguishable smoking mass of fuming burning flesh.

"Here sizzling before your very eyes is your great fat asshole king and his not-so-great seven fat shit-head ministers, for as you can readily determine," Hop-Frog bravely declared in a strong and proud voice, "and as you can plainly observe, the expendable fools were all very combustible! For you see," the dwarf eloquently expounded, "I've tolerated their fucked-up invectives for way too long and so my friends, I've decided to *fire* them all! Yes, little old unimportant me' has caused all this wonderful chaos! And much to my day's disappointment, you've all been witnesses to my last and greatest jest! It's now time for me to venture out on my own as a renegade from justice and therefore courageously begin a new life!"

Upon shouting those proud victorious words proclaiming his individual liberty, the opportunistic cripple hurled his torch into the charred stinking stench mass still hanging below, adroitly clambered up to the ceiling and easily exited the arena through the opening in the cupola, thus disappearing from sight.

Trippetta, stationed strategically on the roof of the indoor theater, was Hop-Frog's ready, willing and able accomplice. Apparently both fugitives from the kingdom's austere justice system had safely escaped their slavery, since neither dwarf has ever again been seen in the strange country that had so egregiously exploited them.

.

"Diddling"

Many amateur pundits have a distorted and erroneous stereotype of Edgar Allan Poe as the literary genius being an extremely disillusioned maniacal self-destructive masochist whose sole preoccupation day in and day out was exploring and ultimately achieving death. Descriptive adjectives such as "morose," "macabre," "morbid" and "moribund" often describe Poe and his transcendent esoteric works but in reality, the celebrated short story author actually did possess and exhibit a decent sense of humor and a once-in-a-while jovial personality, which is both evident and exemplified in the writer's classic manuscripts, "Dr. Tarr and Professor Fether" along with the very curious work "Diddling."

* * * * * * * * * * * *

Diddling: an abstract-oriented verb usually pertaining to either the act of dawdling or the act of loitering in public. *That* specific identification of *diddling* is in terms of the standard dictionary vernacular definition. The word *"Diddling"* was not invented by Mr. Beauregard "Beau" Diddling as many' contemporary pseudo-intellectuals falsely profess. But a new-age usage of the present participle/gerund *"Diddling"* has radically departed from the traditional *verb* vernacular with the avant-garde slang having more to do with the words *conning, scamming, ripping-off* and *tricking* than with historical meanings like "just idly hanging out" or "just hanging around." Needless to say, *diddling* represents some relatively heavy bullshit and in order for the amateur lexicographer to master the very difficult advanced concept, the accomplishment requires great academic scrutiny to be fully achieved.

Now in ancient times, the Greek philosopher Plato (who often had too much on his plate) had been confronted (by several sophists) with the old "picked chicken problem." Plato defined a picked chicken as a "biped without feathers," but then some asshole skeptics in his midst found fault with the great thinker's description by claiming that man is also a "biped without feathers." Those asshole cynics, by virtue of their criticism of dearly beloved Plato, had (without their knowledge) established that civilized man loves to *diddle*: that is, everyone has entirely too much freakin' time on his or her hands and while idly dawdling and loitering around, some imbecile always invents some outlandish example or some outrageous dictionary rule that makes even the smartest philosopher look and feel like an incompetent asshole. What Plato didn't realize was that no animal (including the chicken) *diddles* except man. In other words, it takes intelligence, guile and cunning for a conniver to *diddle*, so *that* vital prerequisite automatically eliminates dogs, cats, alligators, bears, parakeets and the like.

Diddling can easily be broken-down into its chief components, better know as "characteristics." The ingredients that constitute the essence of *diddling* are: minuteness, interest, perseverance, audacity, nonchalance, originality, impertinence and finally grinning, which instantaneously communicates to the skilled *diddler* great self-satisfaction derived from really effectively and shrewdly scamming some unsuspecting and unassuming asshole right up the old yazoo.

Now here are some brief paragraphs about the various elements that constitute well-implemented *diddling.*

Minuteness: The most successful *diddlers* are minute and do neat and cute stupid-ass things to trick others. He or she usually operates a small retail business dealing mostly in cash, although many hoodwinked customers give the *diddler* credit after he or she has decisively enacted his or her con. *Diddlers* never want to evolve into big-time operators because then they would have to make the radical ascension/transition from being a minute entrepreneur to being an important executive or financier. But as the eminent Beauregard "Beau" *Diddling* once feasibly professed, "It is much better to be a *diddler* in Lilliput than being a doomed *diddler* in Brobdignag because the diminutive Lilliputians would need an army of at least ten thousand soldiers to capture, incarcerate and execute one six-foot-tall itinerant American *diddler* visiting *that* totally fucked-up isolated island of miniature assholes."

Interest: A highly skilled *diddler* feigns showing genuine interest in his customer or target and he or she is mostly concerned about his' or her' own well being and survival. He or she scorns the principle of *diddling* as existing only for the sake of *diddling* but instead sees *diddling* as a viable means of ripping-off someone and then feeling "really fuckin' good" about doing it. The best cream-of-the-crop *diddlers* always take care of Number 1 and they religiously insist that Number 2 belongs floating in the goddamned toilet bowl because the sophisticated *diddler's* sacred mantra essentially is, "Shit generally floats and I don't!"

Perseverance: The ideal *diddler* is never discouraged by rejection and can endure a thousand failures without ever complaining or bitching once. And remarkably, the most highly acclaimed *diddlers* actually enjoy horrible things like bankruptcy and destitution, especially when those catastrophic consequences happen to others and are directly caused by the *diddler*.

Ingenuity: A good *diddler* understands how to effectively plot against others of his or her species and he or she is an expert at circumventing legal prosecution, in addition to being versatile at inventing and innovating new ways of ripping people off. One particularly prosperous retail merchant *diddler* used to confuse customers by saying, "Hey *diddle, diddle,* the cat and the fiddle, the cow jumped over the moon!" while pulling-off a creative flimflam or possibly wickedly cheating the gullible buyer by implementing some imaginative-but-detrimental bait-and-switch tactic.

Audacity: A top-of-the-line *diddler* is both bold and brazen and never fears the notion of getting caught, thinking that he or she can talk his or her way out of any emergency fuck-up. King Louis the XVI had to be an atrocious *diddler* because the dumb shit' monarch (*head* of state) was decapitated by incensed French revolutionaries experimenting with a sharp-bladed guillotine. It is one thing to lose your head over a goddamned piece of ass and it is another totally asinine thing to lose your friggin' head over being a poorly trained amateur *diddler* trying to rip-off the naïve public, especially a pissed-off public that had recently gotten wise to your poorly executed attempt at *diddling*.

And yet still another incompetent *diddler* wannabe' who got caught exploiting the victimized French citizenry was Louis XVI's slut paramour Marie Antoinette who instead of proclaiming "Let them eat cake!" had (as an alternative remark) intelligently yelled out with passionate conviction from the palace balcony, "Let the men all eat cunt and the ladies all suck dick!" then quite logically, the stupid royal ostentatious bitch's life would have never been in jeopardy.

Nonchalance: The most highly regarded *diddlers* in the United States are never anxious or nervous when diligently engaged in cleverly scamming someone. He or she is calm and collected throughout the entire ruse and is as they say, "As easy as an old glove." The oblivious dupe being scammed still thinks that the deft *diddler* is a "nice guy" or a "suave lady" even after the dumb-shit victim has been robbed, conned or deviously tricked.

Originality: The most revered and esteemed *diddler* stands head and shoulders over other more inferior *diddlers* principally because he or she is definitely the *diddler* that is the most original plotter and deceiver in the entire vicinity. He or she refuses to imitate any other damned *diddler* but instead takes tremendous pride in practicing superior *diddling* independently. He or she only believes in one special notion, the age-old aphorism, "Imitation is the sincerest form of flattery!" but only when he or she is being mimicked, impersonated, emulated or imitated by other less adroit and novice-type *diddlers*.

Impertinence: The most inconspicuous and most trusted on-the-prowl *diddlers* are those that have swagger and are animated in their methods, essentially, those audacious individuals who will sneer or sneeze in your face both before and after pilfering your money, before and after kicking your poodle, before and after kissing your girlfriend or boyfriend or before and after violently screwing your wife or husband.

Grin: The truly inspired *diddler* is always grinning, but mostly to himself' or to herself in the mirror while dreaming up how he or she is going to diabolically deceive the next prospective "mark." He or she (the self-infatuated egocentric *diddler*) is completely enamored with himself or herself. A really good professional *diddler* would prefer ripping someone off and egregiously fooling *that* intended vulnerable person in some sinister capacity rather than enjoying masturbating or rather than having supremely excellent unending sex with a beautiful member of the opposite gender.

* * * * * * * * * * * *

The first *diddler* in antiquity was probably the raunchy Biblical bitch known as Eve, who out of sheer curiosity and pure ingenuity, mercilessly tricked Adam into eating a rotten apple from the accursed Tree of Knowledge, thus, when the core got stuck in the poor guy's throat, the first living man quickly discovered that he had acquired an Adam's Apple. And so, the idea of "evil Eve" never dawned on Adam, and as a result, the fabled Tree of Knowledge ironically was "the genesis" of all human ignorance along with all human misery.

But to further illustrate the complicated functioning of *diddling* in everyday American society, here are some concrete examples of the rather dynamic process as it' is presently exercised by some very adept *diddlers.*

A housewife in need of a new comfortable fully upholstered red sofa goes out to her town's main street and visits a highly reputable cabinet and furniture warehouse. A polite salesman offers her a sturdy new couch that is priced twenty percent lower than what the frugal bitch had originally expected to pay. But then when no one else is in the shop, the beautiful promiscuous woman rips open her dress and invites the bug-eyed salesman to rub her pussy, and after he eagerly obliges, she asks him to give her another quote on the red sofa just as he's joyfully preoccupied getting his middle finger wet. "Sixty percent off!" says the salesman as he reaches a volcanic climax and soon creams his pants.

The week passes and no sofa has been delivered to the woman's residence. The concerned lady dispatches her obedient wimpy husband to the warehouse to discuss the matter with the experienced *diddler* salesman, who confidently and nonchalantly claims that no contract with the man's wife had ever been signed and that the almost negotiated price was now "null and void" because the good husband's presumptuous spouse had carelessly violated the standard "grace period of oral agreement without signing a written covenant.". Hence, the savvy furniture salesman was a much more proficient *diddler* than the horny greedy housewife was.

And then of course there is the proverbial "reverse *diddle*" where the wily *diddling* customer craftily victimizes the unwary shopkeeper. A well dressed individual steps into an ordinary shoe store and suavely makes a purchase but then in a calm mellow voice claims that he had left his wallet in his other pair of black pants. "My dear Sir," says the foxy *diddler*, "I've left my wallet in my other black pants. But unfortunately, the shoes cost forty-six dollars and the least denomination I have in my wallet is a fifty-dollar bill. Please send your ambitious delivery boy to the address I've scribbled on this piece of paper with the four dollars change along with the package of shoes."

"Very well Sir," the stupid-assed shoe store man answers, happy of course to be making a sale. "I'll send my delivery boy Arnold out as soon as he arrives at the shoe store from his afternoon school dismissal."

The swindling *diddler* purchaser of the handsome leather shoes intercepts the delivery boy, who is en route to the fraudulent address that had been legibly scribbled on the phony note. "Ah Young Arnold, I see that you have my package of shoes!" the *diddler* says to the not-too-astute lad. "Go to my home on the address provided on the note and my dear wife Mrs. Trotter will giver you the fifty dollars for the shoes. Now Arnold, I have an important meeting to attend so I need the new shoes and the four dollars change to tip the pretty waitress at the restaurant where the affair is taking place. So give me *my* shoes and the four dollars change," the proficient *diddler* politely demands, "and then proceed directly to my house and my wife Mrs. Trotter (non-existent, of course) will give you the fifty dollars and a handsome five dollar tip to boot." And that's the classic model of a "veteran stranger-in-town *diddler*" taking full advantage of a wet-behind-the-ears' post-pubescent dumb-ass errand boy by coyly demonstrating an admirably firm, austere, educated and uncompromising attitude.

Here is another nifty *diddle* that's one of my personal favorites. A religious camp meeting' is scheduled to be held in the woods outside a distant town and the rustic site is only accessible by means of a wooden bridge. An enterprising *diddler* (with brass balls) stations himself upon the bridge and respectfully informs the traveling arrivals from afar that a new county law specifies that a toll of one dollar for foot passengers and two dollars per horse drawn carriage and three dollars for four-passenger coaches had been recently passed by the freeholders' board and that he had been hired by the all-powerful county commissioners to collect the tolls or be obligated by law to report all alleged violators to the very dedicated town constable. At least three hundred pissed-off people grumble and bitch about the surprise demand but all soon fear the penalty of legal fines being levied and as a result, the compliant shit-heads voluntarily contribute to the cocky *diddler's* request. And so, the very scrupulous *diddler* is five hundred or so dollars richer for simply slickly impersonating a non-existent toll collector.

Another certain efficacious *diddle* goes like this. A well-talented Southern *diddler* trains his mongrel dog to jump-up and snatch a blank piece of paper that has been dipped in soup. This routine exercise is practiced every day for two consecutive weeks. A rich citizen of the town has lent the crackerjack *diddler* ten thousand dollars and the due date for the outstanding loan has finally arrived. The grim-faced creditor shows-up at the *diddler's* door and politely demands his money back plus accumulated interest. The master *diddler* removes his checkbook and meticulously writes out a draft for the owed sum plus amassed interest and on cue his hungry dog suddenly leaps up and bites and swallows the signed check.

"Sorry Mr. Reynolds, but that was my last check in the book that my dog just consumed," the artful *diddler* solemnly apologizes. "I hate to inconvenience you but I'm expecting new ones to arrive in the mail next Monday."

"Okay, I'll return late Monday afternoon to reclaim your debt to me plus the added two-day interest," the somewhat disappointed creditor replied. "But I strongly suggest that you oughta' feed that damned canine of yours more often."

The lender leaves a little frustrated but the very mentally swift *diddler* moves to another town early Sunday evening.

Another fabulous *diddle* that's especially popular in northern Pennsylvania materializes in this manner. A lady of good breeding is verbally insulted and abused in the street by a detestable crude stranger, the lowlife male being a subordinate accomplice to the principal *diddler*. The chief *diddler* comes like a knight in shining armor to the besieged woman's rescue and pretends to be administering a major thrashing to the foul-mouthed assailant jerk-off. The dignified and refined woman is quite grateful for the gallant intercession so she takes the principal *diddler* to her expensive home, performs fellatio on him, gives him access to her furry love tunnel, gives him a hundred dollar reward and then sincerely thanks him again for his indispensable aid in a time of need.

Now the sexually relieved and happy *diddler* and his trusty accomplice have enough excess money in their possession to amble over to the local bordello and get laid and blown before going to the next town on the evening train to pull the same time-proven *diddle* all over again.

A not so common diddle occurs in taverns, mostly middle-class establishments up and down the Eastern Seaboard. The haughty *diddler* enters the targeted bar and orders several packs of chewing tobacco. After the bartender hands them to him, the on-a-mission *diddler* loudly complains, "This goddamned chewing tobacco is a brand that my taste buds are extremely allergic to. Take the shitty things back and kindly give me a double of scotch whiskey to gulp down instead."

After swallowing down the double jigger of scotch, the scheming *diddler* rapidly gets off his bar stool and heads toward the tavern door. The bartender becomes alarmed at the impertinent *diddler's* rash deportment.

"Sir, I believe that you haven't yet paid for your double shot of scotch!" the bartender squawks. "You owe me eight dollars for the choice expensive whiskey!"

"What the fuck are you talking about?" the *diddler* vehemently yells back. "You fucked-up scoundrel! What's wrong with your goddamned memory? I just handed you two packs of chewing tobacco valued at ten dollars in exchange for the scotch. If anything Asshole, you still owe me two bucks!"

45

"But Sir, you never paid me for the chewing tobacco in the first place!" the unnerved bartender insists in a rather confused and perplexed state of mind.

"No buts about it!" the incensed *diddler* angrily shouts back. "You oughta' stop trying to rip off innocent travelers just passing through your community!" And next the very bold *diddler* opens, exits and then slams the tavern's front door shut while the befuddled bartender just stands there first scratching his round bald head and then scratching his big fat ass.

Still another modern-day scam is often initiated in large cities like Boston. A woman advertises in the Lost and Found newspaper section that she has lost a valuable diamond ring in a downtown park and that a two hundred dollar reward will be given to the lucky finder. The lady promises to give her two sister-in-laws the lost diamond ring if it is returned. A handsome mustached man shows-up at the woman's residence with the ring but only the two sister-in-laws are in the house waiting in the living room for their *diddling* sister-in-law to return from the local furrier. The dumb broads agree to pay the ring's finder the published two hundred dollar reward bonus in exchange for the prized gem.

An hour later, the scorned woman that had placed the solicitous ad in the morning edition's Lost and Found column meets her gigolo boyfriend in the city park where the pair anxiously reviews the result of their wise strategy.

"Jim, do you have the two hundred dollars we need to elope?" she asks. "Was it easy getting the money from my two ugly old hag sister-in-laws or what?"

"Like a piece of cake," Jim answers and smiles. "Like taking candy from a sleeping baby!"

"Good. I hate those two hideous-looking witches more than I despise my goddamned drunk of a husband," the bitter woman spitefully declares. "I'm glad that the two repugnant bitches gave you the two hundred dollars in trade for a worthless ring put together from some really deceiving pinchbeck and some cheap carpenter's paste. Here's my old expensive diamond wedding ring Jim that Bob had given me," the brazen female *diddler* indicated. "Proudly put it on my finger when we get to the Justice-of-the-Peace's place over in New Hampshire."

One final *diddle* must be presented and thoroughly appreciated. A well-dressed man wearing a top hat and cravat to complement his appearance arrives by train in a somnolent New England town and smoothly negotiates modest lodging at a reputable boarding house.

46

"I'll pay you my full rent and my meal board on the first day of each month, starting in two weeks," he promises the warty-faced landlady. "I'm a very important hiring agent for a large national catalog company and if you'd like, you can see my large ad in tomorrow morning's newspaper."

The young-but-unruffled *diddler* had advertised in the city newspaper for him hiring "six honest, responsible and reliable office clerks" that would have to handle and deposit in banks large sums of money received through the mail for the said nationally known catalog company. But according to the young *diddler's* objective, the half dozen new employees would be professionally *diddled* because each one would have to put up a hundred dollars' security deposit to convince the no-nonsense job interviewer that each candidate was a sober, moral and capitalistic free-market Christian citizen. Naturally, the slick confident *diddler* intends to blow town *after* receiving his money bonanza from the ambitious prospective office clerks and *before* not paying his promised rent.

All in all, fifty aspiring new clerks were hired at different times to work for the non-existent company Bogs, Hogs, Logs and Frogs, Enterprises, Incorporated, the bamboozling "official agency" for the large national catalog corporation.

On the morning of the first day of the next month, the busy *diddler's* warty-faced landlady rapped on the scam artist's door, but the daring fellow had furtively left town on the morning train and had carried with him the sum of five thousand dollars of freshly obtained revenue, generously and voluntarily donated by the fifty grateful *diddled*-but-unemployed clerks.

Area constables and sheriffs are feverishly combing all over Vermont and vicinity looking for the gifted and talented itinerant *diddler* but the odds are that they'll never be able to match his wit and equal his incredibly amazing *diddling* ability, for his favorite philosophical maxim is, "Offer a man a whale in exchange for a minnow and then leave town as quickly as possible after receiving the tiny fish!"

"The Masque of the Red Death"

Edgar Allan Poe (1809-1849) has to be the original master when it comes down to writing great murder/suspense/horror stories. Poe possessed an erratic temper to complement his chronic alcoholism and suspected drug usage, the addictions employed to alleviate physical pain. In addition to his celebrated horror and detective style mystery stories, E.A. Poe also wrote haunting poetry as exemplified in "The Raven" and "The Bells." Some of his most fascinating horror/suspense/murder stories are "The Pit and the Pendulum," "The Murders in the Rue Morgue," "The Fall of the House of Usher," "The Tell-Tale Heart," "The Black Cat" and "The Masque of the Red Death."

I remember once touring downtown Baltimore with my wife. We located Edgar Allan Poe's gravesite in an old cemetery and I spent a minute paying tribute to the father of the American detective story and of the macabre tale. A sign with a pointing arrow read, "Edgar Allan Poe House" so I convinced my wife to walk the quarter mile to the famed author's former Baltimore residence. The dwelling was difficult to locate. I decided to ask a black woman coming out of a neighborhood bar "Could you tell me where the Poe House is?"

"Poehouse!" the woman screamed and then hysterically laughed. "Mister, I've been livin' in the 'poehouse' ever since I've been born!" Now here is a humble retelling of Poe's classic tale, "The Masque of the Red Death."

The "Red Death" had killed millions of people in Europe hundreds of years before there were any Communists, Windsors, Social Democrats or Fascists around to perform the eliminations. The plague had long decimated populations and was regarded both as a scourge and as a pestilence. An assortment of bloodspots on the skin was the disease's principal trademark and once the devastating germs were contracted, people began bleeding like hemophiliacs from their assholes, dicks, tits, balls, pussies and skin pores. It all was rather gruesome and hideous to watch or to endure.

Sharp pains were accompanied by giddiness and dizziness and then the victims began bleeding from their orifices and pores all over their bodies, usually starting with their assholes. Scarlet stains were all over bedrooms, kitchens, halls, and all over sanitary and unsanitary napkins too. Those unfortunate individuals that acquired the fatal affliction were quarantined and nobody wanted to fuck with

49

them in any way, shape or form. And after someone's vulnerable asshole began bleeding profusely, the doomed victim would expire in less than a half-hour of delirious agonizing and accompanying suffering.

Prince Prospero was very rich, arrogant, happy, defiant and fucked-up. He believed he was sagacious and fearless but everyone in his retarded father's kingdom knew *he* was the ultimate asshole and predictably a prime candidate for contracting the seemingly vindictive Red Death.

"Half the jerk-offs and the majority of filthy sluts in my kingdom have died of the Red Death and are no longer paying taxes to support my opulent lifestyle," Prince Prospero vehemently complained to his already bleeding chief counselor. "If I don't get some new revenues to support my luxurious extravagant lifestyle soon," he continued in a pessimistic mood, "I'll have to change my name to Prince Pauperus."

"And many of your subjects and predicates are moving to other countries to escape the relentless Red Death's menace," the chief advisor added as he scratched his bleeding asshole. "They think that their asses will be safe if they could change their physical location and run away from the problem. Why the hell couldn't we be born in a future century where they have science and medicine to cure all of this inexplicable bullshit that kills *your* people? Your fucked-up country needs drugs and it needs them now!"

"What should I do to keep my remaining taxpayers living in my mentally retarded father's kingdom?" the depressed Prince asked. "I mean those stupid assholes are going to screw around and sodomize and get the disease no matter where the hell they live. The Red Death is definitely a sexually transmitted pain in the ass. That's one thing I'm most definitely sure of. And my granite-headed taxpaying nobles won't change their fucked-up lifestyles either! They're no smarter than my fucked-up peasants, dregs and serfs are!"

"Yes, your mentally challenged father knew what the hell he was doing when he had you castrated as an infant," the chief advisor reminded the haughty Prince. "And because you have no balls and consequently are impotent, you have no sexual desire, don't get laid and are ironically safe from dying of the Red Death because you can't realistically sodomize anyone."

"But what could I do to keep my taxpayers paying taxes during this most troubling crisis?" the beleaguered Prince asked his already afflicted principal adviser. "My taxpayers might rebel if I can't guarantee them government protection from the friggin' implacable Red Death."

"Why don't you have a big Masque Ball where everyone except you can get laid in your illustrious Ballrooms?" the counselor intelligently suggested. "Then your residents will all make merry and forget all about screwing around in ghettos like Luxemburg or Flanders, or some other despicable remote backward barrio countries similar to those two antiquated pigsties! And finally Prince Prospero," the loquacious court scholar attested, "all of the gay union musicians in your kingdom can legally and with impunity make overtures to one another when not playing their instruments at your exquisite Masque Ball!"

So the highly influenced Prince Prospero made an official proclamation all throughout his kingdom inviting the thousand most prominent taxpaying aristocrats to a Ball Masque to deliberately spite the wicked incursion of the Red Death into his land. Nobles, dukes, duchesses, Dutch asses, knights, bishops, counts (that didn't know arithmetic) and barren barons all received formal announcements requesting their eminent presence.

The basement of the eccentric Prince's abbey was chosen for the extraordinary Ball Masque. Prospero had designed the magnificent edifice and modeled it after a famous bisexual bordello situated in downtown Florence.

"This is my dear Abbey," the spiritually rejuvenated Prince related to his chief advisor, who wished that he could have his Red Death condition accelerated and have his fat ass terminated in thirty minutes so that *he* wouldn't have to listen to his boss's inane bullshit any more. "My sturdy Abbey is girdled with an impregnable wall that resembles a lady's girdle. The twelve-foot-wide obstacle will prevent any nasty germs and sperms from impregnating my guests' sensitive exposed assholes."

'You royal stupid shit!' the chief counselor thought and mentally criticized. 'The asshole guests that are carrying the disease in their dicks and in their' pussies will enter the dear Abbey through doors and portals and not through your impregnable walls!' Then the chief advisor regained his rationality and diplomatically answered his superior, "Yes Prince Prospero, you have the most excellent precautions and ideas of anyone residing in your dumb-ass kingdom! By not having any balls or scrotum," the counselor elaborated, "I think your intelligence is much keener than that of the average person, who is just thinking about getting laid all the damned time instead of considering how to improve the general welfare and happiness of the country's taxpayers!"

"The deleterious contagion will only be rampant outside my dear Abbey fortress," the emotionally buoyed Prince boasted to his normally apathetic subordinate, "and let the external world including the legendary American Indians and the mythical Alaskan Eskimos moan and suffer from the goddamned Red Death. I shall entertain my illustrious guests with buffoonery, sexual *aids*, naked ballet dancers, and many jesters from antiquity, ha, ha, ha!" the royal asshole chortled and exclaimed. "Even my hundred and five year old wrinkled-up feeble-minded great-grandfather will want to get laid at my masquerade ball!"

"Your hundred and five year old great-grandfather will attend the masque ball simply wanting to contract the goddamned Red Death so that he can die in half an hour and be put out of his goddamned misery," the important counselor candidly replied. "The only thing keeping your decrepit great-grandfather alive is that he has a mild case of arthritis in his dick! That particular dickular advantage gives him a stiff chance of surviving the devastating Red Death!"

"Yes, and a local musician has invented for the special occasion a new instrument called a *sex*ophone that is reputed to give tremendous blowjobs to its first fortunate listeners," the Prince reminded his red-spotted chief' counselor. "I hope no one present gets hearing AIDS! Ha, ha, ha! That's almost as fuckin' bad as the damned Red Death. Ha, ha, ha!"

It was in the sixth month of the Red Death epidemic that Prince Prospero held his spectacular Ball Masque for his thousand most loyal royal taxpayers. All of the invitees were required to wear costumes that covered their entire bodies with the exception of the genital areas between the hips and the knees. Then Prince Prospero amused himself' by cleverly guessing the identity of each attendee by carefully examining and fondling his or her exposed genitals. When the royal inspector accurately guessed someone's name, that person would then remove his or her mask and was then allowed to enter the Grand Ballroom located below the secluded dear Abbey of the kingdom's gay/pedophile monks', who were inadvertently excluded from the affair because not one of the rusty *monk' keys* would open the goddamned cellar doors.

After entering the main portal to the Ball Masque, the attendees were allowed to cavort and get laid in seven exceptional colorful chambers. The Prince had designed each room according to his bizarre taste, which was demented in addition to being effeminate.

Many normal palaces in normal kingdoms had a central vista with mirrored ballrooms adjacent to the main corridor. The various chambers were accessible through mirrored French doors. But Prince Prospero's layout had to be original.

Every *thirty yards* the main corridor had a right angle turn, so the guests had to get laid and then have three "first downs" (just like in American football) before they could enter the next Ballroom to advantageously get laid again. Tall narrow Gothic windows were to the right and left of each angled corridor bend so that various voyeurs (in addition to gay horny heterosexual and homosexual monks) could kneel outside, spy on the party through partially concealed windows and simultaneously jerk off on the outer perimeter of the dear Abbey. The impressive edifice's windows were of stained glass (that was creatively stained with semen, dead insects', bird shit and dried up pussy juice).

Each of the seven chambers was decorated in a different color and the stained glass windows nearest each new suite were of the same color as the room's velvet drapes, sable rugs and general décor. The most eastern room was blue because most female guests were to get blue in the face as they intensely blew their mate or date when the designated castrated faggot musician entered and played his *sex*ophone. The second chamber's windows and matching decor were purple because whoever got blown or eaten in that second large room looked like purple-people-eaters when viewed in the purple-hued light. The third room's vertically rectangular windows and drapes were green since that was the color everyone's face turned when they realized that their' delicate assholes were starting to bleed or hemorrhage.

The fourth chamber was orange with bowls of oranges all over the friggin' place because the dumb idiots that resided in the Prince's fiefdom thought that *Vitamin C* (taken in excess) could cure the Red Death. Twenty servants were assigned to the Orange Room to keep the bowls and people's bowels stocked up, and the naughty haughty Prince amusingly dubbed two of his weirdo vassals William and Mary of Orange. The fifth chamber had been ornamented in white in honor of semen ejaculations and the sixth auspicious room was decorated violet since it was widely believed among the superstitious citizens that ultra-violet rays and rubbing one's shrinking genitals with shrinking violets could satisfactorily cure the evil Red Death.

The seventh apartment was quite macabre in that it was shrouded in black velvet drapes and tapestries hanging from the ceilings and the aforementioned embellishments were nailed with heavy spikes to

53

the solid granite walls. The sable carpet was also dyed black and had been personally purchased on the black market by Prince Prospero. The accompanying windowpanes in the eerie black chamber however, were of a scarlet hue and strangely did not correspond to the basic black theme symbolized by the creepy drapes and corresponding rug. Every guest that made it to the morbid black seventh chamber thought the same thing. 'The scarlet panes symbolize my pains in my ass and the notorious Red Death and the black drapes symbolize Death without any fuckin' red in it. I knew I should've moved to either Luxemburg or Flanders!' every distressed individual that scrutinized the macabre black chamber thought.

None of the seven rooms had any lights or candles flickering in wall sconces but next to the windows before each suite was a tripod lamp emanating fire. Each lamp produced a glowing brazier of fire, and each woman arriving on the scene would have to take off her brassiere and place it into the fire before entering the next color-themed chamber. That is why Prince Prospero had specifically instructed in his invitations for each woman to wear seven bras (and no chastity belts) to his illustrious party.

The entire sensational Abbey was a combination of gaudy and fantastic visual impressions guaranteed to stimulate the libidos of the guests so that they then automatically desired to get laid in the first several rooms and next, in a fantasy adventure, seek an imaginary cure before eventually succumbing to the voracious Red Death in the final black chamber.

But when the guests ultimately arrived at the last black chamber, they were both horrified and terrified by the room's morose appearance and there wasn't one erect dingle or one erect nipple or clitoris in that dreaded section of the doomed Abbey. The blood stained' windows were most ghastly, ominous and hideous in appearance and not even the idiotic guest that came to the strange masquerade as the Grim Reaper wanted to stay five seconds alone in the evil-looking place.

The peculiar foreboding suite had a gigantic clock on its western wall, and the mechanism was made of ebony and built by a local crafty craftsman named Ebenezer Screws, who specialized in working with dark woods. The enormous clock's pendulum vacillated slowly back and forth as if it was pronouncing a death sentence upon anyone that viewed the monstrosity whenever it chimed. And every hour the immense clock's monotonous dull haunting clang made the musicians pause from playing their instruments, and even the blithe gay/pedophile *sex*ophone player ceased having his *minstrel cycle*. Even those couples screwing in the blue, purple and green rooms stopped their sexual activity in mid-stroke until the disturbing dull clanging had finally terminated. As a result, many of the men lost their erections because it took the damned gigantic ebony clock a full three minutes to finally chime ten o'clock.

At the stroke of ten p.m. the whole party went silent as the dancers, musicians and screwers all temporarily stopped their activities, and even the gay cross-dressers that were exchanging costumes stopped all of their movements (including their smelly bowel movements). Even the giddiest of shitty partygoers grew pale and also the somber party-poopers (with chronic diarrhea) stopped their perpetual crapping. Old and young attendees alike were almost mesmerized by Ebenezer's ebony clock's tone, which was indirectly communicating to everyone in attendance: "It's almost time for all you shit-headed son-of-a-bitches to die!"

But after the last echo finally ceased its odious reverberation, laughter again pervaded the assemblage; the men screwing their partners reacquired their hard-ons and everyone returned back to their merrymaking. The musicians, the accomplished *sex*ophone player and the women all returned to blowing away, the cross-dressing gays enthusiastically exchanged their gaudy masquerade costumes and Prince Prospero scratched his obese ass and then noticed abhorrent scarlet liquid embedded under his long fingernails. But unaware of their eunuch host's urgent problem, most of the guests had gotten over their nervousness and continued indulging in carnal pleasure.

"The next time that ebony clock chimes at eleven I'm going to ignore it completely," Duchess Morehead told her paramour. "That way I'll be able to ring your chimes!"

"You really blow me away!" *Duke Cain* answered. "Give me more head Duchess Morehead! This party really sucks, and that's exactly what I really like about it!"

"My ass is grass!" Prince Prospero exclaimed to his' scheming and jealous ass-scratching royal adviser. "Put a sanitary napkin and a diaper on my goddamned butt right away!" he commanded as he stared at the blood from his corpulent ass embedded underneath his fingernails.

Three thousand and six hundred seconds later the clock began chiming eleven. Everyone paused to listen to the dismal low tone that symbolically signaled a death knell. And as soon as the nerve-racking chiming stopped, the musicians, the dancers, the gay faggot cross-dressers and the straight erect males proceeded with their frivolity and continued screwing their women (and mates) to death before the Red Death could even kill their sexual partners.

And to thumb his nose at the Red Death menace Prince Prospero (with his sore ass still bleeding) loudly announced that he would generously award a free weekend at a popular suburban whorehouse for the lucky couple than had worn the most grotesque costumes to *his* extravaganza. The maniacal Prince gleefully reveled when he saw arabesque men prancing around his perverted masquerade without any apparent appendages and peckers and voluptuous Arab-bare women flaunting suggestive silver and gold earrings meticulously fastened to their pink beaver slits and succulent breasts.

"The more Satanic and primitive, the better it is!" the regal hedonistic nutcase declared to his thoroughly entertained imperial courtiers. "These imaginative barbaric sado-sexual fantasies are deliriously impious!" Prospero disclosed to his almost dead chief adviser. "If I had any balls I would surely be getting aroused and laid right now at contemplating all of this most stellar bizarre and immoral activity!"

The drunken celebrators then merrily marched into the various colored chambers kissing, hugging and engaging in straight and perverted sex with any other human or available animal they could latch onto.

But everyone that was rollicking around the dear Abbey stayed a safe distance from the morbid black seventh chamber, preferring life, hedonism and partying to the suggestion (and reality) of death and all of its awesome connotations. So the spirited inebriated guests preferred rolling around on the varicolored sable carpets and sharing body fluids all over the damned place, and even squirting sticky substances on each and every dear Abbey marble column.

"My apprehensive subjects are not entering the black room because of fright," Prospero indulgently laughed to his main adviser, who was slowly disintegrating from the inside out. "My guests are *lacking the balls* to do so just like I'm also too deficient in what could be characterized as 'the courage and audacity department'."

"And they are also evading Ebenezer Screws's ebony clock," the chief counselor answered while bending over and holding his heart. "And if the clock falls on yonder piano we'll all have to fuckin' sing "Ebony and Ivory!"

And the intense revelry went on despite the pervasive presence of the stalking Red Death in Prince Prospero's doomed kingdom, and as spirited bodies danced and whirled around and as the extended orgy progressed, the sinister ebony clock eerily began tolling twelve times making everyone aware of the gloomy potentially formidable midnight hour. Again the startled musicians stopped their orchestration, the dancers ceased their blithe activity and the sex maniacs halted their boring humping and pumping in deference to Ebenezer Screws's melancholy-sounding ebony clock chimes.

When the clock finally struck twelve times the nervous guests stepped back with their mouths agape and scrutinized a tall gaunt masked gray-robed figure standing in their midst holding a long scythe in his bony hands.

"Who is this hideous-looking intruder?" Prospero asked his official census taker. "The fellow looks like he's been dead for many decades. Just look how tattered his robe is! See if that jerk's listed on our friggin' tax rolls!"

Certainly no ordinary costume could simultaneously generate so much sensation and so much disgust. Anyone attending the party had license to wear any outrageous outfit that he or she desired, but the detestable-looking newcomer's wardrobe selection had indeed exceeded all customary discretion. Even the usually unabashed Prince was somewhat appalled.

"This vile encroacher is even more fucked-up than I am!" Prospero adamantly stated to his virtually deceased chief adviser. "He's so skinny I believe he doesn't even have an asshole let alone an ass to shit out of, and his huge dick really looks like a horrendous fleshless boner. This fucked-up son-of-a-bitch has an extra damned bone in his body! And the all-too-serious bastard looks like he wants to all-too-seriously sodomize everybody at my damned orgy!"

"He looks like he just climbed out of a goddamned grave," the chief counselor gravely noted to his superior as he desperately struggled for his next breath. "And he probably used a damned skeleton key to get into the friggin' Abbey."

"His repugnant face is fleshless just like his boner is," Prince Prospero gasped, "and the specter's gray robe is stained with blood and a trace of crimson appears on his forehead!" the speaker marveled with an awful degree of awe. "I suspect that this son-of-a-bitchin' trespasser is the Red Death! Oh no! My sore asshole is really throbbing and bleeding right now! Christ! My rear fender is really tender!"

"I feel like adopting all of hell's ghouls because the villainous unearthly creature definitely gives me the creeps!" the intimidated chief counselor agreed while sticking him left thumb into his asshole to stop the bleeding. "Holy shit Prince Prospero!" the alarmed adviser yelled to his royal pain in the ass. "You're bleeding most profusely from your freakin' butt hole too!"

The party crasher then stalked through the flabbergasted invitees randomly seeking out victims to contaminate, who immediately also began bleeding exuberantly from their newly ruptured assholes. Everyone was terrified from the spectacle they were witnessing as the mesmerized invitees shuddered and retreated from the interloping Red Death's company.

"Who dares insult the dignity of my orgy with this licentious blasphemous demonstration?" Prince Prospero hoarsely screamed at the intruder. "Guards, seize and unmask that contemptuous culprit so that we shall hang this foul fart from the fort's friggin' ramparts at dawn and see exactly how well the impostor is hung!"

Prince Prospero's vain command from the center of the blue room rang throughout all seven chambers of the Abbey's spacious cellar, even the condemned black room. The Prince was a bold but spoiled demanding sucker' who always got his way, but this time the bratty bleeding asshole and his spoiled bleeding asshole guests knew that their rectal hemorrhaging problem went far beyond mere hyperactive hemorrhoids.

All the guests attending the queer masquerade orgy immediately and spontaneously panicked and popped every champagne bottle, and each pale invitee was hastily looking for the longest and widest corks to valiantly plug up their partners' butt holes.

"Stop acting like a bunch of stupid crazy assholes!" Prince Prospero yelled at his main political constituents. "Someone seize and arrest the gaunt son-of-a-bitch so that he shall be hung as soon as daylight breaks! Then we'll scare the living daylights out of the bony prick by lynching his ass at the gallows!"

Each of the hysterical mummers in attendance ignored the Prince's imperial decree while looking out to specifically cover, cork and protect his or her own ass. And those more hyperactive guests with indigestion that had begun loudly farting were suddenly squirting blood of all types (A, B, O) all over the fuckin' place. Everyone *shrank* away from the insidious frightful sight, but no one's hemorrhoids shrank one iota whatsoever. Each mummer's back was against the proverbial wall in an effort to guard his or her ass from imminent penetration or further contagion.

Prince Prospero was in a rage as he followed the grim melancholy invader from *his* eastern blue room, past *his* purple room and then into the green chamber. Next the Prince slowly followed the wretched mysterious Red Death figure past the orange and violet

58

rooms and then into the bleak and depressing black chamber. The royal personage was so intensely out-of-kilter assessing his own cowardice that he promptly grabbed a dagger from a scared-shitless' guard and then impulsively rushed toward the frightening encroacher.

When the infuriated Prince Prospero came within three smelly feet of the ghostly trespasser the Red Death instantaneously turned and its evil avaricious eyes invaded the Crown Prince's heart and soul. Before the defeated victim could collapse to the cold stone basement floor, the immortal visitor penetrated and sodomized the host's big fat ass with his incomparable supreme death boner.

The useless dagger harmlessly dropped upon the black *rugged* carpet directly opposite the dark ebony clock.

Everyone that had witnessed the crazy phenomenon stood shocked and stunned. Then a royal prostitute came out of her stupor and shrieked, "Long live the Red Death! The big pricked scourge of the entire earth!"

And then all of the other befuddled attendees chanted and repeated the excited hooker's praise. The Red Death had come like a thief in the night to vanquish Prince Prospero's audacity. The spectral visitor had locked each door of the impregnable dear Abbey and then had a most exhilarating time sodomizing each of the thousand uncooperative mummers, forcing the corks up their delicate assholes all the way to their duodenums with his yard-long bony erection. That ungodly desecration was done until the last of the straight and the gay celebrators had been thoroughly penetrated', drilled and punctured.

"Ha, ha, ha!" the Red Death roared as he deftly and methodically sodomized and riveted each asshole at the party with his long thick bony dick. "Prince Prospero is no longer fuckin' prospering and neither are *you*! I'm systematically giving each of you one by one a dishonorable *discharge* from this non-exotic potentially lethal existence!"

"A Descent into the Maelstrom"

My very elderly Norwegian guide and I had finally reached the summit of the ridge's loftiest crag, which majestically lorded over a beautiful deep fiord situated within the valley below to our right. The climb to the pinnacle had been arduous and I suspected that the old wrinkled-faced gray-haired fellow was exhausted from his three-hour-long labor. Finally the old codger inhaled a quantity of oxygen and began speaking.

"You know Mr. Poe, not too long ago there happened to me an event of terror that to my knowledge no mortal man other than myself has ever survived," Hans Jorgensen claimed before having a three minute allergic sneezing fit. "Just look at my goddamned hair! It's fuckin' white as snow! But let me explain to you Mr. Poe, the color had changed from pure black to snow white in just six hours of extremely horrifying danger!"

"Ha, ha, ha," I lustily laughed, believing that I was being lured into listening to an obscure Norwegian tall tale. "Your hair fuckin' sounds like Snow White without the dick-head Seven Dwarfs and your dandruff must've been the goddamned snow, you old flaky Asshole! And probably you had had your hair dyed but you forgot to die yourself, ha, ha, ha! Hans, it's a good thing I'm not made out of glass because your story's already cracking me up and you haven't even gotten past the friggin' preface!"

"Laugh if you must Mr. Poe, but I can scarcely look out over this cliff without feeling sick in my stomach and giddy in my head," Jorgensen continued his tale's lengthy and monotonous introduction. "If you think our vantage point on top of this wind-blown crag is precarious, it is nothing when compared to the perilous adventure, or should I say *misadventure* that I had once experienced in that treacherous strait of water down there," my guide elaborated. "It was so horrendous that I had shit my pants five times a day for a full year until I finally decided not to wear any goddamned underwear or pants at all. And sure as sin, that's the honest-to-God naked truth I'm telling you Mr. Poe."

"Sounds like you had been suffering from a rare combination of diarrhea, colitis and dysentery to me," I ridiculously jested. "Your good heredity should've given you a more efficient colon and a more durable asshole. And how the hell do I really know Hans that you

61

still aren't farting around using your hyperactive mouth instead of your irritated asshole?"

"Stop acting like my asshole *used* to behave after I had endured and survived my crisis misadventure," Hans chastised. "As you can perceptively fathom from our present mutual high-in-the-sky observation point, we're overlooking the Norwegian coast in the great Nordland Province."

"I never overlook overlooking," I foolishly joked. "Just as long as the coast is clear, ha, ha, ha!"

"Keep fuckin' making asinine remarks like that and I'll tell the whole fuckin' story in medieval Norwegian Viking words," my thoroughly aggravated guide threatened. "Now then Mr. Poe, we're precisely in the sixty-eighth degree of latitude in the always dreary district of Lofoden. We're currently sitting on top of Mt. Helseggen the Cloudy," Hans academically related as I yawned. "Now I strongly recommend Mr. Poe that you look-out beyond the vapor belt below us and focus your eyes on the sea."

Feeling dizzy from my high altitude (and from my guide's lofty attitude), I gazed out, grabbing and holding onto thick grass clumps so that I would not be suddenly sent airborne by the gusty winds. In the distance a certain group of small islands randomly dotted the dark blue water and to my left and right were impressive-looking promontories, the total panorama suggesting to my vivid imagination a deplorably desolate-yet-pristine landscape.

"That island in the far distance is called Vurrgh," Hans knowledgeably informed me, "and the larger island in the middle is Moscoe, which incidentally is not in Russia, you dumb ass! I thought I would say *that* dumb-shit remark before you ever fuckin' thought of uttering the idiotic comment," Jorgensen sternly lectured. "Then a mile to the north is Ambaaren, and yonder are Islesen, Hotholm, Keildhelm, Suarven and Buckholm. And further off between Moscoe and Vurrgh are Otterholm, Flimen and finally Sandflesen.," my ancient-looking encyclopedic mentor said in what sounded like a rather boring Homeric catalog. "Do you now hear anything inordinate or see any dramatic change in the water Mr. Poe?"

"No, I don't hear a toot, I don't smell a fart and I don't see shit!" I sarcastically answered. "Wait a minute Hans! The sea is becoming disturbed over there in the distance near Moscoe and it's rapidly moving towards Vurrgh. Now look!" I pointed in an animated fashion. "It's bubbling and whirling and appears to be almost boiling as it approaches. It looks like a fuckin' tsunami coming our way! It's a good thing we're way up here otherwise we could be wiped into oblivion by a mammoth tidal wave!"

A minute later the distant sea's surface ceased its awesome swelling and eventually became rather smooth. The separate swirling whirlpools gradually dissipated one by one while prodigious streams of white foam became abundant almost everywhere, forming an enormous circle surrounded by a gleaming girdle of spray approximately a mile in diameter.

And then a fantastically huge and powerful sea-funnel appeared, dizzily swirling around, its erratic motion and size easily capable of sucking up the entire cataract discharge of the great Niagara Falls. This mind-boggling phenomenon that my disbelieving eyes and brain were interpreting immediately gave legitimate credence to Hans Jorgensen's fantastic narrative. I then felt the mountain's base trembling as the recently generated terrible waves smashed against its rock foundation several thousand feet below.

"I almost pissed my pants!" I screamed at Hans above the roar of the pounding surf surges. "That giant whirlpool out there would easily suck Zeus' dick off if the Olympian ever got caught stranded here off *his* mountain! Does it have a name?"

"Yes, it's the Maelstrom of Moscoe, but we native Norwegians simply call it 'the Maelstrom!' Just like you Mr. Poe, that colossal mother-fucker out there really sucks!"

"What's the depth of the water out near Moscoe?" I curiously asked, suddenly turning serious in defiance of my normal stupid-shit obnoxious personality.

"About forty fathoms deep, can you fathom that Mr. Poe?" Hans challenged my academic acumen by cleverly employing the use of a poly-semantic English word.

"Yes, about two hundred and forty feet deep, one fathom being equivalent to six feet," I replied as I remembered how Mark Twain had acquired the first and last parts of his pen name. "I'll tell you Hans, that must fuckin' be Jupiter's brother King Neptune down there' having a goddamned orgasm!"

"I've seen several large fishing vessels get vacuumed down inside the hungry Maelstrom and I also witnessed a bear on one occasion and a whale on another disappear into its voracious throat," Hans recollected and disclosed. "And once Mr. Poe, I even saw an immense oak tree and a huge pine get ripped to splinters and then violently deposited onto the shore."

I could not resist the opportunity to again clown around and aggravate Hans. "Once my girlfriend back in Baltimore wanted me to buy her a mink coat for Christmas but I bought her a Douglas fir instead," I inanely quipped. "You should've opened a toothpick factory Hans. It looks like that friggin' Maelstrom had done most of the goddamned hard work for you!"

"Mr. Poe, it's been chronicled in various historical accounts that in the year 1645 on the morning of Sexagesima Sunday, the Maelstrom had raged with such impetuosity that the stone buildings and homes of the village residents all collapsed to the ground. The only survivors were those devout souls that had remained inside the safety of the church."

"Hans, those stupid assholes that stayed home and were having sex on Sexagesima Sunday had to have the greatest most sensational climaxes of their lives, dying while achieving tremendous orgasms. What a fuckin' way to go!"

"Mr. Poe, are you for real? Aren't you ever serious or earnest?" Hans austerely asked.

"Mr. Jorgensen, first of all Sirius is a bright star in the constellation Canis Major, and furthermore, if I were Earnest then quite obviously, my fuckin' name couldn't possibly be Edgar Allan!" I crazily answered.

* * * * * * * * * * * *

"Okay Mr. Poe," Hans Jorgensen said with palpable conviction, "I'll now tell you all about my more than decent descent into the Moscoe Maelstrom even though talking to you is like trying to communicate with a deaf, dumb and blind mute on opium. And if you had half a brain," my illustrious guide added, "you'd be only one-fourth as sagacious as I am!"

My impatient storyteller then related to me that he and his two brothers were famous area fishermen that owned a schooner-rigged smack that got caught in the turbulent eddies smack-dab between the familiar islands of Moscoe and Vurrgh. "We three dumb-ass sailors were the only assholes around that had the balls to venture out there in those wicked straits and soon thereafter, we really found our dumb asses in real dire straits," Hans obtusely explained. "For you see Mr. Poe, the fishing was really excellent between those two islands, but if you're there throwing nets over the gunwales at the wrong time, then there's a really heavy penalty the ambitious fool has to pay, namely risking the loss of your life."

"Come on Hans, get on with your glorious story," I begged. "Surely you must've survived your major problem otherwise you wouldn't be here reliving it at my auditory expense!"

"Well Sir, on July 18th of that epic year a really nasty hurricane invaded the Norwegian coast that afternoon while the three of us were out sailing between Moscoe and Vurrgh casting our nets," the decrepit old man shared. "But let me now emphasize something important. That freaky storm was enough to scare the living semen out of any seaman."

"Stop trying to be so melodramatically funny and resume orating your damned exaggerated story," I entreated, feigning heightened anger. "And please stop attempting to imitate my propensity for telling irrelevant jokes. Now I'm beginning to understand exactly how annoying I must seem to others. I'm finally learning to detest hyperbole, falsehoods and the like."

"Well Mr. Poe, the wind was for once calm and then it began blowing our smack all over the fuckin' place and my brothers and I were suddenly caught up in *current* events, so to speak," Hans preposterously told me. "In less than ten minutes the devastating storm was upon us and literally kicking the shit out of our schooner. Then my happy-go-lucky youngest sibling Thor said, 'Let's get the fuck out of here, the *schooner* the better,' the pathetic jokester yelled as he adroitly tied himself to the main mast. Well Mr. Poe," Hans proceeded with his oddball recollection, "no sooner had that dumb fuck Thor hollered those stupid-assed words that a titanic gust of wind broke the fuckin' mast off and the whole beam and Thor, who was already lashed to the object, went flying off the deck and both he and the sheared-off mast were hastily deposited into the choppy white-capped sea."

Before I could even fart, Hans then orally recounted to me that after what he had witnessed happening to Thor, the storyteller fearfully slid his body over to a ring bolt that had been fastened to the deck near the second mast and then the desperate man securely grasped the metal loop and held on for dear life, fearing that the boat would certainly capsize. Then Jorgensen's other brother Ingemar came sliding over to the ring' bolt and frantically struggled to also hold on in a genuine effort to save his own life.

"Ingemar could've taken your cap size during the capsize," I moronically jested. "Did you let Ingemar have a piece of the iron ring after he rolled to your location?" I ignorantly asked. "Surely you must've exhibited brotherly love despite the fact that you're definitely not from Philadelphia."

65

"Well Mr. Poe," my accommodating guide elucidated with a mild sneer evident on his visage, "brotherly love only goes so far. Even though I loved Ingemar, when self-preservation is involved in the equation, I soon learned that I loved myself more than I did him. I wildly kicked, pushed and shoved Ingemar away from the iron ring', which in fact was only big enough to allow one man to grip properly. And then before I could succinctly yell 'Fuck you Ingemar!' the ship canted and then tilted and my middle brother joined Thor down in Davy Jones' locker. But at that moment Mr. Poe," Hans stressed and reiterated, "I felt that I was just as doomed to die on that half-demolished schooner the same as if I had been cowardly hiding in the hull of a hundred gun warship."

"So Hans, you were courageously battling two very formidable enemies, the savage hurricane on the one hand and the omnipotent Maelstrom on the other," I perceptively comprehended and interrupted. "I'll bet you didn't even have time to wipe your ass or scratch your balls!"

"Mr. Poe, if I dared to do either of those dumb-fuck things I'd be sailing right off the deck and wind-up joining my kin Thor and Ingemar in the drink," Hans insisted. "Surely, I didn't have an icicle's chance in hell of living through my traumatic dilemma but somehow basic instinct gave me the courage to persevere. But then Mr. Poe," Hans pontificated before coughing-up and spitting out a green lunger that splattered against my chest, "I heard a loud sucking sound that made my wet jet-black hair stand-up on end. I thought that some prehistoric dinosaur or prehistoric sea creature was either going to devour my ass or take a healthy shit on top of me and sink the goddamned boat right down to the bottom. But truthfully Mr. Poe," Jorgensen said before again clearing his lungs with me instantly ducking-down, "my terror had all been used up and I was no longer petrified to either act or die. In my heart I didn't give a goddamned shit about dying and in reality, I was actually resigned to the fact that it should fuckin' happen pretty soon. Pretty soon or ugly soon Mr. Poe, it just didn't matter to me! I remember thinking, 'Dying isn't so fuckin' bad. Look how easily Thor and Ingemar managed to do it'!"

I again felt compelled to open my big mouth and articulate something fucked-up. "Yes, plunging down into the bowels of the abyss would certainly be pretty abysmal," I chuckled and then again involuntarily farted. "What the hell happened next Hans? Did a gorgeous mermaid with big succulent breasts rescue your grungy ass when you heard her alluring siren's call? Did you finally wake up from your mind-boggling heinous nightmare?"

"Well Mr. Poe, the devastating Maelstrom then sucked up the entire schooner as if it was a chicken feather and I was being whirled around like a spinning top as I still desperately clung to the metal ring bolt," Hans articulated. "Despite the fact that the ship was whirling around in an orbit all along the circumference of the Maelstrom, in sheer desperation I managed to use my right hand and grab a rope and tie my torso to an empty cask that had rolled over to my vicinity on the deck."

"Was it the Cask of Amontillado?" I idiotically jested. "Excuse me Hans, but *that* reference was a private joke that only I could understand and appreciate."

"As I glanced out at the churning sea," Hans said, pausing a moment to recapture his faltering breath, "I noticed all sorts of junk drifting by: bones, fish skeletons, wine racks, barrels, hogsheads, bottles, chests, liquor cabinets, dildos, well, you name it, all rapidly swirling around in concentric orbits that paralleled the schooner's orbit. It was far worse than the most peculiar bizarre fucked-up nightmare a man could ever have! If I was insanely drunk and on marijuana and cocaine addiction," Hans hypothesized and unconvincingly communicated, "then Mr. Poe, I couldn't have hallucinated anything more outlandish!"

"I'm getting pretty damned dizzy just listening to your fanciful nautical bullshit," I disgustingly opined. "I mean, who in the world could jerk-off let alone get laid under such non-propitious conditions? If a half decent whorehouse had flown by your accursed schooner," I insisted feigning seriousness, "you could've hopped from the swirling schooner directly inside the front door and maybe gotten laid or blown during the climax of your abominable ordeal. Don't you agree?"

Hans was not humored or impressed by my fertile imagination. "Well Mr. Poe, more freakin' fragments went zooming and zipping by the spinning schooner; weird things like furniture, desks, chairs, lamps, cartons, drawers, the kind of drawers in desks and not the kind that's men's or women's underwear, and also timbers and snuff boxes were twirling and swirling all over the goddamned place," Hans narrated with a poker face. "I hadn't been that fuckin' dizzy since I was a kid in kindergarten getting sick and nauseous playing 'Pin the Tail or the horned helmeted Fat Lady singing at the end of the opera' or 'Spin the Bottle, with *me* being assigned being the goddamned bottle!"

"A spendthrift sort of woman might describe your Maelstrom misadventure as a whirlwind shopping trip," I giggled and then indulgently laughed. "I can't believe it but I actually find your terrifying story quite amusing. It's so damned hilarious that I think I'm becoming delirious, ha, ha, ha! This fucked-up fisherman's tale could make a fairly enjoyable comic short story if not the premise for a cornball novel."

"Well in conclusion, my hands, legs, wrists, fingers, shoulders, elbows along with my knees and testicles were all chafed-up and badly lacerated," Hans Jorgensen regretfully testified and then spit a huge lunger into the wind, the green glob instantly being deflected right onto my face. "Now Mr. Poe, I thought I was going to fuckin' bleed to death before I ever had a chance to drown or commit suicide. It was the biggest friggin' bummer of my life and I wished that I was dead and playing strip poker with Thor and Ingemar down there' in Hell, or Hades, or Purgatory, or wherever the fuck my immortal soul was heading."

"Well, it certainly wouldn't be Heaven," I cynically commented. "Paradise would certainly reject your wrinkled-up ass," I facetiously *anal*yzed. "That St. Peter at the Pearly Gates is a pretty damned fussy son-of-a-bitch, or so I hear. But please Hans," I diplomatically urged, "finish-up your goofy story because I think I'm going to have an intense bowel movement within the next five minutes. My erratic intestines won't allow me to sit here and listen to your absurd jargon much longer."

Hans lucidly communicated to me that he had calculated that lighter objects like the pine tree parts that had drifted to the beach from previous Maelstrom activity would tend to rise and not sink during the culmination/termination phase of *his* whirlpool's "spin cycle." And he continued his spectacular story by saying, "So I intrepidly let go of the iron ring, lifted up the empty cask with my girth still lashed to it and then without hesitation jumped off of the schooner into the Maelstrom's swirling mass."

"Did you collide with either Thor or Ingemar after your valiant plunge?" I asked with an expressionless face, enunciating each word tongue-in-cheek. "You three knuckleheaded fuck-heads sound to me like you were already way *out there* revolving around and rotating in some distant solar orbit long before your doomed schooner ever began swirling and orbiting around inside the Maelstrom. Are you a fucked-up space alien or what?"

"Stop being so nasty or I'll refuse telling you the unbelievable ending of my Maelstrom misadventure," Hans angrily reprimanded me. "Show me more courtesy and respect."

I figured that I had to be a bit more contrite and considerate. "Well who the heck rescued you from the formidable waves? Was it John Paul Jones or was it Eric the Red?" I laughed, loudly farting and thus ripping a large hole along the crotch seam of my pants. "How about that dumb-fuck barbarian Viking rascal, Leif Erickson?"

"Some very surprised fishermen from my village salvaged my ass from the great waves and then lugged me aboard their boat," Hans recalled and maintained. "But unfortunately the avid tuna hunters hadn't detected any vestiges of either Thor or Ingemar. My brothers must've really enjoyed Death because they never returned after experiencing it!"

My felicitous mood was about to sober up in a hurry. Much to my consternation, Hans patiently and persuasively divulged to me a statement that sent my skeptical mind shifting into a sudden reality check. I was absolutely unprepared to hear his startling revelation, which quite candidly, scared the living feces out of my rear end and also frightened the yellow piss out of my kidneys.

"After my fishermen colleagues pulled me on board, the sailors were shocked to see that my hair had turned from raven jet-black to snow white in less than a day. Furthermore," Hans Jorgensen stated with a grim countenance that thoroughly expressed his sincerity, "I had aged over fifty years in less than twenty-four hours. More specifically Mr. Poe, I had aged over half a century during the six-hour crisis I had experienced swirling around and around in my drastic descent into the Maelstrom."

"The Black Cat"

Edgar Allan Poe (1809-1849) has to be the original master when it comes down to great murder/suspense/horror stories. E.A. Poe possessed an erratic temper to complement his chronic alcoholism and suspected drug usage, self-administered to alleviate physical pain. In addition to his celebrated horror and detective-style mystery stories, E.A. Poe also wrote haunting poetry as exemplified in his classic works "The Raven" and "The Bells." Some of his most fascinating horror/suspense/murder genre stories are "The Pit and the Pendulum," "The Murders in the Rue Morgue," "The Fall of the House of Usher," "The Masque of the Red Death," "The Tell-Tale Heart" and most certainly "The Black Cat."

I remember once touring downtown Baltimore with my wife. We had located Edgar Allan Poe's grave in an old cemetery and I respectfully spent a somber minute paying tribute to the father of the American detective story and of the macabre tale. A sign with a pointing arrow read, "Edgar Allan Poe House" so I convinced my wife to walk the quarter mile from the downtown cemetery to the famed author's former Baltimore residence. The house was quite difficult to locate but my wife and I eventually found it.

* * * * * * * * * * * *

Two of my favorites Edgar Allan Poe tales are "The Cask of Amontillado" and "The Black Cat," both of which I had first read at the age of twelve in the sixth grade and have read several dozen times each since 1955.

I don't expect anyone to believe the insane story I'm about to relate because the world is fucked-up, the story is fucked-up and I'm fucked-up too. Even I can't believe the abnormal occurrences that had happened and I'm now an avowed atheist and believe in absolutely nothing except that everyone and everything on this planet and in the Universe is fucked-up. Yet I maintain that I'm not *mad*; I'm just thoroughly pissed off and simply am "angry-mad" but not "crazy-mad."

I know I'm not dreaming because presently I have a goddamned excruciating toothache that won't quit and my hemorrhoids are three times their normal size and make my asshole feel like there's a saguaro cactus stuck inside it. But tomorrow I'm scheduled to die,

71

and today I must confess the true circumstances that have led up to my scheduled execution by lynching.

My main objective in producing this writing is to inform the insensitive world about my dilemma, but the world is not a person having ears so why the fuck should I even endeavor to do such an absurd thing? And besides that self-destruct life-curtailing bullshit, I have already established that the world is fucked-up even without having any ears to listen to and sympathize with my distasteful plight. But I'll describe my tale plainly and briefly hoping that in the future some reader will vindicate my conviction about the significance of life and about my accompanying legal conviction by the fucked-up American judicial system.

I'll not try to explain the series of events but instead will simply diligently describe them in detail in a sequential manner. Recently I've experienced nothing but terror, terror of my environment, terror of other people and terror of myself and the attendant demons associated with virtually every fuckin' thing in this whole goddamned world ranging from pets to cellars. I am literally a tortured, maligned and defeated man and I can't wait to die and escape this son-of-a-bitchin' horror-laden existence so inappropriately misnomered as "life on Earth."

Some cynics may consider my account more strange than terrifying. I say to those asshole skeptics "Fuck you!" because I'm the one that has to carry the extreme burden and bear the horrid reality every single minute of every single hour of every single day. A rational calm person thinks that he or she is normal and will interpret my demeanor as being too excitable and as too impetuous, but those cavalier objective idiots are more fucked-up than I'll ever be because they'll never admit that they are fucked-up in the first place. If someone reading this tale sees my tragedy as a mere sequence of causes and effects, then I say to that asshole "Suck my dead dick!"

From the time after I had been protectively rocked in the cradle I was always known and regarded as a cooperative, pleasant and subordinate person possessing an affable temperament. My few teenage hooligan friends made fun of my wimpy personality and often exploited my soft heart and took advantage of my propensity for compassion. The antagonistic jerk-offs all thought that I was a naïve and gullible asshole since I always attempted to please my peers instead of beating the fucking shit out of them like I should have done to achieve the lofty supreme position in their bully-oriented pecking order.

My heart had always been very fond of animals and I quickly learned to like them better than I valued people. I enjoyed owning a great variety of dogs and cats throughout my late childhood and adolescence and I found that my pets showed more honesty and truth in their emotions than my so-called arrogant scumbag facetious untrustworthy friends did. Unlike my mercenary fucked-up peers, my pets were loyal and wise, and in many instances more human than those uncouth imbeciles I associated with at bars, dances and taverns ever were. The animals in my house provided me with unselfish love and faithfulness, traits that my shit head human acquaintances never acquired or developed.

I married young and my pretty wife had a cheerful benign disposition that generally corresponded to my own. She loved animals too and we always had birds, dogs, goldfish, rabbits, gerbils and even a small monkey inside the house. But the one pet that stood out amongst the rest was a very large black cat with beautiful soft fur. The creature exuded a docile wisdom that seemed to transcend all human knowledge and I intensely felt its sagacity and serenity every single day, even without the perceptive animal ever saying a word.

My wife was very superstitious in addition to being a cold frigid piece of ass. "Black cats are really witches masquerading in disguise!" she often commented.

"Well what about your black pussy?" I would occasionally jest. "Is there also a treacherous witch inside that wet pink frigid mama too?"

"Please take my apprehension seriously," my wife sternly admonished. "There is something demonic about that black cat of ours. I can't put my finger on it but our furtive pet always seems to be in a walking *cat*atonic state!"

The black cat's name was Pluto, coincidentally named after the Roman ruler of the dark afterworld. At first Pluto was my favorite pet in the whole house (which as I've already stated was sort of a menagerie) and it followed me all over smelling every damned silent or loud fart I would blast out of my asshole. My wife was absolutely afraid to feed the black cat so I assumed that particular twice-daily responsibility. As I've already mentioned the curious creature would follow me everywhere, even along busy thoroughfares and avenues and also up and down narrow side streets and alleyways.

My friendship with Pluto remained intact for several years but then one by one the goldfish, the birds, the dogs, the rabbits, the gerbils and even the small monkey were viciously killed. Claw marks appeared all over their limp bodies. My wife and I never observed or heard Pluto kill any of the other pets, but one by one they all met their deaths by "inexplicable mutilation." My wife could not endure her emotional duress.

"I'm scared out of my wits," my spouse told me one afternoon when she had discovered the monkey's face, throat, head and chest brutally clawed almost beyond recognition. "I believe that Pluto has killed and abused all our other pets. That cat's turned into a horrible monster!"

"Don't be ridiculous!" I strongly replied. "A cat probably would have eventually eaten the goldfish and the birds!" I insisted. "Their bodies were found clawed and mangled but quite obviously they had not been devoured. And besides," I said, "an adult monkey ought to be able to aggressively defend itself and beat the living shit out of any ordinary black housecat!"

"I think you should call the police!" my wife ranted. "Something has killed our pets one by one over the last year and it certainly wasn't you or I! I'm deathly afraid to stay in this house! It's more like an insane asylum!"

"Look," I said in an attempt to sound plausible, "the police aren't going to waste their time and energy investigating the death of house pets with murders and robberies occurring out there on the city streets! They have better things to do like delving into homicides, suicides and grand larcenies," I stubbornly maintained. "Pets aren't *murdered* even if it appears that another animal had *killed* the goldfish', birds, dogs, rabbits, gerbils and monkey! Only humans are murdered and only humans are murderers! Our pets were killed and not murdered!"

It was during that bizarre pet-killing rampage in my house that I felt compelled to increase my consumption of alcohol. I loved rye whiskey, gin and bourbon and became quite addicted to all three Demons. As time passed I became more cantankerous and more intolerant of criticism. I didn't give a flying shit about anyone else's feelings any more and began behaving exactly as my old hedonistic friends had acted ten years before. I swore at my wife, beat her violently on several occasions and would deliberately piss on the floor to demonstrate my general animosity towards her and towards the cold cruel insensitive world.

Pluto sensed this radical fundamental change in my personality and avoided contact with me, but still I favored the wise creature and petted it whenever I found it hiding from me. My drinking problem became more acute and Pluto was now growing old and aggressive, once fiercely scratching me on my right wrist. 'My wife was right about Pluto being evil!' I thought as I cleaned my wound and then wrapped a bandage around it. 'That fucked-up black cat has somehow transferred its satanic wickedness from its own heart and now that ugly evil shit is wickedly inhabiting mine!'

One summer night I arrived home late intoxicated from imbibing liquor at a neighborhood tavern. I literally stumbled over the sleeping black cat in the hallway located between the living room and the bathroom. I lifted up the diabolical creature and squeezed its neck, but before I could strangle the despicable furry mongrel tomcat it clawed my hands and blood was dripping all over the wood-planked floor.

Maybe it was my inebriation or my great fury or both that motivated me, but a primeval hatred instantly consumed my spirit. I cornered Pluto in the parlor and then surreptitiously removed a penknife from my pants' pocket with my bleeding left hand. Next I callously grabbed the savage black cat's neck with my right hand, lifted the hissing evil creature up from the floor and with a surgeon's precision I frantically cut its left eye right out of its fuckin' socket.

Presently as I recollect and accurately document that gross damnable atrocity I feel intense shame and guilt. But nevertheless I cannot deny that the brutality had occurred and that I had deliberately performed the abominable deed and at the time had delighted in doing so.

The following morning I had sobered up and my random meditations were more lucid and less nebulous. I felt a degree of sorrow for my crime and an element of pity for the partially blinded black cat. But my regret was only superficial in magnitude and I began heavily drinking my whiskey again to erase the memory of my uncivilized horrid deportment, and when the bourbon, rye and gin bottles became empty I switched my harmless addiction to wine.

Pluto had slowly recovered from his abuse and the black cat's left eye socket looked rather grotesque and frightening in appearance. The tomcat seemed to not carry any grudge towards me and walked about the house as if he were a prince strutting around *his* palace, but every time I approached the creature its fur would then rise, it would hiss and next the disturbed animal would scurry away to evade my scrutiny. It was evident that Pluto plainly loathed and dreaded me, and my antagonism towards the creature, towards my abused wife and towards the fucked-up world ascended to the level of perverseness.

'Perverseness is a suppressed characteristic of the human emotional spectrum!' I objectively and academically thought. 'It is primitive and atavistic. It's a baser emotion shared by everyone and the negative quality is also a taboo frowned upon by civilized society, but nevertheless it dwells in the deepest pit of every human being's heart!'

I intensely and compulsively felt like leading the life of a contrarian, not only in thought but also in deed. Every shit head deep down in his or her inner *core* wishes to be a rebellious Law Violator and a defiant Ten Commandment Maverick. But the superego and one's fear of public condemnation discourage those primal feelings from surfacing up to one's more docile learned-behavior world from the goddamned dark and mysterious subconscious. And I so desperately wished to spite the holy morals and the legal principles that bond fucked-up society and law and order together, preventing most of us from becoming the sinful hard*core* criminals our dark side would like us to be. I firmly believe that laws and rules prohibit and inhibit us from being our honest happy selves.

This inner turmoil gradually triumphed over my common sensibilities. I felt an overwhelming obsession to self-destruct (to emotionally implode) and did not have the necessary fuckin' wherewithal to combat it. I felt a terrible diabolical need to become violent and to traduce and attack anyone I could. I feared I would *kill* my wife as if she were an animal rather than merely *murder* her as a human being. 'I gotta' get the fuck out of this accursed house before I enact that dreadful perverted fantasy my mind is fabricating!' I seriously thought.

I left the row house and ambled to the all-too-familiar neighborhood bar. I drank four double shots of bourbon and my mind was swimming in silly numbness that adequately transcended the fuckin' mundane world that keeps us all civil and polite and imprisoned inside our socially acceptable behavioral cages.

Then the most beautiful well' built blonde woman I had ever seen entered the crowded bar and ambled over next to my stool. "Could I buy you a drink?" I politely asked.

"Yes, a scotch on the rocks would do just fine," she coyly answered.

We conversed and drank for over an hour and when I was thoroughly wasted, the now-standing vivacious lady took my left hand and shoved it deep down into her skirt. I immediately knew that she was not wearing any undergarments. My palm touched her wonderful hairy pussy and the exotic female gently rubbed my supersensitive fingers against her magnificent thick bush. The wonderful thrilling tantalizing sensation made me instantly think of Pluto's soft fur. I could not control my fury and my sense of survival that had buoyantly surfaced up to my consciousness. I suddenly wrenched my hand out of her very magnificent pubic zone.

"Leave me alone you fuckin' whore!" I screamed, getting the attention of every envious sex-starved male patron in the crowded bar. "Fuckin' leave me alone to my own misery you promiscuous filthy pig slut!" I boisterously raved like a possessed stark-raving-mad maniac.

I stormed out of the popular bar leaving a generous tip on the counter and also leaving a distinct hush in my wake. I was dominated by a *perverted* urge to enter my corner row house and perform a most heinous act.

Precisely at midnight I had cornered and captured Pluto, carried the black beast outside, and despite the animal's writhing resistance, clawing and biting, I held its neck tightly and before I had strangled the squealing creature to death, I took a rope and wrapped it around the screaming frenetic animal's neck. I creatively hung the black cat from the lowest limb of a nearly dead birch tree in my small backyard. I simultaneously laughed and cried in response to my perverse perverted maniacal sin.

'I have lynched Pluto because it loved me and because I had loved its noble spirit!' I thought as I then sobbed and whimpered. 'I have destroyed evil lurking in its heart! I know I've *killed* the evil lurking deep in his animal soul just as *he* had honored a similar instinct and had viciously killed my other pets!' I sentimentally cried with the bitterest sense of remorse.

My heart didn't give a shit at that moment if I had jeopardized my goddamned immortal soul and had condemned it to the eternal fires of hell. 'Even the most Clement and Just God might not be able to salvage my wretched soul following such inhumane and atrocious mal-conduct,' I suspected.

After I had eliminated what my mind considered the source of my evil by cruelly suspending the black cat from the birch tree, I slept in the spare bedroom fearing that I might also be inclined *to kill* my already abused wife. I was awakened from my slumber with hysterical shouts of "Fire!" originating from voices outside my dwelling. The curtains around my bed along with the sidewall were already in flames. Soon the entire house was engulfed in a raging inferno.

My frigid wife and I had separately escaped the dangerous blaze. I remember staggering out of the front door and falling down the white marble steps, clumsily landing on the pavement. 'Everything I've diligently worked for all my life will soon be reduced to ashes and cinders!' I despairingly thought. 'My life has been cursed and my soul has been doomed! This fuckin' devastating fire is symbolic of the eternal flames of hell my immortal soul will surely experience!'

Now I'm logically and objectively presenting a series of irrefutable facts in the form of a sequence of events, but I'm not such a fucking fool to suggest that there exists any scientific cause and effect relationship between me dramatically hanging and killing Pluto and the terrible conflagration that ensued shortly thereafter. But there are other very troubling goddamned links to this chain of events that undeniably challenge my intelligence and accentuate my fears.

On the day following the devastating fire, after a night of sobering up and pacing the lonely city streets, I felt a need to visit the ruins of my demolished home. Only one wall remained vertical, and it was the one situated in the center of the house. The head of the bed in which I had been sleeping had rubbed against that accursed wall. Remarkably the plaster had withstood the fire's rage and I speculated that its survival had been because the material had been recently applied and was still fresh enough to fend off the intense heat the blaze had generated.

A dense crowd had gather around the standing wall and neighbors were gossiping and marveling about a certain phenomenon. I heard the adjectives "Strange!" and "Odd!" being babbled among the goddamned disgusting horde of curiosity-seekers. I approached the lone standing wall to examine it more specifically. An impression of a rope wrapped around a huge cat's neck had been mystically embedded in the plaster.

My wonder quickly ascended and evolved into terror as I further scrutinized the fucking hellish configuration. 'It's Pluto's ghost returned to further haunt my ass right into fuckin' insanity!' I naturally concluded. 'Try to settle down and get a grip of your emotions!' I recall thinking. 'The special advantage you have over these weak minded curiosity-seekers is that you have the capacity to be stoic and objective.'

My mind evaluated all of the evidence and reviewed all of the extraordinary circumstances. Pluto had been hung in the backyard from the birch tree. My keen eyes then looked at my hands with their many lacerations and scratches as observable residual proof of that indisputable event happening. 'Someone in the neighborhood must have cut down the animal from the tree immediately after he or she had trespassed upon my property after being attracted to it by the house fire!' I theorized. 'Then the contemptible do-gooder must have hurled the dead cat through an open window (for it was then summertime) into my infernal bedroom and I had been awakened by the thump and soon heard the loud screaming outside.

'When the other walls collapsed, Pluto's body must have been pressed into the freshly applied wall plaster making a permanent impression. And then the plaster's lime had been chemically converted into ammonia arising from the cat's sizzling carcass!' I methodically and deductively realized. 'This infallible hypothesis scientifically proves how the black cat had disintegrated and how its' outlined form still eerily remains embedded into the wall's plaster.'

My brain rationalized that fantastic theory and believed that I had made the correct and reasonable conclusion. My impeccable flawless analysis represented adequate confirmation of my intelligent assumptions explaining what had actually transpired. There was nothing mysterious or supernatural about the fucking reprehensible comprehensible event whatsoever. The fucked-up incident just had the appearance of being incredible but was entirely explainable if one rationally applied the science of chemistry to account for what had actually occurred.

But still my suspicions and my fears agitated my already maligned sense of judgment. My discretion had been tinkered with, no fucking doubt about it. For the next half-year I could not discard the image of Pluto embedded in plaster from my psyche. 'I must vanquish these irritating manifestations so that my mind can again enjoy tranquility!' I kept repeating to myself. 'Pluto's terrifying image in that standing wall can be explained by elementary science and that's all that really fuckin' matters!'

The next year my wife and I lived with separate relatives. In the meantime I managed to borrow some money from reliable friends and from several well-to-do cousins and I had my former row house reconstructed to the exact same dimensions to the ones that had been obliterated in the unfortunate fire. But still each night I had crazy fuckin' nightmares haunting my spirit about Pluto with his heinous animal soul crying out to me from the deepest fiery pit of Hell.

My psyche was haunted by the notion that I had to replace Pluto with a substitute cat to redeem my killing of him. I went in quest of a comparable black cat on all neighboring streets but had the fucking bad luck of a born loser. Undaunted by failure, I resumed my search until I reached absolute fatigue.

I dejectedly entered a tavern notorious for its debauchery and decided to get *plastered*, or at least as plastered as Pluto had been before being disintegrated by the intense heat of the house fire and the subsequent chemical reaction that had mercilessly incinerated the dead creature somewhere into oblivion. After becoming groggy from an excess of liquor I espied through a doorway a sinister black cat lying peacefully upon a large rum barrel in the tavern's warehouse. 'That goddamned animal is indeed Pluto reincarnated!' I observantly thought. 'This is my opportunity for redemption. I shall possess the stray and give it the loving home that Pluto had been denied!'

I carefully approached the sedate creature and gently caressed it with my hands. The cat was virtually identical to Pluto except for one outstanding feature. The fucking thing had a white blotch on its breast, which I naturally presumed symbolized an island of goodness amidst a vast sea of sin and decadence. 'This son-of-a-bitchin' black cat is begging me to be its master!' I conjectured. 'It's definitely a docile mature friendly creature worthy of my compassion and affection!'

The appreciative cat was purring loudly, apparently enthused about the good vibrations its sixth-sense radar' had been perceiving' and interpreting as human kindness. He rubbed his soft fur against my sweaty hands and I was fully aware of our genuine compatibility.

"How much for your black cat?" I asked the suddenly surprised tavern proprietor.

"It's not mine and I've never seen the thing before," he tersely answered. "You may claim it for your own for I'm certain it's only but a stray tomcat looking for a warm meal and a comfortable home."

I thanked the pleasant landlord for his indulgence and hurriedly returned to my recently constructed home proudly carrying my new acquisition. The novel addition quickly found favor with my reconciled wife, who treated *him* with more respect and dignity than the frigid cold bitch had ever treated me. I soon became jealous of the new cat receiving more goddamned attention and approval in the house than I had been getting.

My interest in the new black cat gradually turned to jealous resentment. After several months I abhorred and then despised the odious detestable animal. Being somewhat paranoid I avoided the creature, knowing full well that I could be inspired to kill it on instinct for simply breathing anywhere near my face and eyes. 'I must not violate and abuse this cat as I had done with Pluto,' my mind guiltily pondered. 'I shall regard it as if it's diseased and totally ignore its presence in my newly constructed house.'

My conscience knew I was thinking and behaving like a derelict scumbag, but what could I fucking do? I never placed much credence in coincidences until the following morning. I shuddered when I observed that the second black cat had its unlucky left eye missing and now looked more than ever like Pluto (except for the singular patch of white fur on its chest). My wife then loved *him* even more and I selfishly envied the cat for meriting her devotion and tenderness, which I had been neglected throughout our marriage. I was livid and my suppressed emotions were ready to volcanically explode into a tirade.

The more I hated the fucking second cat the more it seemed to like me. It faithfully followed my footsteps as if it were a determined animal private detective stalking me down. It crouched at my feet whenever I sat my ass down. Sometimes the son-of-a-bitch would hop onto my lap begging to be cuddled. And whenever I sauntered down the hallway the annoying animal would pass between my feet and almost trip me into a tumble. Sometimes the cat would insert its long sharp claws into my pants and playfully climb up to my chest. I was both puzzled and alarmed at those excessive liberties the furry Pluto incarnate was exhibiting.

I soon desired to kill this second offensive cat and was contemplating appropriate methods of eliminating it from my daily experiences. 'This is absolutely fuckin' preposterous and silly,' I thought. 'Why should I feel unwarranted terror and dread from such a dumb dependent stray cat? Even if it attacked me in my sleep I would wake up from the surprise assault, grab the mother-fuckin' piece of shit and wring its neck until it ceased breathing!' I graphically imagined. 'Sometimes I think that I'm almost as fucked up as the mother-fuckin' world is!'

My wife kept reminding me how beautiful the new cat's white patch was and that declaration instantly reinforced my certainty that the new pet had its own identity and its own agenda and was not Pluto's spirit reborn into another kindred animal. And besides, when I had found the second fucked-up cat in the tavern it was at least three years old and Pluto had been dead for less than a year, so any possibility of that new black cat being Pluto reincarnated was both chronologically and realistically infeasible.

I pensively thought about and seriously considered the white blotch. At first it appeared shapeless without any particular definition but now the vivid image I observed formed on its breast was the outline of *a gallows*! I recollected hanging Pluto from a limb on the backyard birch tree and suddenly the symbolism of the white gallows' formation on the second black cat's chest made me skeptical of the existence of such things as accurate science and a normal life on this goddamned grace-forsaken planet. And soon I felt an irresistible inclination to kill that second brutish beast, for it was not its physical appearance that I detested but instead its evil soul that was undoubtedly that fucking vicious stalker Pluto reincarnated.

I never thereafter had a decent night's sleep. I tossed and turned anticipating with great trepidation that the bitchin' monster would go berserk, leap up onto my bed and slash my jugular vein with its sharp claws and fangs. I tried sleeping with my hands over my neck to prevent that feared incursion from occurring, but to no avail. I was restless, weary, incensed, frightened and on the brink of becoming a fucking raving psychopath.

One October night I arose from a light sleep and discovered that the evil creature had been breathing on my face. I hopped out of bed in a wild frenzy and chased the alarmed creature out of the spare room and pursued it down the hall into my wife's chamber. When I flung open the door in a rage my estranged frigid spouse became startled and sat up straight in her bed. My eyes glared red when I witnessed the second black cat peacefully resting besides her right arm.

The following afternoon my wife and I were stepping down to the cellar to obtain some vegetables preserved in glass jars. We were poor and my spouse began unjustly criticizing why she and I had reached an almost destitute existence.

"You can never hold a job and we have little money to pay our many bills," she persisted, "and you're nothing more than a drunken failure and a pathetic loser!" she wickedly instigated our quarrel on the cellar steps.

I wanted to take my hostility out on my wife but then I noticed that the black cat was descending the steps down to the dismal dank cellar. When the frightful animal nearly tripped me on the fourth step from the basement's floor I went into an uncontrollable hysteria. I decided to transfer the intense hate I had felt towards my wife to the very vexing black cat.

"What the fuck did you say?" I shrieked while lunging toward an axe that had been leaning against the cellar wall. But instead of taking my animosity out on my frigid wife, I aimed a blow at the ubiquitous black cat. But my interfering wife jumped into the way to

82

protect the tomcat from my wrath and instead of killing the despicable Pluto incarnate I had accidentally murdered her by mistake.

The axe's blade had penetrated her skull and was then buried deep inside her brain. She fell to the cold cement basement floor and blood spouted all over the goddamned place. It was a gruesome scene and as I stood there' crying at my malicious crime I saw the hungry black cat eerily licking up the puddles of crimson. I was afraid to kill the demonic beast since I was so distraught from recently butchering my beloved wife.

'I can't afford a funeral and a decent coffin and the police are sure to conduct an intensive investigation! I must act with dispatch!' I quickly decided. I thought of dismembering her body into small fragments and then efficiently burning them in a fire. 'I could fling her limp corpse into the backyard well!' I imagined. 'Or I could dispose of her remains by burying them under the cellar floor and then resurfacing the section with fresh concrete.'

Finally my mind recollected an ancient practice that had been utilized by crafty European monks during the *Middle Ages*. 'I can seal her body up in the recently *plastered* wall over there. The cellar has been damp and the plaster has not hardened,' I reckoned. 'Any new plaster would easily blend in with the original composition and almost magically conceal my cunning camouflage!' I determined. "Fuck your damned remains, you no good frigid bitch!" I screamed at my spouse's lifeless corpse.

'If I remove the loose bricks from that false chimney construction over there,' I theorized, 'I could stealthily hide her cadaver in the wall and then cover it up with fresh plaster and then deftly conceal my heinous misdeed. No one will ever suspect that I had been capable of such a marvelous expedient stratagem! The fucked up world is full of stupid fucks not half as clever as I am!'

I adroitly used a crowbar to further loosen and remove the aforementioned bricks. When sufficient space had been made to accommodate a standing corpse, I almost mechanically lifted my wife's body and squeezed and finally successfully manipulated it inside the designated area. Next I meticulously reset the bricks and then blended mortar, sand and some of *her* cut hair into a splendid plaster that when applied, looked identical to that which appeared throughout the rest of the wall. It was indeed a most fabulous mixture I had imaginatively concocted and my excellent scheme would be far above and beyond any human detection.

I was perfectly convinced and satisfied that everything had been properly planned and deviously implemented. 'You're a fuckin' genius!' I commended myself. 'I've picked up all clues of debris from the floor and it appears almost immaculate after I had slyly eliminated all bloodstain traces with a powerful solvent that had been kept under the kitchen sink. Only the supernatural is aware of my dastardly deeds, that is to think if an omniscient Supreme Being actually exists!' I deliriously laughed. 'Now I must capture and execute that troublesome fucked-up black cat, which has caused all of the unnecessary pain and suffering my heavily-laden heart must live with for the rest of my goddamned fuckin' life!'

After deciding that I must put the miserable fiendish animal to *his* death, the perceptive creature sensed my nasty mood and evaded my scrutiny. I searched and searched the house but to no satisfaction. Finally I took a nap, being exhausted from burying and sealing my wife in the cellar wall and from futilely ransacking the upstairs rooms madly scrambling all over looking for the goddamned Hell-sent replacement black cat.

I had slept fairly soundly as I hadn't done in many months. Then three days elapsed and still no sign of the evasive cat was evident anywhere. My elation was virtually exultant. 'The fuckin' black bastard has fled the house to escape my prescribed death sentence!' I gleefully thought. 'Its persistent evil will vex me no more!'

On the fourth day after I had conveniently executed and disposed of my wife, the police arrived at my residence to conduct a preliminary inquiry as to her whereabouts. Several neighbors had complained about a minor disturbance and after her relatives had conveyed to the authorities that she had not been in contact with them, the idiotic cops were compelled to make an official report. The police carefully searched all rooms in the premises and then I confidently (without guilt or embarrassment) led the men-in-blue down to the cobweb-infested basement. The resolute investigators left no corner of the property unexplored. Four times they made a rotation of the total cellar and the officers found nothing suspicious or irregular.

I remained calm throughout the inquiry and did not tremble or show any indication of regret or emotion. I folded my arms in front of my chest and freely conversed with the dumb-assed detective and his incompetent asinine crew of notepad scribblers, joking about the weather and jesting about why my wife had mysteriously disappeared and had possibly fled to Florida. 'I fear she's unfaithfully abandoned me for a richer man,' I stated. 'My wife was

84

lazy, kept a poor dirty house and hated washing clothes and cooking meals,' I stated. 'She had always sought a better life with a wealthy man and did not hesitate to repeatedly emphasize those selfish desires to me!' I persuasively testified.

The concerns of the police had been satisfactorily addressed and their superficial doubts about my integrity had been thoroughly alleviated. I felt victorious and exuberant as I began leading them up the cellar steps.

"Gentlemen," I said, "if you need to come again, feel free to do so and also be aware that you'll enjoy my full cooperation. May you return in good health and I anticipate again greeting you with my utmost courtesy."

Then I felt an alien compulsion to say something casual in nature and totally irrelevant to *their* purpose in being there but what I uttered also happened to be very material to the truths that dwelled deep within my soul. "Gentlemen," I continued my concluding remarks, "you must admit that this house is superbly constructed. The walls are dense and solidly built."

And during the culmination of my rather frivolous bravado I deliberately and heavily rapped my black cane against the solid wall. But to my absolute horror I had initiated a bizarre diabolical reaction.

'May the mercy of God protect and isolate me from Satan's poisonous fangs!' I desperately thought. No sooner had my cane's blow echoed throughout the dank dark cellar that the five of us discerned a pitiful cry originating from within the formerly nondescript wall where I had furtively deposited and concealed my wife's corpse.

At first the horrible moan was that of anguish and agony, and as it increased in volume the goddamned fucking noise swelled to a continuous hideous and surreal scream that sounded like it had ascended from the very bowels of Hell. It was a most disconcerting combination of howling, wailing, shrieking and fright. The spine-chilling tone was half victory and half horror, half joy and half damnation.

I felt thoroughly faint and then staggered around the dank cellar in a giddy dizziness. Thoughts and ideas and emotions whirled around inside my head and became jumbled up into one confusing unbearable tornado of mental activity. The four horrified police officials stood frozen on the steps closely evaluating my strange and unsettling behavior.

And then the next thing I remember were eight strong arms hacking away with various clubs and tools at the recently plastered wall. The policemen were hammering and banging away next to the artificial chimney from where the peculiar sensational howling and groaning were still emanating. As a large section of plaster fell to the floor my wife's corpse suddenly stood before *our* horrified eyes. Then I too panicked and quickly shared *their* extreme terror. My wife's morbid face appeared decayed and gory and gruesomely covered with soot and wall dust.

On her head was a one-eyed back cat with an opened-red-mouth. The beast's remaining eye blazed with a scarlet fire. The black demon's screams had alerted the police to the recently plastered wall and had simultaneously condemned me to the gallows. And then in the midst of my mania I recalled one insular fact. I then shamefully recollected that I had walled up the still-alive black cat with my wife during her most unorthodox burial.

"A Tale of the Ragged Mountains"

In the autumn of the year 1827 I had been wasting my life away and residing near Charlottesville, Virginia around a mile or so from the late Thomas Jefferson's famous Monticello estate and my modest dwelling being within sight of the majestic Blue Ridge Mountains, the Ragged Mountains being the local division of that particular sector of the great Appalachian Chain.

It was there in Charlottesville that I had casually made the acquaintance of a certain Mr. Augustus Bellamy Bedloe, who was a fastidious eccentric oddball loner that always insisted on sleeping in the upper mattress level of his bunk-bed frame even though the psycho' didn't live or sleep with anyone else.

Mr. Bedloe was indeed a lone wolf-type of fellow although he was a strict vegetarian and in no way, shape or form was the gent a glutinous carnivore. But the townspeople had nothing better to do than to often gossip about poor Augustus, rumoring that "the crabby hermit" was "an atheist anarchist homosexual," but I would usually politely argue in his defense that the man was merely "effeminate" and not "a faggot" as others so maliciously maintained and that even if Mr. Bedloe were an avowed "gay bird," he still habitually and "religiously" practiced celibacy and abstinence. Well, in looking back, *that* last inauspicious occasion was the first time I ever had rocks, pineapples, cactuses and tomatoes hurled in my direction.

But one thing was certain about Mr. Bedloe: no one knew where the hell he came from, who the hell his parents were, what the hell he did as an occupation to earn a living and exactly what the hell his morals and ethics were, if indeed he had any salient and noteworthy morals and ethics. So in essence and in retrospect, I really suppose I didn't know the mysterious Augustus Bedloe too damned well after all and I now fully appreciate that I would be much better off today if I had never met the neurotic paranoid oddball.

One observation I had made about Mr. Bedloe: I had known him in a rather remote way for twenty-five years and he looked exactly as he must have appeared back in 1802 before the goddamned Louisiana Purchase had been signed. The slender weirdo was six-foot eight inches tall with exceedingly long arms and legs, had a very pallid almost-ghost-like complexion, an extended pointed chin that looked like an acute angle of an isosceles triangle, and was sort of an anachronism because Augustus Bellamy Bedloe dressed similarly to the style that aristocratic men had clad themselves a full century ago.

And when the scuttlebutting assholes in this western Virginia community would incessantly emphasize these glaring-but-irrelevant coincidences I would answer with aplomb, "At least Mr. Bedloe still dresses like a man and does not wear evening gowns, petticoats, corsets, bloomers or skirts, even though he lives on the outskirts of town. And praise the Lord that the gentleman in question most certainly is not one of those appalling cross-dressers that according to tabloid newspaper depictions, happen to be the sensational rage up in Boston, Philadelphia, Baltimore and New York."

But Mr. Augustus Bedloe's front teeth were abnormally huge and had uneven spaces between them, giving his open mouth a jagged and almost jack-o'-lantern-type of frightening smile. But whenever the enigmatic Bedloe did manage to grin, it was an absolutely false grin that somehow engendered and reflected both pessimistic melancholy and chronic suffering. The general impression I had received from being in Bedloe's morose company was that the man was both full of gloom and full of shit, but it was hypothetical shit that nobody knew anything about.

"You don't have to apologize to anyone in this ass-backwards community for anything," I once told the apathetic who-gives-a-shit asshole, "and whatever you do, pay no heed to the insinuations and the braggadocio of your fucked-up neighbors, including me. Everyone on this bizarre Earth is a stupid asshole for thinking that he or she is important in the first place!"

"I should share with you that I have certain neurological problems that transcend the skills of present medical science," Bedloe once confided to me outside a popular local bed and breakfast. "My very competent physician Dr. Willard Templeton, whom I had first met at the racetrack up in Saratoga, New York State, intelligently claims that nature has egregiously gotten under my skin, thus causing my aggravating neuralgia to act up. This Templeton genius is eighty-seven years old and I think my doctor's mind is rapidly disintegrating," Bedloe confidentially related to me outside his favorite morning eating hangout where he kept a table all to himself in a private dining room that had been labeled by local churchgoing gossip-sharers as 'The Satanic Bar and Pub.' "And as far as me not working is concerned," Augustus continued his fascinating monologue, "I'm very independently wealthy and self-sufficient because of fabulous inheritances I've received from rich ancestors and incidentally, I also support Dr. Templeton financially, for as you are aware, I am his sole patient."

"Templeton, didn't he study his craft in Paris and thus learned all about Paris-sites?" I stupidly and glibly remarked. "I think your doctor knows all about the teachings of Franz Mesmer and the experimenter's purported revolutionary magnetic treatments to alleviate all kinds of pain. Hey Augustus," I said, "*that'* recollection gives me a terrific idea. Maybe I should shove a magnet up my rectum because I find you Mr. Bedloe to be a real pain in the ass."

"Yes Poe my friend, over the years Dr. Templeton and I have developed a very distinct rapport where we sometimes engage in mental telepathy and know exactly what each other is thinking or planning, even sometimes when we're actually miles apart. Oftentimes he and I even communicate graphic mental color transmissions in our sleep, commonly and inadvertently sharing both our phenomenal dreams and our hair-raising nightmares."

"As long as you two perverts don't share white dreams and disgusting asshole penetration nightmares together," I said with phobic alarm, "because then if that were the case, I'm certain that both you and Templeton would be tarred and feathered, tied to a long splintery timber and ultimately tossed into a deep lake or river with jagged rocks in the downstream rapids. But tell me the basic honest-to-God truth Mr. Bedloe," I continued with my subtle and mannerly information gathering, "the most recent town gossip is that you're a drugo? Is that rumor true?"

"Yes, I do take concentrated doses of nerve-soothing morphine while honoring Dr. Templeton's prescriptions, and the sedatives sometimes induce hallucinations on my part," Bedloe whispered and explained although no one was within a thousand feet of our dialogue. "I mean like right now for instance Mr. Poe, as I'm privately speaking to you, I just don't know for sure whether or not I'm fuckin' talking to an illusion or conversing with a goddamned mirage. But all in all, morphine is a terrific way to escape from reality. I find it a positively wonderful asset to be intermittently delusional and hibernating on Cloud Nine, wouldn't you agree?"

"And why the hell do you take those long rambles up into the Ragged Mountains with your dog?" I wondered and asked. "It seems like a considerable distance of perhaps seven miles or so up into the precipitous hills. That's a long way to take your pet just for the sake of relieving his dysfunctional kidneys and his spastic colon."

"That's my fuckin' business!" Bedloe furiously bristled in a rare outburst of emotion. "Get your own goddamned canine, walk him up into the rugged Ragged Mountains and fuckin' find out for yourself why I might possibly make that daily expedition into what I describe as 'hillbilly oblivion'."

"Okay Augustus, I'll see you tomorrow," I replied, quite glad to have escaped being brutally assaulted. "I just hope you're in a better friggin' mood than you are right now and have always been since your ignominious pal Dr. Willard Templeton had first introduced us by erroneously having our goddamned names in reverse."

* * * * * * * * * * * *

On a cold misty morning toward the end of November in what is commonly referred to in America as "Indian Summer," Mr. Augustus Bedloe departed on his usual trek onto a trail that meandered into the seldom-explored Ragged Mountains. Eight hours later dusk had settled in and yet the introverted jerk-off had not returned to town and so Dr. Templeton and myself, being concerned about our friend's protracted absence from the human population, were about to conduct a two member search-and-rescue operation because none of the other citizens of Charlottesville either gave or cared a shepherd's shit about the fate of the often shunned and ostracized missing man. And so Templeton and I appointed each other to act like practicing moralistic Christians.

On our fairly arduous expedition up the path leading from town to the foreboding mountain range Templeton and I soon unexpectedly encountered Bedloe descending from his most recent exploration, his spirits seeming remarkably high and his energy level and stamina being exceptional. Naturally the physician and I wished to learn every detail of the queer man's mountain adventure so we allowed him to catch his breath and then begin rehashing his exploit.

"As usual I had left Charlottesville around nine this morning and several hours later discovered a gorgeous gorge that I had never before trespassed into," Augustus began his narrative in his standard monotonous monotone voice. "The general environment was very desolate and quite virgin so naturally my communion-with-nature mind wanted to fully integrate with the myriad rocks and trees because as you two Gentlemen perfectly well know, my motto is 'screw the world and fuck everybody in it.' Anyway Gentlemen," Bedloe proceeded with his zany exposition, "the philosophical thought suddenly occurred to me that where I was merrily treading, the fantastic landscape, being so primitive and so pristine, well, *that* virgin territory had never before been seen or experienced by any

90

other person venturing out from American civilization. Do you Gentlemen identify with my enthusiasm for ecology and for the environment?"

"Your mind is having sex with rocks and trees and you expect me to relate with that?" I vehemently challenged. "And you're fuckin' screwing virgin land too!"

"Mr. Poe, please don't try to mock my testimony and make a travesty of my presentation," Bedloe pleaded.

"I say with conviction Augustus that you had overdosed on morphine back in Charlottesville and that your demented brain was already having mental manifestations that were sending you on a bad drug trip before you ever left town," I sincerely expressed, exhibiting rare candor. "You're going to probably next tell Templeton and me that on your momentous mountain trek this morning you then heard the dead Italian astronomer Galileo inharmoniously pretending to be an opera tenor singing some strange motley loud Bohemian rhapsody to a captivated teenage audience!"

"Pay no attention to Mr. Poe's uncanny sense of humor that is often laced with decadent skepticism," Templeton implored Bedloe. "Now please continue with your intriguing recollection of events up in the enchanting Ragged Mountains."

"I was fearful of stumbling or tumbling into an abyss and being captured by some uncouth race of men that according to legend, are said to dwell up there in dark shadowy caves and caverns," Augustus stated. "Next my normally dependable legs began trembling when I suddenly heard the distant beating of a drum. 'Perhaps Michael the Archangel has lost his coveted golden trumpet and is using a drum to announce the looming departure of my soul from my body,' I anxiously and apprehensively surmised."

"Bedloe, you need hospitalization, medication and a month's rest mighty fast," I strongly advised and suggested. "Have you ever considered enacting suicide or committing euthanasia on yourself?"

"Mr. Poe, you're disrupting our dear friend's train of thought, which incidentally might have several loco-motives as you've been redundantly inferring and stating," Templeton absurdly punned. "Please permit him to resume his extemporaneous rhetoric. Go on Augustus, enlighten us!"

Bedloe cleared his throat of heavy thick green mucus and then began deluging us with some more of his unprecedented bullshit. "Well Gentlemen, a few seconds later, that is after the distant drum beat, a half-naked shrieking hysterical man sprinted by me with the speed of Mercury, that is to say, the Roman god and not the chemical element. Soon the delirious human-like specimen disappeared like magic into a shroud of high mountain mist."

"That shrieking scampering asshole you think you saw could've been either the mayor or the chief-of-police of Charlottesville," I quipped and then giggled. "Both of those fat cornball assholes are currently running for office!"

"Mr. Bedloe, just ignore Mr. Poe's disrespectful asinine comments and continue expounding on your past visualizations," Templeton encouraged. "Perhaps Edgar Allan here doesn't relish your story but I most certainly find it meritorious."

"Well Dr., after the shrieking man rushed by, I turned my head to the right and spotted a fierce-looking animal, a hungry carnivorous hyena I believe, accelerating straight by me and wildly chasing the intimidated human. Although the antagonistic beast was three times the regular size of an animal of that species', I'm thoroughly convinced that the brute was definitely a hyena."

"Was the hyena laughing, telling jokes, doing slapstick comedy or the like?" I chuckled and then guffawed. "Was the hyena just the beginning of a well-trained menagerie relay race team? Ho, ho, ho! My fuckin' guts are going to split open from too much laughing! Ha, ha, ha!" I loudly communicated.

"Go on with your most interesting monologue," the quack doctor implored the somewhat confounded and disoriented Bedloe. "Poe is your typical American cynic that likes to harass and criticize what he doesn't understand. Sometimes I think the stupid bastard is Diogenes reincarnated!"

"Well Dr. Templeton, after getting over my initial shock I gathered my scattered wits and ambled down a path that was entirely unfamiliar to me," Bedloe declared without a trace of emotion evident on his pale albino-like face. "I stopped my walking and momentarily leaned against a tree but upon looking up, I was astonished to recognize that the object was a tropical palm tree, quite indigenous to a place like Florida or Barbados or the Bahamas, but the majestic palm tree was thriving right up here in the Ragged Mountains of Virginia!"

"Maybe the shrieking jerk-off that dashed by you was Ponce de Leon in mad pursuit of the Fountain of Youth," I gushed and giggled, "and perhaps the hyena was chasing after him for stealing its marching drum. After listening to this ton of illogical horse manure," I ascertained and recounted, "I do think that the Charlottesville Mental Clinic's new psycho' ward must quickly prepare three new beds immediately to accommodate *this*, how should I express it, *this* psychologically disturbed triumvirate having an intense inordinate nonsensical conversation at nightfall up here in the fuckin' cold and alien Ragged Mountains."

Bedloe then went on to say that he soon found himself at the foot of a high ridge that overlooked an enormous unknown city that had buildings and structures of foreign architecture and design. According to the questionable eyewitness's account, there were many intersecting streets and alleys along with a variety of balconies, bazaars, elephants, banners, camels, minarets, mosques, donkeys, turban-headed males and an abundance of exotic veiled women abounding everywhere throughout the greater hustle and bustle. "Even from my remote vantage point looking down from several thousand feet away," Bedloe narrated in his one-pitch voice, "the merchants in the marketplace were busy bartering cutlery, food, vegetables, fruits, silks and muslins."

"Wow, Muslims bartering muslins!" I laughed, nearly pissing myself. "What a fucked-up nightmare you were having under the influence of that morphine! Hope you aren't taking any other drugs like opium or cocaine besides the morphine! Tell me Bedloe," I deliberately continued my obnoxious levity, "did you spot any alluring brothels or bordellos down there in that foreign city? How about your common everyday proletarian whorehouse? Ha, ha, ha!"

"Heed not Mr. Poe's unwarranted verbal diatribes," Templeton sternly advised Bedloe. "He's both typical and emblematic of what the hell's wrong with contemporary American Christian churchgoing society. They all still think and behave like prehistoric uncultured men like Abraham, Isaac, Solomon and Moses. Now then," Templeton declared, "let's assume that what you're telling *me* is not a dream or an illusion. My professional psychological opinion is that somehow Augustus you had traveled both in time and space, essentially voyaging inside your regular body to an earlier age setting depicting a thriving Oriental trade center. Now then Augustus," the nutcase physician enunciated, "did you have the audacity to descend down into the foreign metropolis and opportunistically mingle with the citizenry? Were you able to speak their language?"

"A foreign medieval metropolis somehow transported from Asia through time and space to wind-up being right here in the Ragged Mountains of Virginia only several minute miles from where we're standing," I discourteously interrupted and screamed and then indulgently laughed, thoroughly amusing myself as I loudly farted thrice in addition to wetting my pants. "This is fuckin' richer than

93

those new wealthy Wall Street banker tycoons, ha, ha, ha! It's fuckin' richer than all the freakin' czars of Russia put together! Ha, ha, ha! What a trip and a half!"

Bedloe pretended that I was not harassing him. "Well Dr. Templeton, I entered the city rather unobtrusively without any alert guards or soldiers intercepting my passage," Augustus disclosed. "But after visiting the crowded and hectic marketplace, I became somehow mixed-in with a few vociferous political dissidents, who were then pursued by crazed soldiers and policemen of the established authority. I was being jostled around in the mad frenzy and as you can plainly see, my shirt and my pants are ripped from my defensive participation in the ongoing melee," Bedloe insisted. "Now Dr. Templeton, the impetuous rabble to which I was a part scurried hither and thither throughout the narrow streets and alleyways, but at every turn *we* were met and attacked by the weapon-carrying militias. In fact, closely look at my forehead if you doubt my veracity Mr. Poe. I was struck hard on my cranium several times by batons and clubs and was bleeding rather profusely from my scalp wounds. Look here," Bedloe said, leaning his head downward. "I still feel some dried-up blood in the temple area."

"Ha, ha, ha," I shouted, holding my rumbling intestines and growling stomach intact. "You first say that the city was loaded with mosques and now you fuckin' state that you were hit in the *temple* area, when obviously there weren't any damned Jews living in the whole goddamned place! That's what you fuckin' get for hanging out with a bunch of political anarchists and nihilists, ha, ha, ha! How come you were hit in the temple and not in the goddamned synagogue? Ha, ha, ha!"

Templeton didn't savor me toying with a word that was part of his sacred last name. "Are you trying to tell us that you had died from your multiple abrasions and wounds?" the loony doctor seriously asked Bedloe in a coarse hoarse voice. "It couldn't have been a nightmarish dream if you had died during your altercations in the Oriental city! I'm finally beginning to comprehend the essence of what you're stating! Please proceed with your fascinating discourse."

"Well, for many minutes I felt suspended a full fifty-feet up in the atmosphere and I then understood that I was a non-entity having no tangible or palpable corporal existence," Augustus revealed. "And upon peering down at the marketplace scenario my mind's eye spied my dead body lying prone on the cobblestone street, still unattended. It was a totally horrendous dismal helpless feeling that I'm trying to re-create and describe to you."

94

"Mr. Bedloe, you should've drowned in a river if you wanted to do the dead man's float," I laughed, pissing myself some more and then nearly farting a pile of crap out of my aching asshole. "Who then came around to get you? Floating medics in a floating ambulance, floating undertakers in a floating hearse? Ha, ha, ha! I think my goddamned balls just severed themselves from my torso! Ha, ha, ha! I haven't laughed this hard since that no-good bastard Benedict Arnold died, ha, ha, ha!"

"Hurry up with your marvelous recollection Augustus!" Willard Templeton demanded. "Assholes like Poe here never contribute anything worthwhile in the way of knowledge or technology to advance the causes of science and humanity!"

"I seemed to have no concern about my mortal demise lying below and I had lost all detectable desire to exercise my volition, or what the Constitution defines as 'free will'," Bedloe divulged. "I slowly floated away from the foreign city and a minute later miraculously landed on the Ragged Mountain path where I had encountered the sprinting man and the ferocious hyena. And before I could think any more about my misadventures," the nutcase continued, "my fleeting spirit had instantaneously and miraculously been re-united with my body and I was whole again as a complete human being."

"Well Augustus," I analyzed and quipped, "you' were right about one thing. That sprinting old man couldn't have been a dashing young man, ha, ha, ha! I just couldn't resist inserting *that* bit of levity into this insane three-way conversation. Ha, ha, ha! Only a horny woman with sexual motives in mind could recognize a dashing young man, ha, ha, ha!"

"Augustus, that was a wonderfully incredible yet perfectly fathomable story you had just shared," Templeton summarized and praised. "I presume that soon thereafter you trekked down the trail and met Poe and me ascending the hill to find you."

"Yes Dr. Templeton, that's my entire story and I swear to you that all of my epistle was as true as Gospel," Bedloe ineffectively proselytized, attempting to convert me into being a believer of his absurd bullshit. "It's as true as Gospel," he repeated, "however I'm not quite so sure about that wacky Book of Revelations."

But then Dr. Templeton really blew my mind by making certain outlandish and outrageous claims that only a warped psychologist such as himself would ever have the sage imagination or the keen insight to produce. From his coat pocket he casually removed a small color portrait done in 1790 of a dead friend of his, a Mr. Harold Oldeb, a British fellow Templeton had known in Calcutta, India

95

under the administration of a certain martinet governor named Warren Hastings.

"Calcutta," I ridiculously said to Templeton. "Wasn't that a big cow slaughterhouse in India?"

"If you had any damned sensitivity to Hindu culture," Templeton strenuously and angrily responded, "then you would surely know that in India the cow is a most sacred and revered animal and would not be fuckin' slaughtered in any goddamned meat slaughterhouse!"

"Well, what's the big deal with the picture of this deceased Oldeb jerk?" I asked and then cackled. "Did he write the catchy lyrics to the song 'Ol Deb Golden Slippers'?"

"You stupid Asshole!" Templeton bellowed like a demonized maniac. "Can't you see the strict physical resemblance between Mr. Bedloe and Mr. Oldeb? When I first met Augustus here' gambling up at the Saratoga Racetrack, right away I picked-up the facial similarity of him' to Harold Oldeb. The two could've been twin brothers because they looked so much alike."

"Are you trying to tell me that Augustus Bedloe is really Harold Oldeb reincarnated?" I laughed, gasping and panting so hard that I thought I was going to choke to death from sheer amusement. "If I crap and piss myself again, I'll surely dehydrate! Ha, ha, ha!"

Then Templeton profoundly blew my mind with the impact of his next statement. "Mr. Poe, I do truly believe that our chum Augustus has just returned from the Indian city of Benares situated upon the holy Ganges River. The riots in which he had involuntarily participated in yet sustained serious life-threatening wounds were led in the year 1780 by an insurrectionist named Cheyte Sing. Administrator Hastings' life had been put in jeopardy because I happen to know that fact, for you see, I was there in Benares when my dear friend Officer Harold Oldeb fell to the cobblestones and subsequently died. But I'll be able to tell you more Mr. Poe about Mr. Bedloe's extraordinary out-of-body experience once I painstakingly corroborate and substantiate some new salient data that I've been collecting and analyzing."

* * * * * * * * * * * *

The following week I was staggered to learn some harrowing news that instantly made me guiltily regret my disrespectful behavior and my disparaging comments directed toward Dr. Templeton and toward Augustus Bedloe that were spoken at the foot of the Ragged Mountain Ridge. A short dispatch appeared in the Charlottesville newspaper's obituary page announcing the death of Augustus Bedloe, quiet citizen and gainfully unemployed resident. Dr. Templeton had been at bedside attending to Bedloe's neuralgia symptoms by using leeches to achieve topical bleeding, especially to the victim's temple area, the wound which I had originally theorized had been caused by a sudden fall in the steep local mountains. But unfortunately, a venomous sangsue, a pond creature very similar in appearance to a leech, had been mistakenly placed in the medicine jar that Templeton was using and Bedloe shortly thereafter succumbed to death as a result of being accidentally poisoned. Feeling very Christian and also quite penitent, I visited the shaken Dr. Templeton to console the experimental physician about our friend's unexpected demise.

"In the newspaper on the obituary page," I began my condolences, "Augustus' last name was spelled Bedlo instead of Bedloe. Was that a misprint?"

"Yes, it had to be a typographical error, to be sure," Templeton disgustingly answered. "The name is Bedloe ending in an *e* and I've never known it to be spelled any other way."

"Holy shit!" I realized and exclaimed. "Bedlo without the *e* at the end spells Oldeb in reverse. This ironic coincidence is indeed stranger than fiction! Space and time could actually have been breached by the arcane powers of the mystical Ragged Mountains! Perhaps Templeton, just perhaps, Augustus Bedloe was really your old friend Harold Oldeb reincarnated after all!"

"The Cask of Amontillado"

Edgar Allan Poe (1809-1849) has to be the original master when it comes down to authoring great murder stories. Poe possessed an erratic temper to complement his alcoholism and suspected drug usage. In addition to his celebrated horror and detective-style mystery stories, E.A. also wrote haunting poetry as exemplified in "The Raven" and "The Bells." Some of the literary genius's fascinating horror-murder stories are "The Pit and the Pendulum," "The Murders in the Rue Morgue," "The Black Cat" and "The Tell-Tale Heart." One of my favorite Poe tales has always been "The Cask of Amontillado," which I first read at the age of twelve and have read several dozen times since 1955.

That bastard Fortunato is ironically going to encounter and experience a very 'unfortunate' tragedy of *his* own doing. The repugnant rogue has irresponsibly insulted me for the last time. Fortunato has poisoned my dog, drowned my cat, porked my daughter, screwed my wife, but most importantly, the heinous nobleman scoundrel has been having an ongoing affair with my gorgeous mistress. Now I'm so pissed off that I could kill and mutilate the no good shit head just at the mention of *his* despicable abhorrent name.

'I intend to be so clandestine and so secretive about my need for satisfactory revenge that the arrogant asshole will never in his wildest imagination' suspect my malicious scheme,' I shrewdly reasoned. 'I shall minimize risk of failure and my retribution shall be swift and decisive. My vengeful heart shall efficiently execute my subterfuge with impunity from justice,' I decided. 'Fortunato will be punished and will know my callous wrath only when his knowledge of it' will no longer matter. *He* has wronged me and will die an animal's death unfit for a man that has lived as a decent human being. My feigned *smile* of friendship shall be that dirty mangy mother-fucker's guide that will ultimately escort him to the afterlife,' I vowed to my conscience. 'The obnoxious creep deserves to be my victim!'

Fortunato never had any cause or reason to doubt my good will or my motivations. I didn't mind when the son of a bitch killed my dog and mutilated my cat for the sake of diversion. I paid little heed when he continuously fornicated my daughter and had had intercourse with my attractive wife, but when *he* began hitting on my lovely mistress, then that was what had converted my normally tranquil nature into a raging desire to punish the horny perverted philanderer. I intended to first humiliate the devilish villain and then effectively eliminate the city's biggest ball buster from mortal existence.

Every man has an obscure weakness, a concealed bad habit or a fragile predictable behavior that can be scrupulously converted into *his* Achilles heel. Fortunato was vulnerable and was no exception to that marvelous axiom of human interaction. Although respected, honored and feared by his more gullible acquaintances, I happened to know that above anything in life the devious man has loved including my daughter, my wife and my treasured mistress, Fortunato was a connoisseur of excellent wines, especially Amontillado. In many subjects such as oil paintings, politics, investments, religion, philosophy and education Fortunato was a quack, a veritable charlatan, but the repulsive man was no impostor when it came down to outstanding vintage wines. There he was an unrivaled authority, and I planned to use that impeccable knowledge of his to adroitly lure the scummy cock' sucker to *his* unexpected doom.

I also prided myself on being an epicure of extravagant gourmet foods and premium wines and although I was always a mere dabbler I was never in Fortunato's supreme league of discriminating tastes. I had sufficient general acumen in the matter of distinguished wines to connive and then lure the reprehensible scumbag into a brutal inescapable trap. I myself have always been the possessor of an enviable collection of old wines and my many casks I plotted to make into my modus operandi to imaginatively entice the loathed Fortunato to his final resting place.

One evening at dusk during the culmination of merriment and lunacy of the late winter' carnival season I encountered my fiendish friend in front of the city's cathedral. He externally demonstrated a fake warm reception, and I immediately discerned that the braggart was intoxicated both with wine and with his own egomania. The motley real-life jester was appropriately wearing a tight-fitting pin-striped dress, pretending to be a cross-dresser and exhibiting outrageous sin just before the end of carnival and the advent of the sacred fasting' time. On his big fat oval head was a cap cluttered with an array of imbecilic bells that jangled my nerves when I heard them merrily ringing and jingling.

The two of us shook hands in a long extended wringing manner as we stared into each other's cunning eyes. I was the first to initiate

100

conversation with my most bitter adversary, who was aware that I knew of his many transgressions against me. But because of social reasons and the matter of our mutual reputations it was expected of us to extend insincere camaraderie to each other in public, especially during the winter' carnival season. "My dear Fortunato," I falsely and pretentiously began, "you're looking well today and seem to be in a most jovial frame of mind. But I must tell you that I've received from a distant merchant friend a cask of delicious Amontillado, or at least I believe it's genuine vintage Amontillado. But not being a connoisseur such as yourself I do indeed have my doubts about its authenticity."

"Amontillado!" Fortunato euphorically exclaimed in his drunken state. "Ha, ha, ha! What a farce this is! Ha, ha, ha. You, my friend must be a glutton for travesty!"

"Yes, and as I've already told you," I slowly emphasized so that the diabolical ingrate could perceive my every syllable, "I have my doubts."

"A pipe of Amontillado you say?" he inquired. "In the middle of carnival season? Impossible!" my most hated enemy laughed and evaluated.

"Well," I keenly interrupted, "I was foolish enough to pay my reputable merchant friend the full Amontillado price. I realize I should've consulted you for verification of the wine and also to obtain a comparison price, but I could not locate you anywhere in the city on that particular afternoon and I didn't desire to lose what appeared to be a most outstanding bargain. I trust you understand my predicament."

"Amontillado!" the wine' profiteer bellowed once again. "You dare buy expensive wine from someone other than myself! Who was the rascal that sold you the cask? What exorbitant price did you pay?"

"I shall tell you those pertinent details later," I adroitly lied. "I'm sorry that you're enraged at my story. Right now I'm on my way to see Luchesi to ask *him* to come over to my cellars and sample my acquisition to determine whether or not the cask is indeed Amontillado," I informed the drunken and now infuriated Fortunato. "Luchesi will gladly tell me if…"

"Luchesi cannot tell Amontillado from pedestrian merlot or from crude port for that matter," Fortunato sarcastically ridiculed his chief competitor, "and the frivolous jerk off doesn't know his dick from his asshole and always attempts defecating his solid wastes out of the former instead of out of the latter!"

"And I must confidentially confess that many famous aristocrats and clergy in this city actually believe that Luchesi's tastes are parallel to yours," I cleverly said and exaggerated, "but in all honesty I deem that your impeccable taste in wines is superior to his!"

"Come, let me accompany you," Fortunato suggested. "You have a refreshing air of truth about you that transcends all pretense. I volunteer to determine whether your Amontillado is legitimate or a crude imitation sherry."

"To Luchesi's place?" I shrewdly asked. "You want to accompany me to Luchesi's mansion?"

"No, to *your* vaults so that I can confirm the validity of your claim of owning a pipe of Amontillado."

"My dear friend," I replied to the advanced super jerk off, "I shall not impose upon you to deviate from your marvelous carnival merriment. You undoubtedly have an appointment with a powerful government official or a scheduled engagement with distinguished members of the nobility later this evening."

"I have no appointments or engagements with anyone, rich or poor, fertile or impotent or powerful or weak," Fortunato laughed as he awkwardly staggered before me shifting his weight from left to right to disguise his own wretched drunken condition. "I insist on accompanying you to your vaults."

"No my friend," I dissuaded. "You seem to be afflicted with a severe cold tonight. My cellars are extremely dank and damp this winter's evening. The walls and floors are encrusted with dense moss and thick algae and they're certain to trigger severe allergic reactions. You'll be sneezing your lungs out all over the fuckin' place!"

"Enough of this meaningless debate and let's proceed with dispatch anyway," Fortunato confidently insisted. "The cold is really nothing that concerns me for I once survived a severe winter in Siberia with minimal clothing, ha, ha, ha! On the contrary, I *am imposing* on you and not you on me. And as far as that idiotic dick-licker Luchesi is concerned," my nemesis vehemently ranted, "he cannot differentiate the taste of Amontillado from the sweet flavor of pussy because that gay alchemist has never gotten laid or ever even tasted the abundant delicacy known as hair pie! Ha, ha, ha!"

Fortunato possessed himself of my arm, pretending to be the gay pervert' Luchesi that he had been mockingly describing. The conceited ignoramus handed me a black silk mask to camouflage my familiar face in the raucous crowd of festival celebrators, and holding my hand like a bona fide homosexual the pantomiming

102

faggot/jester escorted me incognito to my mansion to show me how much he knew about rare vintage wines.

None of my servants were at my palace. The crazy bastards and bitches were all getting drunk, getting laid or having porno' sketches of themselves being drawn by sex-addict artists renting booths and stalls at the sinful carnival. I had given each of my domestics a small amount of money as a bonus so that they would stay away from my *sanctuary* until the next morning. In that way I would have sufficient time to creatively dispose of my deceitful flamboyant lustful archrival.

I took from wall sconces two torches, wishing that I could then and there shove *my* flambeaux through his gown and straight up Fortunato's enormous rectum, welding his sickening lesbian carnival dress right to his colon. I bowed to my guest, showing him standard courtesy but all the time contemplating castrating the son of a bitch and then solidifying and using his testicles in a neighborhood marbles' tournament.

I escorted my dupe to an archway, a portal leading to stone steps that descended down to my sinister dark and dreary vaults. I advised my still droll visitor to be cautious as we stepped down a cold stone spiral stairway en route to my glorious subterranean wine cellars. At the base of the dangerous curving steps was the burial ground of the Montresors, my venerable deceased ancestors. A rectangular-shaped fifty-by-seventy-foot catacomb had been excavated twenty feet below the mansion's foundation and the tunnel wove its way two hundred and forty feet back to *our* vantage' point.

"What's in these eerie crypts? *Dungeness* crabs?" my irreverent half-inebriated enemy cackled. Fortunato's gait was wobbly, almost as if the bastard was walking with a limp. The nonsensical juvenile bells on the moronic jester's cap jingled as we proceeded to descend to an even deeper level.

"The pipe!" my enemy snorted and chuckled almost simultaneously as he wiped saliva foam from his mouth with the back of his wrist. "Where the fuck's the cask of Amontillado you promised to show me Montresor?"

"It's farther down, perhaps two more winding flights of steps," I indicated as I rubbed my left hand along the wall and stopped it near a web of niter gleaming on the solid masonry. I glanced at *his* ugly face and noticed mucus running out of both nostrils of his enormous nose. "Fortunato, you're sick," I melodramatically implored, "and you cannot languish down here too long because the egregious combination of nitrogen and potassium could have a most detrimental effect on your health. You're not totally well to make this underground expedition at this time," I humbly related with a well-concealed undercurrent of derision. "Perhaps it's best if you sample the sumptuous Amontillado another time!"

"Niter," he irrationally mumbled. "Niter! Fuck niter I say!" he nastily exclaimed. "I assure you that no friggin' niter is gonna' keep me away from imbibing a well-earned quantity of your alleged vintage wine!"

"How long have you had that terrible cough and that waterfall of a running nose?" I innocently asked, seeing that Fortunato was gagging and about to choke from the distinct concentration of niter in the limited breathing air and space that was available.

"Ugh, Ugh! Ugh!" my rival replied like an Iroquois Indian with a severe speech impediment. "Ugh! Ugh! Ugh!" he choked out like someone being strangled. My encumbered foe found it impossible to clearly speak for several minutes. "It's nothing," he weakly uttered at last while trying his best to transmit audacity. Then the lunatic spit a huge green lump of mucus onto the stone floor. I pointed my flaming torch toward the disgusting discharge. "It's nothing!" he repeated while still attempting to reflect strength and pride.

"Come Fortunato," I melodramatically begged, "we'll go back upstairs where the air is fresh and clean. Your health is in jeopardy," I facetiously warned, "and you are a man cherished and revered by most everyone in our great city. If I die down here," I continued, "no one would notice or care a week after my funeral. But if *you* perish, it would be disastrous for both the economy and the politics of our fair metropolis. *Catastrophic* would be a much more accurate adjective to use than *disastrous*. I don't want to be responsible for any injury or affliction this all-too-arduous trek might cause Your Eminence."

"Enough of your mealy-mouthed bullshit flattery!" Fortunato aggressively reprimanded. "The cough is only a cough, a temporary hindrance and nothing more. It and your flagrant fragrant miter certainly will not kill me as you're so naively suggesting. I shall not die of a lousy fuckin' cough," the vain wealthy merchant maintained. "Maybe I'll keel over from fuckin' syphilis or perhaps from loss of sperm after a month-long orgy but definitely not from excessive coughing. Ha, ha, ha, ugh, ugh, ugh!"

"Look Fortunato," I cunningly answered, "your competitor Luchesi is in excellent health. I'll simply ask him to come over and sample..."

"Nonsense!" my aggravated guest loudly bellowed. "That ninny gay fuck-head thinks that a woman's vagina is a sink dispenser to get gook out of to wash his hands. Ugh, ugh, ugh, ugh!" he demonstrably coughed like a tuberculosis victim searching for *his* last breath on *his* deathbed.

"Okay, I suppose you win," I cordially agreed. I removed a large flask dangling from a cord wrapped around my right shoulder. "Perhaps a few snorts of this dry sherry will clear your blocked trachea and your throat of all that disgusting phlegm. Then you wouldn't be so sluggish and so damned *phlegm*atic*!"*

"Ya know," Fortunato giggled in a weak tone of voice, "you do have a sort of humor about you that amuses me. Remind me to invite you to my next bisexual orgy, ugh, ugh, ugh, ugh!" After clearing his throat and blowing his nose on his dress's long silk sleeve, the chauvinistic uninhibited swine muttered, "I have drunk most of the Medoc in honor of your deceased ancestors in repose all around us! Long live Montresor I declare!"

"Drink more of it! Finish it off!" I cunningly recommended. I had never been so odious in my entire life. "In fact I think you oughta' chug the whole damned flask down! It's guaranteed to clear the snot out of your snout and the painful congestion right out of your chest!"

My ornery visitor stared me in the eyes searching for an iota of deceit, slowly raised the flask to his pallid lips and clumsily drank down its remaining liter of content. His headdress's jester bells jingled and jangled, echoing their haunting melody all throughout my macabre subterranean cellars and my sacred family burial grounds.

My famous companion again grabbed my arm in imitation of the notorious faggot Luchesi and we gradually descended another flight of narrow stone steps. "These vaults are rather extensive," he observed and marveled. "I had no idea that your family was so wealthy!" he deliberately manipulated in a statement designed to simultaneously berate and belittle me. "Do you have any poles in these vaults? Ha, ha, ha!"

"The Montresors have for centuries been a great and noble family all over the continent," I gleefully boasted. "My ancestors were first warriors, secondly military officers and finally prominent merchants in numerous European cities. I'm most proud of their numerous accomplishments."

"I forgot your coat of arms," Fortunato replied while attempting to again indirectly insult my honorable kin and me by minimizing *our* contributions to society and to culture. "What is on it?" the lousy sick drunken pompous pig requested.

"It's a huge human foot in a field of azure crushing a serpent with vicious fangs embedded in the man's heel," I explained. "Our family has always abhorred and vanquished evil, and the viper symbolizes the general treachery I've just alluded to."

"And what is your family crest's motto?" the curious excuse for a human being inquired.

"Nemo me impune lacessit!" I sternly proclaimed.

"Speak goddamned Italian or dignified French!" the wine connoisseur demanded. "I loathe Latin. It's such a terribly dead and forgotten friggin' language!"

I searched his sparkling eyes and knew that the wine had had a heavy impact on diminishing his stamina level. We descended to an even lower stratification and passed by piles of bones with casks, pipes and barrels intermingled with the skeletal remains of past gallant Montresors. Each level down signified a descent further into my family's illustrious past, which was a rich historic legacy paying tribute to the dignified and knightly Montresors of yore.

I grabbed Fortunato's left arm above the elbow and hesitated for a moment before delivering my next salient remark. "The niter is now hanging like moss upon the walls," I dutifully noted, "which indicates to me that we're now below the river's bed. The moisture is trickling down these rocks and when we finally get to our destination it'll be almost cascading," I deceptively embellished. "Come, we shall ascend before…"

"Look you asinine dip shit!" Fortunato angrily rebuked. "It's nothing I haven't experienced before. Ya' know," my intended victim continued in a cocky tone of voice, "I got a pretty damn deep cellar of my own! Ugh, ugh, ugh, ugh!" the stubborn suffocating fool repetitiously coughed.

I reached to a side recess where I had deliberately stationed a flagon of De Grave to capitalize on the opportune moment. I handed the powerful substance to Fortunato, who then greedily consumed all sixteen ounces in ten consecutive ravenous swallows. His eyes flashed with both envy and malice. The avaricious maniac didn't say any threatening words but I could *feel* his enmity and his jealousy vibrating out towards me. The arrogant jerk off laughed and then nonchalantly tossed the empty bottle into the air. It fell to the stone steps and shattered upon impact. I could not fathom the basis for his bizarre deportment. I stared at the evil man with a surprised expression on my face. He repeated the gesticulation without employing any glass bottle.

"You do not comprehend my antics?" the imbecile laughingly and mockingly asked.

"No, I honestly don't," I candidly replied. "What did that strange fucked-up gesture mean?"

"Then you're not of the brotherhood," he articulated and laughed. "You ain't nowhere in the 'hood, bro'! Ha, ha, ha, ugh, ugh, ugh!"

"What in the world are you insinuating or implying?" I defensively responded. "Your vague words are indeed incomprehensible!"

"You're not a mason," he chuckled. "Any dolt in the organization would instantly recognize my mystic procedure with the wine bottle! Ha, ha, ha, ugh, ugh, ugh, ugh!"

"Oh yes, a fuckin' fucked-up mason," I finally understood and said. "The clandestine guild of master craftsmen! The secrets of the trade, I presume. Don't tell me that you're one of those jerk off wackos?"

"You do know the mason's sign?" Fortunato further verbally pursued. "There is a distinct sign that when conveyed symbolizes the brotherhood."

I alertly reached into a small alcove and produced a familiar tool of the mortar and stone trade. I showed the trowel to the half-cognizant wine authority.

"Yes, you're certainly jesting," my unassuming guest laughed and accused. "You're making a fiasco out of my sacred Masonic membership. But let's proceed to the Amontillado before I decide to make you pay for your most recent insensitive indiscretion. Ugh, ugh, ugh, ugh!" he choked out while desperately struggling to catch his breath.

I deftly placed the trowel in a belt beneath my cloak, grabbed the tipsy aristocrat-womanizer by the arm and led him deeper into *my* private catacombs. Fortunato latched onto my arm tightly as we passed through a series of narrow arches and then descended to an even lower level where the air was most thin but where the foreboding smell of niter was very heavy. We eventually arrived at a crypt that appeared quite eerie in the ghostly light produced from our flames, and the thin air glowed and the torches' surreally illuminated from the faint trace of oxygen and from the surplus of niter that enveloped us.

We slowly entered another dark crypt adjacent to the first pitiful one on that lower level. My weak associate was breathing in a very labored manner so I boldly held up my torch to show him the piles of ancient bones heaped up to a height of four feet in a similar fashion to burial practices that had recently been discovered in the famous Paris catacombs. Three sides of this present vault were ornamented in that way, with the fourth a solid rock wall covered with dense niter deposits. When we were well into the interior of the second more remote cold dank chamber I had some good news for my suffering "friend."

"Proceed with joy Fortunato," I audaciously informed, "for here's where the splendid supply of Amontillado has been stored, and as for Luchesi, he will…"

"Luchesi is an pusillanimous pussy that squats down to piss! That retarded bastard's never stood up like a man to take a damned leak in his entire life!" Fortunato exhaled, aggressively gasping for air. "Where the hell is the goddamned Amontillado? Ugh, ugh, ugh!" he coughed, discharging another quantity of green-colored mucus from his flu-infected lungs and spitting it onto the cold stone floor.

My grand scheme had been ingeniously designed and efficiently employed. Fortunato awkwardly leaned against the solid rock wall, his eyes rolling. And when I held my blazing torch up, his wrinkled face looked both grotesque and bewildered. I securely placed my torch in a wall sconce near where I had recently installed shackles and then I proceeded to fetter the dazed philanderer to suspended manacles that had cleverly been embedded in the granite wall. The iron fixtures were horizontally three feet distant from each other and I soon quickly and deftly tethered Fortunato to my secret compartment's filthy wall. Next I wrapped the links of a chain around his wriggling waist and in ten seconds secured the chain with a third lock to an iron hook I had spent days pounding into the wall with a sledgehammer just the week before.

I held the *skeleton* key to the three locks (up to the wall sconce's torch) to show Fortunato the vital object. "Try passing your hand over the wall," I challenged my almost unconscious drunken prisoner. "Feel the damp niter if you can, you mangy no good mistress-fucker!"

Apparently my captive did not yet realize that his shrewd vengeful host had competently shackled him to *his* area of slow methodical execution. "The Amontillado! Where's the goddamned Amontillado?" my intoxicated victim boomed almost out of breath. "Ugh, ugh, ugh!"

Beneath a heap of bones I had stored a cache of building stones and mortar. I quickly disassembled the pile and happily uncovered my masonry treasure. I detected that Fortunato's inebriation had been gradually wearing off. His words sounded more rational, more sober revealing a detectable trace of anxiety in his present emotional condition. As I gathered my essential materials I heard a low moaning sort of cry coming from *his* place of entrapment. I chuckled to myself at *his* futility, at *his* desperation and at *his* well-earned ultimate destiny.

Soon I listened to the loud vibrations of *his* chains as the dastardly Fortunato maneuvered around endeavoring to liberate himself from his wicked confinement. My prisoner was in anguish, terror-stricken, evaluating the magnitude and the severity of his dilemma. The chains vibrated even more furiously, and I thought to myself, 'He'll not be a prisoner much longer. Soon this disgrace to humanity that has insulted my integrity for the last time will be dead! He's met his implacable foe and soon his heinous spirit will be conquered!'

I sat down on another pile of bones to momentarily rest from my toil. Already I had built a wall thigh-high between Fortunato's chamber of incarceration and my route to the four flights of stone steps leading up to my cozy residence. When the annoying clanking of the chains against the granite wall finally subsided I resumed my *constructive* enterprise. Soon I had mortared the sixth and seventh tiers and my new masonry wall was now nearly up to my chest. I paused to honor an impulse I was feeling. I held the second flambeaux up over my masonry masterpiece so that the suffocating Fortunato could perceive its' flickering light.

A succession of violent screams and frightening shrieks burst forth from his mucus-infested lungs and I was keenly aware of the terror originating from the pit of my hostage's heart. I hesitated for a moment to garner the right words to demean and castigate him, for I hated the educated scum wagon with a passion for what he had done to my dog, to my cat and to my mistress. 'To hell with my harlot wife and my whoring daughter!' I determined with great enmity in my heart. 'The two bitches are morally corrupt swine just like that condescending dickhead Fortunato is! He's not even worthy of the four-sided cell I'm personally finishing for *his* final resting-place!'

I touched the thick miter encrusted on the crypt's walls and my heart felt both satisfied and inspired to thoroughly complete my most gratifying task. It was almost midnight and soon the boisterous reveling above ground would cease. 'I must finish my skullduggery before the raucous carnival terminates and the holy time of fasting commences,' I seriously considered.

Working in haste like a desperate man whose eternal soul was being gambled away I very diligently assembled the eighth, ninth and tenth layers of my magnificent well-conceived architecture. A portion of the last layer of stones had been mortared and only one more had to be inserted and plastered to form my very splendid partition. As I strained to lift the object up to its designated resting place a low laugh echoed from the niche's inner recess. The hairs on my head bristled erect like those on a vicious cat when it has been threatened. A shrill melancholy repentant voice addressed me and I had difficulty recognizing that the solicitation belonged to the eminent nobleman Fortunato.

"Ha, ha, ha, ha!" the vile instigator then laughed with his last amount of dexterity being virtually exhausted. "That was a very fabulous joke indeed you've performed. A fantastic jest worthy of my admiration," he cumbersomely and insincerely commended. "We shall enjoy many future hearty laughs when the two of us are reminiscing' your brilliant ruse at the palazzo. Ha, ha, ha! All this trouble and that new wall you've constructed, all over stupid wine! Ha, ha, ha, ugh, ugh, ugh, ugh!"

"The Amontillado!" I yelled with newfound authority. "You Fortunato are indeed a gullible stupid shit if I've ever seen one!"

"Yes, the Amontillado, ha, ha, ha, ha, ugh, ugh!" he sputtered and coughed. "Will not our lovely wives be awaiting us at the palazzo! Release me from this incredible joke you've masterfully demonstrated. Ugh, ugh, ugh!"

"Yes," I snidely replied and concurred. "Let's depart to enjoy the end of the celebrating. Our festive wives are waiting, waiting for *me*!"

"Montresor, for the love of God!" my victim hoarsely vociferated with his last bit of strength. "Tear down that terrible wall and unchain me from this most imaginative prank! Ugh, ugh, ugh, ugh!"

"Fuck you asshole!" I yelled like a raving madman. "You've porked my mistress once too often, you pathetic miserable piece of rubbish! Now *you* must pay the price for infidelity and for fuckin' with the wrong jealous man!"

"But Montresor, what are you saying?" my victim incredulously pleaded. "Surely I'll compensate you for any reparations that need addressing! Forgive me Montresor', please forgive me for any harm I might've committed! I'll gladly pay a king's fortune to ransom myself! Ugh, ugh, ugh, ugh!"

"Up yours you filthy piece of vermin shit! Up yours!" I bellowed as my loud voice rumbled throughout my subterranean graveyard without any other ears than *his* to interpret their meaning.

I listened for a suitable reply to my accusations and to my admonitions but none was forthcoming. All I could hear was disconsolate whimpering, delirious sobbing and then desperate weeping. "Fortunato!" I brazenly called three times.

Hearing no answer from the doomed rogue, I squeezed the torch through the remaining small aperture and then assiduously sealed up the cavity with the last necessary stone. The only discernible sound my sensitive ears could detect was a gentle jingling of bells. I felt exhausted and nauseous, but not because of enduring a guilty conscience. I felt sick because of the catacomb's noxious dampness and I had endured fatigue from my great labor. After stubbornly forcing the last stone into place with all the energy I could muster, I very meticulously plastered up the final shred of evidence to my brilliant nefarious deed.

Finally I rearranged the bones that had been scattered on the stone floor back into a tidy neat pile. Presently I am now an old man and can attest that I had restacked those sacred bones fifty years ago and I am privileged to report that no one has viewed or disturbed them in the interim. In pace requiescat! May the souls of my valiant Montresor ancestors be vindicated and rest in peace but may Fortunato's black soul burn for all eternity in hell!

112

"The Fall of the House of Usher"

In the early autumn of 1842 I had received a letter from an old college friend (or should I say acquaintance) Roderick Usher, whom I hadn't seen or heard from in over twenty years. "Reticent Roderick" was a standoffish loner and basically, to tell the truth, so was I. But in contrast to Usher, I did belong to a heterosexually-oriented drinking fraternity, attended parties (several of them wild orgies) and even got laid six times with different inebriated promiscuous girls but Roderick just vegetated and degenerated inside the confines of his apartment, dropped out of the University of Virginia in 1820 and according to my sage suspicion, never could amount to anything because he was a total asshole who even had trouble finding his asshole.

I had known that Roderick had a twin sister, Madeline Usher, who back in 1820 said she would never marry either a man or a woman but instead wanted to always live with her eccentric brother. 'They can't be identical twins,' I thought after considerable pondering, 'because then either Roderick would have to have tits, ovaries and a vagina or Madeline would have to have a dick and balls. They must therefore be fraternal twins,' I deductively reasoned. 'But who the hell would want to fraternize with either of those two oddballs when they probably don't even fraternize with each other? What a fucked-up pair of psychos Roderick and Madeline Usher are!'

After re-reading the content of Usher's letter, my naughty mind did fancy certain other things too about Roderick and Madeline. 'Could they be having an incest-type of relationship and not be sleeping in *twin* beds?' I wondered. 'Even Socrates was more than platonic with his protégé Plato!' I theorized.

But then a more serious conjecture dominated my contemplation after reading for the third time Roderick's invitation (or I should say solicitation) to visit the annoying paranoid reckless recluse and his stranger-than-fiction twin sister.

'I've read in medical journals where twins are believed to have some magical telepathic power of consciously communicating with each other through a weird type of mental signaling, even over great distances,' I recalled. 'The two assholes could've had a stage or circus act with them performing as mentalists,' I mused, 'because if I remember correctly, the two assholes were classic mental cases to begin with! I'll journey up north and visit Roderick and Madeline just out of curiosity. I'm unemployed, have little money or savings, and who the hell knows?' I guessed. 'Maybe Roderick has become rich and can lend me a couple of thousand bucks so that I can open a bordello for horny gays and kinky lesbians just like I've always desired doing but never had the initiative or the required capital to get the sex boat project to float!'

It was a long and difficult weeklong ride on horseback from my remote humble shack outside Richmond, Virginia all the way to Roderick's abode up in Massachusetts, twenty-five miles northwest of Boston. I slept in the woods, begged from farmers and strangers along the route for oats to feed my old horse Nads, who I would encourage to go faster than a foxtrot by relentlessly imploring, "Go Nads, Go Nads, Go Nads!" And yes, my tender ass really hurt and was badly chafed when Nads and I finally and gratefully crossed the Connecticut state line and entered the land of Samuel Adams and Paul Revere, Massachusetts.

'I suppose I'm riding way up here in response to Roderick's letter mostly out of sheer curiosity, if nothing else,' I remember thinking as I politely solicited donations for Nads (and mine) next meal outside a country inn near Plymouth, for Nads had made a wrong turn after leaving Connecticut and wound-up in the vicinity of Cape Cod instead of heading north towards Boston. 'Maybe that wallflower Lady Madeline has developed into a decent-looking hussy and I can get laid and blown while Roderick's out chopping wood or jerking-off in the outhouse,' I nefariously thought as some generous churchgoing asshole dropped two pence into my stove-pipe hat that had a big hole in the bottom and was torn and quite shabby in appearance. 'And according to my daily diary records, I haven't gotten laid or blown since college so when the next opportunity *rises*, I hope I remember what the hell to do with my dick besides taking hour-long pisses.'

As Nads slowly trotted along a lonely dirt trail through a dismal tract of forestland and with shades of evening drawing near, in the far distance as *we* rounded a bend the House of Usher (as Roderick called his residence in his melancholy-sounding letter) came into view. My comical instinct stupidly thought at that moment, 'I'm glad it's not a country theater with only two ushers in it!' and then I further evaluated, 'Well Poe, it's fuckin' time for you to usher in a new day in your life!' I further assessed. 'And 'I'm extremely fatigued and my fuckin' ass really hurts from riding all the way up here just to see this bullshit decaying brick and mortar mansion when as a standard shopping habit I ordinarily boycott brick and mortar stores and buildings back in Virginia!'

114

The walls of the three-story House of Usher dump were rather bleak looking', covered with soot and ivy and looking like they hadn't been properly maintained in over fifty years. 'I've seen plantation slave shanties in better condition than this dilapidated eyesore,' I fancied as Nads plodded ahead and approached the residence, which truthfully looked like it should have been condemned by some blind building inspector decades before.

'Even the goddamned oak and maple trees around this ramshackle estate are in a sad state of decay,' I observed and concluded. 'There's algae and fungus everywhere on this wreck's exterior and I think I'm going to contract some sort of venereal disease just looking at the fucked-up place from three-hundred feet away. If Lady Madeline's tits and cunt look anything like the house she lives in,' I seriously imagined, 'I'd be much better off sodomizing Roderick right up the old yazoo!'

A scruffy-looking midget-sized servant who looked like he hadn't taken a bath since infancy took Nads to the barn, which would have been better off if it had collapsed into rubble a week before my arrival. The dwarfish jerk-off then returned to my company and escorted me into the dank and dreary House of Usher without ever uttering a damned word, which led me to believe that the miniature weirdo was indeed a potentially dangerous deaf mute with certain psychological issues.

The inside of the sinister and ominous-looking house was analogous to that of a funeral parlor with every shadowy room lifeless, macabre and morbid-like in atmosphere, and my first inclination was that I had to relieve my bowels because the place in general was literally scaring the shit out of me.

A doctor carrying his signature black bag (without his autograph engraved on it) descended the rickety wooden steps with a grim expression on his face and the asshole walked right by me without even acknowledging my presence, in fact, almost knocking me over in his hasty departure down the musty dark corridor and then swiftly exiting out of the building.

'I don't blame him!' I thought. 'I'd like to run out of this fucked-up house too! Oh crap! My diarrhea's acting up! I hope Roderick isn't taking a shit in the outhouse, or 'the Necessary' as he used to call such an outbuilding back in 1820! There're two main things I have to remember when entering into a new unfamiliar environment. Where's the crapola and where's the kitchen located, in that particular order.'

I cautiously stepped into what I believed to be the home's living room and sat down on a couch when at least five pounds of accumulated dust billowed up into the air, nearly choking me to death, for I have very bad allergies and am prone to having long extended sneezing and sinus attacks.

The dreary room's wooden floor was planked and warped, the long thin rectangular windows looked like filthy mirrors and I also noticed feeble glimmers of crimson light somehow managing to filter through the transparent panes and refracting inside. The house's furniture all looked antique, giving me the distinct impression of an abandoned museum with cobwebs hanging from the ceiling, from the rotting cornices, from the fireplace mantel and from the ugly walls. The descriptive adjective "gloomy" would have been entirely too complimentary to accurately describe the very hideous-looking and reprehensible-in-appearance House of Usher.

Then in the dark I became startled when I saw the outline of a man who was just lying there on a side couch, and upon recognizing my presence, Roderick sat up like a mummy rising from its coffin and then rose off of the side sofa and stared at me. He was still six-foot eight inches tall and apparently the cretin still weighed about ninety-three pounds, just as I had remembered him back inside his secluded apartment at the University of Virginia.

Roderick, who at best was always laconic and introverted, stared at me for a full mysterious minute without even gesturing to shake my hand or give me a lethargic high-five. Then the gaunt-looking gentleman (I use the term loosely) commenced speaking.

"Is that you Edgar?" Roderick said in almost a trance-like state. "I see that you've ridden all the way up here from Virginia. Your buttocks and rectum must be really sore from your ordeal."

Roderick's high and mighty demeanor and his eloquent formal tone of voice really pissed me off. "You still can't say common ordinary words like ass, asshole, jerk-off, shit, bitch, cock sucker, mother fucker, balls, cunt, bastard and, fuck, can you Roderick?" I angrily quipped. "Once an asshole, always an asshole! That's what I've always said over and over again since grammar school. How the hell have you been Roderick? From the looks of your dump, er, I meant to say 'your exotic mansion', not too well!"

"My twin sister Madeline is very ill and listless," Roderick said.

"Why the hell does she need to keep a goddamned list in the first place?" I foolishly jested, as was my wont. "If she never kept a list, she would never be listless!"

"You don't understand *our* terrible plight, my dear Edgar," Roderick enigmatically answered. "Madeline is suffering from an incurable disease that the doctors cannot accurately diagnose. She's losing weight everyday and is now quite emaciated as if my twin sister is egregiously dying from starvation, although frankly, she eats incessantly all day long, in fact, eight pounds of food each and every day. If you were to see Madeline right this minute Edgar, she'd have to be directly facing you. If she' were to turn sideways," Roderick explained, emphasized and exaggerated, "then she's so thin and skinny that you'd have trouble seeing her."

'Well, it looks like I'm not going to get laid in this house,' I preposterously thought. 'The truth is I don't even feel like jerking-off anywhere inside this hellish disaster.' Then I figured I had better mention something else, especially if Roderick really could practice mental telepathy and really could read the dastardly and disparaging thought transmissions of my dirty greedy mind.

"Perhaps if you were to take Madeline out of the house and visit Cape Cod, Coney Island, Atlantic City, Bunker Hill, Lexington and Concord, well just about any damned place in the Universe except here," I suggested, "and maybe, just maybe such excursions would prove beneficial for both you and your twin sister's health."

"I don't think that either Madeline or myself is physically capable of making any long trip away from the House of Usher," Roderick eerily replied. "As you know from your college education Edgar, the interesting word 'travel' is fundamentally derived from the nomenclature 'travail,' which means 'hard and arduous labor.' Now tell me Edgar, who in Hades needs that kind of bull feces?"

"Can't you ever say the simple word 'bullshit' without feeling embarrassed?" I admonished, raising my voice. "Listen to me Roderick. Ever since I've known you that first day at college, you always said 'fellatio' instead of 'cock-sucking,' you always said 'cunnilingus' instead of 'cunt-licking,' you always said 'urinating' instead of 'pissing,' you always said 'intercourse' instead of 'fuck,' you always said 'testicles' instead of 'balls,' you always said 'Hades' instead of 'hell,' and instead of uttering 'farting' you always said 'passing intestinal gas,' and besides *that*, you always said 'vulva' and 'vagina' instead of 'cunt,' you always said 'toro feces' instead of 'bullshit,' you always said 'penis' instead of 'dick' or 'cock,' you always said 'male dog' instead of 'bastard,' you always said 'sexual relief' or 'masturbating' instead of 'jerking-off,' you always said 'mother copulator' instead of 'mother fucker;' and right up to today Roderick, you'd rather say 'female canine' than the word 'bitch' and

117

you'd rather say 'rectum' or 'buttocks' instead of 'asshole'," I loudly chided and vehemently criticized. "And now you have the unmitigated audacity to tell me that you're sick! Well Roddy baby, I'm pretty goddamned sick and tired of this fuckin' sanctimonious holier-than-thou bullshit you've been laying on me ever since we were freshmen in college. What the hell's the matter with you anyway, you dumb ass prude! I'd rather curse than be accursed like you are living in this garbage heap of rubble any goddamned day of the week!"

As Roderick ignored my protestations and methodically delivered his polite, defensive boring and monotonous justification for his lackadaisical prudishness, out of the side of my eye I caught a glimpse of Lady Madeline flitting by inside the adjacent corridor, the pallid-faced frail woman seeming like a panic-stricken whitish ghoul, her clandestine passage giving me the creeps and making my foul-smelling colitis act up. I then began farting incessantly as Roderick Usher completely ignored (or was oblivious to) the noises emanating from my hyperactive asshole as he redundantly continued spieling his lackluster monologue.

* * * * * * * * * * * *

Over the span of the next week I actually began relishing my stay at the very eerie House of Usher because its ramshackle appearance made me feel good about my humble shack back in Virginia and it's pathetic residents also made me feel encouraged about my own mediocre existence. When someone witnesses the problems and the struggles of others that are far worse than he or she has to deal with, then conversely, that person's perception almost always makes the evaluator feel much better about his or her life.

Roderick and I seldom spoke during that entire seven-day period but I felt that we understood each other perfectly, with *that* rather peculiar observation lending credence to my secret "Usher telepathy theory." My friend Usher and I sat quietly at nights in either his mildewed-smelling library or in his cobweb-infested living room reading books, painting landscapes on canvas, crocheting socks, knitting bed quilts and practicing elementary basket weaving.

At midnight each evening my friend would quietly leave my company to check the condition of Lady Madeline, whom I had only seen once (during my entire stay) as a spectral-type figure zooming like a zephyr by the dusky living room. Everything seemed tranquil and copasetic until five minutes past midnight on Halloween Eve.

118

"Edgar, you must come with me immediately," Roderick imperatively ordered.

"Are we going to celebrate All Saints and All Souls Day?" I all-too-ignorantly asked. "I could use a nice glass of cold champagne right now to soothe my nerves!"

"No Edgar, you narrow minded Dolt! Madeline has passed away and the angels are escorting her to Heaven as I speak," Roderick ironically related, much to my chagrin. "I need you to help me carry her body from her bed down to the cellar vault room. There under candlelight, we'll place my beloved sister's mortal remains on a granite slab where I shall in the privacy of my grief apply lipstick and make-up to her face and hands to simulate her appearance as it might look at a public viewing, and then in two days Edgar, we'll slide her corpse into her crypt and seal it up!"

Normally having a facetious and frivolous nature in terms of personality, I remained reticent while standing in the center of the House of Usher living room, merely nodding my head in tacit agreement, for I didn't wish to say anything alarming or blatantly hypocritical during Roderick's time of mourning. Even my own heart, which usually rejoiced in revelry and ordinarily scorned any facet of suffering, disease and illness, felt a genuine compassion for the terrible burden my friend Roderick was enduring.

My companion could have been a funeral director as verified by the meticulous way he was *undertaking* Lady Madeline's corpse in its preparation for burial. Lipstick, mascara, rouge and nail polish together made the dead woman seem almost like a contemporary Sleeping Beauty, but I was so petrified from the overall ordeal that I shuddered upon thinking that Roderick might appoint and assign me as Prince Charming to awaken Lady Madeline with a kiss.

"I'm afflicted with the same degenerative malady that has led to my twin sister's demise," Roderick verbally explained to me rather cold and matter-of-factly. "I shall die soon Edgar and hopefully, you'll be here to attend to my corpse and bury me too!"

"I'm generally not a superstitious person but your House of Usher along with the scary passing of Lady Madeline gives me the creeps," I divulged to my almost incoherent host. "Let's leave this cellar vault room, stroll into the parlor, open a bottle of red wine and drink to settle our frazzled nerves," I suggested. "That's why liquor and wines are called 'spirits.' They'll change *our* spirits Roderick from absolute melancholy and despair into positive tolerance and hope."

"And what shall we talk about while we're sipping our wine?" my disconsolate friend asked. "Truly Edgar, I can count on your comfort and support during my hour of need without us imbibing any alcoholic beverages."

"Well, if we get juiced-up enough," I remarked rather insensitively, "we could discuss all about our bygone college years and conscientiously review the fascinating topics of urinating, fecal depositing, intercourse, vaginas, vulvas and ovaries, testicles and penises, fellatio, cunnilingus, Hades, male canines, female canines, masturbating, buttocks and rectums and also passing large quantities of intestinal gas; you know Roderick, all of the idiotic toro feces that immature college kids normally talk about."

My friend and I were soon downing our second bottle of rose wine and I had the feeling that Roderick was finally shedding his heavy depression and coming out of his deep stupor. Suddenly there was a disturbing clanging sound as if a great chain was being rattled and *that* startling interruption was followed by a frightening loud clang. Before I could swallow another ounce of rose, Lady Madeline shockingly appeared standing erect in the doorway, her pallid face and her total image being gruesomely cadaverous. Roderick rose from his seat to grab onto his faltering twin but the pale woman collapsed into his arms and instantaneously died a second time.

Momentarily I was completely petrified and incredibly freaked-out, but then gaining some semblance of rational cognition, I was so disoriented that I failed to say even a perfunctory 'goodbye' to my old friend as he knelt down on the floor and affectionately caressed the body and cheeks of his again-deceased sister.

I scampered like an obsessed demon down the dark drafty corridor not even bothering to enter my assigned bedroom and retrieve my overcoat. Rushing out the front door in a panic, I accidentally collided with Roderick's deaf mute servant, knocking the surprised victim on his ass in the haste of my exit. I scurried as fast as my legs could carry me to the dilapidated stone barn, saddled Nads, rose-up from the stirrup, hastily clambered upon my shabby steed's mangy back, grabbed the reins and then my faithful horse trotted out of the dark enclosure and into the lane leading to the accursed House of Usher.

'I gotta' get the fuck away from this House of Usher, this diabolical House of Horrors as quick as a meteor,' I thought. 'Who the hell needs a goddamned fucked-up horrendous nightmare like this one while they're fuckin' sober and awake? I feel sorry for Roderick but I must first look out for #1 while I can still do #2, whether I'm sitting on my horse's back or whether I'm shitting a flurry of wet farts inside the nearest Necessary!'

My mind was so disheveled at that moment that I was virtually oblivious to the overhead thunder and lightning and the hard pelting raindrops that externally constituted my physical environment. Suddenly my ears heard a great crumbling that sounded something akin to a violent explosion or volcanic eruption.

At first I thought that a catastrophic earthquake was in progress but then my logical mind reasoned that such a geological phenomenon would certainly be an anomaly in an eastern state like Massachusetts. Being both awed and curious in *that* particular order, I abruptly tugged the reins and stopped Nads on the summit of a hill. Next I turned around to inspect the source of the tremendous ground-shaking reverberation that my auditory senses had heard.

Beneath a blood-red full moon and amidst the relentless torrential rain, my disbelieving eyes witnessed a calamity like I hope to never again see. My disarrayed mind was reeling from the great tragedy my pupils were beholding. 'This is worse than Joshua blowing his horn outside the walls of Jericho!' I marveled.

My eyes perceived a cloud of luminous dust glowing in the distance, signifying to me that Roderick had finally joined his cherished twin Lady Madeline in the hereafter. The House of Usher and its occupants were no longer in existence on the face of this all-too-fragile Earth. God rest your soul good friend Roderick.

"Tell-Tale Heart"

Edgar Allan Poe (1809-1849) was a gifted short-story author, a most effective poet, an accomplished critic and reviewer, and the generally recognized creator of the detective story. His tales often reflect morose gloomy atmospheres, and many literary authorities suspect that disappointment and frustration in Poe's personal life had been responsible for the macabre characters and themes represented in many of *his* works. Grief, alcohol, alienation and tragedy all contributed to an angry vindictive mindset that is evident throughout the great master's impressive catalog of stories. Herein lies a humble retelling of one of the prolific writer's most famous tales.

I am truly nervous, dreadfully nervous, and have been jittery for many years. Some will say that I am mad and my inclination is to partially agree with that harsh judgment. I will be the first to admit that only a thin line separates brilliance from insanity, anger from craziness.

Yes, the affliction has honed my senses and made them keener. They are comparable to those of a stalking carnivore, for power and purpose goes to the predator of the hunt and not to the targeted prey. My hearing has become especially acute and I can easily identify the slightest sound, even one originating at a great distance.

I hear all things in heaven, all things on earth and all things in hell, sometimes coincidentally. How could I be mad then? Listen carefully and heed the essence to my narrative. Perceive exactly how furtively-how calmly I can recall and divulge the entire scenario.

It is beyond my recollection to isolate the precise moment or day the damned idea first entered my mind; but once the seed germinated, its power inhabited my head every minute of every day. My motivation was not inspired by greed for money or property. Forget materialism. And passion was absent from my cold and calculated intent. At one time I loved and cared for the old bastard but that insignificant fact has been buried in the past.

The old man had never wronged me in any way. In hindsight he never had given me abuse or ridicule. I had no lust for his gold or possessed no avarice for his money. As I contemplate the basis for my motive I believe I was compelled to rationally commit the murder because of *his* detestable eye.

Yes, the old bastard had the eye of scavenger, the disgusting eye of a vile vulture. The horrid thing had a hideous pale blue tint, a most hideous iris indeed with a dull film veiling it. Whenever its stare fell upon me it seemed to penetrate inside my very being and minutely scrutinize my heart, my soul and my conscience. I often found my blood running cold, and so by degree, each successive day, I became obsessed with the notion of eliminating the old man's existence, and thus ridding myself of the terrible daily haunting of the old bastard's obscene evil eye.

Now allow me to get directly to the point. You imagine that I am mad, emotionally disturbed. Madmen are not nearly as cunning, as deliberate and as calculating as I had been. But you should have seen *me* carefully scheming my illustrious plan all during my premeditation. Then you could have discerned how wisely I proceeded-with what shrewdness and precaution I acted-with what foresight and secrecy I organized my ingenious plot. Yes, I was very deliberate and deftly concealed my wonderful dissimulation. Soon I worked hard at stealthily implementing my impeccable strategy.

I was never kinder to the old son-of-a-bitch than during the entire seven days before I frantically killed him. And every night, just around the stroke of midnight, I rotated the latch of his bedroom door and then very meticulously opened it—oh, so very slowly and stealthily. And then, when I had achieved an opening wide enough to accommodate my sweating head, I inserted into the dark space a black lantern to hide my covert intent. No light shone out from the well' designed shutter and that fine maneuver gave me the daring to proceed with competently consummating my grand secret ambition.

'*He* will die at my choosing,' I furtively thought, 'and soon *he* will know of my sinister plan, but then it will be too late!'

Oh, you would have marveled and appreciated how cleverly, how adroitly I thrust my head into the doorway. I held the dark lantern very cautiously so as not to make the slightest sound to interrupt the intended victim's deep sleep.

It required a whole hour for me to enter my entire head inside the space I had created so then I could clearly see the old unsuspecting bastard lying upon *his* bed. 'Fool!' I objectively thought. 'Soon you will be dead. The naïve gazelle should be more wary of the cheetah's presence and stalking!'

Ha—would a madman have been so wise as I had been? Madmen act out of emotion; my scrupulous hunting was predicated on reason, on method, on rationality, on purpose and on objectivity. I wanted the old man dead, and that was the long of it and the short of it.

Then I undid the dark lantern cautiously—so very, very cautiously—for the hinges creaked and I did not want to expose my anxiety for the old man's attention and evaluation. A single shaft of light fell upon the dreadful eye, but at that moment I was not sufficiently compelled to enact the flaccid commands of my volition.

And for seven consecutive nights, exactly at midnight when mystery and intrigue reach their joint crescendos, I entered *his* dingy room in a similar fashion only to discover that his horrid evil eye had been closed. So for seven long and tedious nights I found my well' conceived crime impossible to perform. For it was not the old bastard who bothered me: it was his wretched Evil Eye.

And every morning thereafter just around dawn I intrepidly stepped into his chamber and spoke courageously to his unsuspecting heart, calling him by name in a bold steadfast tone, and inquiring how well *he* had journeyed through his slumber. So as you can plainly determine, *he* would have had to be a very perceptive old bastard indeed to comprehend that every single night, precisely at midnight, I investigated his privacy while he trustfully slept completely unaware of any potential malice or threat.

Upon the eighth night of my stalking I was more than normally deliberate in opening his chamber's door. The minute hand on a wristwatch moves more quickly but less methodically than mine had on *that* particular night. Never before had I ever felt the extent of my own potency—my will was absolute—I had dominion over *his* doom, according to *my* flexible timetable. That night my sagacity had reached its ultimate pinnacle and my confidence abounded as never before. I could scarcely contain my feelings of triumph, my urge for conquest, my thirst for victory, my need to be the savage ruthless predator in the predictable struggle.

And just to consider that there I was, opening that damned door for the eighth consecutive midnight, little by little, and the old buzzard not even dreaming or night-maring about my clandestine thoughts that my mind and conscience had dually conspired.

I almost chuckled at my keen intelligence and at my superior discretion, and perhaps *his* sixth sense perceived my presence, for he suddenly moved upon his mattress, as if remotely aware of some indefinable lurking danger.

Now you may imagine that I retreated from the challenge—but no, I became more resolute in my desire to initiate my felony. His room was as black as coal. There was thick, palpable darkness all around, for his shutters had been closed out of fear of burglars. But true danger was closing in on the elderly bastard and *his* lack of apprehension would certainly trigger his demise should his Evil Eye be open. And so, I became aware that the old son-of-a-bitch could not see the wide crevice between the bedroom door and its commonplace frame, and my left-hand kept steadily pushing the doorknob so that my entire head could pass into the space created by my assiduous effort.

Finally my face was inside the aperture I had so diligently made and I was about to open the lantern to cast a ray upon his unsuspecting Evil Eye. Betraying my designs, my thumb clumsily slipped upon the lantern's tin fastening, and the old bastard sprang up in his bed and frighteningly shrieked—"Who's there?"

I remained exceptionally still and absolutely quiet, for I realized that both power and fate were at my disposition and command. I did not move one iota for a whole hour and in the interim, I never heard the old coot lie down upon his pillow. He was still sitting up and intently listening in his bed—listening just as I have done night after night, contemplating his murder while harkening to the ticking of small wall insects foreshadowing the approach of death's cold ruthless specter.

I heard the old son-of-a-bitch's throat emit a steady low groan and I instinctively knew it was the fearful admission of mortal terror. It was not a picayune groan of agony or of shock—it was the low muffled sound that ascends from the pit of the soul when one is overwhelmed with extreme awe. I personally knew the sound all too well.

Many nights, just at the stroke of midnight, when all of humanity comfortably and securely slept in their warm soft beds, that horrible sound brimming out of my chest vexed me with its dreadful repetitious echo. Indeed, those awful terrors distracted me from focusing on my immediate mission.

I say I knew the terror well, must I repeat myself for *your* unwarranted satisfaction! I comprehended exactly what the old bastard was feeling and deep down inside I actually pitied his plight, although I must confess I chuckled deep in my heart for my own amusement. I was cognizant that the old recluse had been lying awake ever since my careless thumb had awkwardly slipped on the lantern's tin fastening.

'It is *my* call that soon *you* will prematurely meet your Maker!' I remember thinking. 'I am in control! My will shall prevail!'

The old man recklessly tossed and turned in his bed, inciting anger to erupt inside my mind and inside my heart. 'He should have exhibited more proper caution!' I speculated and rationalized. 'He has now sealed *his* doom!'

I conjectured that the old resident had been fancying the strange alien sound had been a mere manifestation of *his* fearful imagination, believing that the troublesome noise had been causeless in *his* reality. The old codger had probably been attempting to convince himself, 'It is nothing but the wind rustling and eddying about in the chimney,' or, 'it is only a timid mouse crossing the floor in quest of a food scrap,' or 'it is only a lonely scared cricket that has produced but a single chirp.'

Yes, the naïve' decrepit aged fellow was about to become an inadvertent martyr to *my* supreme cause, and his attempts at comforting *his* unstable fears by fabricating rash futile explanations would all be in vain. *All in vain;* surely, because the certainty of Death had been mechanically stalking him like a precise machine and its shadow was about to envelop *his'* sorry spirit and then suck *his* miserable soul right out of *his* body. And it was *his* awareness of Death's indisputable presence that caused him to vaguely understand the gravity of the situation, although he neither saw nor heard but instead felt the intrusion of my head encroaching within *his* private sanctuary.

After I had waited for what seemed a long time, very prudently, very deliberately, without even hearing *my prey* lie down, I became determined to open a tiny-a very, very tiny crevice in the black lantern. So I skillfully opened it-you cannot imagine how surreptitiously, how furtively, how stealthily I opened it-until, at last, a single dim ray, a scintilla analogous to a spider's thread, shot out from the tiny crack and fell directly upon the old bastard's ghastly vulture eye.

The eyelid was open-wide, wide open I say-and I became incensed as I peered upon it. I observed the veiled iris and dull pupil with perfect clarity-all were a pale blurry blue, with that repugnant horrendous film cover that seemed not of this world. The spectacle froze the very marrow in my entire anatomy; but I could not distinguish any other characteristics of the old man's facial features; my entire concentration and the lantern's ray were focused precisely upon the damned grotesque Evil Eye.

And need I remind you that what you have mistaken for insanity is merely the over-acuteness of my senses? Now, there came to my auditory perception a low, dull, pulsating sound, similar to a watch's ticking when the object is enveloped in cotton. I knew *that* singular sound well, yes, all-too-well. It was definitely the beating of the old pathetic bastard's heart. The disturbance intensified my mounting rage', just as the pounding of military drums gradually stimulate an infantryman into courage.

But even then I refrained from my felony and stayed motionless, scarcely inhaling and exhaling, waiting for the most opportune moment to effectively pounce like a leopard. I lifted the lantern and then held it' stationary, trying to locate the shaft of light onto the ugly target I despised so much. Meanwhile the hellish repetition of the very irritating heartbeat simultaneously accelerated and amplified my audacity. It increased quicker and quicker, louder and louder with every passing second.

Indeed the old dupe's horror must have been unbearable! The very annoying beating grew louder in volume', do you now assess the magnitude of my fury? I have disclosed to you that I am neurotic and a trifle paranoid, and so I was and am.

And now, at the culmination of the nighttime, amid the sinister silence of that old eerie house, so peculiar a noise as the one I have described motivated me to engage in uncivilized terror. Yet, I momentarily resisted my impulses and refrained from action. But the incessant irksome infuriating beating persisted and rose to an intolerable decibel level. I nervously imagined that the old bastard's heart would explode right out of his chest!

And now a new apprehension gripped my shameless soul; the old geezer's curious neighbor might hear the evil heightening sound! I then determined that the old man's hour of execution had finally arrived. With a boisterous yell, I flipped open the lantern and bounded into the room, now instantly transformed into a savage animal's killing pit.

The old bastard was totally traumatized. He shrieked once-and once only. I dragged *his* petrified body to the floor, and after considering strangling my prey, I decided to pull the heavy bed over his feeble frame', which was desperately struggling to escape my domination. I then gaily smiled, proud of my accomplishment so far completed.

But for many minutes the old man's stubborn heart beat on with a continuous muffled sound. I became more livid than before and sat trembling on top of the mattress, using my full weight to help decisively crush the old bastard's throat and chest, thus causing *his* very labored breathing to cease.

Finally I sensed that the old man was dead. I tugged the bed from atop his neck and sternum to delightfully examine the corpse. Yes, he was stone cold dead, as dead as any floor peg in the wooden planks lying below my feet. I touched his throat and his wrist but

128

there was no pulse. The son-of-a-bitch's grotesque Evil Eye would trouble me no more.

If you still consider me certifiably insane, you will think so no longer when I reveal the coy precautions I took for the concealment of the old man's mortal remains. Morning was approaching, and I hurriedly worked in the silence of shadows. First of all I systematically dismembered the corpse, decapitating the head and then severing the flaccid arms and the wrinkled legs from the trunk.

I next cleverly removed three planks from the chamber's oak floor and then slyly placed the appendages between the joists. I then replaced the boards over the scantlings so adroitly, so deftly, that no human eye-not even *his*-could have detected any deviation from the room's normal appearance. There was nothing left to wash, to rinse or to cleanse. All traces of blood had been wiped on rags that had been buried with the severed body parts. A tub had caught all, and that too was sealed between the scantlings under the sturdy tight-fitting floor planks.

When I had completed those extraordinary endeavors it was already four o'clock, but still as dark as midnight, the time I had cunningly initiated my very necessary deed. As the chimes in the hall grandfather clock struck four I heard a wrapping and then a louder knocking at the front door. I advanced to the foyer with a light heart, for I had nothing to fear. I slowly opened the door and much to my surprise, three men formally introduced themselves as police officers. I suavely asked for identification and after inspecting *their* credentials, I allowed the trio admission into the house.

"A neighbor reported hearing a shriek during the night," the first deputy of justice indicated in a mellow baritone voice, "and we have come to investigate any evidence of criminal behavior in the vicinity."

"That is correct," a second shorter keeper of the peace verified, "and certain information has been lodged at police headquarters. We have come to thoroughly search the premises."

I was strongly inclined to insist that the patrolmen obtain a search warrant from a judge, but I was so arrogantly confident that I had committed the perfect crime that I ignored my initial reaction to demand my *Constitutional Rights* in deference to personal pride. I smiled, for *what* guilt had I to conceal? I invited the reputable gentlemen to explore the dwelling to their hearts' content.

"The shriek," I asserted, "was my own during a bad dream."

"Where is the old man?" the third average-height policeman inquired.

"He's absent visiting friends in the country," I shrewdly answered. "He's not scheduled to be back in town until the weekend, four days from now!"

I accompanied my three guests all over the house and I boldly encouraged them to either randomly or carefully search whatever room, niche, or cranny they so desired, for I had no regret or remorse about anything that had recently transpired. I led the authorities at length to *his* tranquil sleeping chamber, where I showed them all of *his* treasures and *his* prized possessions intact, secure and undamaged.

In my exuberance and overconfidence I had brought four wooden chairs into the bedroom and after asking the constables to rest from their labors, I had the distinct audacity to locate *my* chair over the very spot where the old man's dismembered body had been insulated under the oak floor planks.

"How long have you been living here as a boarder?" the first officer asked.

"Five years now," I calmly replied. "Yes, it's already been five years now!"

"Has the old man ever cheated or wronged you?" the second policeman inquired while obviously attempting to establish a motive.

"No, actually I loved the gentleman. We often played cards together," I diplomatically added, "and we shared mutual interests in chess and in backgammon."

"Are you mentioned anywhere in the old man's will?" the third patrolmen asked. "He is reputed to have amassed a considerable fortune resulting from some very intelligent investments and from frugal living!"

"No, I know nothing about *his will* or his finances," I intelligently lied. "But as you can easily determine, all of *his* valued possessions are on display on counters, bureaus and mantels all over the house."

The investigators were satisfied by my persuasive testimony and I was certain that my self-assured demeanor had convinced them of my innocence, transcending all possible suspicion and doubt on their part. They attentively sat in their squeaky wooden chairs, absorbing the profundity of my every statement.

Then the rogues began chatting about simple familiar things like the weather, families and retirement. Soon thereafter, my head began to ache and I imagined hearing a discernible low ringing in my sensitive ears. But still, the gregarious scoundrels continued their mundane conversation, then discussing and gossiping about history, town officials and certain national figures.

The ringing in my delicate ears became even more distinct, more powerful. I talked more vociferously to alleviate my obvious physical discomfort but the auditory sensation increased in volume and also in intensity. It became more and more definite until at length I soon discovered that the source of the haunting noise was not originating between my ears.

No doubt, my face became very pallid and my eyes receded into their sockets. I foolishly spoke more fluently and became more garrulous, which was contrary to my ordinary introverted disposition. As my voice heightened, so did the horrid sound I heard until I entered an overpowering panic attack. What could I do? What should I do? The sound I perceived was *a low, dull, hurried sound, much like the sound of a watch enveloped in cotton.* And yet the police officers feigned ignorance of the vexing disturbance and persisted in talking more vehemently, more loquaciously as the bothersome noise further increased and quickened.

I arose from my wooden chair and began arguing about trifles, drawing attention to my bizarre departure from my usual suave behavior. My contrived cockiness had deteriorated and then soon eroded, finally abandoning me. My voice was high-pitched and accentuated with violent hand and arm gesticulations. Why *would* the police not be gone?

I paced the floor to and fro in long strides using my arms and hands to emphasize in an animated fashion certain irrelevant points. The fascinated policemen momentarily stopped their dialogue and closely studied my exaggerated and seemingly involuntary gestures. The men's observations excited me into a new wild frenzy. But still, the noise I heard increased in volume as my pacing became more and more intense. 'Oh, what could I do?' I mentally grieved. 'What should I do?' I anguished as I noticed the constables again continuing their casual, critical verbal exchanges.

I foamed at the mouth. I raved. I swore, vainly attempting to disguise my guilt. But alas, my human conscience prevailed. I swung my wooden chair and then grated the object against the three wooden floor planks, but the persistent annoying background noise I heard ascended in intensity and widened in magnitude. It became louder, louder, louder. And the all-too-knowledgeable police investigators simply sat there in their wooden chairs unruffled, still commiserating about trivial contemporary facts and events, while pleasantly smiling and evaluating my general erratic deportment. Was it possible *they* heard not what I had been painfully listening to?

No, no! They heard while pretending not to be listening! They had suspected all along and fully knew of my monstrous misdeed! They were making a travesty of my horror, a mockery of my guilt! This I thought and this I believed. But truly, anything was better than the agony I was then experiencing! Anything was more tolerable than their reprehensible scrutiny of my culpable behavior!

I could bear their hypocritical grins and mocking no longer. I felt I must scream or die from overwhelming anxiety. And then, again, listen. I heard the external noise growing louder, louder, louder.

My formerly dormant conscience was now commanded by guilt! A swift confession was imminent! "Villains!" I shrieked. "Conceal your suspicion no longer. I confess to the vulgar crime! Tear up the planks and see for yourselves! It is the beating of the old bastard's hideous heart!"

"The Purloined Letter"

It was a blustery evening in the autumn of 1839 and the north wind was blowing and gusting with real gusto. I was visiting my old friend private investigator Cedrick Auguste Dupin in his little back library at his residence, Number 33, Rue Donut Faxbourg, St. Germain. We had been conversing for an entire hour, both of us coughing amidst the swirling and curling eddies originating from Dupin's fractured and ruptured pipe. But then as my companion was enjoying contemplating his pipe dreams, I audaciously brought-up the topic of the mystery associated with the murder of a certain Marie Roget, whose former husband was in the Thesaurus publishing business. But just as I was finishing spieling my oral preface, the apartment's front door slammed open and in stepped our old acquaintance, Monsieur Gustav Ghent, the imperfect Prefect for the Paris Police Department.

"Dupin, I wish to ask you a question or two about a matter that has as of late caused the Department a great deal of concern," Monsieur Gustav Ghent addressed my companion. "To be quite candid, it has me more than a trifle bewildered so I figured I would approach you for your sage advice and sound opinion. So please hear me out, for my job and career might depend on your acumen."

"I shall extinguish the candle wick because as you know perfectly well Prefect," Dupin confidently replied, "for some inexplicable reason, I tend to think better in the dark. I find darkness to be a much more illuminating environment than actual lamplight."

"And what exactly is this massive difficulty that has recently arisen?" I curiously asked. "Nothing short of a major assassination I should hope! Did the American President abdicate to France? Have some unscrupulous crooks simultaneously clogged-up all the city sewers? Did the flamboyant Italians demolish the French in a highly-contested tennis tournament?"

Gustav Ghent pretended that I wasn't even present in the small dark library. "For God's sake Dupin, you smoke more than a goddamned chimney does in the height of winter," the Prefect admonished his host, whom neither of us could see in the total blackness save for the dim light escaping from Cedrick's holey pipe. "But getting back on subject, this baffling conundrum that's bugging the crap out of my pea-brain is nothing like anything else that I've ever been exposed to in my history with the Paris Police. The details of my present excavation of facts are quite off the mark and I believe that my old drinking buddy Cedrick Auguste Dupin here would be interested in hearing them. This problem I'm alluding to is not only very odd, it is also very simple in structure, if *that* asshole comment of mine makes any sense to you two apathetic gentlemen."

"Stop trying to be dupin' Dupin!" I jested, slapping the arm of my rocking chair while aiming in the dark at my right knee. "What the hell is perplexing you and your colleagues Prefect? I always thought that you were as cool as a cucumber but now you impress me as being an encumbered cucumber."

"My honorable friends, let me sit down here in the dark before I fall on my goddamned ass," the clumsy Prefect requested. "Ah, this chair is quite comfortable," Gustav Ghent said and then loudly farted. "Now then, I must swear both of you distinguished gentlemen to secrecy for the affair I'm about to mention involves an affair alright, an affair involving a noteworthy aristocratic woman who wishes to avoid being implicated in an embarrassing public scandal. I mean, if it became known that I've divulged the diplomatically-sensitive incident to you two imbeciles, er, I mean fellows, I could jeopardize losing my prestigious position on the police force."

"Good, then my friend and I will broadcast the alleged scandal to all of Paris and also to the surrounding suburbs all the way to Marseilles," Dupin joked and then coughed like a tuberculosis victim. "What is bothering you Prefect besides your double hernia, your notorious kidney stones, your spastic colon and your distended hemorrhoids that hang-out of your smelly underwear like a pair of blue suspenders?"

"The problem is clearly inferred, so allow me to explain why the probable illicit act was not originally provable," Gustav eloquently informed us. "Here is the essential difficulty. A certain document involving a clandestine love affair has been purloined from the royal apartments. We know who stole the letter, which I conjecture contained plenty of juicy tabloid gossip-type stuff that could cause a revolution if it ever filtered into the public domain. The suspect, or should I say individual, was seen taking the letter and more than likely the damaging missive is still in the absconder's possession."

"Obviously," the very august Cedrick Auguste Dupin interrupted, "the owner of the privy information could hold a certain power over those that govern this inferior nation's highest levels of power where even international sex relations could be impacted and affected. I find this newly learned bullshit rather intriguing."

"And who might the letter's thief be since you've already indicated to us that you claim you know his identity?" I inquired. "Someone of a nefarious villainous character who no doubt has blackmail as a motive."

"The suspected culprit is none other than Minister Claude DeVries who as you know, is my brother-in-law's other brother-in-law," the Prefect shared. "But Claude DeVries' method of theft was ingenious in addition to being extraordinarily bold. The female aristocrat in question was in her boudoir with her secret lover when a messenger delivered the aforementioned letter, which was originating from another lover and admirer of this all-too-famous woman. The royal woman in the center of this love triangle didn't want her bedroom lover to learn about the just-arrived letter from her other lover, so she discreetly placed the missive on the fireplace mantel."

"Oh this is so neat," I expressed and giggled in the dark. "The prime suspect is a Prime Minister! Ha, ha, ha!" And then I could not resist a frivolous continuation of my general stupidity. "Prefect, you had mentioned that Dupin here smoked like a chimney. It's too bad that our mutual pal good old C. Auguste wasn't the chimney in the royal apartment and smoking away," I mused and then laughed. "As a smoking chimney Dupin could've gotten the letter of disgrace off the mantel and incinerated the document with his own excessive heat, thus destroying the evidence altogether and effectively preventing the scandal from ever occurring in the first place."

Dupin ignored my idiotic drivel and asked Gustav Ghent, "I'm a little confused Prefect by your seemingly illogical statements. If the one lover was in the royal apartment's boudoir supposedly literally giving this high class harlot the royal shaft and the other paramour had the letter delivered, how does this sticky business involve Minister Claude DeVries if he isn't one of the two lovers?"

"Well, the wily Minister Claude DeVries gently knocks on the royal apartment door, enters with his private key and quickly his eagle eye perceives the delivered scandalous letter right there on the mantel. He immediately recognizes the handwriting and the return address," the Prefect divulged to Dupin and me. "Then the cagey Minister asks the woman being framed if she still has his wallet, which he had left in her boudoir the day before, since the lady's famous husband was out of town on a business excursion. The promiscuous female goes to retrieve *his* wallet and then DeVries stealthily paced to the mantel and exchanged the letter atop it with one that he coincidentally had concealed in his coat pocket. When the licentious rich lady returned to the living room she noticed DeVries grabbing something from the stone mantel but when…."

"But when she saw that there was still a letter on the mantel," Dupin deducted and articulated, "she presumed that Prime Minister Claude DeVries had confiscated something else other than the original letter. But the whoring woman must be aware that DeVries had purloined the letter after she realized that the one left on the mantel was a fake."

"And who is this aristocratic nymphomaniac who has all of these big-wig suitors walking around with stiff erections?" I asked. "It sounds as if the insatiable bitch has at least three vaginas."

"Her name is Lady Marie Antoinette DeClement," the Prefect related. "And quite frankly, she doesn't even need one vagina because she specializes in oral sex!"

"Yes," Dupin butted-in. "In fact, among the High Society Scuttlebutt Society, ten years ago Lady DeClement was known as code words 'Deep Throat' but after a decade of practice and experience, she's now affectionately called 'Deep Esophagus'!"

"Wow, instead of 'Let them eat cake," I chortled in the dark library sitting and smoking room, "this fucked-up Marie Antoinette probably says 'Let me eat dick'!"

"Our searches have been very comprehensive and very discreet," the Prefect said, paying my ludicrous remark no particular heed. "We've methodically sorted through the surreptitious Prime Minister's dwelling on four separate occasions and yet the missing letter has not been found. DeVries has two gay Neapolitan servants who are always drunk and at nights are preoccupied sucking each other's dingles, whether they're sober or intoxicated. And as you know," the Paris Prefect related, "I have keys in my possession that will open any door in the whole fuckin' city except the goddamned door to success! If only I were born into nobility I wouldn't have to do this stupid-ass detective work!"

"Yes, it seems that you've investigated every nook and cranny except Lady DeClement's never used vagina," I said and then coughed and choked from the dense smoke continuously permeating the dark room. "But obviously and in a more serious vein Prefect, the all-too-slippery Prime Minister Claude DeVries must either have the letter in his possession or he has concealed it in some other place other than his posh residence."

"Yes, he dares not destroy the missive and would be a complete moron to do so," Dupin intelligently concluded and said, "because that foolish act would be analogous to destroying his only tool for

136

committing blackmail, either for money ransom or for obtaining more political influence through unethically acquiring an unearned government appointment."

The grim-faced gent Prefect Ghent then provided Dupin and me with some additional irrelevant background that made both of his disenchanted listeners wish that we didn't have ears. "DeVries has been searched twice on the street by my competent men and once I even had three plainclothes' detectives disguised as dangerous bandits assail the Minister on the Champs E'lysees, beat the living and dead shit out of him, and then following my good directions to the T, my loyal subordinates ripped off all the Minister's clothes and finally left the Monsieur DeVries standing there stark naked. But still, the jerk-off's pockets contained no libelous purloined letter that had been cunningly stolen from the royal apartment."

And before either Private Investigator Dupin or I could tell Prefect Ghent that he was on the wrong track and that he was more-than-evidently full of shit, Gustav relentlessly deluged us with more of his monotonous piss-poor rhetoric, claiming that his crew of inspectors had taken apart the expensive furniture in Minister DeVries suite, checking the legs of tables, chairs and sofas and peeking for possible hollowed-out bedposts in quest of hidden compartments. And next he boringly vociferated about dismantling the bureau and credenza drawers while delving for secret areas where a scandalous letter might be furtively stashed. And then while I was yawning in the dark and beginning to doze off from boredom, the Prefect stated that his expert forensics' team had industriously examined all of the bricks outside the front and back doors to determine if any space or crevice existed where a letter might be concealed. "We even checked all of the mortar between the red bricks on the outside walls and the similar bricks on the front and back porch steps," the befuddled police administrator shared with us. "Alas Gentlemen, my brain now feels as impotent as my flaccid dick!"

"While you were looking for crevices and apertures," Dupin criticized his eminent guest, "you overlooked one basic thing: the biggest cavity was inside your narrow-minded skull."

"Yes Monsieur Prefect," I concurred with my good chum Cedrick. "It stands to reason that the obvious place to have looked was inside Minister DeVries' hollowed-out dildos."

"You dumb-ass Retard," Prefect Ghent yelled in my direction in the dark, abruptly knocking me out of my lethargic and fanciful state of mind. "If you knew anything about the ladies of French high society, you'd be very aware that Lady DeClement does not do sex with any goddamned dildo, but instead, she very skillfully gives men oral sex. That's her fabulous specialty, her modus operandi, and I know *this* particular truth quite well because I myself am one of her most appreciative clients. Now stop trying to pump my ass for more information because I'm not a fuckin' gay homo' faggot! And furthermore, I know for a fact that Minister DeVries loves whores and abhors the use of dildos but instead prefers using giant freshly-picked cucumbers to stick-up horny kinky ladies' crotcholas!"

"That hot whore Lady DeClement sounds like she really sucks and can easily blow her competition away," I inanely answered. "And Lady DeClement probably blows harder in imitation of the wind during inclement weather than she does in the more clement summer months when the breeze is hardly blowing."

"Look Knucklehead," the Prefect rankled in the dark, "everything that's both inside and outside the Minister's suite was thoroughly scrutinized and analyzed with the magnifications of both a microscope and a telescope. We meticulously went over the entire residence with a fine-tooth-comb, unfortunately mine, so that's why my fuckin' hair is in such disarray because of all the many missing teeth! Next time I'll go to Normandy and comb the beach rather than break the poorly made son-of-a-bitch in Minister DeVries suite."

"Did you intensively search behind the mirrors, between the floor boards and planks, under the decorative plates in the china cabinet or hutch, under the mattresses as well as extensively probe the curtains and the carpets?" I inquisitively asked. "How about sticking your fat nose inside the damned medicine chest?"

"Yes, and my exhausted men even ransacked, or should I say *rummaged* through the cellar and all throughout the attic too," Gustav Ghent reported, "and yet not a trace, not one iota of said scandalous letter was ever discovered. Now Dupin, what do you recommend for me to do? I'm at wits end and I don't savor the terrible feeling one bit."

"It's glaringly apparent to me that your outdated methods are so traditional and so standard and so predictable and so obsolete that you tend to overlook the obvious," Dupin dubiously communicated to his out-of-breath over-the-hill visitor. "Come back in one week's time. In the interim, I'll ponder your tight fix and try and invent some plausible explanation that will guide us to the missing purloined letter. Oh well, it's time to put the lights on so that I can locate my favorite sex doll and go to sleep! And if I'm lucky over the span of the next seven days," my pal Cedrick Auguste stated, "I won't burn my humble house to the ground from smoking my
138

defective pipe in the dark! And please don't worry Prefect!" my good friend exclaimed. "I'm only half as clumsy and half as fucked-up as you are!"

* * * * * * * * * * * *

One week later the three of us again met and then assembled in the dark miniature library to consult and confer about the inappropriate purloined letter exchange that had taken place inside Lady DeClement's royal apartment.

"I've just visited Prime Minister Claude DeVries' suite and I believe I can get the letter in question for you," the incomparable Dupin calmly told Prefect Ghent with me being his listening witness vigorously scratching my itchy testicles in the dark. "How much of a reward are you offering that I may claim and democratically split with my newfound partner sitting here with us?"

"Fifty thousand francs!" the astounded policeman replied. "Fifty thousand francs!" he emphasized again, breathing heavily in the dark, sounding much like a goddamned warthog in heat.

.   "Well, if you want possession of the fuckin' letter, you'd better cough-up a hundred thousand francs to fully compensate my cohort here and me," Cedrick Auguste Dupin dictated to the now-obligated government official that sounded like he was having a full-blown epileptic seizure.

"That's right Prefect," I piped-up in the dark, feigning courage and conviction. "When your asshole inspectors had violently raped Prime Minister DeVries on the Champs E'lysees and savagely removed all his clothes to be looked through later, the purloined letter was obviously stashed-away somewhere in the culprit's suite and not in any of his suit pockets. And every time you and your fucked-up detectives and henchmen examined his suite, the sought-after letter obviously was on his person. Any kindergarten asshole kid could've figured that elementary shit out!"

"If I pay you the hundred-thousand francs tonight," the almost flabbergasted Prefect said to the suave-speaking Dupin, "when will you have the letter in your possession for my perusal?"

"You can stop by on Saturday morning," Dupin promised his prominent acquaintance. "My friend and I will have two spectacular ruses to accomplish in order to adroitly pull the caper off on Friday afternoon. I've already arranged an appointment with Prime Minister Claude DeVries and threatened him that if he were to carry any documents on his person within the next two weeks, then my hit men along with *your* hit men Prefect would attack, rape, pound, pummel, pulverize and sodomize his ass and then throw his butt-naked anatomy into the Seine from the top of the Cathedral of Notre Dame in the middle of the river."

"Why' that's impossible!" Prefect Ghent gasped and weakly challenged. "From that distance and from that height atop the Cathedral, the Prime Minister would never splash into the water."

"As I had also told the Prime Minister, that's *his* fuckin' problem!" Dupin answered Ghent in the darkness of the tiny library. "Now Prefect, despite my nervous condition, I'm going to light the oil lamp. Get out your checkbook and your plumed pen. I want to see in bright illumination exactly what the hell one-hundred-thousand francs look like in your personal writing having your friggin' personal signature!"

* * * * * * * * * * * *

On the following Friday at precisely noon I arrived at Dupin's ramshackle (about to be condemned) dwelling and we conferred in the dark (after he had closed the opaque shade on the lone window) in the small library room and then lit his undependable pipe in the dark, complaining about scorching his left hand with his lit match and later his right palm with his hot smoking apparatus. But despite those two "minor second degree-burn adversities," Cedrick Auguste was in an uncharacteristic jovial and optimistic frame of mind as he conscientiously reviewed "our strategy."

"Have you acquired the musket that I had requested you use in today's enterprise?" Dupin asked me. "That weapon might turn out to be a key element."

"Yes, I got one from my close friend Little Richard, who as you probably know has a small penis and a bad Napoleon complex as a result. Anyway," I explained to my shrewd cohort about that afternoon's proposed pilfering of the scandalous letter session, "Little Dick is one of three musketeers that I know who sings both alto and soprano in my church choir."

"And don't forget to rap on Prime Minister Claude DeVries' door exactly five minutes after I enter and initiate a conversation with him. Keep knocking for ten seconds," Dupin reminded me, "but just remember, you can keep-a-knocking but you can't come in. Don't forget to run out the front door and hurry down the steps after you rap without chanting either an alto or a soprano mantra for a full ten seconds. Are my easy instructions perfectly clear?"

"Where is the letter hidden in the Prime Minister's residence?" I nervously asked the inimitable Dupin.

"It's not hidden at all," the most excellent Cedrick Auguste shockingly related to me. "Do you remember when I had accused Prefect Ghent of being too old-fashioned in his fuddy-duddy police methods? Well, I attribute *that* phenomenon to common sense, which nowadays is not too common and I also attribute *my* theory of resolution to what psychologists call 'the power of suggestion.' Since Prime Minister Claude DeVries had picked-up the original defamatory letter from Lady DeClement's fireplace mantel," Dupin expounded after several seconds of introspection, "and when I had met with the ingrate asshole at his residence, Minister DeVries had asininely placed the letter-in-question on his own goddamned mantel piece in subconscious imitation of what Lady DeClement had done. I mean to say that the degenerate government asshole couldn't be more fuckin' stupid if his name was John Duns Scotus! Ha, ha, ha! If DeVries wasn't such a damned riot, he'd surely be a goddamned mob, ha, ha, ha!"

"And of course our word *dunce* comes from John Scotus' middle name," I etymologically contributed to our intellectual conversation. "Any other directions?" I asked my crime-fighting tutor. "I'm quite anxious to get started."

"Yes, but first I must alert you, as usual you have your pants on backwards," Dupin informed me in the dark. "I noticed them on you wrongly being worn when you had first entered my humble abode five minutes ago. I trust that your ignorant mannerism *slacks* off before we get Lady DeClement's self-indicting letter back from that dastardly weasel DeVries."

I accompanied Dupin over to Prime Minister Claude DeVries' suite and waited patiently in the side corridor for five minutes and then loudly knocked on the door for ten seconds. Quickly I exited the premises, nearly colliding with a wrinkle-faced elderly woman (a domestic servant in an adjacent suite, I believe) who had been ascending the front marble steps leading into the building.

Prior to my rapping distraction, Dupin had been bullshitting with and also threatening Prime Minister DeVries at the dining room table. When DeVries rushed to the door to escape Dupin's derogatory comments, Dupin slipped a powerful fast-acting laxative into his host's full cup of coffee.

Exactly fifteen minutes later, Claude DeVries had to evacuate the room in order to evacuate his large intestine's free-flowing fecal matter in a "sudden diarrhea attack" as the magnificent Dupin had wonderfully described it earlier to me.

Seeing DeVries' mad rush to find a large enough pot to crap in, my inventive accomplice hurried to the living room mantel and exchanged an envelope with the one that had been addressed to Lady DeClement by her second anonymous amorous consort. And when I fired Little Richard's musket out on the street fifteen minutes later, the paranoid Prime Minister, who already had the runs and was in danger of dehydrating, wildly dashed to the window (followed by Dupin) to see what the commotion was all about.

After seeing that the musket firing was of no special consequence, DeVries did a one-eighty to return to either the dining room table or his crapping pot. With the speed of Hermes, Dupin swiftly raised the window and tossed Lady DeClement's letter outside where my good friend Little "Dick" Richard grabbed the fluttering missive out of midair and then handed it to me a block away in exchange for his already agreed-upon twenty-five franc reward. Thus *our* imaginative second diversion involving the firing of the borrowed musket had been remarkably successful and thank goodness that no man, woman or child had been injured, for that instance was the first time I had ever shot off any potentially lethal weapon.

A half hour later Dupin and I held our "post pilfering rendezvous" inside *my* apartment where I insisted and stubbornly maintained that the internationally acclaimed private detective should review the entire "expeditious counter-heist exploit" in broad daylight.

"At first I was thinking about leaving an empty snuff box under the sofa inside Minister DeVries' suite but then I switched to *our* more adventurous 'dual diversions' plan'," Dupin elaborated on his complex letter reclamation scheme. "You know as a matter of fact that I prefer things when they're more complicated and more challenging. That's why I quickly dispensed with the snuffbox idea as an excuse to return to DeVries' apartment but instead visited him and then made a second appointment to be scheduled a week later. And I must congratulate you!" Dupin genuinely praised. "Your invaluable services were commendably performed indeed," my good friend complimented.

"Do you plan on giving Prefect Ghent the letter tomorrow evening?" I asked. "He seemed rather anxious to get it back into his possession, at least *that* was my take."

"Yes, but the tricky asshole did have a motive other than keeping his fine reputation in law enforcement intact with the newspapers and with the public," Dupin keenly elucidated. "The goddamned sex-starved Fool! I suspected immediately that the friggin' love letter that had been addressed to Lady DeClement was from our dear friend the esteemed Prefect Gustav Ghent, who in addition to myself, was a regular fellatio client of the fantastically immoral-but-pleasurable Lady DeClement, who incidentally will be receiving a new set of kneepads from me for her upcoming Christmas gift!"

"And will I be receiving my share of the reward for assisting in pilfering the purloined letter to be given to Prefect Ghent tomorrow evening?" I asked. "My damned rent is due and I need groceries in my cupboard and pantry and I need the cash desperately."

"Well, allow me to be the bearer of good news; you're in for a decent bonus to boot," Dupin surprisingly announced. "After that egotistical asshole Ghent gives me a hundred-thousand-francs for a job well done, I'm going to demand an additional hundred thousand for blackmail compensation now that I know the all-too-sultry contents of the Prefect's scandalous letter to the naughty Lady DeClement."

"I should've pieced all of these mosaic fragments together and figured out the puzzle myself," I regretted and gasped. "There had to be a feasible reason why the horny Prefect desired obtaining *that* letter from his love triangle rival DeVries other than *his* concern for Lady DeClement's good reputation in French aristocratic society. You're a veritable genius Dupin!"

"As I had stated to you on many occasions," my sagacious associate remarked and laughed, "I detest things, or should I say, I detest utilizing *methods* that are too simplistic to perform. But when matters are made more complex to solve or to execute," Dupin evaluated and said, "then that's when I derive the most satisfaction in solving crimes, or in this particular case involving Claude DeVries and Gustav Ghent, solving an immoral enigma."

"I'm going to invest my portion of the reward money into stocks and bonds," I excitedly told Dupin. "What the hell do you intend to do with yours?"

"Well confidentially, I happen to owe Lady DeClement over ninety thousand francs in back payments for her stellar professional services, so therefore the remaining ten thousand I'll use as an advance payment for another month of the irresistible woman's specialized lip-o-suction technique, ha, ha, ha!"

"Dr. Tarr and Professor Fether"

Someone might think my tale is humorous but to me, it was all quite disconcerting. During the mild autumn of 1840, I was touring France's southern provinces trying to locate a certain *Maison de Sante*, or a notorious local nuthouse that specialized in advanced psychology methods and techniques. Since I had never had the pleasure of visiting an eminent "experimental asylum" of that kind, I proposed to my French traveling companion that we should set aside an afternoon so that I could avail myself of the opportunity to gather some pertinent research for a short story on mental health I had wished to write.

"This place to which you allude is a lunatic magnet and I wish not to visit it," my Parisian friend replied. "If I were you, I'd fuckin' seek asylum from that wacky asylum and avoid the goddamned place as quickly as you can. But if you insist, I'll tell you how to get there but I intend to ride on to Marseilles and rest my weary bones. I'll meet you at the designated waterfront inn that is expecting us later tonight. Then we could enjoy an excellent supper together."

"Do you know the superintendent of *Maison de Sante*, a distinguished fellow named Monsieur Maillard?" I asked my friend Gaston. "I had heard his renowned name mentioned while I had been speaking with some notable published men in the medical profession back in Paris."

"Unless you have some meritorious letter of recommendation or an official state certificate of admission from the national government," Gaston said in a regretting tone of voice, "then I doubt whether this Monsieur Maillard will allow you to enter and tour his avant-garde facility. Quite frankly, I've heard that Maillard is a trifle fucked-up in his organization skills and that he's quite suspicious about unexpected or uninvited visitors," Gaston confided. "But Edgar, since I'm a medical doctor and had known this Maillard five years ago back in Lyons, I'll accompany you to his clinic and introduce you to him. The rest will be entirely up to you."

"I see," I answered Gaston, my ordinarily rational mind being somewhat confused. "You *are* a doctor of the body and just like your Parisian colleagues, you condescend those that study the activities of the human mind, thinking that they're all a monstrous gaggle of fucked-up incompetent quacks!"

We rode our fatigued horses on a dirt trail that meandered through a dank and dismal forest and at the base of a mediocre-sized mountain we finally arrived at *my* destination, the *Maison de Sante*. At first glance the edifice was a fantastic-looking chateau, but upon closer scrutiny, its appearance was a bit dilapidated from neglect and from lack of maintenance. My initial inclination was to turn around and head towards Marseilles with Gaston but then my heart gathered the courage to stay and satisfy my original curiosity about the rather intriguing place.

Monsieur Maillard was quite a vigilante administrator who immediately detected our presence while peering out of an iron-barred window. The short portly superintendent anxiously exited his clinic and upon recognizing Gaston, courteously invited him and me inside. Maillard at first impression struck me as a man of genteel and polished manners whose general demeanor reflected dignity and authority. 'Always trust your first perception,' I thought as I keenly evaluated the strange-looking fellow.

"My friend Mr. Poe would like to stay the afternoon and tour your nationally famous *Maison de Sante*," Gaston blandly disclosed. "Unfortunately I have important business to attend to in Marseilles and will have to take a rain check on your offer to stay. Would you mind accommodating my dear friend Mr. Poe in my absence?"

"No, not at all," Superintendent Maillard graciously indicated. "Why don't you alight from your horse Mr. Poe and I'll gladly give you a guided tour of the premises."

After I thanked Gaston for his invaluable assistance, and after he rode off in a fury towards Marseilles, Monsieur Maillard politely ushered me into his "experimental facility." A cheerful fire blazed upon the hearth and a very beautiful and talented young woman was preoccupied playing an aria from Bellini on the piano. She paused upon realizing my intrusion into the room, casually greeted me with a graceful smile and then continued with her rehearsal of the complicated composition.

I had instantly detected an element of sorrow and melancholy in the young woman's disposition but being a refined gentleman of good breeding, I never explored pursuing *that* possibly embarrassing aspect of conversation. I had heard at the recent academic conference in Paris that the acclaimed *Maison de Sante* (under the direction of Monsieur Maillard) had been managed (by the vulgarly used term) "system of permissive soothing" so I asked the now-garrulous superintendent about his innovative method of mental care.

"Well you see Mr. Poe, according to my revolutionary creative method, all types of punishments have been disposed with and the novel concept of 'rewards' is implemented whenever possible," the superintendent enthusiastically explained. "Although the patients are secretly watched, they do have liberty of the house, that is to say, they have and enjoy complete freedom of mobility. And instead of wearing uniforms like inmates in prisons do, my pampered patients are allowed to cavort around at will in civilian apparel and mingle and bond with their peers whenever they so desire," the esteemed executive of the asylum informed. "Such a tolerant atmosphere could only engender the development of independence and self-sufficiency among my 'guests' as I like to call them."

"I see Sir, you run your remarkable institution as if it were a high society hotel," I commented. "Very interesting indeed Mr. Maillard. Very fascinating too if I may add."

At that time I had resolved in my always-skeptical mind to confine my remarks to general topics so as not to offend either Monsieur Maillard or his sensitive-minded patients. A footman then brought a tray of fresh fruit into the room along with wine and other refreshments and I made myself comfortable taking a glass of merlot along with a red ripe apple.

"Was that young lady in the other room playing the piano one of your patients?" I diplomatically asked my host. "She seemed very normal to me."

"No Mr. Poe, that pretty young lady is pretty young and she happens to be my beloved niece Florence, just visiting here for the week," Monsieur Maillard laughed and then loudly burped, nearly regurgitating a large chuck of cheese he had just swallowed. "Flossie as I call her is a most accomplished musician and plans to do some major theater concerts in the near future. All she needs right now is a booking agent and a manager!"

"Are you feeling all right?" I asked Maillard as he began burping and farting loudly. "I do have adequate knowledge about gastro-intestinal remedies, you know!"

"You must excuse my chronic belching," Maillard said while exhibiting a degree of mortification. "For you see, under the previous system that was in place here, a harsh system that enforced martinet discipline and punishment, the inhibited patients were often abused. So that's why with the utilization my new 'permissive soothing method' I had to exclude visitors from the outside interfering with its administration. My patients must learn to trust the friendly staff in the building and not be subject to the prejudices and discriminations of those encroaching outsiders that can't relate to *their* often complex mental health issues."

"How long has your permissive soothing system been in operation?" I innocently asked as I began to think that Maillard was an idealistic impractical dumb fuck university academic doing irrelevant quack research on his own. "I would like to analyze and document the entire intricate process if I may?"

"Why that would be impossible Mr. Poe!" Monsieur Maillard surprisingly exclaimed. "Just last week I found it necessary to return to the formerly obsolete martinet discipline approach. I'm sorry Mr. Poe that you had not visited us last month when the controversial permissive soothing method was being employed."

'This dumb fuck is really a fickle doltish asshole,' I concluded. 'No doubt he farts and shits out of his mouth and probably eats out of his asshole. What a fucked-up hypocritical omnivore' this pathetic jerk-off Maillard is!'

"You see Mr. Poe, while I was utilizing the 'permissive soothing method' of mental treatment," Maillard defensively stated and equivocated, "some of the men actually thought that they were chickens, more specifically roosters, and the fellows would run around the house trying to screw any female whether the ladies said or screamed cock-a-doodle-doo or not! And then we had several gay roosters in the pack that were trying to have sexual intercourse with other male patients! And then a few of the more serious hens spent their entire day attempting to lay eggs! The entire psychological experiment proved to be an abominable abysmal failure where all semblances of civility had been abandoned with the ineffective ultra-liberal permissive soothing philosophy going completely amuck!"

"Did you still have dancing, music, sports, card playing and reading books as alternative amusement activities?" I inquired.

"Well Mr. Poe, for a while we did try those standard therapeutic things and we also relied on the patients admonishing each other for alleged misbehaviors and indiscretions," Maillard lectured without a lectern, "but the really bad maniacs we had to discharge to a local regular hospital for rehabilitation. We wanted to find a perfect medium, somewhere between those punitive methodologies of the ruthless Marquis de Sade and those Christian charity-oriented methods of Jesus Christ. But Mr. Poe," Maillard warned, "I strongly advise you to believe nothing that you hear and only half of what you see in regard to you assessing the *Maison de Sante*. Whatever you do," the rather strange superintendent cautioned me, "don't be misled by the false teachings of those medical ignoramuses over in Paris!
148

Now then, I'll show you the gardens and the conservatories and then we'll have a delicious dinner after six."

"Mr. Maillard, where the hell are your patients?" I inquired. "I haven't seen one of them since I've been here."

"Oh, they're around here somewhere," the chief administrator obtusely answered. "I'm sure they're hiding from us somewhere in the dense foliage or perhaps playing Hide and Seek behind sofas and chairs just to break our balls!"

And before I could explore the next uncultivated garden and weed area, I heard around twenty zany voices all' zestfully yelling in unison, "Cock-a-doodle-doo!" in a queer dissonant cacophony, sounding much like some sort of out-of-control lunatic chicken coop.

* * * * * * * * * * * *

At six o'clock dinner was announced and the superintendent and the footman conducted me from the chateau's comfortable-but-sterile living room through in-need-of-repair French doors into a large dining area containing a huge eight-leafed solid oak table with what I assumed to be thirty dignified people seated around it. Twenty-five of the chatty diners were well dressed women, all of whom were wearing expensive-looking evening gowns, necklaces, wrist and arm bracelets, gold medallions and finally, jeweled diamond rings. The ostentatious women all seemed gregarious and also appeared to be dominating the myriad conversations that were occurring.

I next noticed that the warped floor was rug-less, that the dirty windows were indeed barred (both horizontally and vertically) and that the oak table had been set with an abundance of food with veal and ham as the principal meats and with rice, salad, potatoes, yellow squash and corn being the main vegetables. A great many anecdotes were being exchanged among the guests and my mind tried to absorb all that was being discussed around the gigantic oval table.

"We had a gentleman here about a year ago," prefaced a man two seats down from my right, "and the old geezer fancied himself' being a goddamned teapot, always whistling, not like a human mind you but like a goddamned common ordinary kitchen stove teapot. And do you know what?" the self-serving speaker continued his monologue. "The dumb shit jerk, I think he was from Cannes, would polish himself every night to stay shiny and silvery."

"It's a good thing he didn't think there was a hurricane inside of him or else he would've been a wicked tempest in a teapot!" I mused and then foolishly declared.

Next a tall gentleman seated three down from Monsieur Maillard piped-up, "About eight months ago we had a stubborn asshole staying here who thought he was a hungry donkey and he would eat pine cones, hay and thistle all day long," the fellow with the good memory stated. "Well then, when I kindly asked to see his pecker I saw that the lying son-of-a-bitch didn't have any goddamned donkey-dick after all, ha, ha, ha!"

Immediately Superintendent Maillard felt obligated to reprimand and chastise the loose-tongued fellow. "Mr. DeKock," the flustered administrator said, "stop acting so naughtily. You're beginning to make an ass out of yourself just as our former guest Mr. Muleskin had done when he was hee-hawing his damned tonsils out every single morning, noon and night."

Everyone at the table was merrily drinking wine as if it was fresh cold water. Bottles of chardonnay sauvignon, of cabernet merlot and of white zinfandel were randomly scattered (or distributed) all over the immense table. I was busily feasting on ham and veal and was so engrossed in my consumption of food that I paid little heed to the nonsensical hubbub happening all around me. But in retrospect, the scenario was even worse in magnitude than any chaotic nonsensical episode out of *Dante's Inferno*.

And then a cadaverous-looking lady sitting six chairs down to my right testified, "We had a screwed-up patient living here at the chateau a while back that thought she was a slice of Cordova cheese and every time she picked up a knife at breakfast," the raunchy old bag emphasized, "at lunch or at dinner, a naked Lady Cordova would attempt to slice off a sliver of herself, honestly thinking that she was the goddamned Big Cheese around here!"

"I'm Mr. Chardonnay and I'm a chilled bottle of red wine," the transsexual cross-dressing woman four chairs down to my left announced as she put her finger inside her mouth and made the popping sound of a cork flying off a champagne bottle. "Now which of you asshole men wants to corkscrew me so that I can pop your weasel too!"

"These weird stories are not only amusing, but they're quite visceral and graphic too," I leaned over and confidentially related to Monsieur Maillard. "Are these people fucked-up, or are *we* fucked-up just sitting here and listening to their incredible bullshit?"

Before Maillard could reply to my keen observation, the asshole woman sitting thirty-feet down at the far end of the table boisterously yelled out to Maillard and me, "Hey you two shit-heads down there! Don't you know I'm a frog? Yesterday I was a horned toad, but now

150

I've changed into a horny frog that doesn't want to croak until I get laid at least twenty times tonight." And next the dumb shit toothless woman noticed a huge disgusting insect crawling on the wood-planked floor, got down on her hands and knees and then extending her long tongue, captured the very large black bug in her mouth and began chomping away."

My mind was in a quandary but I was again subjected to listening to additional bizarre bullshit. "And what about that fuck head Petit Gaillard who thought himself to be a box of snuff and wanted everyone in the house to sniff his smelly asshole that he thought was his box's opening?" a woman in the center right of the expansive oak table hollered-out for all to hear. "And don't forget that dumb shit Jules Descartes who believed he was a pumpkin and who would beat up the cook before every meal because Jules suspected that the always bruised-up chef was going to change him into a pumpkin pie to be eaten by all at dinner."

"What the hell is this stupid shit all about?" I demanded to know from Maillard. "Either these pea-brained fuck-heads are all raving imbeciles or they're an insolent pack of retarded morons? Which is it Monsieur?"

Before the beleaguered superintendent could ever garner and utter a response to my imperative/interrogative statement, a really ugly lady who was now half naked shouted out, "What about good old Bouffon Le Grand who thought he had two heads, the first one being Cicero and the second one being Demosthenes. And then good old debonair Bouffon would leap-up upon this same dinner table and render to us in a an extemporaneous speech saying, "That asshole Greek Demosthenes might have pebbles in his mouth but that fuckin' roamin' Roman Cicero always had rocks in his head! Ha, ha, ha!" the female zoo candidate shrieked. "And then good old bonny Bouffon finally graduated into being a top and would spin around all night long until he finally shit and pissed his pants!"

'My riding companion Gaston was indubitably right,' I finally realized and concluded. 'I too need asylum from this fucked-up asylum! These son-of-a-bitches sitting here have to be the fucked-up patients and I now think that they certainly aren't goddamned sophisticated aristocratic guests at all!' I determined.

But before I could grab Maillard by the collars and start strangling a feasible explanation out of his throat, an elderly gray-haired promiscuous bitch (with her hideous flabby tits hanging out of her dress) stood up and began redundantly bellowing, "Cock-a-doodle-doo, any cock'll do! Cock-a-doodle-doo! Any cock'll do!"

"Monsieur, she's trying to start a sex orgy at the dinner table! Do something Maillard! I say fuckin' do something before I violently squeeze your neck until your goddamned windpipe disintegrates!" I boomed as I took out my frustration by pounding my right hand against the asshole superintendent's chest, but to no avail or personal satisfaction.

"Mr. Poe, I must tell you that Madame Honeywell is in heat," Maillard explained to me with a very pallid face. "She thinks she's a female poodle in estrous. There's little I can do to salvage Madame Honeywell, or 'the Bitch' as she wants to be called! And incidentally Mr. Poe, Madame Honeywell sometimes thinks she's a modest young lady who when she meticulously dresses herself, she always gets outside rather than inside her clothes."

"Just like the goofy Cicero/Demosthenes jerk-off that was just discussed, your Mrs. Honeywell is what the modern psychologists call a person suffering from a split personality, yes, I believe that the mental condition is now referred to as schizophrenia! But truthfully Monsieur Maillard," I screamed above the ever-ascending dining room din, "I now truly feel like I'm the goddamned chief cashew inside the nuthouse!"

And before basic order could be intelligently restored, Mrs. Honeywell again stood up and once more cockily yelled out, "Cock-a-doodle-do! Any cock'll do! Cock-a-doodle-do! Any cock'll do!" while ripping off her ornate dress and accompanying undergarments and then the crazy old bag "Bitch" began wildly masturbating her vulva and her clitoris in public.

"Maillard, who has devised this retroactive treatment of a compromised medium existing between your former liberal permissive soothing method and the more Draconian Marquis de Sade martinet punishment method?" I hoarsely gasped.

"Why it was none other than that famous dynamic duo Dr. Tarr and Professor Fether," Maillard recollected and loudly replied. "Don't tell me you've never heard of those two very prominent contributors to the psychology field?"

"I must admit that I'm forced to acknowledge my uneducated ignorance," I confessed in a raspy hardly audible voice. "If I recall, those two gentlemen were not in attendance at the recent Paris medical conference."

Suddenly a massive food fight originated at the other end of the colossal oval table with apples, oranges, bananas, ham, veal, and hot potatoes flying all over the damned place and soon the airborne objects were accompanied by torrents of wine from recently opened

152

bottles of chardonnay sauvignon, cabernet merlot and white zinfandel. I stood up and weakly screamed, "You're all going berserk! Stop this bullshit buffoonery right this second!" at the top of my faltering lungs and vocal cords but regrettably, the voice of a minnow swimming under faraway Niagara Falls could have been heard much better at that crazy fiasco scene located not far from the Riviera in Southern France. "Maillard, if you can't immediately put these thirty insane lunatics in straight jackets, then I suggest that you get out the fuckin' crooked jackets instead!"

"Certainly Mr. Poe," the short obese baldheaded superintendent loudly articulated into my ear, "these thirty patients need one-on-one individual attention, which because of economic reasons, cannot be supplied. I have only two reliable employees assisting me and we're pretty damned overwhelmed, wouldn't you agree?"

"Well then," I yelled in a puzzled frame of mind, "where the hell are Dr. Tarr and Professor Fether? Can't they help you re-tool and reorganize this fucked-up place?"

"I'll tell you a little secret Mr. Poe. They're both locked-up in the chateau's cellar," Maillard confessed without remorse. "They had taken over this institution from me but then I became an activist patient here myself, shrewdly coordinated a counter-revolution just like Napoleon Bonaparte had done, and I coyly got together these thirty uncouth rebels and convinced them to recapture the asylum from the control of those two quack shrinks Tarr and Fether."

"Holy shit!" I exclaimed amidst the tumult of the ever-escalating dining room food fight. "Then really and truly Maillard, the patients have taken over the goddamned asylum! That's fuckin' even worse than the goddamned chicken hawks and foxes being given the keys to the chicken coop!"

Three nude men then clumsily hopped onto the table and started kicking plates and serving bowls and eating utensils off the already abused oak surface while the deranged triumvirate simultaneously and in-harmoniously were singing "Yankee Doodle."

And while all of the unbearable noise and frenzy was in progress and reaching a crescendo, a formidable army of experimental baboons and chimpanzees (that had been caged-up in the asylum's cellar) savagely invaded the dining room and the vicious animals were led by the demented Dr. Tarr and the equally demented Professor Fether, who both had broken free of their shackles and had gotten the Simian troops to support *their* battle assault.

Needless to say, during the hectic and ferocious combat that ensued, I had received a tremendous brutal thrashing and was maliciously scratched all over my face, hands, chest, testicles and arms. I instinctively feigned mortal injury by falling to my hands and knees and then accelerating my ass by swiftly crawling out of the terrible madhouse *Maison de Sante*. I staggered and hobbled outside to the chateau's outbuildings, and I next struggled to saddle and then mount my refreshed horse, which had been moved to the nearby stone barn. Five minutes later my rested steed was ambitiously galloping in the direction of Marseilles.

After my hasty departure from the crazy asylum, I traveled extensively throughout France and researched inside each and every Paris, Marseilles and Lyons library for the collective thesis works of Dr. Tarr and Professor Fether, but alas, in the end my well-intentioned efforts all proved to be abject failures.

"The Facts in the Case of V. Valdemar"

I have had the total displeasure of knowing that parsimonious and ultra-frugal stingy son-of-a-bitch Mr. Vladimir Valdemar for thirty-three years now, and I absolutely despise the no-good bastard specifically because in my life I've personally had many traumatic relationships with the detestable asshole, and principally, the annoying unimaginative fuck-head happens to be my avaricious ball-breaking father-in-law. As is often said, you can choose your friends but not your relatives, in-laws or outlaws.

But since I am a nationally renowned psychologist studying both life and death in conjunction with the multiple functioning of the human mind, I sagely decided to objectively analyze Mr. V. Valdemar in a clinical case study that (I thought) would undoubtedly benefit other behavioral scientists and university graduate students in the future. However, in a more cautious vein, it is axiomatic to state without equivocation that in order to do quality re*search*, the inquiring mind must first intensely *search* and catalogue vital data and then painstakingly *re-search* his findings many, many times. But in the end game I was quite confident in my ability to proceed with developing my unique treatise.

As a general rule, I have never been a superstitious man dependent on priests, ministers, rabbis, or imams for spiritual and emotional guidance. In American culture, this business of death is indeed a taboo subject to most ordinary commonplace people but in order to probe its defining elements and characteristics, the psychologist must first transcend human fears and apprehensions and focus his labor on addressing the fundamental topic at hand. In short, most untrained *civilians* might be inclined to exaggerate the major tenets presented in my case study so therefore its erudite essence and premises must be kept confidential and only exclusively available to specialists and future experts in the psychology/psychiatry field of endeavor. That was my intention from the outset.

Since I've always had an extensive animosity towards my fucked-up egotistical asshole father-in-law (that coincidentally is shared by his daughter, my adoring wife), I can say with *relative* assurance that I'm looking forward (as I pen these words) to working with my devious and greedy father-in-law as his tainted spirit departs from his deathbed and filters into the so-called supernatural dimension. I understood that my ambitious project was destined to make me' and my work internationally famous. And right before me was the ideal opportunity to launch my grandiose enterprise.

For the last three years I've been concentrating my research on a new social science called Mesmerism and it soon occurred to me that I could advantageously explore the principles of this new knowledge by intelligently communicating with a dying person as his spirit exits the body and journeys (or evaporates) into the hereafter. Of course I would be professionally using hypnosis to stay in touch with the in-transit soul as it makes its mysterious excursion into the afterlife. And since I utterly abhor the case study in question, the detestable and heinous prick Mr. Vladimir Valdemar, I was more than anxious to commence my gathering of facts and the implementation of my soon-to-be indispensable thesis, which I maintained would be a valuable academic contribution to the advancement of my fledgling specialty area of theoretical discipline.

In summary, my primary motivation was to become a pioneer engaging in avant-garde breakthrough discovery in *Psychology*. My paramount goal was to make, sustain and document contact with a dying soul as it miserably leaves this predictable Earth and then enters (or vaporizes) into the unclassified and uncharted afterworld. It is widely believed that a thin demarcation separates a madman from a genius and I was resolute to pursue *that* division for fame and fortune. I had desired to push the envelope to the maximum.

In a biographical sense, my skinflint millionaire father-in-law was a well-known author who had written various classical works under the nondescript *nom de plume* Isachar Mars. Some of his more popular texts are *Wallenstein, Gargantua* and the obscure-but-controversial published manuscript titled *Testicle and Penis Expansion and Reduction in Dwarfs and Midgets*.

And oh yes, Mr. Vladimir Valdemar's lower limbs and upper appendages resemble those of Washington Irving's fictional character Ichabod Crane, who also had an *icky*-type appearance and his *bod'* had certain physical similarities to a skinny long-beaked bird. After Mr. Vladimir Valdemar's more adventurous globetrotting days, my fucked-up father-in-law, despite his extraordinarily fantastic wealth, chose to reside as a lowlife mendicant in a Harlem ghetto and democratically distributed his great mammon to undeserving homosexuals, lesbians, anarchists and disease-infected whores and hookers while all during his irresponsible humanitarian philanthropy, the butt-ugly white bearded black-haired decrepit asshole was completely ignoring his struggling daughter Alice and her most-deserving husband. Such was the marital arrangement in which I soon found myself entangled.

On a trial and error basis, my failing and mentally deficient father-in-law had remarkably consented to going under deep hypnosis three separate times after learning that he was dying from old age, syphilis and senility. I had found the mental case Mr. V. Valdemar to be totally obnoxious in his value system beliefs, hardly clairvoyant or inventive in either imagination or creativity. The listless shit-head was simply a lucky businessman that hit it big in publishing his lackluster journals, anecdotes and notes, and I've honestly wound-up being somewhat jealous and envious of the non-talented cock-sucking fortunate shit. It had always bothered me that such an inferior intellect could gain worldwide acclaim. My secret aspiration was to exceed my father-in-law's accomplishments.

Last month I had learned from his attending physicians that my father-in-law was finally approaching his unscheduled meeting with the proverbial Grim Reaper, of course modeled after Charon, the ferryman on the River Styx that transported the dead person's soul from the Land of the Living to Hades, the dreadful and un-inspiring Kingdom of the Dead in Greek mythology. Yes, I had diligently studied the most significant ancient civilizations in graduate school and (unlike deranged Vladimir Valdemar) possess a more-than-adequate knowledge of heroes and antiquated empires and cultures.

Now to be perfectly frank, from past experiences I had never expected any tokens of sympathy or gratitude from Mr. V. Valdemar, so I was somewhat surprised that the arrogant fuck had agreed to fully cooperate in my landmark case study. In addition to old age, syphilis and senility, my devious father-in-law was also suffering from *acute* tuberculosis, cancer, heart disease, gonorrhea, phlebitis, brain tumors, kidney failure and *a cute* hussy with polio, but since the phlegmatic bastard had been living with those horrible conditions for well over twenty-five years, I feared that I myself' would die standing next to his deathbed (before ever completing my distinguished research involving him) prior to the no-good scumbag degenerate ever ceasing to breathe. Even as death approached, the enigmatic son-of-a-bitch's vital signs remained strong in spite of his myriad maladies. Certainly I had not anticipated my wife's father being so defiant to both his and my needs.

'His character has always been his most flawed disease,' I remember thinking and concluding. 'I can only describe the emotionally worthless mendacious jerk-off as being 'the asshole of all assholes'. I am not a planet and he is not the sun and I wholeheartedly resent that over the years my life has perpetually revolved around *his* wealth and *his* achievements.'

It had been arranged between the two of us that V. Valdemar's medical doctors would summon me to their dying patient's deathbed when it was clearly obvious that the pathetic wretched fuck-head had less than twenty-four hours time left in his symbolic hourglass. My interest in the lousy bastard was promptly aroused the minute I received an urgent messenger-delivered memo' from his physicians.

Dear Dr. Tidwell:

This brief missive is to inform you that our patient Mr. Vladimir Victor Valdemar is showing signs of rapid organ dysfunction and tissue degeneration and that his tenure as a human being has entered into his last day on Planet Earth.

Sincerely,

Dr. Alvin Neuron (Neurologist)
Dr. Henry Busch (Gynecologist)

It was a rather hectic scramble for me to race and cover the half-mile trek from my modest Baltimore row-house residence to the hospital. On the way I had gotten into a loud protracted argument with a belligerent cab driver over the right of way at a congested intersection so I angrily and decisively beat the shit out of the ill tempered asshole and then had his horse use its front hooves to kick the remaining crap out of the fat jerk-off as the wise-assed big-mouth lay near a sewer. And I felt no guilt or shame in administering that well-deserved pummeling, for I had abandoned the notions of *conscience* and *morality* a year after getting married and a year after I had to deal with my fucked-up father-in-law.

Upon arriving at the downtown hospital, I was amazed to discover that the emaciated pig-head Mr. Vladimir Victor Valdemar was still alive and propped-up in his bed with pillows and the asshole was assiduously endeavoring to drink a yellow liquid from his bedpan. I approached the vicinity of his bed with extreme caution, knowing full well the jerk-off's tempestuous behavior and the type of bizarre temper tantrums the unpredictable psychopath would ordinarily vociferate. My shaky hands removed the patient's chart from the wall and I conscientiously interpreted and assessed the numbskull's
158

decline in health, wondering how the dumb arrogant fuck had wondrously remained in the hospital bed and was not lying horizontally on a cold slab in the facility's morgue. It was as if the dirty prick was immortal and had somehow transcended Death itself.

'Holy shit!' I evaluated while reading the chart. 'His left lung has collapsed and he hasn't urinated or defecated in the last four days despite the fact that he has a bad case of chronic colitis. He's had a severe aneurysm of the aorta and I don't have to be a goddamned oracle to understand that his right auricle isn't fuckin' working,' I read and determined. 'His doctors think that *this* medical anomaly will die around midnight tonight. My fucked-up father-in-law is much more durable than your typical run-of-the-mill invalid invalid!' I thought in a rare instance of self-amusement. 'If the doctors' prognosis happens to be correct then *this* room visit gives me' a time window of less than ten hours to satisfactorily conduct my revolutionary research experiment,' my brain ascertained. 'Even while dying, my father-in-law is still calling the goddamned shots.'

I then bent over to converse with the man I despised. "You have nothing to fear. Do you wish for me to mesmerize, or should I say hypnotize you right now?" I asked the dying specimen lying before me. "The prescribed activity might help you better cope with your circumstance!"

"Yes you Dumb Fuck, get this goddamned thing over with before I decide to leave this fucked-up world and its plethora of difficulties behind!" my demented subject stated. "When you feel the way I do, you want to shit your brains right out of your ass if that will allow you to pass-on better!"

I felt like amputating his shriveled-up dick and castrating his tiny balls right there and then, but my professionalism prevailed over my anger and I managed to persevere through all of my deep subconscious urges and angst. The no-good bastard was in his death throes with his pulse being almost imperceptible and his irregular breathing was now at a dying pace of taking in air every half minute and then exhaling thirty seconds later.

I attempted my thorough and efficient hypnosis and soon Vladimir Valdemar's frightening eyes became glassy and almost opaque. I bent over his chest to hear his faint heartbeat but the recalcitrant asshole (even under hypnosis and his existence very near death) inadvertently pissed in my face. After drying off my cheeks, chin, mouth and forehead with a dirty towel, I patiently held a clean mirror up to his nose and determined (by the subsequent surface haze' which eventually formed) that the detestable son-of-a-bitch was still very

159

much alive. Still I was somewhat intrigued by my subject's general stamina even though he was never half as physically fit as me.

But then out of sheer frustration and basic accumulated hate, and knowing that *we* were alone in the room, I savagely punched the patient in the stomach and then in his chest with intentions of bludgeoning him to death. The patient's limp prone body bounced up from the mattress twice but the uncooperative fuck showed no facial expression that denoted any positive or negative emotion whatsoever. Feeling quite exasperated, I was in an extremely livid mood that was characteristically based on my very difficult two-decade history with the intolerable patient along with the personal embarrassment of him just recently urinating onto my bearded face, hence, me still having to breathe-in the unnerving disgusting odor.

"Are you asleep Mr. Valdemar?" I calmed-down and asked, effectively disguising my voice.

"Yes Asshole, I am asleep so why don't you leave me the fuck alone!" the mesmerized shit-head answered in a stupor-type trance. "Do you hear me? Go into the other room and take a long shit and leave me the hell alone!"

"Do you still feel pain in your breast as has been reported on your medical chart by the very competent doctors?" I authoritatively questioned the total imbecile. "You have a myriad of things wrong with you."

"Yes, a slight pain throbs in my chest but more importantly, I have an immense pain in the ass, namely you!" my despicable father-in-law blandly-but-nastily replied. "Now get the fuck out of here before my goddamned kidneys fill up again! Your ass should've been exterminated several decades ago!"

"Mr. Valdemar," I objectively said, speaking through a small megaphone I had carried with me to cleverly alter my regular voice, "are you asleep, or are you dying?"

"I don't give either a Chinese or an American shit what the fuck I'm doing!" the crazed loon exclaimed and opined. "Just leave me the hell alone or go out and find a good-looking nurse to screw silly in the other room. If you're lucky she'll jerk you off and then give you a decent blowjob too!" the eccentric asshole eerily articulated as his large scary eyes rolled after his eyelids had flapped opened. "Stop fucking my daughter! Even though you're legally married, stop fucking my daughter!" Valdemar emphasized and repeated. "I don't want any retarded grandchildren! I don't want any asinine retarded grandchildren! I want you the hell out of my legacy! I want you out of my legacy you goddamned irresponsible parasite!" the crazy fuck insanely reiterated.

All vital signs then diminished and the patient's yellowish-brown tongue creepily curled up inside his open mouth and then the ugly organ began vibrating in his throat as if the son-of-a-bitch was twenty-one years old again and greedily eating delicious pink wet pussy. Then my dopey father-in-law's larynx and jaws emitted a confusing flurry of almost indiscernible and peculiar intonations. At that pivotal point I was totally baffled and puzzled, for I had never before ever encountered anything so incomprehensible.

Well, as I've just alluded, my overtaxed brain was in a quandary. I didn't know what the frig' to ask him next so I went back to basics, the postulates of my science. "Are you still sleeping, or are you presently dying?"

"Are you fuckin' dense or what?" Valdemar obtusely and rhetorically challenged my intelligent line of interrogation. "Fuck the world! Fuck everybody! Fuck Satan and all the cock-sucking gargoyles and all of the holier-than-thou winged angels too! But most importantly, fuck *you* Asshole!" the now unconscious-but-incensed nutcase bellowed from his trace-like state. "Now then, if you must have a response, I'm no longer sleeping. I'm fuckin' dead and gone! You got your answer Asshole! I'm fuckin' dead and gone!"

Naturally I shuddered upon hearing those fantastic words, for I truly believed that I was then actively communicating with a dead person and that *we* had demonstrably bridged the gap between Heaven or Hell and Earth. My ascending awe was indeed a form of ecstasy. The whole entire situation was absolutely incredible. My insolent subject had been talking but not a trace of 'breath fog' appeared on the mirror that my quivering hand held under his enlarged snot-clogged nostrils. I then honored a sudden compulsion and endeavored to draw blood from his right arm but the rusty hairpin I was using broke and became stuck in his lifeless artery. Nothing was going right so I paused to collect my wits.

But then to my consternation, the crazy asshole began breathing again so apparently, my mesmerism session had temporarily interrupted the supernatural death process and had also greatly interfered with its manifestation. In fact as has been professionally recorded in my journal and in my corresponding notations, for the next six weeks the ornery stubborn truculent conniver refused to die and still answered my probing questions with the same inane declarations that have already been mentioned.

161

Finally on a dismal dreary rainy Friday morning in late December I resolved to awaken the pretentious asshole (even in death) from his extended recalcitrant and defiant slumber. My psychology skill attempted employing the same usually successful cause-and-effect/ stimulus-and-response cues on my rebellious subject but Mr. Vladimir Victor Valdemar was obstinate and the obdurate asshole (still in his subconscious condition) resisted all of my scientific initiatives.

Ultimately I made one last-ditch request to verify my scientific breakthrough. "Mr. Valdemar, this is your one and only son-in-law. Do you have any feelings or wishes you want to express right now? Here is your chance to say your final words."

The circles on Valdemar's wrinkled and withered cheeks wiggled and his yellowish-brown tongue convulsed and his pallid face turned purple and his ghastly oversized eyes incessantly opened and closed. My mind was completely perplexed.

"For God's sake, learn to make a goddamned decision for once in your comedy-of-errors life and stop being a gigantic fucked-up loser!" my hypnotized subject indicted his all-too-aggravated evaluator. "Make up your fuckin' mind, will you! Either put me to sleep or pronounce me dead! I don't give a shit whether or not you bury me alive, or bury me sleeping! Just get the fuck out of *my* life and out of *my* death! That's my final goddamned wish!"

I was in a state of general shock. Out of genuine trepidation and physical weakness, I soon fell to the floor and my body and head impacted the brown planks. In my fainted state of mind I had rationally theorized that Mr. Vladimir Victor Valdemar did not want to die in a docile subordinate position in the bed with me (his loathed nemesis) standing over him in a dominant posture. That recollection I recalled as I got off the floor and rubbed my aching elbow.

Upon standing up from my unanticipated fall, I was then in for the most horrendous and mind-boggling ordeal of my mediocre life. According to my dependable watch and my detailed notes, within the space of a mere ten minutes Mr. Vladimir Victor Valdemar had somehow crumbled and shrunk in his bed and the vestiges of those inexplicable processes were presently exhibited before my very eyes. I was witnessing something both nauseating and appalling.

And then accompanying the incongruous visual aberration, a putrid horrifying mass of loathsome pungent liquid was randomly scattered all over the top of the hospital bed and the man's ugly face had become a hideous grotesque skull and the remainder of his gaunt body a horrific anatomical skeleton lying (and almost floating)

162

beneath the terrifying mound of protoplasm and stench-laden tissue. Then my notorious deductive reasoning finally comprehended exactly what had happened.

'My father-in-law had died over a month ago but I had kept him alive in his mesmerized state for the full five week duration. When I had eventually severed his continuous trance, his earthly body had finally caught-up with his departed spirit!' I fully understood. 'In reality, before me upon this sickening bed is what Mr. Vladimir Victor Valdemar should really look like after not being embalmed and dead for at least several weeks! It is not right to tamper with the omnipotent Powers-That-Be!' I solemnly concluded. 'I only hope that I am not wickedly punished for my transgression into and interference with the hereafter!'

"The Gold Bug"

Many years ago I had the distinct pleasure of developing and cultivating a fine friendship with Mr. William LeGrand, a genteel descendent of a French Huguenot family that believed in and practiced voodoo rituals. Although LeGrand had been born into wealth, a series of financial calamities had bankrupted him down to the level of destitution. Being both mortified and alienated from cruel societal scorn because he had gambled away his substantial inherited fortune, William (in defeat) left New Orleans and took up residence inside a glorified shack rudely constructed on Sullivan's Island, an uninhabited natural paradise located near Charleston, South Carolina.

Sullivan's Island is only about three quarters of a mile long and a quarter of a mile wide and the barren land is bounded by the Atlantic Ocean to the east, the Isle of Palms to the north and a swampy marshland (not even fit for toasting marshmallows) to the west and finally, to the south, the isolated strip of land is bordered by that hub of Southern culture and hospitality, metropolitan Charleston.

Reeds, slime and stagnant ponds populated most of Sullivan's Island, but on the western tip is decrepit-looking Ft. Moultrie, a poorly equipped distant outpost of Ft. Sumter, situated in Charleston Harbor. Sweet myrtle, much of it growing to an exceptional height of ten foot, along with a variety of thorny beach shrubs cover much of the island's sandy shoreline. And then there are of course scads of palmetto growths, or miniature palm trees that would make Sullivan's Island a haven for horticulturists more so than a destination paradise for summer vacationers allergic to mosquito and alligator bites. In the early 1800s even a man with purple skin would not want to be marooned on Sullivan's Island.

LeGrand had built his dilapidated domicile on the remote eastern side of the island where I had first made his acquaintance while I was scouting around for bargain-priced beachfront properties to be sold to the highest bidders at a scheduled public auction. "Being a hermit out here in this island wilderness," I had once joked to LeGrand, "you never have to worry about being arrested for *recluse driving* of a horse-drawn carriage like you would have if you were residing in downtown Charleston."

"I happen to like idiots and assholes," LeGrand peculiarly answered, "and since you're both of those things, I especially am enamored with your odd style. But let me tell you Mr. Poe, I also happen to like the primitive life out here without any constables, sheriffs or policemen to harass me or without any insidious crooks around to rob or attack my vulnerable ass."

I found William LeGrand to be eccentric in demeanor, but more importantly, his oddball moods vacillated between extreme euphoria and extreme melancholy, an abnormal condition that contemporary psychologists presently describe as being "a manic depressant." But my host was very well educated and fluent in the ancient classics and rather familiar with the ideas of the great Greco-Roman philosophers from antiquity, and so I found his overall personality to be quite intriguing to say the least.

A certain old gray-haired loyal Negro slave named Jupiter always seemed to be orbiting around LeGrand, the strange master being the center of the illiterate servant's very limited solar system. Jupiter was LeGrand's only remaining inheritance from the downtrodden heir's parents' vast Louisiana estate that unfortunately had recently been liquidated because LeGrand couldn't solidify his assets.

It should be chronicled herein that the winters in the geographic latitude of Sullivan's Island are rather moderate temperature-wise, the mercury seldom declining into the near-freezing zone. In the middle of October of 1833 there had occurred a very chilly day so feeling rather cold and *ice*-o-lated, I abandoned my perfunctory surveying of beachfront properties and scurried through the sandy brush en route to my friend's shack to warm up a bit. At the time I was staying nine miles away from LeGrand's place, merrily residing inside a cheap flophouse on Meeting Street in downtown Charleston where I had (on more than several occasions) become nearly dehydrated from continuously pumping the poop out of blonde, brunette and red-haired pussy day in and day out.

After entering LeGrand's small flimsy home, I was euphorically greeted by my weird ever-changing-moods' friend, who then allowed me to warm my hands, feet and genitals next to a stone fireplace that was blazing with roaring logs upon the hearth.

"Guess what Poe!" LeGrand then enthusiastically exclaimed. "This morning I discovered a unique bivalve of an unknown genus but more significant than that bullshit," William gushed like a geyser, "I also found in the reeds an incredible scarabaeus that I've nicknamed 'the Gold Bug' because of its magnificent copper hue' on its shell! I'm so happy and thrilled that I could piss myself!"

"That's hardly enough incentive for you to get an erection and start jerking-off about!" I cynically commented. "Let me take you back into civilization to Meeting Street where you don't have to rely

166

on hand and wrist action to squirt your reproductive juices into the air. Instead you can either expel your fluids into a nice warm pink love tunnel or into some tooth-less bitch's suck-happy mouth! That's the kind of stimulation you really need! But William," I said, "let me see this unusual Gold Bug so that I can examine it and then have a legitimate basis for declaring you legally insane."

"I wish I could accommodate you in that respect concerning the Gold Bug," LeGrand answered with an element of regret evident in his tone of voice, "but only an hour ago I had met Lieutenant Goodwin from Ft. Moultrie, who incidentally is an amateur entomologist so I lent him the marvelous-looking sacrabaeus, which is actually the size of a hickory nut, or more specifically, the size of my enlarged left testicle, for the officer's own studious satisfaction until Saturday afternoon."

"Does the bug also have gold-colored antennae?" I sarcastically inquired. "Is it also clairvoyant and can it read the minds of objective-minded non-superstitious assholes like myself? I gotta' confess to you, a beetle lover I am not. Even empty spider webs scare the shit out of me!"

"There ain't nothin' in that bug Masta' Will, nutin' spesh-all at all," Jupiter adamantly declared. "It's da cursed ghouly bug, yes it is! Sent straight from Hell by Lucy-fur hisself. That scary bug gives me the fucked-up heebie-jeebies, yes it does!"

"Listen-up Poe and don't be influenced by Jupiter's silly prattle. Now as I was about to convey, the scales of the insect that's been bugging my mind for the past several days do emit a fantastic luster that is actually incomparable," LeGrand insisted, his mercurial disposition suddenly turning defiant, angry and egocentric. "But right here and now Edgar, I'll draw the goddamned insect for you on this piece of dusty foolscap, which I think both you and Jupiter ought to be wearing on your fuckin' heads."

LeGrand removed the writing paper from his coat pocket, picked up a pen from his cluttered desk and began sketching from memory his "Gold Bug." After my strange erratic friend handed me his bug rendition, I innocuously stepped over to the fireplace to warm my hands, for I had poor circulation, which truthfully was even far worse than that of a defunct city newspaper. Just then a large Newfoundland blasted through the door, rushed into the shack and the canine, who was very familiar with my petting of him from previous encounters, leaped up and began aggressively caressing and licking my face in a display of unbridled affection.

LeGrand helped calm-down the canine's frenzy, so then I had leisure time to pick up the bug drawing that had fallen upon the hearth and that had nearly been incinerated by the blazing fire. I casually scrutinized LeGrand's sketch and was more than a tad astounded at what my disbelieving eyes perceived.

"Look William, there isn't any damned bug drawing here!" I exclaimed. "Are you trying to deceive me? Jolly Roger, over and out!" I nonsensically shrieked. "You had drawn a goddamned skull; a morbid-looking death's head with cross-bones underneath it! You call yourself a fuckin' artist? Why Billy Boy, you couldn't even be a striptease artist at the iniquitous downtown Charleston Gay and Lesbian Burlesque Theater or a friggin' con artist huckstering porno' magazines outside the riverfront straw market!"

"Well now," my slightly demented friend stammered, "I'm not a bona fide blockhead as you might suspect Mr. Poe. I did draw the exact dimensions of the Gold Bug that I had located in the nearby marsh. I'm not a scientist by trade, but I'll venture to guess that the heat from the raging fire caused some sort of chemical reaction to occur on the paper and that the Gold Bug had mysteriously vanished and simultaneously and almost magically," LeGrand contended, "the image of the cranium, or I should say numb*skull* oddly appeared in its place. Edgar, there has to be a feasible explanation to account for this illogical paper drawing anomaly."

LeGrand seemed to be quite peevish in his deportment and was about to crumple the paper in disgust when he slowly ambled over to his sea chest and sat down to privately examine the remarkable skull. I didn't wish to interrupt his tense concentration with some insulting comment because such an exacerbation might represent a total exasperation to him. William experimentally turned the paper upside down, right and left and next futilely peered at it from behind. After watching LeGrand tinker and toy with the uncanny skull drawing for a full five hours, I decided that I had had enough of his repetitious irrelevancy so I said "Farewell" (without receiving any detectable acknowledgement on his part) and quietly and unobtrusively exited the shack to return to the Best Little Whorehouse in the South on downtown Meeting Street.

* * * * * * * * * * * *

A full month had soon elapsed when quite unexpectedly, Jupiter showed-up at my upstairs door just as I was sending a cute strawberry blonde virgin into orgasmic ecstasy with my powerful

168

thrusting and cherry busting. The old Negro was in terribly sad spirits so I reluctantly dismissed the knockout young hussy from my fleabag bed and in a frustrated frame of mind, initiated an undesired conversation with William LeGrand's thoroughly bewildered, volatile ignoramus slave.

"Well Jupiter, you look down in the dumps. Have you been rummaging through the local trash, rubble, garbage and rubbish?" I condescendingly began. "How's lovely Juno treating you up on Mt. Olympus these days?"

"What the fuck ya' tawkin' bout Mr. Poe?" Jupiter wondered and asked, removing his straw hat with his left hand and scratching his gray-haired scalp with his right. "Ya' ain't makin' any dammed sense ta' me! Say what?"

"I meant to say Jupiter, how's your boss Mr. William LeGrand doing these days?" I adjusted and rephrased my initial comments. "Is he well?"

"Well Sur, my Masta' is not berry well," Jupiter disconsolately attested. "In fack, he's berry sick in his head."

"Is he confined to his bed?" I seriously asked, finally assessing the gravity of the crisis. "Does he require medical treatment? What *ails* him? Too much beer I wonder?"

"Masta Will is sick in the head but I think hiz boddie is all right," the slave answered. "He's white as a goes or a gobbling! He go walkin' all over the dammed islin' lookin' for something' dat ain't dare! Now Mr. Poe, I have a big stick ready to hit Masta wit to knock some sense into his head, and I plan on usin' it soon if Masta duzzin' change his fucked-up ways."

"Er Jupiter, I suggest that you not act too severe toward your sick Master. Don't flog him, whatever you do!" I cautioned the almost moronic slave. "Now tell me, has anything unpleasant happened since I last visited Sullivan's Island?"

"I think Masta Will was bit in the head by dat Gold Bug of hiz," Jupiter claimed. "Masta no have flu bug; he got brain bug! He's all fucked-up inside hiz own skull!"

"And you believe that William LeGrand was bitten by the gold beetle once it had been returned to him by the army lieutenant?" I recollected and demanded knowing. "But wasn't the bug dead? How could a dead insect bite your Master?"

"Mr. Poe, Masta dream about the ghouly google bug and talk about it in hiz sleep all night long," Jupiter reported. "And den he talk about lots of gold in hiz dum-ass nightmare. I mean Mr. Poe, if

Masta Will was awake sayin' that same fucked-up stuff, I'd say and tell him he waz full of shit!"

"Well then, did you bring me any written message from your Master for me to read?" I questioned my unannounced visitor. "Perhaps your Master William LeGrand has something essential for me to consider and for my mind to digest."

"Dat's why I came here," Jupiter recalled and then awkwardly reached into his pants' pocket. "Dat's why I came here Mr. Poe," the ordinarily obedient servant reiterated, handing me the brief note. "I fig-yur dat somethin' impor-teent is on dis here paper. I wish I wuz as smart as you and can read it myself!"

> My Dear Mr. Poe,
>
> Why have I not seen you for such a long time? Screwing around as usual on Meeting Street in downtown Charleston I presume! I hope you aren't pissed-off at me examining the skull drawing for five and a half consecutive hours, are you?
>
> Now Poe, I have something quite urgent to tell you that cannot be communicated in a mundane letter. I'm quite anxious about my phenomenal discovery, a great find that I'm afraid my man Jupiter can't comprehend. The dumb shit thinks I'm crazy and has threatened to beat the crap and the urine out of me with a huge stick. As you can sympathize Poe, I don't deserve to be disciplined or chastised by an asshole of his low magnitude on the genius scale, but I do maintain to you that my sickly pallid appearance has temporarily salvaged me from Jupiter "Beatin' the dammed demons of Satan outa' you Masta Will!"
>
> If you can come over to Sullivan's Island immediately Edgar, you'll soon recognize the significance of my invitation to you as has been vaguely addressed in this memorandum.
>
> Yours in truth,
>
> William LeGrand

I immediately accompanied Jupiter in the direction of Sullivan's Island and we boarded my friend's skiff, hurried to William LeGrand's shack and I was happy to discover and observe my old chum in fairly decent health and apparently glad that I had come in swift response to his "urgent letter."

"Did you receive the Gold Bug back from the army lieutenant?" I asked after we had exchanged salutations.

"Yes, and Jupiter was at least partially right in his evaluation of the Godsend bug," LeGrand stated with a certain alacrity in his tone of enunciation. "I'm convinced that the scarabaeus will bring me great fortune and I'll be able to re-acquire my lost wealth and then return triumphantly back to the glamour of New Orleans' high society. But first I must employ the practical use of the Gold Bug very discreetly. Now Jupiter," the Master imperatively ordered his slave, "go and fetch me the Golden Insect and please don't answer me with the fucked-up word 'Humbug'!"

"Masta Will, ya' gotta' get dat dare bug on your own because I'm not goin' through the trubble or else I might die or somethin' bad like dat from an evil goes getting my ass," Jupiter weirdly answered. "I knows I'm just a super-stitches dumb nigga' Masta, but I fraid of dat dammed bug!"

LeGrand ambled over to a nearby glass case, removed the Gold Bug from its interior and then showed the beautiful creature to me. "This Gold Bug will lead me to great fortune," my mentally unstable friend predicted. "And I must enlist your support and cooperation Poe to venture-out on a great expedition with me."

"William, you aren't well and should remain in bed for several days," I spoke-up. "I'll nurse you back to good health even though I'm an adult male and have no milk in my breasts. But if you'd like, I could travel back to the Meeting Street brothel and bring you a well-endowed woman who has just given birth to a fat little sucker."

"Bullshit and poppycock Poe!" LeGrand screamed. "I'm perfectly well without any goddamned fever and I need not listen to your hideous ludicrous doggerel. My pulse is especially normal and I feel as strong as an ax, er, I meant to say 'ox.' Now My Friend," William excitedly proceeded, "I need you to come along with Jupiter and myself to the rough jagged hills on the mainland. I promise we'll be returning back here on the island at sunrise, well, at noon tomorrow at the latest."

"Okay, I'll go away with you as long as we both don't wind-up living on Weird Street in Looneytown, USA," I conceded as I checked my watch and it reliably read four o'clock. "Let's expedite this expedition expeditiously!"

We boarded LeGrand's well-hidden skiff and Jupiter rowed us to the mainland with (in our possession) a scythe, two lanterns, two picks and two digging spades along with the now deceased Gold Bug, which LeGrand had for some arcane reason attached to a long ball of string.

After easing the small boat into a rocky cove and tying it to a sturdy palmetto, my 'sick' companion led the way on ground through a patch of very desolate swampy land that LeGrand, showing his familiarity with the rugged terrain, had apparently already explored on his own. We laboriously trekked up and over a steep ravine and soon reached an area of interspersed crags surrounding a dense aggregate of bramble bushes. In the center of the thick inhospitable vegetation was a massive tulip tree that vastly towered over the eight oak trees in the immediate vicinity. The immense tulip was majestic in appearance with its widely spread branches and abundant foliage dominating our perception of it. Then the surreptitious LeGrand shocked my mind when he asked Jupiter if *he* was capable of climbing up the giant gnarled tree.

"Yes Masta Will, I can climb that sucker as if it was my mama's lap," Jupiter proudly insisted. "But don't spect me to take that fucked-up evil ghouly bug up dare wit me!"

"You can whip the crap out of any man I know," LeGrand praised the old slave, "and yet you're afraid of a harmless dead beetle? But if you refuse to take it up there with the bug being suspended from this long string, I'll be compelled to violently split open your noggin with this heavy shovel. And besides Jupiter, the dead bug will for the most part be dangling six feet below you as you make your dramatic ascension up the gnarled trunk of the tree!"

"I ain't scared of no man, but the Devil's work, dat's another shit-eatin' story," Jupiter smartly replied. "But I'll do as ya' say Masta Will. It's the only fuckin' way a dum-ass slave nigga' like me can make my way up in the world!"

And soon Jupiter (armed with his stringed Gold Bug) began his precarious climb and showing fantastic dexterity for a man over seventy years of age, the slave assiduously and cautiously labored and eventually made it to a prodigious dizzying height of around seventy feet.

"Now go out slightly on the large branch to your right," LeGrand shouted up to his man. "I hope you're limbered up," LeGrand joked, "because according to my mathematical calculations, you must get to the fork of the branch and then go up one more limb!"

"Okay Masta, I'm where you says I should be!" the slave shouted down. "What next? And please don't co-man me to fuckin' fall!"

"Keep moving out as far as you can go and if you see anything strange," LeGrand hollered up, "then stop and let me know!"

Now at that juncture I really and truly believed Jupiter's seemingly savvy testimony that my friend from Louisiana was really authentic asylum material. LeGrand was making Jupiter orbit on the verge of committing involuntary suicide should the branch he was crawling on suddenly snap like a weak twig.

"Have you discovered anything unusual yet?" my pal loudly screamed up.

"Hole-ley fuck!" Jupiter boisterously yelled, his voice making chills rush down my spine. "Masta, why da' fuck ya' do dis shit to me? It's a god-dammed skull nailed to da' god-dammed branch! Lord have mur-see!"

"Calm down!" LeGrand yelled up. "If you do your job successfully, I'll reward your ass with a silver dollar. Now Jup, find the left eye of the skull and drop the Gold Bug attached to the string through it. Your left hand should be on the left side of your body."

"Ya mean the side I chops wood on," Jupiter yelled down, not knowing his left side from his right." Okay Boss, but first I gotta' squeeze the piss outa' my pants!"

"Now slowly drop the gold beetle through the skull's left eye and make sure you hang onto the goddamned string, you pathetic horse's ass!" the slave-owner gruffly instructed.

All the while I was totally confused and befuddled by what I was seeing and hearing. *Surreal* would be the best adjective that would most accurately describe my fleeting feelings and my obscure unnatural surroundings. But to my utter surprise, my friend's lunacy was yielding some amazing positive results. When the gold bug finally reached the ground, LeGrand wasted no time in driving a stake at that very spot to mark it for future reference. Then my friend removed a measuring tape from his jacket and paced-off a distance of fifty feet due west until he came to a circular clearing having a crude diameter of approximately five feet across the circumference.

At that designated location we diligently excavated for two hours to a depth of six feet, the precise level where human corpses are ordinarily laid to rest. Then instead of giving up his mad pursuit and heading back towards Sullivan's Island, LeGrand frantically grabbed Jupiter by the collar and bellowed, "You stupid fucked-up scoundrel!

Point to your goddamned left eye! It'll be dark in several short hours! Show me your left eye damn it!"

Jupiter was obviously perplexed and mentally challenged by the assigned task so guessing incorrectly, he pointed his right finger at his right eye. But instead of throwing a wicked temper tantrum, LeGrand rejoiced. "Eureka! That's it! A dumb fuckin' mistake committed by an imbecilica Americanus!" my friend joyfully vociferated. "You must again climb up the tulip tree and drop the beetle through the skull's *other* eye. I'll now give you two silver dollars if you obey my order!"

"What's up besides Jupiter's clambering ass?" I asked my crazed companion. "I'll take you all the way to London if I have to and place you in the last available bed in Bedlam!"

"You don't fathom this scenario right now Poe," LeGrand boomed like a loose cannon, "but if you take the precise distance from the eighty-foot-high skull spiked to the limb and the distance between the two bony eyes sockets, the angle, by the time the stringed beetle reaches the ground, will be very different than it was during our first attempt. In short Mr. Poe," the euphoric maniac said, "we were fuckin' digging in the wrong fuckin' place!"

"Digging for what? Dog bones for your Newfoundland?" I skeptically asked.

"You'll fuckin' see!" William vowed. ":You'll fuckin' see!"

The new digging site was promptly determined and we again strenuously dug for two and a half hours when Jupiter's shovel hit pay dirt by clanking against the metal rings of what amounted to a well-preserved pirate chest. The sturdy wooden box was three feet long, three feet wide and two and a half feet deep.

Our combined strength was renewed as energy liberally flowed throughout our arteries and veins. Exultation and anticipation governed our emotions, our spirits and our rejuvenated bodies. And after finally lifting the heavy chest from its burial hole and then gradually prying the lid open with our work implements, we were astounded to find a treasure trove, the container loaded to the brim with exotic gold coins, magnificent pearls, precious jewels, platinum chalices along with an assortment of sensational cups and rings, all featuring resplendent combinations of enormous diamonds, sapphires, topaz configurations, exquisite emeralds and the most gorgeous ruby gemstones.

"Well Poe, do you now still consider me to be a prospective candidate for Bedlam Hospital?" LeGrand merrily asked. "If so, I now consider *you* to be my fucked-up suitable insane roommate!"

174

"Certainly you're now rich enough to buy the whole goddamned British mental hospital, so it really doesn't fuckin' matter if you're crazy or not," I opined. "Plenty of wealthy assholes are also insane LeGrand, but everyone and their narrow-minded mothers think the psycho' jerk-off with the big bucks is the smartest person around!"

"I still thinks you is one crazy mudder-fucker!" Jupiter insisted. "But if it's my mudder you been fuckin' with Masta, then ya' gotta' deal with me and my two mean-assed fists!"

* * * * * * * * * * * *

It took Jupiter, LeGrand and me several days of arduous toil to finally haul the weighty opulent pirate treasure back from the marshy mainland to my ecstatic friend's shack on Sullivan's Island. Exhausted from completing our grueling project, my illustrious host and I reviewed the fundamentals of our marvelous enterprise and simultaneously celebrated by emptying and consuming a full bottle of sweet and delicious blackberry brandy.

"Despite your obstinate obnoxious negativity Poe," LeGrand mildly scolded me, "I still plan to reward you handsomely for accompanying me on my little treasure hunt ramble and later assisting me with excavating the valuables and then transporting the booty, or should I say *plunder* back to this isolated island. Only a fucked-up jerk-off like yourself would have gone along with me on such a glorious and implausible mission."

"Yes, and now we have to worry about any nefarious robbers or desperate area crooks learning of our miraculous find and rowing out here to endeavor stealing the fruits of our labor," I reminded my all-too-wary host. "What do you plan to do with Jupiter in regard to the dissemination of the booty, er, I mean plunder?"

"Oh, I have a few non-pirate bones to pick with that incorrigible moron," LeGrand stated and then grinned almost ear-to-ear. "But after I finish reprimanding him for wanting to flog my lily white ass to get me to return to his narrow concept of what *he thinks* my normalcy ought to be, I'll probably give him a few of the smaller jewels that will definitely make the swarthy-skinned fuck-head the richest damned Negro residing south of Richmond and farting north of Atlanta. But by Jupiter, I hope that my salve doesn't become, for lack of a better term, nigger rich!"

"That's very prudent and judicious of you," I commended while savoring the rich taste of sweet liquor in my mouth. "But for my benefit and mental stability LeGrand, please explain how you knew precisely where the treasure had been hidden and how the Gold Bug led to finding it in *that* specific location fifty paces away from the Gold Bug's string drop through the skull's correct eye socket near the colossal-sized tulip tree."

"It isn't nearly quite as mysterious as it superficially seems my dear Poe," William prefaced and coyly framed his answer. "After you had left my home while I had been preoccupied contemplating the piece of parchment for a full five hours, out of curiosity I again placed the extraordinary paper next to the fire's heat and soon discovered that my original theory about a chemical reaction was absolutely true. A cryptic message gradually appeared inside the death skull but it was written in some sort of bizarre code with twenty-six different symbols like triangles, question marks, stars and arithmetical plus signs representing what I immediately theorized to be the twenty-six letter of the standard English language alphabet."

"And what if you were wrong in your conjecture?" I asked. "Did that possibility ever occur to you?"

"Why most certainly yes!" LeGrand exclaimed with a brief expression of disdain flashing across his facial features. "My biggest concern was that the message had been authored in a foreign language other than French or Spanish, two European tongues that I possess a degree of fluency in. But I was hoping and trusting that if I could decipher the code, that it would be presented and interpreted in the English vernacular."

I then requested knowing exactly how my now very sane and rational host had skillfully cracked the weird symbol code, which he had creatively and hilariously labeled 'lower-glyphics'." His profundity and methodology had not been nearly as complicated and as difficult as I had first suspected.

"Well you see Poe," LeGrand said before sipping and swallowing another ounce of the delectable blackberry brandy, "as you know from previous conversations, I was once the editor of a fairly large Louisiana newspaper so I'm well aware of the frequency of alphabet letters in word patterns represented in paragraphs, in manuscripts and in missives. For instance," my close friend elucidated, "the letter E is the most commonly used, and so after I had found that *the asterisk symbol* stood for E, then I would look for a two-letter word ending in E, and it could only be BE, HE, ME or WE. And likewise, the word' 'THE' could be easily deciphered and then I conscientiously found out that the symbols 'minus' and 'division' stood for the letters T and H respectively. Next I feverishly and avidly searched out the second most common vowel, A, I believe, and I worked around A and its

176

attendant two and three letter words. Eventually, by the process of elimination, I was able to...."

"You were able to figure out the remainder of the letters, and if all the letters were represented in the secret message as I presume," I theorized and disclosed, "then obviously the letters V, W, X, Y and Z' could easily have been identified and distinguished. Now it all makes perfect sense once I understood how you had obtained the location of the treasure based on the information provided in the coded message, which had been accidentally revealed when your frisky Newfoundland had knocked my hand holding the foolscap close to the fire's heat and thus causing a chemical change in the paper's composition. But who do you suppose buried the treasure? Bluebeard, better known as Blackbeard?"

"No, that heinous treacherous rogue Edward Teach had performed most of his daring raids and thefts in the Caribbean Islands," the very knowledgeable LeGrand lectured. "Instead, I suspect that the crew that did the mainland burial we've unearthed had belonged to the infamous Captain Kidd. In fact, I do believe that the fellow responsible for the burying of the incredible chest was indeed Captain Kidd."

"Now excuse my general ignorance LeGrand," I politely requested, "but how did you ever arrive at *that* extraordinary conclusion? It's like you had just grasped for a straw and then pulled a fluffy spotted rabbit out of your hat. There had to be an element of luck involved."

"You've always been a fucked-up nincompoop Poe ever since you had first set foot on Sullivan's Island," LeGrand spoke and then laughed, spilling the remainder of his blackberry brandy all over my shirt's sleeve and cuff. "Here's my simple hypothesis in a nutshell. The message was written on *sheepskin*-type paper similar to that which is used in college diploma distributions, so employing deductive reasoning," the jolly fellow continued, "a kid is a small sheep, so naturally, the only feasible explanation to your academic inquiry is that the treasure had been buried by that notorious nautical outlaw, the one and only Captain Kidd!"

"That's as good an answer as any I suppose," I reckoned and admitted. "Who gives a donkey shit anyway? We've deftly found your elusive treasure, but the redeeming factor in this entire wonderful adventure is this: I'm happy to confirm that you're not crazy or insane LeGrand; and I'm also quite thrilled to verify that you're only a little bit naïve and perhaps a shade stupid for having a complete fool such as myself as your closest confidante and friend!

177

Your biggest flaw is that you're just a little more fucked-up than the average American citizen is!"

"Oh dear Poe, at first impression in regard to my credibility, I had thought that you were a Doubting Thomas," LeGrand sincerely expressed, "but in the end I was extremely glad to fathom that it is better to have a Doubting Thomas as a close friend than to be deceived by a covetous and jealous Judas Iscariot!"

"The Pit and the Pendulum"

Undoubtedly, my total being was in both emotional anguish and in physical agony. The dual pains were extremely excruciating and every fiber that constituted *me* was aching from my head down to my testicles right on down to my toes. When the anonymous guards finally untied me, I realized two things: I didn't know who the hell I was (apparently suffering from some memory disorder or amnesia), and besides that, I didn't know who the hell the black-robed judges were that were heartlessly pronouncing my sentencing.

Yes, those despicable bastards were in the process of unanimously rendering a verdict of "Death," yet at that bizarre moment in time I was suffering from a distinct loss of identity and my conscience was unaware of what egregious crime I had committed or even in what goddamned country I was being convicted. I recollect deducting that I was at that inglorious moment thinking in English but conversely and illogically, the chief judge was communicating my doomed fate in Spanish. Thus, I reasoned and theorized that I was an Englishman being condemned to die for no apparent rationale or explanation somewhere in Spain.

Yes, those hideous macabre lips that the three black-robed judges flaunted were thin, grotesque and white as if the cheerless objects belonged on the mouths of goddamned albinos. 'Those three inflexible and repugnant sons-of-bitches deserve to be butchered and mutilated,' yes, that's what my disoriented brain had reckoned as I stood there before the trio of reprehensible but all-powerful assholes! Indeed, those fucked-up nightmarish lips were whiter than the paper on which I'm presently writing this incredible chronicle.

My recollection does not betray past reality. My eyes keenly perceived seven gloomy candles flickering on the judges' mahogany table and I remember black drapes hanging above where the three ruthless fucks solemnly and reticently sat in a windowless 'Inquisition Chamber.' At the time I imagined the seven tall candles as being white slender angels especially assembled to escort me either to Heaven or to Hell once my final breath had been inhaled, or perhaps exhaled. But in retrospect contemplation, how could my fucked-up mind be so vivid and observant when I had been experiencing so much agony and so much anguish?

Then my creative brain thought of how serene and tranquil and sweet a cemetery grave (or even a catacomb) would be compared to the horrendous suffering 'this nameless helpless victim is suffering.' 'Death will be my cherished reward, my salvation, my escape from this perpetual torture I've endured,' I hypothesized.

And then the judges, like a triumvirate of omnipotent-evil-magicians, suddenly disappeared, a subtle clue that had momentarily deceived my senses, for as I author these words, the vanishing of the three ruthless pricks was really a blunt signal that I had gone unconscious from lack of strength and from a deficiency in nutrition.

My spirit was falling into oblivion, but perhaps either into Hades or into the infernos of Hell itself. Yes, at *that* queer surreal moment the seven candle flames on the mahogany table had inexplicably become extinguished as my cognizance of my surroundings simultaneously went totally blank. Then quite mysteriously and ominously, my only fleeting sensation was a lone stark recognition that a bleak darkness had enveloped me.

I didn't recall any objects or furniture swirling around or floating in air. I believe that my immortal soul, or perhaps my subconscious post-mortal psyche was passing through a supernatural void or maybe an empty vacant medium of space and time, or perhaps my spirit was swiftly traveling through an obscure alien dimension.

Somehow my present memory suggests that I had been descending, not by my own volition or by employing the use of my legs down stone or wooden steps, but instead being carried by invisible men to some black and dreary place of punishment. My mind recalls that most everything l perceived as being a weird fucked-up nebulous combination of flatness, dampness and most of all, total madness. But then again, my principal comprehension was that I was being conveyed to a designated area of atonement and ultimately, my mortal demise.

Yes, my eyes were open, and I must admit that it required plenty of courage to do *that*, for I was still contemplating whether I was dead or alive. I finally realized that I was breathing and that I had a pulse and I could feel my heart beating in my chest, so Descartes' "I think; therefore I am" axiom had physical verification that I was still a living human being. But indeed, I was frightened beyond reason or understanding, for having no memory as to my name and being in a cold dank damp dark environment with fowl smelling air gave me an instant urge to vomit.

I was soon aware of lying on my back on a hard surface that I presumed was solid stone or granite. My bravery increased as I stretched out and my lacerated fingers and left hand touched a slimy hard wall, which I ascertained was either metal or stone. I was still

180

quite apprehensive about engaging in further exploration and discovery because there was still absolutely *nothing* (no thing) to see or to identify through sight. The intolerable dark air seemed to be strangling me as my lungs labored to perform their simple function. Sweat was profusely rolling down my forehead and neck and was virtually cascading down my back.

Two essential questions dominated my' befuddled thinking: 'Will I have to suffer more torture before being executed?' and 'How much sacrifice and pain can I possibly endure before either dying or attempting suicide?' I decided that I should rise to my feet to determine exactly how large the dark dungeon (in which I was being detained) happened to be. I believed that I was not in a prison cell for indeed no ordinary prison could ever have such deplorable conditions as my present area of confinement.

But still, I dreaded advancing even a goddamned mini-step forward for fear of the unknown could oftentimes paralyze a man's motivation to experiment doing anything. 'Am I in a tomb, my own personalized tomb?' I frightfully speculated. The mounting suspense was unbearable.

My eyeballs were straining (from their sockets) to observe even one scintilla of light, a wonderful phenomenon that would give my soul just one iota of hope. Finally, with my right hand sliding against the wet mildewed wall, I gingerly took several counterclockwise steps along the macabre chamber's perimeter, which I fathomed to be circular in form by virtue of the roundness of the wall, and after twenty or so very slow and deliberate steps, no corner or meeting of walls had occurred. 'Have I been left abandoned in this dreadful fucked-up incarceration to desperately meander around in circles only to eventually starve to death?' I wondered. But gradually, my mind's curiosity became the equivalent of my heart's tremendous fear. 'What fate could be worse than death? What futility should ever overshadow my desire to live?' I intrepidly conjectured.

Then I instinctively felt my body to see what type of garments I was wearing and from my cursory tactile inspection I soon learned that I had no shirt, pants or uniform on my torso but instead had been clad in a thin robe of very cheap and tawdry cotton material. An inspiration filtered into my mind and I quickly honored the suggestion by ripping a flimsy seam at the thin robe's hem and then tearing a sizeable length of fabric that I immediately placed on the slimy slippery floor directly against the wall. 'This way,' my sense of self-preservation dictated to my will, 'I'll know when I've made a full revolution of the room and I'll then be able to estimate its circumference, area and diameter from my basic knowledge of simple Euclidian geometry.' But then my overall hellish fatigue was all-powerful and so I collapsed upon the feces-laden floor and fell fast asleep.

When I abruptly awoke from my nightmarish slumber, my outstretched hand felt a loaf of stale bread and a pitcher of warm water. 'Is the goddamned water fresh? Is it stagnant? Are both the putrid-smelling water and the odorless bread fuckin' poisoned?'

I wasted no further valuable time assessing and debating the issue. I ate voraciously and drank indulgently thinking all the friggin' while, 'Who' in either their right or wrong mind gives a flying shit about food poisoning? I'm fuckin' famished, and if I die from attempting to alleviate my hunger, then what the fuck do I care!'

Shortly after consuming my strange feast in complete darkness I arose and began my exploratory circuit of the foreboding black chamber. A hundred and three paces around the unfamiliar room's circumference brought me back to the discarded piece of hem situated on the cold dank floor. 'Let's see now,' I logically guessed. 'There're two steps in a yard so the circumference must be fifty yards in length, approximately a hundred and fifty feet around. But am I standing in a room, in a dungeon, in a prison cell or in my own personal sepulchre?'

And so wanting to investigate my arcane dark environment some more, I bravely decided to move my feet and proceed in a straight line, my essential purpose being to traverse the chamber's diameter to establish if any useable objects could be found that I could cleverly improvise into tools, and my weak heart so deeply desired that such imaginary implements miraculously occupied the place's stench-laden interior.

My nostrils were keenly aware of a distinct clammy moldy vapor, the peculiar smell of rotting fungus when unexpectedly, my feet slid on the slippery floor and my already abused body, honoring gravity, made contact with solid stone. Despite the pain resulting from the hard impact, my face felt a chilling draft that wafted across my forehead and then my chin and I was suddenly aware that I had nearly plummeted down into the throat of a circular pit, probably intentionally designed to have a prisoner like myself drop into its horrid total darkness.

Through the exercise of diligent effort and excessive concentration, I managed to eventually dislodge a small fragment of stone from a narrow mortar groove located inside the pit's rim and then with a hysterical scream, I flipped the pebble into the well, only

182

to hear a low splash occur several seconds later. 'Are dangerous and ferocious animals down there, perhaps a venomous snake or two, or maybe a very undernourished carnivorous crocodile?' my rampant imagination vividly considered.

And at that alien moment I heard a trap door in the ceiling opening and then closing very quickly. 'I'm being watched and scrutinized!' I pessimistically thought with my knees trembling and my sinuses leaking secretion. 'Yes, my pupils caught a faint glimmer of light,' I anxiously interpreted. 'It soon faded and everything is once again awesome, gloomy, black and intimidating! That timely and ironic accident of me falling near the pit has temporarily averted my shrewdly schemed death by design! But quite frankly I'd rather die than suffer any more of this extreme mental duress! Danger must be ubiquitous in this horrifying black place!'

Shaking and quivering, I carefully sobbed and crawled my way back to the safety of the stench-infested round wall. 'How many other terrible wells are cunningly hidden in this fucked-up chamber's interior?' I contemplated while shuddering. 'Perhaps I should go back and plunge myself into that disgusting abyss and swiftly end it all! But since when have I become a spineless coward? And who the hell am I anyway?'

I fell asleep out of sheer exhaustion, suspiciously believing that the pitcher of water and the loaf of rancid-tasting bread must have been drugged with some ingredient that engendered hallucinating. But upon awakening, I soon perceived that my chest, hips and legs had been strapped-down on a horizontal table. I comprehended that my left hand was able to come into contact with another pitcher of water and a second loaf of crusty stale bread. Again I ate and drank ravenously not caring one precious second whether I crapped myself excessively upon the table or whether I fuckin' pissed myself through my gown, and according to my exaggerated comprehension of things, I soon felt my own urine arching directly into my expressionless who-gives-a-shit face.

I dozed off for an interminable period of time and when my eyes again opened I immediately noticed that 'the dungeon' was no longer black but had been illuminated by a wild yellowish glow, its source or origin not at first traceable. Now I was finally able to decipher the appearance and the size of the loathsome chamber, and I evaluated that it had been constructed of stone masonry walls and 'the dungeon' definitely had a granite floor. The strange sinister amber light revealed to my grateful eyes that the room was around fifty-feet in diameter, and second and third observations confirmed and proved my keen analysis to be accurate.

Certain mentally demented drawings of hellish-looking demons, gargoyles, monsters, skulls and skeletons adorned both the ceiling and walls, immediately suggesting that perverted lunatic monastery monks with a fascination for and an obsession with death had satanically performed the weird and repulsive artwork.

I did gain some low comfort in visually realizing that there was only one pit in the entire area of confinement. And yes, the second pitcher and loaf of bread had been strategically placed upon the top panel of a wooden framed table to my left. 'But why?' I questioned my general ignorance. Although my hands and arms were still free, I was unable to maneuver or manipulate my body from the four tight leather straps that tethered me horizontally upon the table.

Looking upward, my eyes and mind studied the chamber's ceiling, which in its center had a faded painting of Father Time looking exactly like the formidable and invincible Grim Reaper, carrying a gruesome scythe to obviously harvest his next unfortunate soul, which I perceptively gathered and intelligently understood must be *me*. But from out of the traditional curved scythe blade came the gradual sweep of a pendulum, not a standard clock pendulum mind you, but a pendulum in the shape of a warrior's battleaxe possessing an excessively sharp blade.

And as my astonished eyes viewed the object's hundred and eighty degree movement back and forth and perpendicular to my body's prone position, I then fully fathomed that the goddamned thing was descending by degree an inch or so at a time with each successive oscillation. The visual horror made my heart palpitate and I feared I was going into cardiac arrest.

* * * * * * * * * * * *

A slight rustling noise distracted my strict attention from the almost mesmerizing descendent medieval pendulum. 'Oh rats!' I boisterously and coincidentally shrieked. My circumstance would have been humorous if it wasn't (in grim reality) such a drastic terrifying emergency.

Several enormous squealing furry rodents had skillfully emerged from the now very conspicuous well situated in the center of the morbid-looking chamber, apparently attracted by the amber light from above that had seemingly supernaturally permeated my dreadful environment. The disease-carrying creatures seemed to

184

methodically advance in troops but without exhibiting any particular marching cadence. I knew right away that I should not procrastinate but instead should endeavor to scare the terrible vermin away so I redundantly shouted 'Fuck the World!' a dozen times.

My initial exhortations were successful and the result of my hollering afforded me a minute of welcomed relief. The sickening rodents had retreated and scattered but soon they garnered the desire to eat the remainder of breadcrumbs that remained on the little side table. But then I noticed several overlooked globs of raw meat that evidently had been provided to me by my unscrupulous captors as a farewell meal for me to devour. 'I must grab the meat before the goddamned rats do!' I reasoned. 'Those obscene and nauseating disease-laden mother-fuckers will first voraciously eat the raw meat as an appetizer and then start nibbling as a frenzied pack like there's no fuckin' tomorrow upon me!'

And yes, my attention again focused on the descending axe-pendulum, which instantaneously reminded me that I had dual problems to contend with since the deadly weapon had lowered a full yard since I had originally recognized its imminent danger. Its foot long razor-sharp blade from tip to tip was gleaming in the artificial yellow light's glow.

'That sucker is both huge and heavy and will easily plow right through my vulnerable chest like a sharp knife cutting through soft butter! And its wickedly attached to a brass rod that hisses like a snake with each passing vacillation. Oh well, at least I won't be fuckin' decapitated or dismembered!'

And then other disturbing thoughts haunted my psyche. 'Those craven sons-of-bitches black-robed judges! I would love to violently bludgeon each of their asses with a heavy sword, if only I had the fuckin' opportunity! Yes, they're too fuckin' gutless to pick up three sabers and kill me themselves. Or if they had any decent-sized balls,' I angrily concluded, 'they would egregiously and hatefully hurl my ass directly into the rat-infested pit! The weak-spine assholes want to see me accidentally kill myself!'

And then my beleaguered mind had still another consideration. 'Yes, plausible reason must acknowledge that the pernicious pendulum constitutes a much milder death than a screaming plunge down into the dark abyss where I would probably be fuckin' eaten alive by carnivorous rats before I'll ever have a chance to drown! Yet inch by inch, that lethal pendulum continues its evil descent downwards towards my helpless limp body.'

Throughout my colossal despair, all along I sensed that I had not been in the past (nor was I in the present) a devoutly religious man but nevertheless I began praying incessantly for either my fortuitous rescue or in the worst-case scenario, for redemption and eternal salvation. If my moral conversion to a particular creed had been the principal objective of the vindictive robed judges, then the asshole jerk-offs could with jubilation regard their cruel Inquisition and subsequent sentencing as being a veritable success.

But soon my idiotic fantasy/reverie vanished like an illusion from my fatigued and overburdened mind and I once again dedicated my profound survival thoughts to denying the on-the-prowl rats of their precious raw meat, raw meat that ultimately would lead the abhorrent scavengers to my exposed cut skin.

And yes, the terror I was experiencing was indeed quite real and in its twin lowest common denominators, very callous and brutal. To use the nomenclature "sadistic" to describe my diabolical tragedy would be entirely too polite, too courteous, too bland, too benign! But for several hours the pendulum redundantly progressed back and forth above my chest and simultaneously, those revolting squealing rats scurried about the base of the decayed framed table, avariciously sniffing at the raw meat on the ledge above.

But my craving for sustenance suddenly afforded my mind a stellar inspiration. At first I believed that the spectacular thought which had entered my cerebrum was merely a trite triviality, but then I set my mind to executing the crazy idea as a last resort before I myself would be savagely executed by the devastating blade's thrust.

'The relentless sweeping of the pendulum's axe is now traveling only three inches above my chest. I must act with dispatch or else I'll most certainly perish!' I very practically surmised. 'But who gives a shit or a fuck about my picayune earthly plight? I'm just one doomed pathetic insignificant soul about to be systematically eliminated from existence on a tiny insignificant planet in the vast mind-boggling-galaxy in the infinite-sized unending eternal Universe!'

I furiously extended my left arm and finally my hand's stiff bleeding fingers were able to desperately grab the three balls of raw meat, which I then managed to smear against the main strap that fastened me to the execution platform. The distance between the food plate' to my mouth was the length of my grasp. 'There's only one fuckin' chance to evade this maniacal death ordeal but it is not me trying to grab the pendulum and stopping it unless I want my hands horribly severed from my wrists. It would be a lot easier to halt a massive avalanche rumbling down an icy mountainside than to accomplish *that* foolish feat!'

I contracted my chest in with each time I inhaled, my breathing corresponding with the appalling pendulum's predictable sweeping intersection with my pounding heart. 'There's no more time for delay! I must act in a hurry or most certainly I shall be severed in two by this sharp weapon of those craven black-robed white-lipped fanatical religious hypocrites!'

But hope's voice whispered from another dimension into my yearning ear so without hesitation I boldly initiated my sagacious plan. Indeed, with the next several passes, the axe would be indiscriminately scraping away my thin black gown's fabric. But astonishingly, my resilient spirit was no longer petrified beyond rationality! My arthritic hands began working feverishly with an obsessed nervous energy generated solely by my own despair and horror. I instinctively knew that I had to emerge as master of my environment. The numerous rats were wild, brazen and ravenous, yet I calmly resolved to make them my assistants and allies. Here is what ingenious machination I had set into motion.

I frantically smeared the rotting raw meat onto the strap that kept my chest and upper torso stationary on the table and then as if on cue, the hungry rats climbed up the frame's legs and began to bite away at the food that their sniffing noses smelled. Their greediness to eat was the phenomenal miracle for which I had been praying.

By the dozens, the on-a-mission army of disgusting vermin swarmed upon my torso and soon their cold animalistic lips met mine. With their' long probing whiskers the despicable creatures meticulously squirmed and maneuvered around upon my throat, face and neck. Nevertheless I lay still in a virtual panic-attack state of mind. My face was being smothered and I honestly felt like regurgitating but fortunately I lacked sufficient food in my stomach to accomplish performing that rather revolting urge.

Out of the rodents' queer biological necessity, soon the teeth of the sickening stinking vermin nibbled and bit away until finally the uppermost greasy strap encumbering my torso snapped from their jaws' activity and I amazingly had the wherewithal to turn my body and with the shifting of my weight, the sturdy table overturned and in an instant both it and I flipped over onto the cold granite floor just as the sharp blade passed above where my exposed chest would have been pierced. 'Oh how precious air is, basic oxygen that I would ordinarily take for granted!' I momentarily rejoiced.

From my fallen position on the floor I heard a sound and reflexively glanced up. My eyes saw the near-fatal pendulum being hoisted back up to the ceiling by what seemed (to my erratic judgment) a mystical invisible force. My hands somehow garnered the strength to free the remainder of the straps that had harnessed my body to the reprehensible execution bench. But no sooner had that task been successfully consummated that the fickle rats began fleeing back to the safety of their well. I gradually got to my knees and then rose to my feet. Standing there like an automaton, I was then cognizant of a harshly terrifying sensation that immediately diminished my will to live.

The aforementioned yellow light had been originating from a one-inch crack occupying the space between the stone-cold walls and the granite-cold floor that comprised the two major components of the torture chamber. 'The walls are separated from the goddamned floor!' I realized and marveled. 'Oh no! Oh my God! Holy fuck! What the hell is this?'

The final horrifying mystery of the demonic death chamber became quite abundantly clear and threatening. Then the vague amber light gradually became more intense and brilliant. My senses were dazzled and enraptured until the distinct smell of sulfur numbed my mind. 'The air's being contaminated! My already fucked-up lungs are now being poisoned with hot gas that will soon surely choke me to death. Enough of this abominable torture that you've so craftily designed! I want to fuckin' die! Do you hear me Lucifer, you' demented Asshole! How much more pain can I possibly take? Do you hear me Satan? I said that I want to fuckin' die!'

And then another unbelievable ghastly danger plagued and terrorized my all-too-pathetic existence. The dungeon's walls were slowly-but-surely gravitating and (by design) moving in speed and distance at what I estimated to be a foot a minute toward the pit situated in the chamber's center. I coughed and spit and gasped and sneezed. 'My immortal soul's beginning to burn in the infernos of Hell!' my confused and blurred mind acknowledged. 'Hurry! Transform my body into embers before the pain of burning to death becomes entirely too unbearable!'

My grimy bloodstained hands were cupped upon my face in total submission and resignation to my fate. I reluctantly accepted my destiny without any serious defense being rendered. My consciousness was positively and steadfastly resigned to the prospect of dying. My only human reaction was to bitterly weep and anticipate my inevitable demise. The Inquisition had triumphed and

188

my conquered soul was about to surrender. Yes, the sulfuric walls were approaching me on all four sides and within thirty seconds I would have an accursed choice to make: either die by asphyxiation with my body being cremated, or voluntarily leap into the deep dark pit and meet my predictable end upon impact with the bottom. All the while the red steaming walls moved steadily and morosely toward me in all four directions.

"The fuckin' pit!" I concluded and futilely yelled to the apathetic ears of Satan. "It'll definitely be the goddamned pit! My lungs are being stifled and feel like they're being incinerated! This atrocious sulfur is far worse a fate than being strangled to death!"

At the height of my dread there was a discernible cessation of activity. My tired eyes stared between the fingers of my raised cupped hands, and my pupils perceived a stoppage in the sulfuric fumes that had been filling the room. And then the mechanical walls began to slowly recede back to their original positions. What on Earth (or in Hell) was happening?

My vocal cords screamed as loudly as they could, with me sounding much like an insane asylum maniac during an atrocious seizure. I tottered over to the right side wall and astutely listened to human voices conversing in French. Soon the sound of trumpets was heard and my hazy mind then envisioned God's obedient angels arriving on the scene to escort and accompany my soul to some distant afterlife destination. Then a grating noise equal to a thousand thunders frightened the remaining daylights out of me.

I was quickly surrounded by a group of garrulous French soldiers led by the very audacious General LaSalle. Then it all occurred to me in a marvelous flash. The sadistic black-robed white-lipped violators were now in the hands of the benevolent enemy. The cobwebs instantly disintegrated inside my mind. I joyfully remembered that I had been a British mercenary fighting for the French against the wicked and reprehensible Spanish Inquisition.

"The Murders in the Rue Morgue"

The best private detectives are those persistent sleuths that perceive reality in a slightly different vein than the standard police inspectors do. Sometimes what' appears to be a vast incomprehensible crime mystery can be easily solved with the examiner scrutinizing the very minute details that the average investigator tends to overlook.

Essentially the most successful private investigators are shrewd-minded distrustful crackerjacks highly skilled at analyzing, experimenting, hypothesizing, assuming, verifying and concluding. A critic might superficially say, "Well, those are the steps represented in the scientific method!" And that is a perfectly accurate definition on his or her part. But the most accomplished detectives are those serious-minded gumshoes that perform and execute to perfection the six characteristics evident in the "Scientific Method" with much more guile and sagacity than do their counterparts.

In July of 1839 I had arrived with a purpose in Paris, France to conduct some valuable research on obscure materials to use in an upcoming novel I had planned on authoring. I was standing in a narrow aisle in an obscure small library in the Rue Montmartre searching for specific information relative to the Normandy and Brittany peninsulas in Western France and I also wanted to learn about the prominent families that populated those two sectors when I accidentally met Mr. Cedrick Auguste Dupin, who incidentally was much more fluent in English than I was in French.

"Do you have a place to stay in the city?" Dupin asked me. "You look a little like a mendicant to me!"

"No, not a permanent one," I chuckled and said. "But Mr. Dupin, I do plan on staying at a downtown hotel until I can find adequate and inexpensive accommodations on the outskirts of the city. I'm an aspiring writer you see, and I'm trying to amass a reputation and so unfortunately I don't have a large revenue stream. Therefore I must limit my budgetary spending."

"I see," Dupin answered as the chief librarian in the far corner of the room cautioned him to keep his bass voice low, which it already was. "Mr. Poe, you can stay at my residence at 33 Rue Donut Faxbourg, St. Germain if you'd like," Monsieur Cedrick Auguste Dupin invited. "It's not a deluxe hotel by any means but the rent will be cheap, the wine will be good and last but not least, I promise to be exquisite company."

"You aren't a faggot are you?" I discourteously and impertinently asked. "I fuckin' despise homosexuals who don't practice abstinence and celibacy. That's why I positively detest most Popes, Cardinals, Archbishops, Bishops, Monsignors, Priests, Brothers and Protestant Ministers and a few Hebrew Rabbis and Muslim Imams thrown in to boot," I qualified. "Those gay faggots either love to pork each other up the ass, suck each other's dingles or get their rocks off by molesting and sexually abusing vulnerable choir and altar boys. You might say that I have a phobia about those fuck heads that practice unnatural sex, but truly Mr. Dupin," I proceeded with my dissertation, "I find *their* perverted kind of lust to be unacceptably abominable when the gay fucks think that each others' assholes are wet pink vaginas. An asshole is never a good substitute for a delicious hairy wet pink pussy, wouldn't you tend to agree?"

"Absolutely Mr. Poe! Absolutely!" Dupin promptly confirmed. "In fact there's a terrific bordello only a block away from my residence and I'll take you for a most gratifying visit there sometime later this week. But just remember," the keen-minded detective pontificated, "I like to get the sloppy seconds. Please excuse me Mr. Poe, but that's an eccentric fetish of mine to which I happen to be addicted. I just love sloppy seconds!"

A week after my incidental meeting of Cedrick Auguste Dupin, he and I were casually looking over an evening edition of the Paris newspaper *Gazette des Tribunaux* when a certain front page article attracted Dupin's interest involving a bizarre murder scenario. Two women were found dead, one in and one near an apartment, and there were no major clues as to the culprit's identify or any hints about any motive,

"Were these women related to one another?" I phlegmatically asked Dupin. "Or were they lesbian lovers? Or perhaps they were bad-luck prostitutes?"

"The older woman was a certain Madame L'Espanaya and the younger one was her daughter Mademoiselle Camille L'Espanaya," Dupin read from the evening newspaper. "The two ladies lived in an apartment on the fourth floor of a tenement building in the Rue Morgue. Eight neighbors and two gendarmes heard their loud frantic screams, broke down the locked doors, climbed up three flights of stairs, knocked down the entrance door to their apartment and were shocked at what they discovered."

"Well, what was in there?" I implored my new Parisian chum. "Were these ladies a mother-daughter prostitution team and handling a lot of tax-free illicit cash money? Aren't they the two sex-starved

192

nymphomaniac bitches we screwed Monday night over at your favorite brothel? Ha, ha, ha Dupin. That night you got your sloppy seconds twice! Ha, ha, ha!"

"You blundering Fool!" Dupin hollered with a lisp and spit directly into my face. "You never mix business with pleasure. That's rule number one in professional detective work so that the investigator can easily separate objectivity from subjectivity. Now then," my sagacious mentor continued, "the entire apartment was in total disarray with items, objects, drawers and assorted articles randomly strewn all over the damned place."

"I see," I said with little thought or speculation, "so the robbers were breaking and entering to steal personal property and the women caught them in the act and during their struggles were killed by the criminal villains. Those asshole murderers must've been rank amateurs because talented burglars never make the stupid mistake of killing anybody during a heist gone bust."

"Not exactly," Dupin answered with a puzzled expression on his countenance. "Money, jewels, diamonds, necklaces and the like were left lying all over the apartment so whoever committed the gruesome homicides didn't have robbery as a motive."

"Then it just doesn't make a whole lot of sense to wantonly kill two people just for the sake of killing them," I acknowledged. "Whoever enacted these brutal attacks must be a barbaric descendent of Attila the Hun, who incidentally was not gay!"

"Well Mr. Poe, according to the newspaper article, furniture had been broken, legs of chairs, lamps, a bookcase, etcetera."

"Monsieur Dupin, what about a jaded lover, a jilted boyfriend, a jaundiced husband or a fiance with liver disease?" I ridiculously asked. "Love and hate could also represent motivations to extinguish human lives, especially during a crime of passion."

"Here's what is so baffling and mysterious about the entire incident," Cedrick Auguste Dupin elaborated. "The mother, Madame L'Espanaya's hair was pulled-out at the roots and two long gray tresses belonging to her were found near the hearth, all dabbed with blood and dandruff. And also, a blood-stained sharp razor was discovered on the Oriental rug not far from the fireplace."

"So, the razor must obviously be the murder weapon," I concluded and verbally theorized. "The killer must either be a disgruntled or demented barber or tailor! Who else could it' have been? A jealous lesbian hairdresser from the local beauty salon?"

Dupin was not ruffled by my general lunacy. "A small metal safe was found in the main bedroom with the key still in the lock but the contents inside were all still intact," Cedrick Auguste slowly read from the front page account. "And situated next to the ripped-out gray hair tresses were found two cloth bags containing four thousand francs each, and nearby were four gold Napoleons and three silver spoons," my friend monotonously read from the gazette.

"Well Monsieur, I've heard of someone being born with a silver spoon in their mouth but this is the first instance of someone dying with one almost stuck down their friggin' throat," I stupidly remarked. "I mean Cedrick, silverware might've been much more involved than either you or I can ever conjecture. Maybe the two ladies were stabbed with a sharp knife when they refused to fork over the silver spoons."

"Stop speaking like you have diarrhea of the mouth and constipation of the brain," the normally unflappable Dupin cautioned and criticized my' retarded cerebral functioning. "Edgar, now please listen to me. Bona fide detective work requires total concentration and no fuckin' fooling around."

"Okay Monsieur Dupin, I'll get serious for a moment and for one moment only," I fraudulently pledged with my left hand being held over my heart. "Tell me, what had happened to the rest of Madame L'Espanaya in that her pulled-out hair had been tossed all over the whole damned living room?"

"The gendarmes responding to the emergency soon discovered plenty of soot below the fireplace so one of them stuck his head up the chimney and to his utter horror the corpse of the daughter Mademoiselle Camille L'Espanaya was up there with her head upside down, and the girl came tumbling onto the hearth after being only slightly yanked by the astonished policeman."

"Holy shit Cedrick!" I exclaimed. "It's bad enough when a person's nose gets stuffed-up with snot but when your chimney gets stuffed-up with your dead daughter, and you yourself are dead too, that's enough to make the average newspaper reader blow his or her stack. It's far worse than getting the damned flu (flue), that's for fuckin' sure!" I answered in a totally ludicrous dumb-ass response. "But truthfully My Friend, no man would be strong enough to stuff Mademoiselle Camille L'Espanaya that far up a chimney! It's physically impossible to do I would think!"

"Indications are from circumstantial evidence gathered that Mademoiselle Camille had been shoved up the chimney while she was still alive," Dupin reported from his newspaper column comprehension. "She had bruises, abrasions and lacerations on her

194

face, chest, neck and head, all coming from friction happening between her body and the chimney stack."

"And was the mother Madame L'Espanaya ever found?" I asked Dupin. "Where was her hide if her hair had been discovered because usually the incompetent police can't find neither hide nor hair of anybody! H, ha, ha!"

"Well Edgar, you clownish Buffoon, the neighbors and the police then heard shrieks coming from the back courtyard and immediately ran to the apartment's back window. Below them was the body of Madame L'Espanaya lying prone in the weeds. The alarmed searchers then dashed down the three flights of stairs and quickly entered the rear courtyard through a side wrought iron gate. They found the mother's throat cut and her neck nearly severed. Upon raising-up her body off the ground, the mother's head fell right off of her neck. Madame L'Espanaya is now fully decapitated!"

"Who could've done such despicable heinous crimes?" I rhetorically asked. "Remind me to lock the goddamned door to my room tonight. We have enough *cutthroats* already living in this neighborhood ghetto as it is Monsieur Dupin without me having to fuckin' worry about being literally decapitated too!"

* * * * * * * * * * * *

Two nights later at the supper table Cedrick Auguste Dupin and I were seriously discussing a subsequent follow-up front-page article concerning the sensational Murders in the Rue Morgue that had just appeared in that evening's edition of the *Gazette des Tribunaux*. My friend, the singular and autonomous private investigator, was reviewing for my information the reported depositions given to the Paris Police concerning the strange killings. Dupin was in an extraordinarily contemplative mood as his analytical mind was methodically piecing together data that the regular police inspectors could not connect or had overlooked.

"Listen to this preposterous bullshit Edgar," Cedrick Auguste entreated. "Mrs. Pauline Dubourg, the laundress for Madame L'Espanaya claims that she's been washing clothes for the old woman and her daughter Camille for three years. She states in her deposition that the mother and the daughter were on good terms and that they were affectionate towards each other, but seldom in public. And besides that," Dupin continued reading excerpts from the newspaper, "according to Mrs. Dubourg, Madame L'Espanaya always paid her cleaning bills on time and was never late for a payment."

"Well Monsieur Dupin," I said after a brief bit of introspection, "can we really trust Mrs. Dubourg's integrity? How do we know that she wasn't laundering money for Madame L'Espanaya and her daughter Mademoiselle Camille?" I frivolously jested. "Isn't there anything better to read on the Sports Page or perhaps in the daily horoscopes section? What about all the ultra-liberal political bullshit on the editorial page?"

Ignoring my inane facetiousness, my loyal companion (who incidentally was not gay) described a second lengthy deposition given by Monsieur Pierre Moreau, an area tobacconist who sold the toothless Madame L'Espanaya several pounds of tobacco and a pound of snuff every week. "Monsieur Moreau testifies that the Madame was an independently wealthy woman who often did fortune-telling as a hobby for area residents living in and around the vicinity of the Rue Morgue. What do you think about *that* Edgar?"

"Well," I said before clearing my throat, "if the dead old bitch had any advanced skill in fortune-telling, she would've known that she was going to be killed and dropped out of the goddamned fourth floor window of her apartment and she would've gotten the hell out of there before the tragedy ever happened to her. I mean Cedrick Auguste," I editorialized while examining the newspaper's editorial page, "a person can't tell the future if she herself has no goddamned future. But what intrigues me the most about this remarkable case is that all of the doors and windows of the house were shut and locked and the only possible means of entry was through the fourth story window that Madame L'Espanaya had been thrown out of. But the window is a full four to five feet below the roof eaves and I maintain that not even a triple-jointed acrobat could've gained access from the outside. And also, the chimney was way too narrow for anyone of any size to clamber down and enter the apartment."

Dupin remained in deep meditation and heard not a word of my fantastic monologue. "And look here Edgar, Isidore Muset, who was one of the gendarmes on the scene, claims that he had heard some shrill sounds and a voice speaking in another language loudly emanating from the apartment. The language he had heard of course was other than French, possibly Spanish."

"That makes some sense out of nonsense," I lyrically replied. "Madame L' Espanaya has a Spanish name and perhaps she has a secret hot Latin lover, or maybe her daughter Camille was pregnant out of wedlock and the mother had been engaged in an argument with the prospective biological father."

"You think just like the regular police do and you're always fallaciously looking to the obvious in attempting to excavate important clues," Dupin offensively chided. "And the deposition of this policeman Isidore Muset can't be trusted either because he's recently quit the force and is now recovering from insanity in a downtown mental institution. When the dedicated gendarme pulled Mademoiselle Camille out of the chimney, Isidore was so horrified that his mind and emotions automatically regressed back into his early childhood a day later."

"Well Monsieur, what do you make of this male person in the apartment speaking Spanish?" I asked Dupin. "Who the hell was he? Miguel Cervantes or Don Quixote reincarnated?"

"You're a complete horse's ass!" Cedrick Auguste vociferously indicted my true character. "In the paper's account it's specifically stated that a nosy neighbor named Henri Duval claims that he had heard someone in Madame L'Espanaya's apartment speaking in Italian just before the murders had occurred although Duval doesn't understand a damned word of Italian, and some other people giving depositions reported that they had heard words in Russian, German and Hungarian even though all of those other French assholes have indicated in their wacky signed testimonies that they don't know any foreign words in Russian, in German or in Hungarian."

But what really pissed-off Dupin more than anything else was a remote fact mentioned in a related article on page three of the newspaper where it was casually reported that the police had arrested a petty thief named Adolphe Le Bon in conjunction with the Murders in the Rue Morgue.

"I know this lowlife vagabond Le Bon. True, he is a smalltime burglar and a petty crook too but he's definitely not a brutal murderer. Now Edgar," Cedrick Auguste emphatically expounded, "I fully intend to prove Adolphe Le Bon's innocence."

"How do you intend to accomplish that impossible task?" I challenged and then snickered. "The police must know what the hell they're doing! You're waging a losing battle My Friend. After all Bon Ami, they *are* the authorities and they're going to resist and belittle anything of merit that you have to say about this prime suspect Adolphe Le Bon's innocence."

"The police are assholes just like you're an asshole for thinking exactly like they do," Dupin cryptically answered. "This morning I received an urgent visit from Monsieur Gustav Ghent, the Prefect of the Paris Police Department. Ghent is quite baffled by these almost indecipherable dual murders in the Rue Morgue and he's asked me to assist in the ongoing investigation."

"And are you going to aid the police utilizing your great acumen?" I asked. "That could give you an excellent opportunity to clear the name of this petty thug Adolphe Le Bon."

Dupin then spoke as if he was describing the disunited pieces of a complex jigsaw puzzle and I had to listen very intently in order to grasp the full gravity of his lexicon. My pragmatic friend said that he had met with Gustav Ghent earlier in the day and that he had later accompanied the Prefect to the murder scene apartment and that Monsieur Ghent had eventually agreed to allow Cedrick Auguste to keep the straight razor murder weapon in his possession for forty-eight hours in exchange for a definite solution to the baffling dual homicides.

"Did you uncover any new evidence besides the old evidence of the straight razor weapon?" I inquired. "After all, that *is* the murder weapon isn't it?"

"It most certainly is," Dupin quickly concurred. "But sometimes the smallest insignificant discovery could wind-up being the key factor in cracking open a difficult case."

"Like what?" I interrogated my most ingenious colleague in crime fighting. "Like what?" I reiterated.

"Like this orange hair I discovered this afternoon in back of the apartment's living room sofa," Dupin answered as he proudly showed me a long thick orange hair.

"Is it a pubic hair?" I idiotically laughed and then smirked. "I've never seen pussy hair quite that long and come to think of it, I've never seen orange pussy hair either. Some eccentric broad must've either dyed her head or dyed her cunt!"

"Don't be such a dumb fuck Ninny!" Dupin angrily reprimanded me. "I've examined this vital orange hair under a microscope and now I know how the murder was committed. I've already arranged to place an ad in tomorrow morning's newspaper and I hope to have this crime wrapped-up within the next forty-eight hours."

"You're fuckin' nuts, do you know that Dupin! You're fuckin' nuts!" I repeated. "You put more weight in a goddamned orange pubic hair or a goddamned dyed orange head hair than you do in the actual razor blade murder weapon! Forget your stupid-assed microscope. I recommend that you stick your freakin' noggin under a telescope because you oughta' have your head examined!"

"Be here in my dining room two mornings from now at nine o'clock sharp if you want to learn exactly how the murders to Madame L'Espanaya and to Mademoiselle Camille had been committed."

* * * * * * * * * * * *

Two mornings later at a quarter to nine I was in the prescribed place seated at the dining room table and informally conferring with the brilliant and inimitable private detective Monsieur Cedrick Auguste Dupin. At first I felt a trifle fidgety, seriously thinking that I was being exploited as an accomplice to an elaborate hoax involving an orange pubic hair being the principal clue that would unlock the mystery of the intriguing Murders in the Rue Morgue. But then again, I generally trusted Dupin's judgment and his professionalism and I believed that the reputable fellow wouldn't be playing any grandiose trick on me.

"Have you invited Prefect Ghent in on this session?" I anxiously asked Dupin while I twiddled my thumbs in a reverse motion' as was my bad habit. "I mean Cedrick, you do have to return the borrowed straight razor murder weapon to him, don't you?"

"It is always easier to borrow than to invent," Dupin weirdly answered, using some arcane symbolism to establish a relationship that at that time I couldn't fathom. "But as I've told you a dozen times Edgar, the Prefect and his horde of nincompoops don't know bullshit from cat piss or from the smell of boxwood either."

"Well Monsieur, you're doing all of this to exonerate a minor thug named Adolphe Le Bon," I continued our impromptu conversation. "Why are you so concerned about the fate of a petty thief?"

"Because Monsieur Le Bon, if convicted, will be a part of a travesty of justice entirely generated by police incompetence," Dupin replied. "That type of destiny shouldn't happen to anyone: to you, to me or to Adolphe Le Bon. The police are looking for an available dupe to blame, just to cover their own asses."

I was totally miffed and stymied and I needed several concrete explanations to preserve my rapidly diminishing confidence and my totally dwindled sanity. "Cedrick, what was the content of the ad that you had placed in the Lost and Found section of the morning paper?"

"I had advertised that I had in my possession a lost on-the-prowl orangutan and that whoever had misplaced the ape should come to my residence no later than nine o'clock this morning to claim their prize. Is that perfectly clear to you Mr. Poe?"

"Why Monsieur, now I really do think that this entire fiasco is a lot of poppycock," I volleyed back, a bit flabbergasted. "You're telling me that the orange hair you had analyzed under your microscope belongs to a goddamned orangutan that committed the dual murders! I think I'm going to take you to London to be admitted to St. Mary's of Bethlehem. Yes indeed Dupin, Bedlam is where you need to be to fully recuperate from your detri*mental* delusions!"

Just at that point in our important dialogue there was a heavy rapping on the front door and Dupin rose from his chair and answered the knocking. My illustrious friend returned into the dining room with a tall brawny-looking muscular fellow that Auguste introduced to me as Monsieur Jacques Trappe, who then was requested to have a seat. After the three of us were comfortably situated, the private investigator initiated our three-way consultation.

"I see Monsieur Trappe that you're a sailor?" Dupin cordially began. "Am I correct in making that assumption?"

"How in the world did you know that?" our guest incredulously asked. "I am indeed a sailor for fifteen years now."

"It's all not a complicated matter," Dupin declared. "You have an anchor tattoo above your right wrist confirming your occupation."

"I see," Monsieur Jacques Trappe acknowledged with a sigh of relief. "There was nothing mysterious about how you had figured that out after all! Now Sir, I've come to reclaim my orangutan. Do you have it here?"

"No Monsieur," Dupin indicated with a short smile flashing across his face. "It's too dangerous to keep inside a dwelling. It's in a cage at another location and you'll be able to retrieve it in a few hours."

"What about the razor blade?" I awkwardly asked, nearly blowing Dupin's investigative technique. "How is the straight razor involved in this strange caper?"

Cedrick Auguste Dupin quickly produced the murder weapon and the agitated sailor attempted standing up but then the stellar private investigator held a previously concealed pistol in his hand and threatened to use it against Monsieur Trappe should the sailor attempt to flee the premises. Then my wise friend demanded that Monsieur Trappe disclose everything that the nautical voyager knew about the orangutan and about the very bewildering and gruesome Murders in the Rue Morgue.

As it turned out, Monsieur Trappe had acquired the orangutan on a recent sail to Borneo and he had trained the ape to accomplish certain tricks, labors and tasks. Upon arriving at the Paris docks, Monsieur Trappe was shaving in his quarters and the orangutan began imitating the behavior it had just witnessed by applying shaving cream to its face and then dangerously gaining possession of the straight razor.

The concerned sailor reflexively reached for his training whip to punish the ape and repossess the razor but fearing being punitively reprimanded, the Simian creature instinctively bounded out the door and fled the ship, carrying with it the sharp blade. Jacques Trappe chased after the powerful animal right to the vicinity of the Rue Morgue, where the frightened orangutan then skillfully climbed up the side of the building, latched onto a flagpole and using its great strength and dexterity, next swung its frame inside the back fourth story open window, launching himself directly into Madame L'Espanaya's apartment.

"And naturally," Dupin interrupted the sailor's woeful narrative, "neither elderly Madame L'Espanaya nor her ill-fated hundred-pound-daughter Mademoiselle Camille L'Espanaya had the wherewithal or the physical ability to discipline or fend off the excited orangutan wielding the sharp razor. So the impressionable beast felt a compulsion to imitate *you'* as its ideal model of impersonation, after you of course had been shaving your neck Monsieur Trappe, the ape...."

"The orangutan killed the lady in question by slitting her throat with the razor," the guilt-laden sailor finished. "When I heard the screams and shrieks coming out of the fourth floor back window, that's exactly what I then speculated had happened. The ape had gone absolutely ape!"

"And since you were exceptionally scared about what had just transpired," I contributed to the discussion, "you ran away from the crime scene. And I suppose that your orangutan barber is still on the loose somewhere in Paris."

"Not really," Dupin confidently clarified. "Prefect Ghent has advised me just an hour ago that the dangerous creature had been captured while trying to gain admission to the Paris Zoo. The alert zookeepers cleverly lured the animal into an empty cage by leaving peeled rotten bananas inside and then shut the door after the orangutan leaped inside."

"Will I be arrested?" the sailor nervously asked. "I wish to avoid having a criminal record if at all possible! I must be able to re-board my ship that's scheduled to leave port by early Tuesday morning of next week."

"Well Monsieur Trappe, that particular matter is for the Paris Police to decide," Dupin suavely answered. "But since the powerful ape had committed the two brutal murders and not you, I imagine and predict that your charge will be reduced from a major felony to a misdemeanor, that is, your leaving the scene of a crime and then not reporting it to the proper authorities. But since you're a fairly decent fellow Monsieur Trappe," Cedrick Auguste nonchalantly added, "I'll speak to Prefect Ghent personally and I'm willing to predict that you'll be leaving port on your ship next Tuesday morning either with or without your treasured orangutan."

About the Author

Jay Dubya is author' John Wiessner's pen name. John is a retired New Jersey public school teacher, having diligently taught the subject for thirty-four years. John lives in Hammonton, New Jersey.

Counting *Poe: Pelted, Pounded, Pummeled and Pulverized*, John has written and published thirty-five total books. *Pieces of Eight, Pieces of Eight, Part II, Pieces of Eight, Part III* and *Pieces of Eight, Part IV* all contain short stories and novellas that feature science fiction and paranormal plots and themes. *Nine New Novellas, Nine New Novellas, Part II, Nine New Novellas, Part III, Nine New Novellas, Part IV, One Baker's Dozen, Two Baker's Dozen, Snake Eyes and Boxcars and Snake Eyes and Boxcars, Part II* are short story collections all written in the spirit of the *Pieces of Eight* series.

Other Jay Dubya adult-oriented fiction are the works *Black Leather and Blue Denim, A '50s Novel*, and its exciting sequel, *The Great Teen Fruit War, A 1960' Novel. Frat Brats, A '60s Novel* completes the action/adventure trilogy. Jay Dubya also has produced two irreverent Biblical satires, *The Wholly Book of Genesis* and *The Wholly Book of Exodus*. A third satire *Ron Coyote, Man of La Mangia* is a parody on Miguel Cervantes' classic novel, *Don Quixote* published in 1605. *Thirteen Sick Tasteless Classics, TSTC, Part II, TSTC, Part III* and *TSTC, Part IV* are satirical works that each corrupt thirteen classic stories from American and British literature and from Greek mythology. *Fractured Frazzled Folk Fables and Fairy Farces* and *FFFF & FF, Part II* satirize and corrupt famous children's literature stories. *Mauled Maimed Mangled Mutilated Mythology* is another popular adult-oriented satirical/parody work that pokes fun at twenty-one famous classical myths. *O. Henry: Obscenely and Outrageously Obliterated* is another satirical adult rewrite. Finally, *Shakespeare: Slammed, Smeared, Savaged and Slaughtered* and *Shakespeare: S, S, S and S. Part II* poke fun at the famous works of the great playwright.

The author has also penned a young adult fantasy trilogy: *Pot of Gold, Enchanta* and *Space Bugs, Earth Invasion. The Eighteen Story Gingerbread House* is a collection of eighteen new children's stories. And last but not least, two non-fiction works are *So Ya' Wanna' Be A Teacher* and *Random Articles and Manuscripts*.

Jay Dubya really likes '50s music and he also listens to songs by the Beatles, *ELO*, the Carpenters, the Beach Boys, Fleetwood Mac, the Eagles', the Rolling Stones, John Mellencamp and John Fogerty.

CPSIA information can be obtained
at www.ICGtesting.com
Printed in the USA
BVHW071044151121
621686BV00012B/369/J